INVESTING IN UTILITIES

A COMPREHENSIVE

INDUSTRY-BY-INDUSTRY
GUIDE FOR INVESTORS
AND MONEY MANAGERS

DANIEL D. SINGER

PROBUS PUBLISHING COMPANY
Chicago, Illinois

Library of Congress Cataloging-in-Publication Data Available

ISBN 1-55738-125-9

Printed in the United States of America

1   2   3   4   5   6   7   8   9   0

Dedication

For my children: Rick, Cindy, Nick, Bud, Steven, and La La.

Contents

Acknowledgments   xi

Chapter 1   Introduction   1
              The Future for Investing in Public Utilities   2
              Using the "Guide for Investment Profit"   3
              Understanding Public Utilities   4
              Comparing Public Utility and Industrial Stocks   6
              Electric Utilities   6
              Gas Utilities   7
              Telecommunications Industry   7
              Water Utilities   8

Chapter 2   A Guide to Future Stock Prices and
                Dividends Among Public Utilities   9
              Using the Guide to Investing in Public Utilities   10
              Electric Utility Industry Forecasts   11
              Gas Utility Industry Forecasts   20
              Telecommunications Industry Forecast   23
              Water Utilities Forecast   28

Chapter 3   Public Utility Stock Price Determination   33
              Public Utilities as Natural Monopolies   34
              The Utility Rate Making Process   36
              Deregulation and the Breakdown of
                Monopoly Markets   39

Evaluating the Financial Performance of
    Public Utilities   41
Forecasting Utility Stock Prices   47

Chapter 4   **Evaluating the Performance of Industrial and
                 Utility Stocks**   **55**
             Comparing Industrial and Utility Stocks   55
             Comparing the DJI and the DJU   56
             Calculating the Total Rate of Return (TRR)   60
             Applying the TRR to the Industrial and
                 Utility Portfolios   64
             Real and After-Tax Rates of Return   64

Chapter 5   **Electric Utility Fundamentals**   **67**
             Organizational Overview of the Electric
                 Utility Industry   67
             Electric Utility Industry Performance Overview   67
             Future Trends in the Electric Utility Industry   87

Chapter 6   **The Future for Investment in Nonnuclear
                 Electric Utilities**   **95**
             Performance Overview   95
             Forecasting Stock Prices   96
             Specific Utility Forecasts   104
             Dividend Forecasts   115
             Forecasting Stock Prices   115
             Evaluating Investment Return   118
             How to use These Forecasts   118

Chapter 7   **The Future for Investment in Electric
                 Utilities with Nuclear Exposure**   **121**
             Performance Overview   121
             Forecasting Share Prices   125
             The Nuclear Background   126
             Nuclear Facilities and Risk   128

	Forecasting Returns for Electric Utilities with Nuclear Exposure	130
	Identifying Reliably Performing Electric Utilities with Nuclear Exposure	133
	Dividend Forecasts	133
	Specific Utility Forecasts	137
	Dividend Forecasts	144
	Forecasting Stock Prices	144
	Evaluating Investment Return	144
	Risk Among Electric Utilities with Nuclear Exposure	145
	How to Use These Forecasts	146
Chapter 8	**Natural Gas Industry Fundamentals**	**147**
	Organizational Overview of the Natural Gas Industry	147
	Gas Industry Performance Overview	147
	Supply-Demand Fundamentals	152
	The Natural Gas Industry: 1990–1999	158
	Analysis of Diversified Gas Company Performance: 1984–1988	161
	Analysis of Distribution Company Performance: 1984–1988	166
Chapter 9	**The Future for Investment in Diversified Gas Companies**	**171**
	Performance Overview	171
	Future Energy Prices	173
	Returns, Earnings, and Stock Prices Among the Diversified Gas Companies	176
	Forecasting Diversified Gas Company Stock Prices	181
	Specific Diversified Gas Company Forecasts	183
	Summary	210

Chapter 10   The Future for Investment in Local
                 Distribution Companies   213
              Performance Overview   213
              Returns Among Local Distribution Companies   214
              Forecasting Stock Prices and Returns   216
              Specific Local Distribution Company Forecasts   220
              Summary   234

Chapter 11   Telecommunication Industry Fundamentals   235
              Organizational Overview of the
                 Telecommunications Industry   235
              Telecommunications Industry Performance
                 Overview   235

Chapter 12   The Future for Investment in Independent
                 Telephone Companies   261
              Performance Overview   261
              Uncertain Growth Companies   266
              Proven Growth Companies   276
              Summary   289

Chapter 13   The Future for Investment in Regional
                 Holding Companies   291
              Performance Overview   291
              Industry Driving Forces   292
              RHC Return Forecasts   298
              Specific RHC Forecasts   301
              Summary   327

Chapter 14   The Future for Investment in
                 Common Carriers   329
              Performance Overview   329
              Industry Structure   330
              Returns Among Common Carriers   333
              Telecommunication Services   337
              Summary   357

Chapter 15   **Future Returns in Water Utilities**   **359**
                 Performance Overview   359
                 Market Structure   360
                 Water Utility Fundamentals   361
                 Specific Water Utilities   371
                 Summary   394

Index   **397**

Acknowledgments

The author is greatly indebted to many individuals for their willingness to read the manuscript and provide helpful advice. Particularly valuable comments were received from Dave Woolford (Shearson, Lehman, Hutton) on the electric utilities industry; Jim Baker (Merrill, Lynch, Pierce, Fenner, and Smith) on the fundamentals of investing; Bob Bergbauer (Ernst and Young) on the gas utilities; and James Singer (Kober Financial Corp.) on the construction of the Guide.

The author also acknowledges a tremendous debt to all his graduate and undergraduate students who patiently listened to endless lectures on the public utilities sector and wishes to thank them collectively for their many fine ideas and comments which have contributed so much to the quality of this book.

The author wishes to thank Towson State University for its support. Particularly helpful has been the encouragement from Dr. G. Timothy Haight, Chairman of the Department of Finance. The author also wishes to thank his professional colleagues for their encouragement during this project. Particularly worthy of mention are G. Randolph New, Dean, School of Business, Loyola University of New Orleans; William Murray, Associate Dean, University of San Francisco; Harsha Desai, Chairman, Department of Management, Loyola College of Baltimore.

Chapter 1

INTRODUCTION

Public utility stocks in the 1990s present exciting opportunities to the informed investor. Deregulation has created an unprecedented situation among telecommunication, electric, gas, and water utility companies. In an environment characterized by rapid technological change, emerging environmental concerns, consumer activism, and continuing instability in the world energy complex; public utilities will face an additional challenge to be successful in the face of intense market competition. The nature of this challenge has changed the rules for successful investing in public utilities. Earnings and cashflow growth will become increasingly important in determining investor rewards. That the reliance on the market mechanism to meet social goals is not complete or uniform provides an additional element of uncertainty in assessing the economic performance of these firms and creates additional profitable opportunities for informed investors.

Investing in public utility common stocks is no longer a conservative investment strategy. As a result of these fundamental changes, some public utilities will prosper and return considerable profit to their shareholders. Other public utilities will stagnate. Still others will weaken slowly over time, lingering on indefinitely or until they are absorbed by a more competent organization.

The Future for Investing in Public Utilities

The underlying framework for investing in public utilities has changed. As a whole, the investment community has been slow to react to this fact. Utilities are no longer able to invest capital in facilities with the assurance that they will be able to earn a fair return on their investment. Many public utilities have restructured as holding companies, allowing them to aggressively enter unregulated markets. Earnings shortfalls can no longer be automatically remedied by a rate increase, because of the fear of losing existing customers to competitors. Many utilities no longer return the bulk of their earnings to their stockholders in the form of dividends. Utilities no longer have the luxury of phasing in new technologies in such a manner as to fully depreciate their existing assets.

The upshot of this metamorphosis is that returns to investors in the public utilities sector will increasingly be a function of stock price changes. Future stock prices will, in turn, reflect the investment community's perception of current and future earnings.

As a result of the high degree of turbulence in their environment, management's lack of experience with competitive market structures, and regulatory inconsistencies, earnings in the public utility sector may be expected to be quite volatile throughout the 1990s. It is this volatility which creates opportunity for the informed investor.

The increased importance of earnings to stock prices among firms in the public utility sector has two important implications for investors. The first is that investments in public utilities will be subject to greater market risk (the tendency to go up as the market goes up or down as the market goes down) than has been the case in the past. The second implication is that the stock prices of individual firms in a given sector will exhibit greater variability (as their earnings fluctuate) than had previously been the case.

With greater exposure to market risk, investors in the public utility sector will need to be more conscious of the array of forces that tend to move the market as a whole up or down. In this respect, both fundamental and technical factors should be considered. The underlying market fundamentals of inflation, the interest rate complex, foreign trade, unemployment, etc., should be considered in assessing the timing of a particular investment decision. In addition, as evidenced in the October 1987 crash, technical factors can have a considerable impact on stock prices. Identifying individual public utility stocks whose current price is low relative to its potential earnings will yield an investor handsome rewards. The complex and transitional nature of the utilities sector will create many significant investment opportunities in the coming decade. The guide to the anticipated future stock price and dividend levels of individual utility firms presented in Chapter 2 should provide investors with a powerful tool for interpreting future events and assessing specific investment opportunities.

Using the "Guide for Investment Profit"

Despite the attempt in this book to present an understandable and clear picture of what is happening in the public utility industry, the subject is complex and technical. To give the investor ready help in this matter, Chapter 2 presents a guide to the dividend and price performance anticipated for 180 firms in the electric, gas, telecommunications, and water supply industries over the next decade.

The purpose of this guide is to provide investors with quick access to assessing the present situation of a particular firm.

Significant deviations in price or dividend levels from those forecast in the guide should be evaluated in the context of current market conditions and actual relevant events to determine if buying or selling behavior is appropriate. The guide is arranged within the electric, natural gas, telecommunications and water industries alphabetically.

Therefore, an investor following Enron (for example) in 1992 could go to the guide and look up Enron in the gas industry section. The investor could then compare the actual price and dividend level of Enron at that time with those predicted in the guide.

In the absence of adverse general market conditions and events unfavorably impacting a particular firm, a firm whose price is below that anticipated should be considered as a buying opportunity. Similarly, in the absence of favorable general market conditions and promising events impacting a particular firm, a firm whose price is above that anticipated in the guide should be scrutinized as a possible situation in which the investor would want to sell. The actual decision to buy or sell should always be made in the light of current market conditions and actual events. The material in the following chapters will help the investor evaluate the significance of those events.

Understanding Public Utilities

The period 1984–1989 yielded excellent returns to investors in public utilities. The reasons for the relative success of public utility sector investments during this period lies in the nature of natural monopolies and in the regulatory environment that existed during this period. Chapter 3 discusses the evolution of this regulatory environment, with an emphasis on the impact of technology on current and future market conditions. The combined effect of the regulatory and technological changes currently underway and those that may be expected in the future is to transform the service market of most public utilities from quiet and predictable to turbulent and uncertain. Public utilities are thus being forced to change their strategic posture from passive and reactive to aggressive and proactive. These changes portend increased volatility in financial performance, hence, an opportunity for investors.

The failure to comprehend the significance of the changed nature of the public utilities environment may result in missed opportunities and losses for the uninformed investor. For example, investors are frequently advised to purchase utility stocks based on their dividend yield. Such advice is typically misleading. Since 1960, the total return earned by investors in utility stocks has been much more influenced by stock price changes than by dividends declared. Successful investing in the public utility sector requires an understanding of the factors that affect stock price.

Utility stock prices were at one time a strict function of their dividends. This relationship was based on the stability inherent in the market position of a natural monopoly and an unwritten compact between the utilities and their regulators that the utilities were entitled to recover their costs and earn a normal profit on their investment. Under these circumstances, utilities paid out the bulk of their earnings in the form of dividends.

This relationship was fundamentally altered in the 1970s and 1980s. In the 1970s, most public utilities were battered by unprecedented inflation, the two energy crises, and a significant increase in concern over the environmental impact of their operations. The impact of these forces culminated in a significant reduction in earnings among most utilities. This situation was exacerbated by a consumer activist movement that succeeded in politicizing most state regulatory agencies. Utilities were no longer able to effectively pass through their cost of operations and earn competitive returns on their invested capital. The net effect of these changes caused a fall in the value of utility stocks.

In the 1980s inflation began to abate, the memory of the energy crises dimmed and immediate environmental concerns had been successfully addressed. While consumer advocates continued to hold greater power than had previously been the case, many firms in the public utilities sector began to stage a turnaround. By the end of the 1980s, most public utilities (with the notable exception of electric utilities which had an unsuccessful nuclear power experience) had regained a measure of financial health.

However, the 1980s brought with them a new approach to the regulation of public utilities that will have an effect far into the future. A shift in political philosophy evolved that favored local government and market solutions to economic problems over the intervention of big government. This philosophy culminated in the election of Ronald Reagan to the presidency in 1980. The implications of this shift for the utility sector were significant.

The lack of success in overcoming the problems of the 1970s that beset the utility sector had given rise to a general feeling outside the industry that administratively determined price structures in the utility sector were inherently inefficient. The perceived success in deregulating the airline industry gave added impetus to the forces favoring deregulation in the electric, gas, and telecommunications industries.

While deregulation has taken a different form in each of the public utility sectors, the net effect of deregulation is to increase the potential volatility of earnings among public utility firms. The essence of the market mechanism as a regulatory device is to reward "good" firms with profits and punish "bad" firms with losses.

Comparing Public Utility and Industrial Stocks

Chapter 4 examines the relative performance of utility and industrial stocks between 1960 and 1989. This is an especially important chapter because it deals explicitly with the problem of measuring investment performance between industrial and utility stocks: a problem that accounts for a good deal of the misunderstanding about the public utility sector that characterizes the investment community today.

Historically, utility stocks have proved better investments than industrial stocks. As measured by the Dow Jones indexes, public utility stocks have consistently outperformed industrial stocks since 1960—even in the bull market of the late 1980s. Additionally, this stellar performance has been accomplished with less market risk than in the industrial sector.

The reason this is not generally understood is that utilities have historically paid out a much larger portion of their earnings in the form of dividends than have industrial companies. A simple comparison of utility and industrial stock indexes during this period suggests that the industrial stocks were high performers and the utility stocks moribund. This approach automatically compounds the earnings for industrial firms but not for utilities. When dividends are reinvested in the utilities, however, it can be seen that the utilities actually outperform the industrials for most periods in this era.

In addition, stock price changes may be positive or negative, but dividends always positively impact return. This tends to reduce the volatility of utility stocks relative to industrial stocks.

Electric Utilities

Many electric utility stocks will prove solid investments in the 1990s. Chapter 5 examines the fundamental conditions impacting investment performance among electric utilities over the coming decade. Deregulation is found to be the major factor affecting investment performance during this period.

Chapter 6 develops stock price and dividend forecasts for 33 electric utilities that do not have a nuclear exposure. These forecasts are then used to estimate the five- and ten-year total returns which may be expected from an investment in one of these utilities.

Chapter 7 develops stock price and dividend forecasts for 23 electric utilities that do have a nuclear exposure, but investment in which is judged to be prudent, in the sense that the financial performance of these firms will depend primarily on economic variables. These forecasts are then used to estimate the five- and ten-year total returns which may be expected from an investment in one of these utilities.

Forty electric utilities are identified as having a financial outcome primarily dependent on political factors consequent on their involvement with nuclear power. Investment in these firms is not judged prudent for investors who are not willing to trade off potentially high returns for the security of their capital.

Gas Utilities

Gas utility stocks will provide numerous promising investment opportunities in the 1990s. Chapter 8 examines the fundamental conditions influencing profits and cash flow among 48 large gas utilities. Future profitability is seen to be a consequence of a combination of steadily rising energy prices throughout the decade, deregulation, and the depressed price levels of diversified gas companies in 1989.

Chapter 9 focuses on the potential for investing in 18 diversified gas companies. Price, dividend, and investment return forecasts are developed for each firm through 1999.

Chapter 10 examines the present circumstances of 30 local gas distribution companies. Their incredible run-up in value between 1984 and 1989 is unlikely to be duplicated in the 1990s, and investors can look toward only moderate returns among the local distribution companies.

Telecommunications Industry

Telecommunications stocks promise the investor potentially large rewards in the 1990s. Annual returns to investors in the 20 to 30 percent range are likely to be available throughout the decade from telecommunications companies. Risks are commensurately high as a result of the uncertain nature of future technological advances and the ferocious competition characterizing the industry.

Chapter 11 examines the fundamental nature of the telecommunications industry. Particular attention is paid to the evolution in regulatory philosophy leading to structured deregulation.

Chapter 12 forecasts future returns to investors for ten large independent telephone companies. Explicit consideration is given to the possibility of mergers and acquisitions for this group of firms.

Chapter 13 examines the future interrelationships between the seven regional holding companies formed by the breakup of AT&T and the remainder of the industry. Returns to investors in these firms are forecast through 1990.

Chapter 14 probes the future outcome of the fight for market shares among the long-distance common carriers and the implications of this fight for the financial performance of these firms.

Water Utilities

Chapter 15 presents an analysis of future returns among 11 large water utilities. The implications of the run-up of water utility stock prices in the late 1980s for these stock prices in the 1990s are examined.

Chapter 2

A GUIDE TO FUTURE STOCK PRICES AND DIVIDENDS AMONG PUBLIC UTILITIES

The results of the analysis developed in this book of industry conditions and individual firm performance in the electric, gas, telecommunications, and water service sectors of the public utility industry are summarized in the forecasts below. The intent of this presentation is to allow an investor convenient access to expected stock price levels and dividend payouts for 180 utility companies through 1999 based on the analysis of present circumstances and expected future developments as presented. These forecasts can be used by an investor to determine at any point in time if the current price of a utility warrants buying or selling that stock based on the investor's objectives.

A guide to public utility investments is necessary because the role of public utilities in our economic system has changed significantly. Prior to the hyperinflation and energy crises of the 1970s, conservative investors found a safe harbor in public utility equity markets. These two forces, however, led to an erosion of the historical informal compact between the utilities and their regulators that provided for the utilities recouping a market return on their investment.

Conditions in the public utility sector have further been changed by the institutionalization of the consumer activist movement, the intensification of environmental concerns, continuing uncertainty in the world energy market and the acceleration of the rate of technological change.

In the midst of these fundamental changes in the context of the public utilities sector, the election of Ronald Reagan as President in 1980 signaled the beginning of a shift in government philosophy toward deregulation. Evidence of this change can be seen on the federal level with the Federal Energy Regulatory Commission (FERC) and Federal Communications Commission (FCC) at the forefront of the deregulatory movement. However, recent appointments by President Bush to these important administrative agencies suggest that they may moderate the current pace of deregulation.

The net effect of deregulation has been to increase the stakes for investors in the public utility sector. Both opportunities and risks in the telecommunications, gas, and electric industries have been dramatically magnified by this turn of events.

While no longer a safe harbor in the sense that investment in the industry could be made indiscriminately, or simplistically on the basis of dividend yield, the industry will present many superb opportunities for investors in the 1990s. Many investors will find this guide helpful in identifying those situations that present favorable investment opportunities.

Using the Guide to Investing in Public Utilities

The projections summarized below may be used as a guide to determine the desirability of specific selling or buying strategies. Investors interested in electric (Chapters 5-7), gas (Chapters 8-10), telecommunications (Chapter 11-14), or water (Chapter 15) utilities will want to examine the historical conditions in that particular industry and the procedures used to develop the projections below to enable them to apply this guide in the light of current circumstances.

These projections are based on the continuance of current market conditions prevailing in 1990. Changes in the fundamental or technical determinants of market performance (other than those specifically anticipated) may result in a significantly different set of projections.

Thus the forecasts presented below should function as a guide to investors, rather than specific suggestions. That is, as the fundamental and technical factors influencing this industry change, the investor can compare the actual price and dividend levels offered by a utility to those projected in this book to determine if it is an appropriate time to buy or sell a particular stock.

Electric Utility Industry Forecasts

The fundamental factors influencing performance in the electric utility sector are discussed in Chapter 5.

Overall returns to investors among electric utilities were excellent between 1984 and 1988 as the fall in energy costs and general inflation allowed regulators to rationalize price structures without undue political pressure. In the coming decade, the primary factor influencing the performance of electric utilities will be the trend towards deregulation emanating from the federal level. As a result of the pressures of deregulation, as well as technological innovations and changing patterns of demand, electric utilities will continue to do well through 1999, although not as well as in the 1984–1988 period. The impact of deregulation will result in a considerable range in performance levels among electric utilities over the coming decade.

Total return forecasts for the 33 firms without nuclear exposure are presented in Chapter 6. Total returns for the 23 firms that do have an exposure to nuclear power, but are nevertheless in a relatively predictable situation, are developed in Chapter 7. These returns are based on the expected price levels forecast in Table 2.1 and the dividend levels forecast in Table 2.2.

Investments in the nonnuclear segment of the electric utility industry will be solid gainers in the 1990s. Particularly worth looking at are Utilicorp United Inc., St. Joe Power & Light Co., and the Potomac Electric Power Co.

While stock prices in this area will experience occasional volatility, the trend in both dividends and stock prices will be steadily upward. Stock price weaknesses in this sector should be seen as buying opportunities.

Table 2.1 Electric Utility Stock Price Forecast

Utility	1990	1991	1992	1993	1994	1995	1996	1997	1998	1999
Allegheny Power	38.16	39.88	41.68	43.55	45.51	47.56	49.70	51.94	54.27	56.72
Atlantic Energy Inc.	35.38	36.09	37.53	39.03	40.59	43.03	45.61	48.35	51.25	54.32
Baltimore Gas & Electric	28.38	30.08	31.89	33.80	35.83	37.98	40.26	42.67	45.23	47.94
Carolina Power	44.36	45.70	47.07	48.48	49.93	47.81	49.24	50.72	52.24	53.81
Central Illinois Pub. Ser. Co.	22.29	22.85	23.42	24.01	24.61	25.22	25.85	26.50	27.16	27.84
Central La. Electric Co.	33.61	35.07	37.52	40.15	42.96	45.97	49.18	52.63	56.31	60.25
Central Vermont Pub. Ser.	29.98	31.17	32.42	33.72	35.07	36.47	37.93	39.45	41.02	42.66
CILCORP	32.45	33.75	35.10	36.50	37.96	39.48	41.06	42.70	44.41	46.18
Cincinnati Gas & Electric Co.	25.78	26.29	26.82	27.36	27.90	28.46	29.03	29.61	30.20	30.81
Consolidated Edison	23.64	25.05	26.56	28.15	29.84	31.03	32.28	33.57	34.91	36.31
Delmarva Power	19.25	22.79	23.47	24.18	24.90	25.65	26.42	27.21	28.03	28.87
DPL Inc.	18.57	19.13	19.70	20.29	20.90	21.53	22.18	22.84	23.53	24.23
Duke Power Co.	55.00	55.57	58.34	61.26	64.32	67.54	70.92	74.46	78.19	82.10
Empire District Electric	29.00	30.15	31.36	32.61	33.91	35.27	36.68	38.15	39.67	41.26
Florida Progress Corp.	36.68	38.00	40.20	41.40	42.64	43.92	45.24	46.60	48.00	49.44
FPL Group Inc.	30.50	32.00	34.38	35.24	36.12	37.02	37.94	38.89	39.87	40.86
General Public Utilities	43.86	46.49	49.28	49.63	51.61	53.68	55.82	58.06	60.38	62.79
Green Mountain Power	24.00	24.72	25.46	26.23	27.01	27.82	28.66	29.52	30.40	31.31
Hawaiian Electric Industries	33.08	34.73	36.47	39.02	41.75	44.67	47.80	51.14	54.72	58.56
Idaho Power Co.	24.25	24.59	25.46	26.80	28.78	29.64	30.53	31.45	32.39	33.36
Interstate Power Co.	24.51	25.00	25.50	26.01	26.53	27.06	27.60	28.15	28.72	29.29
Iowa-Illinois Gas & Electric Co.	21.25	22.10	22.99	23.91	24.86	25.86	26.89	27.97	29.09	30.25
IPALCO Enterprises Inc.	24.34	25.90	27.57	29.36	31.26	32.83	34.47	36.19	38.00	39.90
Kansas Power & Light Co.	21.69	22.34	23.01	23.70	24.41	25.14	25.90	26.67	27.47	28.30
Kentucky Utilities Co.	19.25	19.50	19.70	19.89	20.23	20.83	21.46	22.10	22.77	23.45

(Table continues)

Table 2.1 Electric Utility Stock Price Forecast (Continued)

Utility	1990	1991	1992	1993	1994	1995	1996	1997	1998	1999
Louisville Gas & Electric Co.	37.57	38.69	39.86	41.05	42.28	43.55	44.86	46.20	47.59	49.02
MDU Resources Group	20.00	20.29	20.69	21.31	21.95	22.16	22.82	23.51	24.21	24.94
Midwest Energy Co.	20.00	20.29	20.90	21.53	22.17	22.84	23.52	24.23	24.95	25.70
Minnesota Power & Light Co.	24.18	25.15	26.15	27.20	28.29	29.42	30.60	31.82	33.09	34.42
Montana Power Co.	19.45	19.84	20.24	20.64	21.06	21.48	21.91	22.34	22.79	23.25
Nevada Power	22.29	22.74	23.19	23.66	24.13	24.61	25.11	25.61	26.12	26.64
No. States Power Co.	36.16	37.96	39.86	41.86	43.95	43.59	45.77	48.06	50.46	52.98
Oklahoma Gas & Electric Co.	34.39	36.11	37.91	39.81	41.80	43.89	46.08	48.39	50.81	53.35
Orange &Rockland Utilities, Inc.	30.62	31.65	32.50	33.48	34.48	35.52	36.58	37.68	38.81	39.97
Pacific Gas & Electric Co.	23.19	23.88	24.60	26.81	29.23	31.86	34.73	37.85	41.26	44.97
Pacificorp	21.18	21.81	22.47	23.14	24.30	25.51	27.55	29.76	32.14	59.16
Pennsylvania Power & Light Co.	41.53	42.77	44.06	45.38	46.74	48.14	49.59	51.07	52.60	54.18
Potomac Electric Power Co.	21.20	22.90	25.07	27.44	30.04	32.89	36.03	38.91	42.02	45.38
PSI Holdings Inc	17.25	18.00	18.25	19.00	20.00	21.00	22.00	23.00	23.50	24.00
Public Service Enterp. Group, Inc.	26.00	26.66	28.00	29.40	30.87	32.41	34.03	35.73	37.52	39.39
Public Service of Colorado	21.28	21.70	22.14	24.00	26.00	28.72	29.29	29.88	30.47	31.08
Puget Sound P & L Co.	19.56	20.71	21.08	21.33	22.24	23.19	24.04	24.76	25.50	26.27
S.W. Public Service Co.	27.81	28.64	29.50	30.39	31.30	32.24	33.21	34.20	35.23	36.29
SCANA Corporation	32.64	33.62	34.63	35.67	36.74	37.84	38.98	40.15	41.35	42.59
SCE Corp.	37.28	38.40	39.55	40.74	41.96	44.48	47.15	49.98	52.98	56.16
Sierra Pacific Resources	21.90	22.56	23.24	23.94	24.65	25.39	26.16	26.94	27.75	28.58
So. Indiana Gas & Electric Co.	29.69	30.58	31.50	32.44	34.06	35.77	37.55	39.43	41.40	43.47
St. Joe Light & Power Co.	26.87	28.75	30.76	32.91	35.22	37.68	40.32	43.14	46.16	49.39
TECO Energy Corp.	29.45	28.35	27.48	28.00	29.00	31.81	33.40	35.07	36.82	38.66
TNP Enterprises	18.11	18.65	19.21	20.95	22.00	23.10	24.26	25.47	26.74	28.08

(Table continues)

Table 2.1   Electric Utility Stock Price Forecast (Continued)

Utility	1990	1991	1992	1993	1994	1995	1996	1997	1998	1999
Tucson Electric Power Co.	11.88	10.50	11.00	12.00	14.00	16.00	22.00	25.20	27.72	30.49
Utilicorp United Inc.	21.00	24.06	26.96	30.30	34.00	36.66	38.40	40.32	42.43	44.72
Washington Water Power Co.	28.84	29.41	30.00	30.60	31.21	31.84	32.48	33.12	33.79	34.46
Wisconsin Energy Corp.	28.46	30.17	31.98	33.26	34.59	35.98	37.42	38.91	40.47	42.09
Wisconsin Public Service Corp.	22.73	22.96	23.19	23.42	23.66	23.89	24.13	24.37	24.62	24.86
WPL Holdings Inc.	24.55	25.29	26.05	26.83	27.63	28.74	29.89	31.08	32.33	33.62

Table 2.2 Electric Utility Dividend Forecast

Utility	1990	1991	1992	1993	1994	1995	1996	1997	1998	1999
Allegheny Power	3.16	3.30	3.45	3.61	3.77	3.94	4.12	4.30	4.49	4.70
Atlantic Energy Inc.	2.88	2.94	3.06	3.18	3.30	3.50	3.71	3.94	4.17	4.42
Baltimore Gas & Electric	2.10	2.23	2.36	2.50	2.65	2.81	2.98	3.16	3.35	3.55
Carolina Power	2.93	3.02	3.11	3.20	3.30	3.39	3.50	3.60	3.71	3.82
Central Illinois Pub. Ser. Co.	1.84	1.88	1.93	1.98	2.03	2.08	2.13	2.19	2.24	2.30
Central La. Electric Co.	2.62	2.81	3.00	3.21	3.44	3.68	3.93	4.21	4.50	4.82
Central Vermont Pub. Ser.	2.10	2.18	2.27	2.36	2.45	2.55	2.66	2.76	2.87	2.99
CILCORP	2.60	2.70	2.81	2.92	3.04	3.16	3.28	3.42	3.55	3.69
Cincinnati Gas & Electric Co.	2.32	2.37	2.41	2.46	2.51	2.56	2.61	2.67	2.72	2.77
Consolidated Edison	1.82	1.93	2.04	2.17	2.30	2.39	2.49	2.58	2.69	2.80
Delmarva Power	1.55	1.60	1.64	1.69	1.74	1.80	1.85	1.90	1.96	2.02
DPL Inc.	1.56	1.61	1.66	1.70	1.76	1.81	1.86	1.92	1.98	2.04
Duke Power Co.	3.18	3.33	3.50	3.68	3.86	4.05	4.26	4.47	4.69	4.93
Empire District Electric	2.33	2.42	2.52	2.62	2.72	2.83	2.94	3.06	3.18	3.31
Florida Progress Corp.	2.65	2.73	2.81	2.90	2.99	3.07	3.17	3.26	3.36	3.46
FPL Group Inc.	2.29	2.35	2.41	2.47	2.53	2.59	2.66	2.72	2.79	2.86
General Public Utilities	2.50	2.65	2.81	2.98	3.10	3.22	3.35	3.48	3.62	3.77
Green Mountain Power	1.98	2.04	2.10	2.16	2.23	2.30	2.36	2.44	2.51	2.58
Hawaiian Electric Industries	2.15	2.26	2.37	2.54	2.71	2.90	3.11	3.32	3.56	3.81
Idaho Power Co.	1.80	1.85	1.91	1.97	2.03	2.09	2.15	2.21	2.28	2.35
Interstate Power Co.	2.00	2.04	2.08	2.12	2.16	2.21	2.25	2.30	2.34	2.39
Iowa-Illinois Gas & Electric Co.	1.67	1.74	1.81	1.88	1.95	2.03	2.11	2.20	2.29	2.38
IPALCO Enterprises Inc.	1.81	1.90	1.99	2.09	2.20	2.31	2.42	2.54	2.67	2.80
Kansas Power & Light Co.	1.80	1.85	1.91	1.97	2.03	2.09	2.15	2.21	2.28	2.35
Kentucky Utilities Co.	1.42	1.46	1.51	1.55	1.60	1.65	1.70	1.75	1.80	1.85

(Table continues)

Table 2.2   Electric Utility Dividend Forecast (Continued)

Utility	1990	1991	1992	1993	1994	1995	1996	1997	1998	1999
Louisville Gas & Electric Co.	2.78	2.86	2.95	3.04	3.13	3.22	3.32	3.42	3.52	3.63
MDU Resources Group	1.48	1.51	1.54	1.58	1.63	1.68	1.73	1.78	1.84	1.89
Midwest Energy Co.	1.63	1.68	1.73	1.79	1.84	1.89	1.95	2.01	2.07	2.13
Minnesota Power & Light Co.	1.86	1.93	2.01	2.09	2.18	2.26	2.35	2.45	2.55	2.65
Montana Power Co.	1.42	1.45	1.48	1.51	1.54	1.57	1.60	1.63	1.66	1.70
Nevada Power	1.56	1.59	1.62	1.66	1.69	1.72	1.76	1.79	1.83	1.87
No. States Power Co.	2.22	2.33	2.45	2.57	2.70	2.83	2.98	3.12	3.28	3.44
Oklahoma Gas & Electric Co.	2.55	2.67	2.81	2.95	3.10	3.25	3.41	3.58	3.76	3.95
Orange & Rockland Utilities, Inc.	2.33	2.38	2.42	2.50	2.57	2.65	2.73	2.81	2.90	2.98
Pacific Gas & Electric Co.	1.62	1.67	1.72	1.88	2.05	2.23	2.43	2.65	2.89	3.15
Pacificorp	1.44	1.48	1.53	1.57	1.65	1.73	1.87	2.02	2.19	2.36
Pennsylvania Power & Light Co.	2.91	2.99	3.08	3.18	3.27	3.37	3.47	3.58	3.68	3.79
Potomac Electric Power Co.	1.61	1.74	1.88	2.03	2.19	2.37	2.55	2.76	2.98	3.22
PSI Holdings Inc	0.80	0.82	0.85	0.89	0.94	0.98	1.03	1.08	1.14	1.19
Public Service Enterp. Group, Inc.	2.08	2.13	2.24	2.35	2.47	2.59	2.72	2.86	3.00	3.15
Public Service of Colorado	2.00	2.04	2.08	2.12	2.16	2.21	2.25	2.30	2.34	2.39
Puget Sound P & L Co.	1.76	1.76	1.76	1.76	1.81	1.87	1.92	1.98	2.04	2.10
S.W. Public Service Co.	2.25	2.32	2.39	2.46	2.53	2.61	2.69	2.77	2.85	2.93
SCANA Corporation	2.55	2.62	2.70	2.78	2.87	2.95	3.04	3.13	3.13	3.32
SCE Corp.	2.61	2.69	2.77	2.85	2.94	3.11	3.30	3.50	3.50	3.93
Sierra Pacific Resources	1.84	1.90	1.95	2.01	2.07	2.13	2.20	2.26	2.31	2.40
So. Indiana Gas & Electric Co.	1.90	1.96	2.02	2.08	2.18	2.29	2.40	2.52	2.56	2.78
St. Joe Light & Power Co.	1.80	1.93	2.06	2.21	2.36	2.52	2.70	2.89	2.80	3.31
TECO Energy Corp.	1.62	1.70	1.79	1.88	1.97	2.07	2.17	2.28	2.20	2.51
TNP Enterprises	1.63	1.68	1.73	1.78	1.87	1.96	2.06	2.16	2.13	2.39

(Table continues)

Table 2.2   Electric Utility Dividend Forecast (Continued)

Utility	1990	1991	1992	1993	1994	1995	1996	1997	1998	1999
Tucson Electric Power Co.	0.00	0.00	1.00	1.25	1.75	2.25	2.36	2.48	2.60	2.73
Utilicorp United Inc.	1.24	1.32	1.42	1.51	1.67	1.83	2.02	2.22	2.44	2.68
Washington Water Power Co.	2.48	2.53	2.58	2.63	2.68	2.74	2.79	2.85	2.91	2.96
Wisconsin Energy Corp.	1.71	1.81	1.92	2.00	2.08	2.16	2.24	2.33	2.43	2.53
Wisconsin Public Service Corp.	1.59	1.61	1.62	1.64	1.66	1.67	1.69	1.71	1.72	1.74
WPL Holdings Inc.	1.72	1.77	1.82	1.88	1.93	2.01	2.09	2.18	2.26	2.35

In the early part of the 1990s, electric utility stock prices will continue to be strongly influenced by dividends. Dividend growth will be strong during this period as a result of rising profits. Towards the end of this decade, the utilities are likely to lower dividend payout ratios to fund the construction of unregulated power generation facilities; stock prices will then tend to be driven more by cash flow than dividends towards 1999.

Profitability will increase slowly in the early 1990s as the cost of existing power-generating capacity is absorbed, then rise with increasing speed as capacity is pressed. Towards the end of the decade, profits will be tempered by the additional power-generating capacity coming on-line and consumer resistance to higher electricity prices stemming from rising energy prices. Profits will increasingly result from the sale of wholesale power by unregulated independent power producers (IPPs) or cogeneration subsidiaries. The industry will largely be structured into unregulated power producers (which will provide almost all additions to power-generation capacity throughout the decade), regulated power producers (the relative size of this sector of the industry will depend on the outcome of the power struggle between state regulatory agencies and FERC), long-distance transmission facilities (which will function as common carriers), and regulated distributors. The emerging energy shortage may be expected to bring about strong increases in the cost of electric power beginning in the middle of the decade. However, the resultant political pressures are unlikely to reverse the course of deregulation in the industry.

Investments in the nuclear segment of the electric utility industry will carry high levels of risk throughout the 1990s. Two groups of utilities among the 63 firms which comprise this market segment have been identified: 23 firms whose future financial performance is primarily dependent on economic and market factors; and 40 firms whose financial future lies almost entirely within the hands of politicians and regulators.

This segment of the industry was brought to the brink of destruction in the 1970s and early 1980s in its attempt to develop a nuclear source of electric power. The incredible unanticipated expenses of nuclear facility construction, resistance to such facilities in the community, the unforeseen slowdown in energy consumption, and *ad hoc* prudency reviews by regulatory agencies (which resulted in the exclusion of significant amounts of expended capital from the rate base) proved a deadly combination.

The mid-1980s saw a partial recovery for this segment of the industry as excess capacity began to be absorbed and the various nuclear facilities either entered service, were refitted to burn conventional fuels, or were abandoned. Investors reaped significant gains during this period as stock prices recovered from unrealistically low levels.

The 23 utilities with relatively successful nuclear power development will not reap any significant gains for their substantial pains. This power is in their regulated base and the lower costs of production will flow through to their customers. Indeed the legacy of this effort for all of these firms is a severely weakened balance sheet and a reduced ability to fund potentially profitable unregulated power-generation facilities.

Among these 23 utilities with a nuclear exposure judged to be able to influence their own financial outcomes, only modest gains can be expected during the 1990s. It may be that stock ownership in one or more of these firms has speculative merit, but the outcome is highly contingent on factors other than those under direct management control. The fate of these firms is dependent on something other than their ability to function as business entities. As a result, it is felt that the risk associated with the purchase of stock in one of these firms is not adequately compensated for by the potential return. These modest returns are associated with significantly higher risk than the electric utilities without nuclear exposure covered in Chapter 6. This risk arises from three separate sources: (1) a nuclear mishap at a particular firm would have a negative impact on earnings and share price at that firm; (2) a nuclear mishap at any firm could dampen investor enthusiasm for this segment of the industry—affecting the stock prices of all firms with nuclear power-generating facilities; and (3) the market has currently (1990) attributed a very low net effective discount factor to these firms—its unlikely this factor would become more favorable, but quite possible for it to become even less favorable.

Prospective investors in electric utilities take a very hard look at nuclear risk-return combination. Better opportunities appear to be available among electric utilities without nuclear exposure.

The 40 utilities with nuclear exposure judged to be highly risky present interesting speculative possibilities. Each of these utilities is a candidate for a significant turnaround, because each is currently down. The experience in this sector of the industry between 1984 and 1988 is that turnarounds can yield investors handsome rewards.

The question is will these utilities stay down? A case can be made that by the mid-1990s the shortage of electrical capacity will be so critical and the need for a healthy utility industry so obvious, that these firms will be made whole by the powers that be. It is unlikely that these firms will extricate themselves from their financial difficulties or judicial morass by the middle of the 1990s. Certainly they will not do it on their own. As the outcomes for these firms will be determined by political factors rather than economic factors, there is hope. Financial health is only a rate increase away.

A list of "risky" electric utilities with nuclear exposure is presented in Table 2.3.

Gas Utility Industry Forecasts

While overall returns for investors in the natural gas industry were uneven between 1984 and 1989, the prospects for this industry brighten considerably in the decade to come.

The current consumption patterns are such that the use of petroleum as an energy source dwarfs that of natural gas. Even though natural gas has notable advantages over its petroleum competitors in handling costs and environmental impact, the basic cause of prosperity or depression in the natural gas industry may be found in the relative supply of, and demand for, petroleum products. This does not mean the two sectors move in concordance. Although the supply elasticities are roughly equivalent, domestically produced natural gas, unlike petroleum, is not subject to the shifts in the supply of oil that result from our dependence on international conditions.

Table 2.3 Speculative Electric Utilities with Nuclear Exposure

1. American Elec. Pwr.
2. Boston Edison
3. Centerior Energy
4. Central & South West's Corp.
5. Central Hudson
6. Central Maine
7. CMS Energy Corp.
8. Commonwealth Edison
9. Commonwealth Energy System
10. Detroit Edison Co.
11. Dominion Resources
12. Duquesne Light Co.
13. Eastern Utility Associates
14. Gulf States Utilities
15. Houston Industries, Inc.
16. IE Industries
17. Illinois Power Co.
18. Iowa Resources Inc.
19. Kansas City Power & Light Co.
20. Kansas Gas & Electric Co.
21. Long Island Lighting Co.
22. Middle South Utilities Inc.
23. Midwest Energy Co.
24. N.E. Utilities
25. N.Y. State Electric & Gas Corp.
26. New England Electric System
27. Niagra Mohawk Power Corp.
28. NIPSCO Industries Inc.
29. Ohio Edison Co.
30. Philadelphia Electric Co.
31. Pinnacle West Capital Corp.
32. Portland General
33. Public Service Company of New Mexico
34. Public Service Company of New Hampshire

(Table continues)

Table 2.3 Speculative Electric Utilities with Nuclear Exposure (Continued)

35. Rochester Gas & Electric Corp.
36. San Diego Gas & Electric Co.
37. Southern Co.
38. Texas Utilities Co.
39. Union Electric Co.
40. United Illuminating Co.

The two sectors are also differentiated by the heavier degree of regulation in the natural gas sector. The current move to deregulate this sector further changes the equation between the two sectors.

Eighteen diversified gas companies are expected to stage a resurgence based upon the presence of significant natural gas reserves; a climate of increasing energy prices; their position in a service market that is characterized by good growth potential; their possession of underutilized exploration and drilling subsidiaries, (which will increase significantly in value as petroleum prices rise); and the extent to which the debilitating excess supply of natural gas during the last half of the 1980s depressed their stock price at the beginning of 1989.

Consequently, investors in diversified gas companies in the coming decade can look forward to the possibility of exceptional gains. Investors should be aware that this pleasant situation may experience a few jarring notes along the way.

The 30 local distribution companies who performed so well for investors in the 1984–1989 period will not fare as well in the coming decade. While increases in capacity utilization through the middle of the decade will help propel a steady increase in profits, as this portion of its activities remains regulated, the increase will be weak. In addition, as energy prices rise to stressful levels, the local distribution companies will experience increasing difficulty in obtaining rate relief for their nonfuel costs.

As a result, only moderate returns may be expected from the local distribution companies. However, these returns will be accompanied by little downside risk.

Forecast stock prices and dividends for the natural gas industry are presented in Tables 2.4 and 2.5 respectively.

Telecommunications Industry Forecast

The perception that the telecommunications industry is mature is inaccurate. Telecommunication firms are just entering an era of dynamic growth and change. Rapid and continuing technological change will result in an ever-increasing demand for telecommunications services, both domestically and worldwide.

The telecommunications industry will enter the 1990s with a vigorous competitive market. Existing firms and new market entrants will jostle side by side for potentially lucrative emerging market niches. The competition will be rough. The Federal Communications Commission (FCC) and the courts will maintain a form of structured competition to ensure a continuation of strong competitive forces.

Chapter 12 examines the potential returns for 12 independent telephone companies (ITCs).

Driven by continual technological innovation, the ITCs will have the chance to enter new market niches and establish profitable market positions. The greatest asset these firms possess is the ability to move more swiftly to emerging markets than the competition and to react more quickly to changing technologies. Potential profits from merger or acquisition activity among the ITCs increases the attractiveness of investments in this sector. If properly managed, these independent telephone companies will become obvious growth vehicles. This would make them doubly attractive to the regional operating companies (RHCs) who have generally taken a conservative approach to exploiting the new growth areas in telecommunications with their existing organizations.

Chapter 13 develops a forecast of financial performance among the seven RHCs, or "baby bells." These seven firms were created in 1984 out of AT&T's basic operating companies (which provide tra-

Table 2.4 Gas Industry Stock Price Forecast

	1990	1991	1992	1993	1994	1995	1996	1997	1998	1999
Arkla, Inc.	23.46	24.84	26.34	27.98	29.76	30.19	30.63	31.08	31.54	32.01
Atlanta Gas Light Company	29.64	30.75	31.92	33.17	34.49	35.89	37.37	38.94	40.61	42.38
Bay State Gas Company	19.95	20.46	21.32	22.23	23.18	24.18	25.23	25.67	26.13	26.58
Brooklyn Union Gas Company	28.70	29.14	29.29	29.44	29.60	29.75	29.44	29.13	28.83	28.54
Burlington Resources	42.25	45.68	51.05	64.82	83.88	119.13	145.85	180.53	181.65	183.43
Cascade Natural Gas Company	16.85	17.22	17.60	17.80	18.00	18.21	18.42	18.63	18.85	19.08
Coastal Corporation	32.13	34.11	38.96	51.41	63.37	75.33	68.32	57.87	48.41	47.70
Columbia Gas System	44.13	50.23	56.14	75.84	106.12	146.83	137.95	114.24	91.22	75.27
Connecticut Natural Gas Corp.	16.46	16.92	17.41	17.92	18.03	18.14	17.92	17.71	17.49	17.29
Consolidated Natural Gas System	45.00	48.37	55.72	73.98	103.71	137.26	139.01	139.31	126.08	126.08
Diversified Energies, Inc.	31.58	32.84	34.17	35.58	37.07	38.66	40.34	42.12	44.00	46.00
Eastern Gas & Fuel Associates	28.95	29.99	31.10	31.43	31.78	32.13	31.59	31.07	30.56	30.07
Energen Corporation	18.31	19.04	19.79	20.58	21.19	21.82	22.47	22.25	22.03	21.81
Enron Corporation	55.88	91.31	134.28	158.96	203.72	264.63	268.09	267.39	233.12	192.36
Enserch Corporation	25.52	30.57	37.44	44.97	59.10	79.29	65.59	63.02	59.09	53.95
Equitable Resources	34.79	40.59	49.03	64.02	93.22	123.38	133.36	130.74	117.77	117.42
Indiana Energy, Inc.	19.39	19.66	19.79	19.93	20.07	20.21	19.93	19.65	19.38	19.11
KN Energy	25.68	29.58	35.62	41.62	49.97	52.91	45.64	39.94	33.02	30.76
Laclede Gas Company	29.75	30.31	30.89	30.88	30.88	30.88	30.58	30.28	29.99	29.70
Louisiana General Services Inc.	20.68	21.33	22.01	22.73	23.48	24.27	24.77	25.29	25.82	26.36
MCN Corporation	20.29	20.81	21.34	21.88	22.44	23.02	23.62	24.23	24.86	25.52
Mitchell Energy	17.48	21.99	27.43	35.14	43.84	49.82	52.72	44.66	39.80	33.43
N.W. Natural Gas	26.77	27.24	27.72	28.05	28.39	28.74	28.56	28.39	28.21	28.04
National Fuel Gas Co.	23.34	24.00	24.68	25.39	26.13	26.71	27.30	27.91	28.54	29.19
New Jersey Resources Corp.	18.98	19.35	19.75	20.15	20.57	20.70	20.82	20.95	21.08	21.20

(Table continues)

Table 2.4 Gas Industry Stock Price Forecast

	1990	1991	1992	1993	1994	1995	1996	1997	1998	1999
Nicor Incorporated	37.82	38.22	38.62	38.82	39.03	38.82	38.61	38.41	38.21	38.01
NUI Corporation	17.50	17.80	18.11	18.44	18.43	18.43	18.21	17.99	17.78	17.57
Oneok Inc.	13.48	15.35	17.57	18.79	23.44	25.80	26.21	25.16	25.36	23.43
Pacific Enterprises Corp.	42.64	43.99	45.40	46.87	47.90	48.96	50.05	50.42	50.80	51.18
Panhandle Eastern Corp.	25.32	28.30	31.05	36.22	41.73	51.50	59.33	53.56	49.68	41.40
Peoples Energy Corporation	24.22	24.80	25.40	26.03	26.36	26.70	26.53	26.36	26.19	26.02
Piedmont Natural Gas Co.	27.25	28.27	29.36	30.53	31.24	31.99	32.37	32.77	33.17	33.58
Providence Energy	23.37	24.71	26.20	27.85	29.19	30.63	31.41	32.22	33.06	33.93
Questar Corporation	34.36	35.88	37.48	38.89	40.38	41.94	43.58	44.27	44.97	45.69
Seagull Energy Corp.	25.60	28.11	33.23	37.06	41.33	43.40	40.51	35.57	32.74	29.32
Sonat Inc.	49.77	52.11	57.47	73.60	77.90	89.54	73.08	64.89	54.69	49.23
South Jersey Industries, Inc.	17.17	18.34	19.61	21.00	22.52	24.17	25.57	27.07	28.67	30.39
Southwest Gas Corporation	17.78	18.46	19.18	19.93	20.56	21.22	21.73	22.26	22.80	23.36
Tenneco Inc.	66.54	69.85	80.01	91.18	98.03	105.40	96.89	86.06	89.37	84.33
Transco Energy Company	41.18	47.50	56.44	68.28	80.28	86.50	71.30	76.94	62.53	62.07
UGI Corporation	36.67	37.76	38.90	40.58	42.38	44.30	46.36	48.56	50.92	53.44
Valero Energy	16.25	17.30	20.76	27.23	29.76	36.44	29.77	28.13	25.67	25.54
Washington Energy Company	19.41	20.10	20.82	21.58	21.98	22.39	22.81	23.24	23.68	24.13
Washington Gas Light Co.	29.64	30.60	31.61	32.69	33.83	34.44	35.06	35.70	36.36	37.05
Wicor, Inc.	22.74	23.45	24.18	24.57	24.96	25.35	25.76	25.55	25.35	25.14
Williams Company	30.91	35.81	40.24	49.62	60.09	69.14	69.31	65.02	68.24	71.62

Table 2.5 Gas Industry Dividend Forecast

	1990	1991	1992	1993	1994	1995	1996	1997	1998	1999
Arkla, Inc.	1.17	1.21	1.26	1.31	1.37	1.42	1.48	1.54	1.60	1.66
Atlanta Gas Light Company	1.94	2.04	2.14	2.25	2.36	2.48	2.60	2.73	2.87	3.01
Bay State Gas Company	1.24	1.31	1.39	1.45	1.51	1.57	1.63	1.70	1.76	1.83
Brooklyn Union Gas Company	1.81	1.85	1.90	1.95	1.99	2.04	2.10	2.15	2.20	2.26
Burlington Resources	0.70	0.72	0.80	0.88	1.13	1.49	2.37	2.93	3.11	3.14
Cascade Natural Gas Company	1.34	1.38	1.41	1.45	1.48	1.52	1.56	1.60	1.64	1.68
Coastal Corporation	0.40	0.45	0.52	0.60	0.70	0.84	0.91	1.21	1.21	1.19
Columbia Gas System	2.20	2.23	2.34	2.65	3.38	4.79	5.45	5.71	5.70	5.65
Connecticut Natural Gas Corp.	1.36	1.39	1.41	1.44	1.47	1.50	1.53	1.56	1.63	1.63
Consolidated Natural Gas System	1.84	2.02	2.17	2.59	3.30	4.37	5.41	6.09	6.30	6.30
Diversified Energies, Inc.	1.59	1.64	1.69	1.74	1.79	1.84	1.90	1.96	2.02	2.08
Eastern Gas & Fuel Associates	1.45	1.50	1.55	1.61	1.62	1.64	1.66	1.67	1.69	1.71
Energen Corporation	0.90	0.92	0.94	0.96	0.99	1.02	1.05	1.09	1.12	1.15
Enron Corporation	2.48	2.48	2.90	3.25	3.50	8.09	9.83	10.50	10.68	10.58
Enserch Corporation	0.80	0.81	0.94	1.12	1.40	1.78	1.97	2.03	2.05	2.02
Equitable Resources	1.34	1.48	1.70	1.96	2.42	3.21	3.85	4.49	4.63	4.61
Indiana Energy, Inc.	1.30	1.34	1.38	1.42	2.59	2.59	2.59	2.59	2.59	2.59
KN Energy	1.13	1.22	1.29	1.50	1.71	1.81	1.85	1.85	1.93	1.92
Laclede Gas Company	2.38	2.40	2.43	2.45	2.45	2.45	2.45	2.45	2.45	2.45
Louisiana General Services Inc.	0.75	0.79	0.83	0.87	0.91	0.96	0.99	1.02	1.05	1.08
MCN Corporation	1.58	1.62	1.66	1.70	1.74	1.79	1.83	1.88	1.93	1.97
Mitchell Energy	0.32	0.37	0.48	0.66	0.95	1.37	1.61	1.75	1.82	1.84
N.W. Natural Gas	1.63	1.67	1.70	1.72	1.73	1.75	1.77	1.79	1.80	1.82
National Fuel Gas Co.	1.35	1.39	1.43	1.48	1.52	1.57	1.61	1.66	1.71	1.76
New Jersey Resources Corp.	1.33	1.36	1.39	1.43	1.47	1.51	1.56	1.61	1.65	1.70

(Table continues)

Table 2.5 Gas Industry Dividend Forecast

	1990	1991	1992	1993	1994	1995	1996	1997	1998	1999
Nicor Incorporated	2.08	2.10	2.12	2.14	2.16	2.19	2.21	2.23	2.25	2.27
NUI Corporation	1.56	1.56	1.60	1.60	1.60	1.60	1.60	1.60	1.60	1.60
Oneok Inc.	0.74	0.77	0.88	0.94	1.00	1.11	1.21	1.26	1.27	1.28
Pacific Enterprises Corp.	3.48	3.48	3.48	3.58	3.69	3.80	3.88	3.96	4.04	4.12
Panhandle Eastern Corp.	2.00	2.00	2.00	2.00	2.00	2.06	2.37	2.47	2.48	2.48
Peoples Energy Corporation	1.65	1.70	1.75	1.80	1.86	1.91	1.84	1.84	1.84	1.84
Piedmont Natural Gas Co.	1.65	1.73	1.82	1.91	2.01	2.11	2.15	2.19	2.23	2.28
Providence Energy	1.40	1.47	1.54	1.62	1.70	1.79	1.86	1.93	2.01	2.09
Questar Corporation	2.00	2.12	2.25	2.34	2.43	2.53	2.63	1.90	1.90	1.90
Seagull Energy Corp.	0.00	0.00	0.00	0.00	0.97	1.09	1.16	1.19	1.19	1.20
Sonat Inc.	2.02	2.08	2.30	2.51	2.73	3.13	3.26	3.29	3.28	3.35
South Jersey Industries, Inc.	1.42	1.49	1.57	1.64	1.73	1.81	1.90	2.00	2.10	2.20
Southwest Gas Corporation	1.40	1.47	1.54	1.62	1.70	1.79	1.88	1.97	2.07	2.17
Tenneco Inc.	3.12	3.38	3.60	3.65	3.92	4.22	4.47	4.69	4.87	5.06
Transco Energy Company	1.35	1.46	1.76	2.21	2.83	3.24	3.56	3.71	3.75	3.72
UGI Corporation	2.33	2.42	2.52	2.62	2.73	2.83	2.95	3.04	3.13	3.22
Valero Energy	0.20	0.29	0.42	0.57	0.62	0.91	0.95	0.70	0.71	0.71
Washington Energy Company	1.30	1.37	1.43	1.50	1.58	1.66	1.74	1.83	1.92	2.02
Washington Gas Light Co.	1.98	2.04	2.10	2.16	2.23	2.27	2.32	2.36	2.41	2.46
Wicor. Inc.	1.40	1.44	1.47	1.51	1.55	1.58	1.63	1.68	1.73	1.78
Williams Company	1.40	1.41	1.59	1.88	2.25	2.59	2.89	3.05	3.20	3.36

ditional hard-wire, local telephone service on a regional basis). These firms remain fully regulated by state regulatory agencies.

It might be thought that the RHCs would continue to function as classic regulated utilities. This, however, will not be the case. The RHCs have become transformed into growth companies. The quickening pace of technological innovation and emerging competition have left them with no other strategic choice to protect their stockholders' wealth.

Chapter 14 looks at future possibilities for investors among the four common carriers. AT&T is seen losing its dominant share of the long-distance telecommunications market to MCI and Sprint, but being able to maintain its profitability despite this situation.

Forecast stock prices and dividends for these telecommunication firms are presented in Tables 2.6 and 2.7 respectively.

Water Utilities Forecast

Investing in water utility stocks has traditionally represented a trade-off of return for safety. The increased popularity of this sector following the October 1987 crash pushed up prices (and consequently pushed down yields) to levels that do not appear sustainable over the long run. The price and dividend forecasts presented in Tables 2.8 and 2.9 reflect the optimistic assumption that this popularity will prove enduring. Chapter 15 concludes that the optimism is likely unwarranted. Prudent investors would do well to look elsewhere for safety and return.

Table 2.6 Telecommunications Industry Stock Forecast

Utility	1990	1991	1992	1993	1994	1995	1996	1997	1998
Alltell Corporation	$31.53	$36.23	$56.04	$71.36	$82.86	$96.09	$90.90	$96.65	$102.87
Ameritech	60.40	63.12	66.02	71.10	80.88	89.55	94.32	99.43	104.91
AT&T	39.60	43.58	45.36	46.78	52.21	53.98	59.57	67.50	75.24
Bell Atlantic	50.00	54.05	58.88	65.18	72.77	78.76	86.02	94.04	102.91
Bellsouth	52.50	56.83	59.63	65.13	67.84	73.49	82.67	92.82	99.34
C-Tec Corporation	20.00	21.83	22.72	25.68	29.02	32.95	39.20	45.15	49.27
Centel Corporation	34.13	36.50	38.74	42.71	45.58	51.23	61.62	72.73	78.64
Century Telephone Enterprises	18.14	21.31	24.95	29.40	33.45	38.11	45.39	51.90	54.01
Cincinnati Bell Inc.	23.88	25.27	26.75	28.34	30.29	32.39	34.65	37.10	39.42
Citizens Utilities Company	35.07	38.40	42.05	43.78	49.99	52.30	54.74	51.80	54.12
COMSAT	33.50	33.38	33.03	33.44	33.50	34.13	34.78	35.45	36.14
Contel Corporation	25.69	28.86	34.27	39.40	49.99	58.44	66.22	69.53	73.70
GTE Corporation	31.33	34.66	38.74	43.69	49.70	56.30	63.56	70.75	78.58
MCI	41.55	51.85	59.23	69.54	77.88	87.46	98.47	111.15	125.72
NYNEX	82.20	83.66	84.47	85.58	86.71	88.59	90.53	92.53	94.92
Pacific Telesis	44.54	48.55	54.18	58.84	66.08	72.18	81.51	92.13	101.07
Rochester Telephone Corp.	31.32	34.64	41.31	46.86	54.90	61.99	69.93	72.83	78.25
So. New England Telecomm.	32.26	36.31	40.68	45.99	51.77	58.78	66.49	73.28	79.69
Southwestern Bell	54.00	60.35	69.20	82.80	91.13	101.12	119.69	134.28	142.52
U.S. West	37.07	38.88	40.80	42.58	45.97	48.02	52.73	56.07	59.66
United Telecomm. (Sprint)	38.13	45.19	51.85	63.38	76.74	93.14	114.66	136.39	162.47

Table 2.7 Telecommunication Industry Dividend Forecast

Utility	1990	1991	1992	1993	1994	1995	1996	1997	1998	1999
Alltell Corporation	$1.20	$1.34	$1.55	$1.96	$2.25	$2.59	$2.97	$3.33	$4.07	$4.56
Ameritech	2.06	2.17	2.33	2.60	3.11	3.57	3.82	4.09	4.38	4.69
AT&T	1.29	1.44	1.47	1.50	1.76	1.85	2.11	2.49	2.85	3.21
Bell Atlantic	2.33	2.52	2.71	3.06	3.49	3.82	4.22	4.67	5.16	5.70
Bellsouth	2.75	3.07	3.26	3.67	3.86	4.24	4.85	5.54	5.97	6.51
C-Tec Corporation	0.00	0.12	0.24	0.27	0.34	0.40	0.47	0.60	0.68	0.76
Centel Corporation	0.85	0.85	0.85	0.96	1.04	1.24	1.49	1.79	2.09	2.41
Century Telephone Enterprises	0.42	0.47	0.54	0.62	0.69	0.75	0.87	0.99	1.14	1.32
Cincinnati Bell Inc.	0.77	0.82	0.92	1.08	1.16	1.26	1.36	1.47	1.57	1.66
Citizens Utilities Company	1.74	1.82	1.91	2.03	2.15	2.28	2.42	2.56	2.71	2.88
COMSAT	1.36	1.38	1.39	1.42	1.43	1.47	1.51	1.56	1.61	1.65
Contel Corporation	1.11	1.19	1.29	1.43	1.63	1.85	2.04	2.25	2.47	2.72
GTE Corporation	1.48	1.58	1.68	1.84	1.99	2.18	2.36	2.58	2.81	3.03
MCI	0.00	0.00	0.00	1.67	2.56	3.68	4.66	5.36	6.16	7.09
NYNEX	4.50	4.55	4.61	4.69	4.78	4.92	5.06	5.21	5.39	5.58
Pacific Telesis	2.05	2.15	2.47	2.64	3.04	3.37	3.87	4.45	4.93	5.47
Rochester Telephone Corp.	1.45	1.53	1.65	1.82	2.04	2.29	2.56	2.82	3.00	3.30
So. New England Telecomm.	1.71	1.85	1.93	1.99	2.17	2.39	2.63	2.99	3.20	3.43
Southwestern Bell	2.77	3.17	3.62	4.25	4.74	5.32	6.41	7.26	7.74	8.77
U.S. West	1.98	2.04	2.17	2.29	2.43	2.56	2.87	3.08	3.31	3.56
United Telecomm. (Sprint)	1.01	1.21	1.38	1.83	2.22	2.68	3.27	4.33	5.10	5.99

Table 2.8 Water Industry Stock Price Forecast

Utility	1990	1991	1992	1993	1994	1995	1996	1997	1998	1999
American Water Works	$16.18	$18.00	$20.00	$21.00	$22.50	$24.00	$25.00	$27.00	$30.00	$33.62
California Water Service Co.	25.00	25.63	26.31	27.36	28.09	29.24	30.02	31.26	32.57	33.93
Connecticut Water Service	17.94	17.94	17.97	17.97	17.97	17.97	18.30	18.64	18.99	19.35
Consumers Water Co.	14.53	15.37	16.26	17.20	18.19	18.74	19.62	20.54	21.51	22.52
E'Town Corporation	35.05	35.70	36.86	37.51	39.62	41.87	44.25	46.77	49.44	52.27
Hydraulic Company	23.38	23.75	23.75	24.00	24.50	25.25	26.00	27.00	28.00	28.75
Middlesex Water Co.	10.00	10.50	11.00	11.25	12.00	12.50	13.00	13.50	14.00	14.50
Phila. Suburban Water Co.	13.70	14.19	14.12	14.41	14.39	14.27	14.21	14.86	14.57	14.26
SJW Corporation	25.42	26.60	27.84	29.58	31.17	32.86	34.66	36.55	38.57	40.70
So. California Water Co.	31.00	32.00	33.25	34.00	35.04	36.71	38.48	40.35	42.34	44.45
United Water Resources	13.49	14.81	14.91	14.87	15.84	17.44	18.42	19.27	20.09	20.15

Table 2.9   Water Utility Dividend Forecast

Utility	1990	1991	1992	1993	1994	1995	1996	1997	1998	1999
American Water Works	$0.81	$0.91	$1.00	$1.15	$1.27	$1.39	$1.50	$1.62	$1.75	$1.89
California Water Service Co.	1.75	1.81	1.87	1.96	2.02	2.13	2.20	2.30	2.42	2.54
Connecticut Water Service	1.48	1.48	1.48	1.48	1.48	1.48	1.51	1.54	1.57	1.60
Consumers Water Co.	1.18	1.25	1.33	1.41	1.50	1.55	1.63	1.71	1.80	1.88
E'Town Corporation	2.91	2.96	3.07	3.12	3.31	3.51	3.72	3.94	4.18	4.43
Hydraulic Company	1.61	1.66	1.68	1.73	1.79	1.84	1.89	1.95	2.01	2.07
Middlesex Water Co.	0.93	0.96	1.00	1.04	1.08	1.13	1.17	1.22	1.27	1.32
Phila. Suburban Water Co.	0.93	0.97	0.96	0.99	0.99	0.98	0.97	1.03	1.00	0.98
SJW Corporation	1.98	2.09	2.20	2.35	2.49	2.64	2.80	2.97	3.15	3.34
So. California Water Co.	2.02	2.09	2.19	2.32	2.46	2.61	2.77	2.93	3.11	3.29
United Water Resources	0.93	1.05	1.05	1.05	1.14	1.28	1.37	1.44	1.51	1.52

Chapter 3

PUBLIC UTILITY STOCK PRICE DETERMINATION

Understanding public utility stock prices in the 1990s requires recognizing that public utilities will be in a transition process throughout this period. The rules that governed investment decisions in the past are being replaced by new rules that have yet to become sufficiently established to rely on with blind faith. As public utilities seek equilibrium in an increasingly difficult and uncertain environment, utility stock values are likely to experience uncharacteristic volatility.

Old investment rules that are losing their validity include:

- Dividends will support stock prices.
- Size equates to market strength and translates into stability of earnings.
- Earnings support dividends.
- When push comes to shove, regulators have the ability to bail the utilities out of a difficult situation.
- Efficiency tends to be less of a priority than egalitarian social goals for regulators.
- Financial leverage greater than that found in comparably sized industrial firms is desirable.

- In the prevailing management philosophy, profits take a backseat to service.

New rules that are gaining validity include:

- Cash flow drives stock prices.
- Position in a growing market niche is more important than immediate earnings.
- Dividend payouts are a lower priority than maintaining future earnings growth.
- Above-normal profits are seen as an appropriate market incentive provided such profits are shared with the consumers.
- In the prevailing management philosophy, service takes a backseat to profits.

This changing scenario has important implications for investors in public utilities. Profitable opportunities and potential disasters will abound in the 1990s. To assist the investor in capitalizing on these opportunities and avoiding the potential pitfalls, this chapter will explore the historical framework for public utility stock prices and the implications of the current environment for future public utility stock prices.

Public Utilities as Natural Monopolies

The historical justification for regulating public utilities was that they were natural monopolies providing a good or service that was essential to the public welfare. Provisioning of such services was not left to a market solution because the presence of substantial economies of scale was thought to preclude competition. In exchange for the "franchise," the public utility gave the state the right to set its prices and, in exchange, received a guarantee that it would be allowed to earn a fair return on its investment.

A natural monopoly has three characteristics: (1) it provides a good or service that is seen as essential to the well-being of the members of society, (2) there are no satisfactory substitutes for this good or service, and (3) the underlying economics (the presence of large fixed-costs and economies of scale) of producing the good or service do not allow a sufficient number of firms to provide a competitive market solution.

The generation, transmission and distribution of electric power; the production, transportation, and distribution of natural gas; and telephone service and water service have been seen as having the characteristics of natural monopolies. To a greater or lessor extent (depending on the sector of the industry) the government has chosen at times to own the necessary facilities and provide these services directly to the public. However, the bulk of electric, gas and telephone services in the United States are currently provided by public utilities that are privately owned.

Investor-owned utilities are allowed to provide these essential services to the general public for two reasons: first, it allows the tremendous amounts of necessary capital to be raised without placing this burden on the taxpayer; second, it is felt that the private sector, being driven by the profit motive, is more likely to operate such facilities efficiently.

Where the government chooses to allow private industry to supply these services as a natural monopolist, it does so in exchange for the right to regulate that service. This concept was enunciated by the Supreme Court in *Munn* vs. *Illinois* in 1877:

> Property does become clothed with a public interest when used in a manner to make it of public consequence, and affect the community at large. When, therefore, one devotes his property to a use in which the public has an interest, he, in effect, grants to the public an interest in that use, and must submit to be controlled by the public for the common good, to the extent of the interest he has thus created.

What a utility may earn from its activities is referred to as the rate of return and generally defined as the amount of earnings above all expenses, expressed as a percentage of the rate base. The basic framework for the rate of return was specified by the Supreme Court in the landmark *Bluefield Waterworks*:

> A public utility is entitled to such rates as will permit it to earn a return on the value of the property it employs for the convenience of the

public equal to that generally being made at the same time and in the same general part of the country on investments in other business undertakings which are attended by corresponding risks and uncertainties; but it has no constitutional right to profits such as are realized or anticipated in highly profitable enterprises or speculative ventures. The returns should be reasonably sufficient to assure confidence in the financial soundness of the utility and should be adequate, under efficient and economical management, to maintain and support its credit and enable it to raise the money necessary for the proper discharge of its public duties. A rate of return may be reasonable at one time and become too high or too low by changes affecting opportunities for investment, the money market and business conditions generally.

As a practical matter, this does not guarantee an investor in a public utility an appropriate return on his or her equity. Certainly, the history of regulation in the industry has created some notable exceptions to this intention, but these were just that—exceptions. As long as social policy is committed to using private capital to finance these essential services, the utility can obtain additional capital from the market only by passing the "market test." That is, if the rate of return (adjusted for risk) offered by a utility is not competitive with comparable investments, then the value of the securities of that utility will fall to a lower level. This can create a situation in which a utility is unable to obtain additional capital to finance improvements or expansion. Regardless of which way political winds blow, sooner or later the regulators must deal with this reality.

The Utility Rate Making Process

Although significant differences exist in the regulatory processes among the different public utility industries, and further differences exist between state and federal regulators and among the various state regulators, all regulatory agencies follow the same basic process in determining a desirable level of earnings.

The basic framework holds that the revenue required by the utility be equal to its cost of service. Cost of service is the sum of all proper expenses chargeable to current utility services plus a return on the assets used in providing that service. The return is equal to the rate base (which generally consists of assets currently being

Table 3.1

XYZ Utility Income Statement
($000,000)

Operating Revenues	1,200.	
Operating Expenses	1,170.	
Operating Income		30.
Other Income	50.	
Income before interest		80.
Interest	30.	
Net Income		50.
Taxes (34%)	17.	
Net Profits after Taxes		34.

used valued at original cost less depreciation) times a "fair" rate of return.

This process can best be understood by considering a public utility's income statement (Table 3.1).

Assuming the utility has a rate base of $500, it has an effective rate of return of 6.8 percent (34./500.).

A firm may apply for relief (a rate increase) from the regulatory agency if its return is insufficient to cover its cost of capital.

The firm's cost of capital is calculated by taking the weighted average of its cost of capital in the following manner. If the capital structure of the utility is 60 percent long-term debt and 40 percent equity, then the actual cost of its long-term debt (30./300 = 10 percent) and the administratively or judicially determined cost of equity capital (assumed to be 12 percent in this case) are averaged to come up with an average cost of capital (i.e., .6 × 10 percent + .4 × 12 percent = 10.8 percent).

The cost of capital is then applied to the asset base to determine if the return was adequate, i.e., if revenues were equal to cost of service. In this case, 10.8 percent (the cost of capital) of 600 (the rate base) equals 64.8. Since earnings were 34, a rate increase should be permitted. The size of the rate increase necessary to raise earnings to the permitted level is dependent on the income tax rate. If the income tax rate is 34 percent, then the rate increase must be "grossed up" to 46.7 (i.e., an increase of net income of 46.7 is necessary to yield an after-tax profit increase of 30.8).

If the regulatory commission grants the increase, then it would normally request the utility to submit revised tariffs (price schedules by type of customer). As the regulatory commission is generally concerned with achieving a number of public goals in setting rates, that is, besides ensuring the adequacy of stockholder return, an extended hearing process may be initiated to ensure that all affected parties are well served by the regulatory commission.

While highly simplified, the above scenario captures the essence of the regulatory rate setting process. This process does not guarantee the investor a fair rate of return; at any point in the process there are assumptions that can be made to bring about whatever outcome the regulators feel is appropriate. For example, there may be disagreements over exactly what assets are permitted in the rate base or what expenses are necessary and proper.

Regulatory commission members are often politically appointed or elected and may be quite responsive to community needs or concerns over the cost of utility service. If the utility disagrees with the interpretation of the regulators, a judicial appeal may be undertaken, these appeals tend to be both lengthy and expensive.

The experience of utilities generally proves that it is much easier to earn an adequate rate of return in an environment characterized by falling or constant service costs than in an environment where the cost of service is rising.

Whatever the mechanics or politics of the process, as a regulated monopoly, the utility must ultimately pass the market test to gather sufficient capital so as to provide adequate service in the long run. As discussed below, if the utility does not have sufficient monopoly power and is unable to pass the market test, or its regulators do not permit the utility to earn a competitive rate of return on its investment, the utility's owners will suffer a continuing decrease in shareholder wealth.

In the transitory environment of the 1990s, long-term decreases in shareholder wealth loom as a distinct possibility for utilities in an unfavorable regulatory environment, or where management is not up to the competitive challenge in a newly turbulent market.

Deregulation and the Breakdown of Monopoly Markets

Deregulation is not a cause of the breakdown of traditional public utility market structures. Rather, deregulation is a response to a shift in political philosophy and a response to technological changes that have broken the monopolistic market structure for many traditional utility services.

The increasing rate of technological innovation weakened barriers that created many natural monopolies. New products that could serve as substitutes for the utility's service (as in the case of long-distance telecommunications) were created. In addition, technological changes have tended to reduce the economies of scale necessary for efficient operation. A smaller scale reduces the barriers to entry and permits new, unregulated market entrants (as in the case of cogeneration in the electric utility industry). Recent advances in solid state electronics, computer technology, solid state physics, metallurgy, energy conversion, and a host of related areas suggest the likelihood of the continuation of this trend.

This situation is often exacerbated by artificial price structures. In their pursuit of social goals, regulators frequently created price structures that did not reflect the cost of providing the service. This situation gave additional incentive to new competitors to enter the market (e.g., where long-distance rates were used to subsidize local service in the telecommunications industry). Under these circumstances, many utilities began to suffer serious loss of revenues to the new competitors. This loss of revenues tended to drive up unit costs, further encouraging competitive inroads.

There were two possible regulatory responses to this situation. One response would have been to extend regulation to the new competitors, thereby protect the existing utilities. The second possible response would have been to allow the competitive market forces to bring about market solutions. If natural competitive market forces proved unworkable, the regulatory agencies could create pseudo-competitive structures administratively and thereby bring about market type solutions.

The second approach has largely been taken as a result of a general shift in political philosophy towards a market ideology. This emergent force found voice with the election of President Reagan in 1980 and has continued with President Bush. The appeal of a movement away from the concentration of power in the hands of government bureaucrats towards a decentralized market mechanism struck a responsive chord with the American public. Notable success with deregulation in the airline industry has given this idea credibility.

It is somewhat ironic that while the initial thrust of the movement towards a market ideology was accompanied by a desire to shift power from the federal level to local government, the net effect of deregulation has been to place increasing power at the federal level. The Federal Communications Commission (FCC) in the telecommunications industry and the Federal Energy Regulatory Commission (FERC) in the electric and gas industries have been in the forefront of pushing for deregulation over the resistance of state regulatory agencies.

Deregulation can be implemented as an explicit policy by existing regulatory agencies. *De facto* deregulation has been occurring since the mid-1970s, as many public utilities correctly foresaw the increasing disadvantages of operating as regulated entities in markets they no longer monopolized. This form of deregulation has occurred as utilities diversified out into unregulated markets. Throughout the public utilities sector, many firms chafed at the thought of being confined to their traditional markets and made every effort to move into new areas where they have some competitive advantage and can employ their capital with better returns. Since public utilities are capital intensive, they often have substantial cash flows to finance a diversification effort. As these firms become increasingly diversified, their financial characteristics will increasingly mirror those of firms in the industrial sector.

The main criterion of performance in a competitive industry is profit. The search for profit will increase innovation and change. New products and markets will emerge, new technologies will be stimulated, resources will be shifted from old patterns, and costs will be put under pressure. As this process continues, some firms will emerge as consistent winners and their stock will appreciate accordingly. Other firms will falter, and this too will be reflected in their stock prices.

Evaluating the Financial Performance of Public Utilities

Evaluation of a utility's financial performance begins with a consideration of its financial statements. For investors, information on the financial performance of utilities is obtained from financial statements presented in annual reports and in 10k and 10q reports filed with the Securities Exchange Commission (SEC). This information is audited by public accounting firms that issue opinions on the financial data presented.

The data is carefully scrutinized by a variety of investment advisory services such as Moody's, Standard and Poor's, and Value Line. A plethora of publications on public utilities is readily available by subscription or in public libraries. In addition, many stockbrokerage firms publish research relating to the financial prospects of individual firms.

There are two problems in using this data: one problem lies in the difficulty of interpreting just what the data means; the other difficulty lies in assessing the quality of earnings.

Interpreting the Data

It is commonly understood that data on financial performance has consistent meaning between firms and for a single firm over time. Even when such data is compiled according to generally accepted accounting principles (GAAP) by a reputable firm, this is an oversimplification. This situation is compounded in the utilities industries by the imposition of additional accounting assumptions required by the regulatory agencies. Utility firms keep no less than four sets of books—one conforming to SEC concepts (which is what investors are most familiar with), one for tax purposes, one for the local regulatory agency, and one for the federal regulatory agency. Given the complexity of these differing constructions, its a small wonder that the utility executives themselves are able to assess the financial performance of their firm.

Little consolation may be taken from the fact that most utilities receive "unqualified" opinions from their auditors. An "unqualified" opinion that accompanies such financial statements means that everything which should have been exposed has been exposed and that the numbers are not materially wrong. The opinion states that the financial statements have been developed in accord with generally accepted accounting principles (GAAP). This does not mean that the numbers presented are suggestive of reality. Reality may well lie in the footnotes. There is plenty of room in GAAP to develop a misleading impression by the judicious combination of data categories and the use of unrealistic or arbitrary assumptions. Reality may well be in such financial statements, but it need not be apparent.

A second category of opinions are "subject to." This means the auditor finds the financial data subject to pervasive uncertainty. This is a judgment call and its infrequent use suggests this opinion should be a red flag to the investor. For example, the depreciable cost of an asset is its original cost, less salvage value plus any clean-up or disposal costs. It is clear that the current practice of estimating cleanup costs for nuclear reactors in the electric utilities sector seriously underestimates these costs. Although the numbers are large and seem to imply "pervasive uncertainty," electric utilities in this situation invariably receive an unqualified opinion. How bad must the circumstances be for the utility to receive a "subject to" opinion?

It is also possible for a firm to receive an "except for" opinion or a disclaimer of opinion from its auditor. An "except for" opinion means that the auditors were unable to examine certain areas of the organization. Such opinions constitute a violation of SEC regulations for publicly listed firms.

A clean, unqualified auditor's opinion does not mean that things are as they seem. It is up to the investor to determine what such data means.

Quality of Earnings

Conceptually, net income on the income statement is the most important indicator of how well a firm is doing. As a practical matter, it is almost meaningless. Net income is an abstraction from reality embodying a boatload of accountants' assumptions and conventions. An investor who relies solely on net income as a measure of performance (as in price-earnings multiples) is walking on quicksand. Furthermore, 1988 saw an increasing deterioration of net income as a measure of anything as a result of new Financial Accounting Standards Board (FASB) rules in the area of pension benefits, health benefits and deferred taxes.

Income

There are two basic kinds of income that do not fit the popular notion of what income is. The first kind of income arises from nonrecurring events and the second type of income (phantom income) has not actually happened but is inferred to be likely to happen in the future.

Nonrecurring Income In the context of the dividend discount model we examine current income in order to infer something about the flow of income in the future. Income that may be expected is generally that from normal, recurring operations. If nonrecurring income occurs it may be regarded as an aberration. Consequently, in considering the net income of a firm, we would ignore (subtract out) any nonrecurring income. From an accounting point of view, a variety of treatments with respect to timing are consistent with GAAP: nonrecurring income may be treated as a lump sum or spread out over a period of time; nonrecurring income may be taken account of when incurred or when realized. The actual treatment is buried in the footnotes.

A further problem in this area occurs in making a distinction between normal operating income and nonrecurring income. In the industrial sector, it is not uncommon for nonrecurring income to occur regularly over time. In this sense, nonrecurring income becomes a pseudonym for nontraditional income, which is quite a different concept. For example, many industrial firms (such as ITT) with volatile earnings have merged with financial services companies in order to manipulate nonrecurring investment to smooth net income for the firm as a whole. As utilities diversify, this may become an increasing problem in determining the "true" level of income.

Phantom Income A big problem, particularly in the electric and gas utilities, is the Allowance for Funds Used During Construction

(AFUDC, or sometimes AFC). From 1981 to 1987, this form of phantom income accounted for more than half of all the reported income of electric utilities. AFUDC is an accounting treatment that credits net income an imputed return on funds tied up in construction work in progress (CWIP). Although occasionally CWIP is included directly in the rate base, this is unusual. As a political matter, the regulatory agencies favor a "lower now, higher later" policy because then ratepayers pay these charges as the facilities are used rather than when they are constructed. This policy is in accordance with the accounting principle that revenues should be recognized at the same time the costs associated with those revenues are recognized.

AFUDC is calculated by applying a firm's weighted average cost of capital to its dollar investment in CWIP. The resultant sum is divided into an equity portion and a debt portion according to their respective fractions in the firm's capital structure. The equity portion is then applied to the income statement as "other income." (In Table 3.1 this would have appeared as "other income.") The debt portion is deducted from actual interest payments (in Table 3.1, it would have been netted out of interest expense). The net effect is to increase income by the combined effect of the AFUDC charges. This amount is then capitalized and included as part of the total cost of new construction.

In theory, at some later point in time this new construction enters the rate base and thus returns the cost of capital to the company, except there is no certainty that this will happen. In an era of excess capacity and slowly growing demand, the addition of new capacity frequently must pass a prudency review by the regulatory agency. If the plant creates what is determined to be excess capacity, its construction will be found not to be prudent and, thus, disallowed from the utility's base. Disallowances under these circumstances (particularly if the construction involves a controversial nuclear plant) have been an all too frequent occurrence. When this happens, the utility forgoes a return on its invested capital as well as the phantom profits.

Expenses

Proportionately increasing or decreasing expenses may hold the key to future profitability in a way that does not necessarily meet the eye.

Increasing expenses may reflect changing underlying economic conditions that management is unable to avoid or they may reflect ineffective management practices. In the former case, the existence of regulatory lag may impose real costs on the firm. In the latter case (if so judged by the regulatory agency), the firm may not be allowed to pass these costs on to the customers.

Increasing expenses may paradoxically harbinger future decreases in expenses: sometimes to save money you have to spend money. Prior to deregulation, utilities were frequently not (and many are still not) organized for efficiency. Competition has put pressure on overstaffing and induced a search for more cost-efficient means of providing service. Achieving lower costs in the long run frequently require higher costs up front. A good example of this situation would be the use of an early retirement plan to reduce staffing levels; expensive in the immediate period, but well worth it over a longer time horizon.

Increasing expenses may also be a function of revenue enhancement activities. As competition and deregulation create new opportunities for utilities in existing and new markets, moving into these markets requires incurring expenses before revenues are received. For example, in the telecommunications sector a number of companies have been moving very strongly into the cellular telephone market, which appears to be potentially quite lucrative. However, this activity has increased expenses and diminished earnings in the short run.

Thus, the impact of expenses on earnings should not be considered in a mechanical fashion. It may be necessary to investigate what lies behind changing expense patterns.

Cash Flows

Many of the problems associated with interpreting the net income of a utility can be overcome by focusing on cash flow. Determining the cash flow of an organization used to be a very difficult. FASB 95 has replaced the old "Statement of Changes in Financial Position" with a "Statement of Cash Flows." This latter statement often proves quite helpful in determining a company's current position and future performance. Unlike the net income concept, cash flow is grounded in reality. In the industrial sector, cash flow has clearly proved a more reliable predictor of stock prices than net income. The great thing about cash flow is you know what it means: cash either comes in and goes out, or it doesn't.

Cash flow is both the source of dividends and the source of internally generated funds that can be reinvested in the firm. As such, cash flow will play a critical role in determining a utility's stock price. Much can be learned from an examination of the components of cash flow and their trends. The Statement of Cash Flows breaks out where the cash comes from and where it goes to—in operations, investments, and financing as separate categories. Thus, this statement will yield a clear view of how healthy a firm's operations really are.

This concept may be further augmented through the development of the concept of "free cash flow." Free cash flow may be defined as cash flow less dividends and necessary capital expenditures. Free cash flow thus represents a source of cash for increasing dividends or diversification outside its regulated markets. An increasing trend in free cash flow bodes well for a potential increase in total return. A decreasing, or negative, free cash flow has the opposite implications.

Earnings are not an unambiguous indicator of financial performance in the utility sector. For example, in 1987 NYNEX reported net income of $950 million for a respectable return on equity of 10.3 percent. However, NYNEX had a negative free cash flow of $304.3 million (one of only two baby bells with a negative free cash flow in 1987). NYNEX is operating in a very difficult market and will need additional capital merely to maintain service, much less explore new opportunities. Without a rate increase, this firm, its shareholders, and probably its customers are in for difficult times.

Focusing on earnings rather than free cash flow is apt to mislead an investor as to this firm's true prospects.

Forecasting Utility Stock Prices

The Changing Framework of Stock Price Determination

The ultimate value of any stock is determined by its ability to generate cash flow, at the present and in the future, whether retained by the organization or distributed to the shareholders in the form of dividends.

In the past, public utility firms typically paid out a larger portion of their earnings in the form of dividends than did industrial firms. Within a traditional natural monopoly environment, the earnings of utilities were characterized by a high degree of stability. It was frequently a source of pride that utilities were able to maintain constant or increasing dividends over long periods of time. Under these circumstances, equity securities in the utility sector behaved a lot like high-grade, long-term debt securities in the industrial sector. Utility stocks were frequently purchased by investors who wanted a reliable source of continuing income. Unlike long-term debt instruments, utility stocks could experience increasing dividends and, thus, were thought to provide some degree of protection against the ravages of inflation. As a result, current yields from utility stocks tended to be slightly below those available from comparable long-term debt instruments.

This situation caused utility stock prices to be an inverse function of long-term interest rates. Increasing interest rates tended to drive utility stock prices down. Decreasing interest rates tended to drive utility stock prices up.

In contrast, although not immune to the impact of interest rate fluctuations, industrial stock prices tended to be a function of future earnings potential. This made industrial stock prices generally sensitive to the stage of the business cycle, foreign exchange rate changes, inflation, and changes in the tax structure. As a consequence, industrial stock prices tended to be a function of their cash flow (cash flow being a more reliable indicator of financial performance than earnings, for reasons described above).

For the industrial stock market as a whole, stock prices might be 12 times cash flow at the beginning of the expansionary phase of the business cycle, when future earnings looked bright. At the beginning of a recession, stock prices might be five times cash flow, reflecting the dim prospects for future growth.

For individual industrial firms, the stock of a firm with good growth prospects might sell for twenty times cash flow, even though its earnings were small. In contrast, the stock of a mature firm with few prospects for increased earnings might sell for three times its cash flow, no matter how large its current earnings.

The relationship between utility stock prices and interest rates is in the process of change. Falling market barriers, aided and abetted by deregulation, have changed the fundamental business context for public utilities. No longer can earnings stability be confidently relied upon. The need to exploit the ever-increasing flow of technological advances and the need to meet competitive pressures are reducing dividend payout rates in all areas of the public utility sector. As the impact of competition, technological change, diversification, and industry restructuring increasingly impact financial performance, utility stock prices will become less sensitive to interest rate changes and more sensitive to changes in potential earnings.

As a result, utility stock prices will increasingly become functions of cash flow. Changes in current cash flows are likely to be interpreted as indicative of future earnings trends. Utility stock prices will increasingly come to behave like the stocks of industrial firms in a highly competitive, turbulent market.

This process of change will increase both the opportunities and dangers associated with investing in the public utility sector.

The Dividend Discount Model (DDM)

The value of a stock lies in its ability to earn future profits. This is the basis of the current emphasis in the investment community on "value investing." The basic model for this concept goes back to J. William's *The Theory of Investment Value* in 1938 and was popularized by Benjamin Graham and David Dodd in their book *Security Analysis; Principles and Techniques*.

To be sure, stock prices can rise and fall dramatically with no apparent changes in underlying earnings potential.   Such price movements are often the result of speculative frenzy and resemble a Ponzi pyramid in which prices go up as long as a bigger fool can be found and come crashing down when one can't be found. Such price movements are inherently difficult to anticipate.

In contrast, potential earnings can be forecast with a fair degree of reliability. Situations can be uncovered where firms have so positioned themselves that earnings will rise inexorably. Similarly, some firms appear to find themselves mired in situations of falling earnings from which they are unable to extract themselves. Consider in the past two decades the meteoric rise of Federal Express and the steady descent of Railway Express—two firms that positioned themselves differently in basically the same business.

The concept of value investing finds expression in what is sometimes called the dividend discount model (DDM). The power and attractiveness of this model lies in its basic simplicity and comprehensiveness. Paradoxically the DDM does not require that profits be immediately translated into dividends. Despite its name, the model relates future earnings to stock price. It does not matter if these earnings are repatriated in the near, intermediate, or long-term. The assumption is that eventually earnings will accrue to the stockholders. A firm may wisely choose to reinvest its earnings in itself rather than pay these earnings out as dividends. As long as the market feels that this investment will yield an appropriate downstream increase in profits, potential earning will support the stock price.

The most common formulation of this model is one in which the price of any stock is equal to the discounted value of its dividend stream over time. This concept may be expressed in the following form:

$$P = \frac{D_1}{(1+r)} + \frac{D_2}{(1+r)^2} + \ldots + \frac{D_n}{(1+r)^n}$$

where P is the price of the stock, D the dividends in any given year, r an interest rate reflecting the value of money over time (which has two components: (1) a risk-free rate of interest and (2) a premium for the market risk experienced by the firm), and n any given period of years.

If dividends (D) may be assumed to be constant and to grow at a constant rate (g) then this formula reduces to:

$$P \ = \ \frac{D}{(r-g)} \ .$$

The use of dividends in this formulation is an abstraction of the assumption that future earnings will eventually be received by shareholders as dividends. What if the firm currently pays no dividends? What if the dividends paid are not reflective of future earnings? As a practical matter, estimates of future earnings can be substituted for the flow of dividends in this model. As a result of the arbitrary nature of accounting systems, estimates of cash flow tend to have better predictive value than net profit as a measure of earnings in this model.

While clearly an oversimplification of reality, the model does provide a basic understanding of what drives stock prices, why some firms with the same basic earnings will sell for five times earnings and others sell for 15 times earnings. The answer lies in differences in the expected growth of earnings.

Critics of the DDM often belabor the fact that small changes in current earnings can have an exaggerated impact on stock price. This occurrence is entirely consistent with the DDM. A relatively small change in earnings can have a dramatic effect on stock price because that current change in earnings signals the market that g is changing as well.

Exactly how this model works may be seen in the following example:

ABC Corporation is currently earning $5.00 per share per year and is expected to experience a 5 percent annual growth in earnings. Under current money market conditions the long-term risk-adjusted rate of interest is 10 percent. Consequently, its per share stock price is $100.

$$P \ = \ \frac{\$5.00}{.10-.05} \ = \ \frac{\$5.00}{.05} \ = \ \$100.$$

A quarterly report is issued indicating quarterly earnings of $1.00. However, the $5.00 earnings estimate above was predicated upon the expectation of $2.00 earnings in this quarter. If the market interprets this event as merely impacting current earnings and not effecting future growth prospects, then the stock price will fall to $80.

$$P \ = \ \frac{\$4.00}{.10 - .05} \ = \ \frac{\$4.00}{.05} \ = \ \$80.$$

However, if the market interprets the fall in the quarterly earnings to mean that the firm's growth prospects have halved, then the impact on stock price is much more dramatic.

$$P \ = \ \frac{\$4.00}{.10 - .025} \ = \ \frac{\$4.00}{.075} \ = \ \$53.33.$$

What the market sees as the growth potential for the firm is clearly the linchpin in determining the future price of a stock.

Any regular reader of financial columns in the daily newspaper or the monthly business and finance magazines will be struck by the frequency with which the DDM is repudiated or refuted. Such frequency is backhanded testimony to the power and durability of the model.

Most of the criticism of the model comes from its misapplication. The market is complex, the model simple. The purpose of the model is not to predict stock prices, but to understand stock prices. "Tests" of the model that purport to show it doesn't work fail, not because the model is invalid, but because the model is misspecified. This misspecification arises because the key component of the model—future earnings—is not observable. Future earnings are in the eye of the beholder, i.e., they are subjective. The market consensus of future earnings is thus subject to emotional and psychological forces, which can produce considerable price volatility. The mass hysteria of October 19, 1987 is a case in point.

Using Earnings to Forecast Utility Stock Prices

Two formulations of the DDM are used to forecast stock prices in the following sections.

Electric Utilities Among electric utilities, the formula $P = D/(r-g)$ is used where: P = Price of a share of stock; D = dividends per share; r = rate of discount, which includes the risk free interest rate (the interest rate on long-term federal government bonds) plus a premium for market risk; and g = the long-term rate of growth anticipated in dividends. Dividends are used rather than cash flow per share because, among electric utility stocks, dividends are much better predictors of price change than cash flow in the DDM. This relationship probably reflects the strength of the traditional perception of the importance of dividends in this industry. Among electric utilities, dividends remain of prime importance in determining stock price.

How long this remains so in the future is open to question. Deregulation and competition are coming to the industry very rapidly. Many electric utilities are diversifying into unregulated electric power generation or diversifying out of the electric industry altogether.

The forecast of dividends developed to predict stock prices among electric utilities suggests considerable variation in cash flow per share (CFS) growth patterns in the industry—and the ability to pay dividends ultimately rests upon the ability to earn profits. Dividend payouts among electric utilities may be expected to become increasingly volatile in the future as these firms respond to the pressures of newly competitive markets. It is not unlikely that within the decade electric utility stock prices will become more a direct function of cash flow and less a direct function of dividends.

Telecommunication, Gas, and Water Utilities Among telecommunication, gas, and water utilities, a formulation of the DDM ($P = CFS/(r-g)$) is used where: P = Price of a share of stock; CFS = cash flow per share; r = rate of discount, which includes the risk-free interest rate (the interest rate on long-term federal government bonds) plus a premium for market risk; and g = the long-term rate of growth anticipated in dividends.

This formulation appears to have good predictive power. The use of CFS as a proxy for earnings recognizes the reality of the strategic focus of these firms. Shareholders are focusing more on future earnings power (and, consequently, future dividends) than on the immediate level of dividends in assessing the value of these stocks.

The specific forecasts in these industries use the DDM by employing a least-square regression model in the form $P = a + b(CFS)$ where: a is a constant indicating that component of share price independent of earnings and b indicates the impact of earnings directly on share price. Thus, the share price estimates among telecommunication, gas, and water utilities are based directly on estimates of future earnings. Dividend payouts are seen as a consequence of both the level of earnings and the strategic posture of the individual firm.

Chapter 4

EVALUATING THE PERFORMANCE OF INDUSTRIAL AND UTILITY STOCKS

Comparing Industrial and Utility Stocks

The conventional perception of utility stocks as investment vehicles has been misdirected by simplistic and inappropriate comparisons between utility and industrial stocks. The most important difference between the two categories of stock, from an investment perspective, is that utility stocks historically have paid out most of their earnings as dividends while industrials have not. A related problem is that the popular indexes are constructed in such a way that the utility stock index usually has a much smaller base than a comparable industrial stock index. Thus, the absolute change in an industrial stock index may be larger than that for a utility index, but smaller on a percentage basis.

As a theoretical matter, this difference is easily accountable. Yet it has significant implications for the way in which data on stock movements are depicted in the press. The distortion in the perception of the public utility sector, resulting from the inherent difference between the two types of stock, has concealed the fact that utility stocks have generally outperformed industrial stocks since WWII.

Two illustrations clarify this distortion:

(1) Stock A (industrial) was purchased at the beginning of 1990 for $100 and sold at the end of 1990 for $110. No dividends were paid. Stock B (utility) was purchased at the beginning of 1990 for $100 and sold at the end of 1990 for $107. It paid $7.00 dividends. It is clear that evaluating stock performance without considering dividends is inappropriate.

(2) On April 7, 1989, the Dow Jones 30 Industrials (DJI) rose 12.83 points while the Dow Jones 15 Utilities (DJU) rose 1.24 points. Which class of stocks did the best? Since the DJI base of 1941.48 on that day was much larger than the DJU base of 167.08, the DJU actually had the larger increase (.67 percent relative to the DJI's .56 percent).

Comparing the DJI and the DJU

While the problem of perception may seem trivial, it has contributed to a general underestimation of the performance of utility stocks in the stock market: utilities tend to be thought of as an area with lackluster performance. Investing in utilities is seen as unexciting: an ultraconservative strategy best fit for widows and orphans. In fact, as detailed below, utility stocks have generally outperformed industrial stocks since 1960. In addition, the impact of deregulation on an extraordinarily turbulent market promises high drama among utility stocks in the 1990s. Opportunities for exceptional profits will be found among the utility stocks by the informed investor.

Figure 4.1 presents the absolute Dow Jones Industrial and Utility stock price averages over the last 28 years on a quarterly basis. The overwhelming impression gleaned from this commonly found presentation is that utilities offer few prospects for successful investments.

Even if dividends are considered to be automatically reinvested as in Figure 4.2, the picture appears not to change dramatically. The performance of utility stocks still seems to be lackluster relative to that of industrials.

This perspective results from the use of a different base in each index. One way to overcome this perceptual problem is to create two $1,000 portfolios and then apply the actual percentage rate of

Figure 4.1   Dow Jones Industrial and Utility Stock Price Indexes

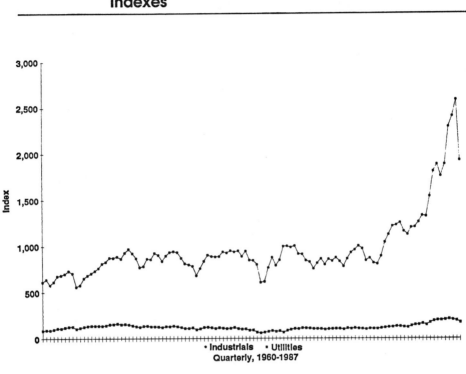

change in the different indexes to the two portfolios. This approach is taken in Figure 4.3. It is evident from this formulation that the utility portfolio actually outperforms the industrial portfolio throughout most of the period.

In addition to offering higher returns between 1960 and 1987, the industrial portfolio exhibited greater variance on a quarter-to-quarter basis than did the utility portfolio. This may be seen in Figure 4.4.

The relative performance of portfolios is quite sensitive to the climate of the period in which they are started. Nevertheless it is

Figure 4.2   Dow Jones Industrial and Utility Stock Indexes with Dividends Reinvested

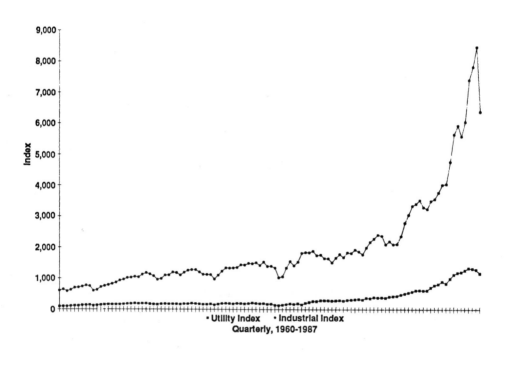

worthwhile to examine more closely the relative performance in the two sectors during the recent bull market.

Figure 4.5 illustrates what would happen if an investor purchased a $1,000 portfolio in each sector in 1978 and reinvested dividends through 1987.

An analysis of portfolios begun in 1978, based on the performance of the two indexes with reinvested dividends throughout the period, suggests that the holder of the utilities-based portfolio would have done better at any point in time during this period. With minor fluctuations, the advantage gained by the utilities-based

Figure 4.3 $1,000 Stock Portfolio
Dow Jones Industrial and Utility Portfolios

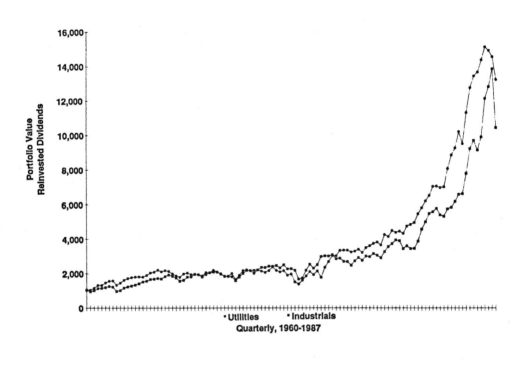

portfolio continued to gain throughout the period, with the notable exception of the third quarter 1986 to the third quarter 1987. The run-up in industrials during this time may well have reflected speculative excesses that the utilities market avoided. Industrials fell more than utilities in the October 1987 price break, and utilities have gained steadily since that time.

Alternatively, the relative performance of two similar portfolios begun in 1982 and extending through 1987 suggests a quite different picture. The run-up of industrial stock prices, relative to utility stock prices, prior to the October 1987 price break produced supe-

Figure 4.4   Quarterly Portfolio Returns

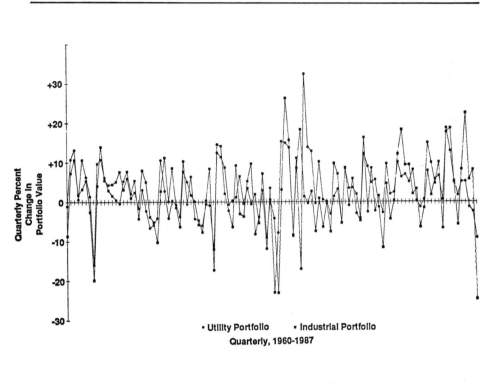

• Utility Portfolio   ▪ Industrial Portfolio

Quarterly, 1960-1987

rior performance for the industrials-based portfolio throughout most of the period. This may be seen in Figure 4.6.

Calculating the Total Rate of Return (TRR)

Despite its intuitive appeal, the foregoing analysis does not yield a clear insight into the relative performance of the two sectors. There are two basic reasons for this. First, the preceding analysis makes it clear that the time selected to begin the portfolio influences the outcome of the portfolio comparison. An additional problem is that the return on reinvested dividends is tied to subsequent portfolio performance. Since utility dividends do not necessarily have to be rein-

Figure 4.5   Dow Jones Industrial and Utility Portfolios

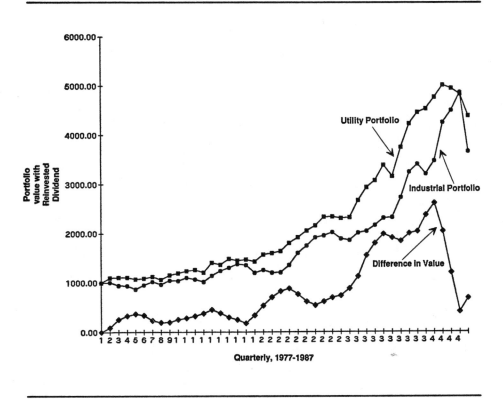

vested, this procedure may understate the return on utilities relative to industrials, i.e., utility dividends are available for investment elsewhere.

These problems may be overcome and a clearer insight into the nature of the comparative performance of industrial and utility stocks may be obtained through an evaluation of the total rate of return (TRR) generated by an investment. The TRR is expressed as an annual percentage rate that averages the total return over the life of the investment, in a way that takes account of the timing of inflows and outflows. (Mathematically, the concept developed here as the total rate of return is known as the internal rate of return, some-

Figure 4.6   Dow Jones Industrial and Utility Portfolios

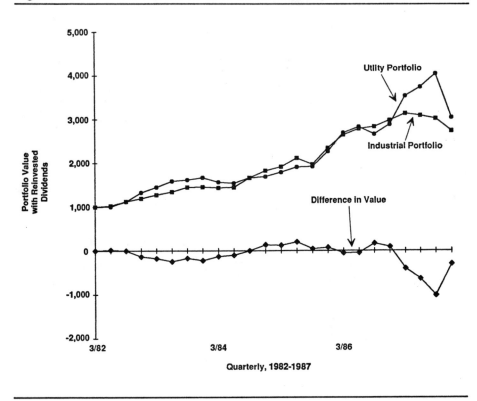

times abbreviated as the IRR. The terminology of total return is used in this book because it is more descriptive of what the technique actually measures.)

Examples of the total rate of return (TRR) are shown on the facing page.

The TRR is a rate of discount that equates a purchase price to all subsequent cash flows. This concept of return is sensitive to the timing of cash inflows and outflows, as well as the amounts of such cash flows. Thus, the TRR effectively measures the average annual return on an investment over the life of that investment. As a result, the TRR can be used to effectively compare investments with different cash flow characteristics.

	Stock A	Stock B	Stock C	Stock D
Purchase Price	$100.	$100.	$100.	$100.
Dividends				
Year 1	0	10.	0	10.
Year 2	0	10.	0	10.
Year 3	0	10.	0	10.
Year 4	0	10.	10.	0
Year 5	0	10.	10.	0
Year 6	0	10.	10.	0
Selling Price	125.	200.	150.	150.
TRR	11.5%	10.4%	10.4%	9.3%

In the example above, Stock A had a TRR of 11.5 percent, indicating its average return over an eight-year period. This may be compared with Stock B's TRR of 10.4 percent. Even though Stock B had significantly greater price appreciation, the level and timing of the dividends gave Stock A an advantage. (Note that the absolute value of Stock A's dividends and appreciation is 85, whereas Stock B's appreciation is 100. Stock A still had the higher average return because the return to the investor was received sooner.)

An advantage with the TRR approach is it recognizes the critical effect of the timing of cash flows. This may be seen in a comparison of Stock C and Stock D. Each receives the same level of dividends and price appreciation, but Stock C receives its dividends earlier and thus experiences a higher average annual return.

The formula from which the TRR is calculated is as follows:

$$\text{Initial Investment} = \frac{NCF_1}{(1+TRR)} + \frac{NCF_2}{(1+TRR)^2} + \frac{NCF_3}{(1+TRR)^3} + \ldots + \frac{NCF_n}{(1+TRR)^n}$$

where NCF_n refers to net cash flows in year n.

While the direct calculation of the TRR is a difficult task, in this age of solid-state miracles, it is not necessary to perform such a task manually. Many hand-held calculators have this as an automatic function. Most electronic spreadsheets also have this capability.

Applying the TRR to the Industrial and Utility Portfolios

The TRR may be used to evaluate the utility and industrial portfolios developed above. The results of this evaluation of portfolio performance (without reinvested dividends) are presented in Table 4.1.

As a result of this analysis, it can be seen that for all practical
purposes, utilities and industrials as investment classes have had
similar yields since 1960 when the timing and size of dividends
were taken into account. Since utility stocks generally have lower
betas than industrials (i.e., are less exposed to market risk), this
means that the investor can generally expect to get the same return
on industrials and utilities, but that the utility stocks will be less
risky. For risk averse investors (not those afraid to take a risk, but
those who require a greater return for being exposed to greater
risk), utility stocks were clearly the preferred investment during
this period.

Real and After-Tax Rates of Return

The evaluation of the TRR also facilitates consideration of the real
rate of return. The real rate of return would be the average annual
return less the annual rate of inflation.

Consumer prices (as measured by the CPI-U) increased 185 percent between the beginning of 1960 and the end of 1987—an average annual increase of 6.6 percent. Thus, in this period of time the

Table 4.1   Internal Rate of Return; Industrial and Utility Portfolios (Dividends not Reinvested)

Portfolio Term	Utility Portfolio	Industrial Portfolio
1960-78	8.58%	8.47%
1968-87	10.14	9.15
1978-87	14.74	14.54
1983-87	17.96	17.97

purchasing power of money declined at an average rate of 6.6 percent. If an investor had invested in the utility portfolio over this period of time, the real return on the investment would be 4.9 percent (11.5 percent − 6.6 percent = 4.9 percent). Thus, investing in either industrial or utility stocks during these portfolio periods would have protected the investor's real wealth from the ravages of inflation. The only time when this effect did not hold during this period was when the rate of inflation soared briefly into the high teens in the early 1980s.

An important caveat to this analysis is required by the issue of taxes. Investors correctly want to maximize after-tax income. The above analysis considers only pre-tax income. Prior to the Tax Reform Act of 1986 when income from earnings was taxed at a much higher rate than capital gains, individuals in high marginal tax brackets may well have had a better after-tax return from industrial stocks than utility stocks. This would result from the fact that capital gains (stock price appreciation) were taxed at a lower rate than earnings (dividends). As the current tax code does not make this distinction, there is no inherent tax advantage in either of the two types of investment. If a lower capital gains tax is reinstituted, this may well impact the relative desirability of industrial stocks to the extent that utilities pay out substantially more of their earnings as dividends.

Chapter 5

ELECTRIC UTILITY FUNDAMENTALS

Organizational Overview of the Electric Utility Industry

The electric utility industry is covered in Chapters 5-7: Chapter 5 examines industry fundamentals, analyzes the recent performance of 96 electric utilities, and identifies the five driving forces which will shape the industry in the 1990s. Chapter 6 undertakes an individual analysis of the future prospects for each of the 33 major electric utilities without nuclear exposure, and forecasts stock prices, dividends and the returns to investors for this group of firms through 1999. Chapter 7 undertakes an individual analysis of the future prospects for 23 of the 63 major electric utilities with nuclear exposure and forecasts stock prices, dividends and the returns to investors for these firms through 1999.

Electric Utility Industry Performance Overview

The outlook for investors in nonnuclear electric utilities during the 1990s is exciting. This segment of the industry presents opportunities for handsome gains accompanied by less risk than those found among comparable industrial firms. An examination of the regulatory, environmental and competitive forces among the 33 major utilities that do not have nuclear exposure facilities suggests that firms in this sector on the average will outperform firms in the industrial sector throughout the 1990s.

This situation presents the investor with the opportunity for extraordinary gains with disproportionately little risk. In this high performing segment of the utility industry, four outstanding firms are seen to be positioned to reward their stockholders with annual gains conservatively estimated to be in the 15 to 20 percent range. These four firms are Utilicorp United Inc., St. Joe Light and Power Company, Hawaiian Electric Industries and the Potomac Electric Power Company.

Significant potential gains are also available to investors among the 63 major electric utilities that own nuclear power generating facilities or have suffered from an attempt to develop a nuclear power source. However, these gains are associated with significantly higher risk than those characterizing investment in electric utilities without nuclear exposure. No investment in firms with nuclear exposure is recommended for investors to whom the preservation of their capital is a top priority.

Among the 63 electric utilities with nuclear exposure, 40 of these are found to be so weakened by their experience with nuclear power generation that investment in these firms is highly speculative. The investment outcome for these firms will be determined primarily by noneconomic factors. Their fate lies within the sphere of complex regulatory and political processes.

Twenty-three electric utilities with nuclear exposure are determined to have an outcome that rests primarily on predictable economic factors. Paradoxically, prospective returns among these firms are expected to average less than for those firms with no nuclear exposure. It is clear that our economic system as it is currently structured has not, and will not, reward forays into the use of nuclear power.

Industry Fundamentals: 1973–1983

This era was an extraordinarily difficult one for the electric utility industry. The energy crisis led to rate shock for electric consumers and politicized the regulatory process. Demand, which had historically grown at 3 percent, slowed and then ceased to increase, leaving utilities under construction with considerable excess capacity. Growing environmental concerns required huge capital expenditures. Attempts to develop nuclear power as an alternative source of energy proved difficult at best and, for many utilities, precipitated an unmitigated disaster.

The impact of these forces was to severely diminish the quantity and quality of earnings throughout the industry. The decline in earnings suggested an impaired ability to sustain or increase dividend levels. Consequently, stock prices were depressed.

Industry Fundamentals: 1984–1989

During this period the effects of the energy crisis abated. Instability among OPEC members resulted in falling oil prices, while the requirements of environmental legislation had largely been addressed. The industry completed a building cycle, resulting in an improvement in the quantity and quality of earnings, and the enhanced cash flows rebuilt the firm's balance sheets and provided many firms with unprecedented opportunities to seek profitable investments.

As a consequence, stock prices in this sector rebounded and many firms were able to increase their dividends.

Industry Fundamentals: 1990–1999

Demand for electric power is expected to increase moderately throughout this period, although considerable regional variation will occur. A period of excess capacity through 1992 will keep electricity prices stable. Following this point, capacity will be increasingly pressed in an era of escalating electricity prices.

The regulatory process will change considerably during this era. As the fundamental changes are significant, the pace of change will be uneven and accompanied by a great deal of uncertainty and confusion. Power will shift from the state regulatory agencies to the Federal Energy Regulatory Commission (FERC). This will create more of a "level playing field" for utilities. Electric power will be deregulated at the federal level and new generating capacity will be increasingly supplied by independent power producers (IPPs) and cogeneration projects.

Environmental concerns are seen to be an important priority, but not a top priority in the 1990s. The issues associated with the deterioration of the ozone layer, the greenhouse effect and acid rain are so complex and knowledge so piecemeal that it is likely to take more than a decade to build a political consensus that will significantly impact the cost of energy production. Consequently, no major legislation is expected during this period.

A significant number of mergers will increase industry consolidation throughout this period as utilities seek to take advantage of operational efficiencies in the deregulated wholesale power market. Some diversification effort will be undertaken, with mixed results. Utilities investing in IPP subsidiaries and cogeneration projects will be richly rewarded.

Utility stock prices and dividends for many firms will increase steadily throughout this period. Investors in the nonnuclear segment of the electric utility industry will generally receive handsome rewards.

Financial Performance: 1984–1988

Investors in electric utilities experienced dazzling success between 1984 and 1989. The 96 electric utilities surveyed during this period recorded an average TRR of 22.8 percent. That is, on the average, each stock in this group (counting price appreciation and dividends) returned 22 percent annually to an investor holding it over this period. This spectacular performance compares favorably with both the Dow Jones Utility Index TRR of 18 percent and the Dow Jones Industrial Index TRR of 18 percent. The range of this performance is illustrated in Figure 5.1

This tremendous performance was accomplished with an average beta (measure of market risk) of .70—suggesting that investing in electric utilities during this period produced higher gains with less risk than the general market.

Not all utilities performed equally well. TRRs ranged from a high of almost 50 percent (General Public Utilities) to a low of 16 percent (Public Service Company of New Hampshire). Understanding the reasons for this variance among electric utilities yields insight into those factors determining returns in this sector in the decade of the 1990s. To facilitate an understanding of the determinants of return in coming years, the industry's recent performance is examined by breaking the electric utilities down into four groups based on their returns to investors between 1984 and 1988: stars, strong performers, average performers and dogs.

Figure 5.1   TRR (1984–1988)

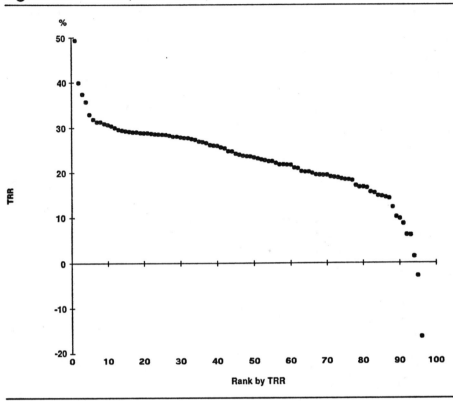

Stars The performance of the top group was nothing short of stupendous. These "stars" of the industry were found to have their values abnormally depressed at the beginning of this period as a result of general industry difficulties in the prior decade. However, they were poised for high growth. They took advantage of improved business conditions and converted additional revenues into significantly higher profits. Putting the difficulties of the earlier era behind them, they used their considerable cash flows to strengthen their balance sheets and reward their stockholders.

It is worthwhile to note that despite the critical role played by the regulators in this industry, none of these firms operated in a particularly favorable regulatory environment. Their performance reflected the strength of their underlying business fundamentals.

Strong Performers A second group of utilities performed solidly throughout this period as well. While exceptional, their performance was less spectacular than that of the first group. To some extent this reflected the fact that they were recognized by the market as being well-managed and well-positioned companies in spite of general industry difficulties. An additional factor was that, as a result of slower growing markets, they were not as effective in converting revenue gains to profits as were the stars.

Average Performers A group of average performing utilities was also found. The returns accruing to the shareholders of utilities in this group were satisfactory, but hardly outstanding. These utilities tended to serve stagnant markets and have difficulties controlling costs. In addition, they tended to be located in relatively unfavorable regulatory climates.

Dogs The final group of utilities were literally brought to their knees by a series of unfortunate events surrounding their attempts to develop sources of nuclear power. The development of, or reliance on, nuclear power during or prior to this period was found not to have any systematic impact on the return received by investors in electrical utilities (refer to Chapter 7). However, this poorest-performing group of utilities can trace its problems to attempts to develop nuclear sources of cost-effective power.

Analysis of Investor Returns in the Electric Utility Industry

TRR Determinants The high TRRs experienced by electric utilities tended to be a function of both stock price appreciation and increasing potential earnings rather than dividend levels. The growth in stock prices during this period reflected the generally depressed level of electric utility stock prices at the beginning of the period. Stock prices were depressed because of the unusually difficult decade that utilities experienced between 1974 and 1984 (discussed in Chapters 3 and 4).

The average appreciation in stock price for this group over the five-year period was 48 percent. The relationship between the

Figure 5.2   TRR and Price Change (1984–1988)

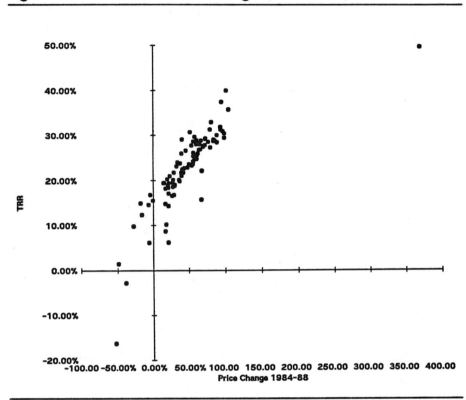

change in stock prices and the TRRs for these 96 utilities can be seen in Figure 5.2.

The closeness of this scatter suggests a strong and significant positive relationship (R^2 = .67). The absence of a comparable relationship between the dividend yield and the TRR is evident in Figure 5.3. This finding suggests that the conventional approach of evaluating electric utility stocks strictly on the basis of dividend yield misses significant opportunities for profit.

It was also found that changes in dividends were not strongly (R^2 = .47) associated with a change in stock prices over this period. This relationship is illustrated in Figure 5.4.

Figure 5.3   Dividend Yield and TRR (1984–1988)

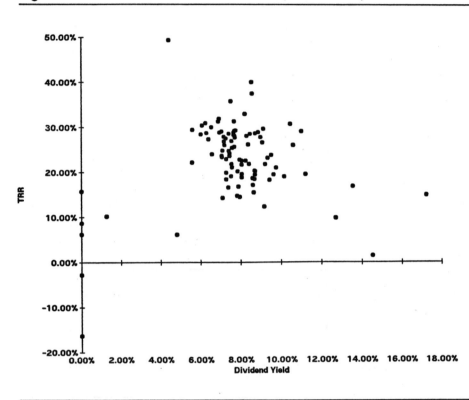

These relationships are quite significant from an investor's point of view. A sophisticated investor is interested in maximizing his or her TRR rather than dividend yield or stock price gain alone; the conventional wisdom in this area can be misleading.

The TRR is primarily dependent on any change in stock price (at least during the period examined). Changes in the stock price tend not to be directly related to a change in dividend levels, but rather to perceived changes in earnings and, consequently, future dividends. This does not mean that stock prices aren't a function of dividends in the electric utility industry—they most certainly are. But the potential returns to an investor are not related to the cur-

Figure 5.4   Price and Dividend Changes (1984–1988)

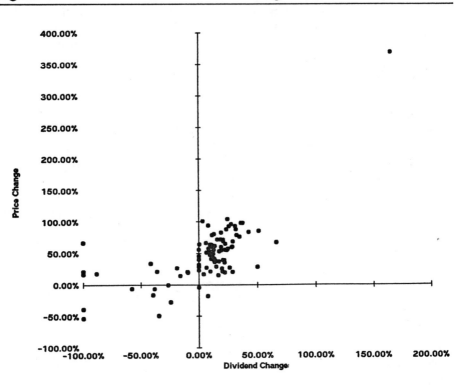

rent level (or change in the current level) of dividends—this is quite a different animal!

Success for the investor in the electric utility industry requires discerning future earnings and dividend levels (which will influence future changes in stock price). Focusing on dividend yield alone is a mistake.

Rising Electric Utility Stock Prices 1984–1988

What factors accounted for the extraordinary price appreciation of electric utility stocks during this period? There can be little doubt that a substantial portion of this increase reflects the fact that the stock market generally was in a very strong bull phase during this period. Nevertheless, even without this support, utility stock prices would have risen during this period for a number of reasons.

The strong financial performance of these stocks reflects (1) an increase in earnings, (2) an enhancement of earnings potential, (3) an improvement in the quality of earnings, and (4) a consequent strengthening of balance sheet fundamentals.

As may be seen from Table 5.1, earnings for the group of electric utilities increased 9.2 percent over the period. The significance of this increase is understated by a number of factors. During this period of time, cash flows increased significantly—during 1988 the ratio of cash flows to net profits was 1.72. In addition, AFUDC as a percentage of profits for the group declined from an average of 33 to 15 percent. Thus, this period was characterized by (1) higher

Table 5.1   Electric Utility Performance (96 Stocks)

Characteristic	Average	Standard Deviation
TRR 1984–1988	22.8%	8.7%
Change in Stock Price 1984–1988	47.8%	46.6%
Change in Dividend 1984–1988	4.0%	33.0%
Change in Sales 1984–1988	12.8%	27.0%
Change in Net Profits 1984–1988	9.2%	26.5%
Change in AFUDC Percentage of Net Profits, 1984–1988	–28.0%	98.7%
Times Earnings Ratio 1988	2.6	0.6
Common Equity Ratio 1988	0.45	0.07
Long-Term Debt Ratio 1988	0.48	0.06

earnings, (2) an improved quality of earnings, and (3) greater available cash flows.

Simultaneous with the improved flow of earnings and cash, the need for capital expenditures decreased as (1) the industry completed a building cycle that left it with substantial excess capacity and (2) the immediate environmental concerns of the previous decade had largely been met. These two circumstances produced a surfeit of cash for many utilities, both cash that could be distributed to shareholders or cash that could be invested in other profitable activities (such as unregulated cogeneration or IPP subsidiaries).

More importantly, the prospects for future earnings enhancement improved significantly during this period. The completion of the building cycle implied that many utilities could look forward to rate relief as the new productive capacity was factored into their rate base. In many cases utilities could now expect to actually receive the profits they had been credited with under AFUDC.

Outlook for Specific Industry Segments

To better consider the implications of past performance for future performance, the industry may be divided into four segments based on their TRR over the last five years: stars, strong performers, average performers, and dogs.

Stars Between 1984 and 1988, the 11 high performing stars of the electric utilities industry identified in Table 5.2 experienced internal rates of return ranging from a high of 49 percent (General Public Utilities) to a low of 30 percent (Hawaiian Electric Utilities).

This spectacular performance reflects strong, well-managed companies who were emerging from a difficult era (i.e., the energy crisis, environmental concerns, inflation and the regulatory lag) well-positioned for growth in favorable markets. The difficulties of the late 1970s, and early 1980s had depressed the price and earnings of these stocks. As general conditions improved, these companies prospered exceptionally to reward their faithful shareholders. The important characteristics of these utilities influencing their price appreciation are found in Table 5.3.

Table 5.2   Electric Utility Stars (1984–1988)

Overall Rank	Rank in Group	Utility	Total Rate of Return
1	1	General Public Utilities	49.37%
2	2	Cincinnati Gas & Electric Co.	39.92%
3	3	DPL Inc.	37.40%
4	4	Eastern Utility Associates	35.73%
5	5	Union Electric Co.	32.96%
6	6	San Diego Gas & Electric Co.	31.85%
7	7	Pennsylvania Power & Light Co.	31.32%
8	8	St. Joe Light & Power Co.	31.32%
9	9	Baltimore Gas & Electric	30.92%
10	10	Ohio Edison Co.	30.71%
11	11	So. Indiana Gas & Electric Co.	30.41%

The primary factor in the outstanding TRRs noted was the run-up in stock prices for this group of utilities. The largest gain was recorded by General Public Utilities (GPU)—369 percent. This stellar performance partially reflects GPU's recovery from the low share-values following the Three Mile Island Debacle in 1979. However, its increase in price also reflects a sustained increase in revenues resulting from the resurgence of heavy manufacturing activity in its Pennsylvania service area and extensive cost reduction activities. GPU's operating profits soared 95 percent between 1984 and 1988.

Share price increases for the remaining utilities in this group ranged from 104 percent at Eastern Utility Associates to 52 percent at Ohio Edison. Even though dividends for this group rose 17.6 percent between 1984 and 1988, the average stock in this group had a yield of only 7.3 percent at the beginning of 1989. This low yield reflects a market valuation of anticipated growth in profits that is reflected in share price and is not reflected in current earnings.

Revenues in this group increased 14 percent. Even though all firms in the group reported a strong upsurge in the actual distribu-

Table 5.3   Star Electric Utility Performance (12 Stocks)

Characteristic	Average	Standard Deviation
TRR 1984–1988	34.3%	5.4%
Change in Stock Price 1984–1988	112.2%	78.0%
Change in Dividend 1984–1988	17.6%	11.5%
Change in Sales 1984–1988	14.0%	17.1%
Change in Net Profits 1984–1988	26.9%	32.5%
Change in AFUDC Percentage of Net Profits, 1984–1988	–16.3%	75.7%
Times Earnings Ratio 1988	2.8	0.6
Common Equity Ratio 1988	0.46	0.07
Long-Term Debt Ratio 1988	0.47	0.06

tion of electric power, as a result of rate reductions imposed by regulatory authorities, revenues did not necessarily rise symmetrically. Revenues increased less than 6 percent for five of these firms and actually showed a small decrease at two utilities. Rate reductions notwithstanding, profits increased strongly for all but three members of the group. Those firms in which profits did not increase were anticipating future increases in profit. One firm (San Diego Gas & Electric Co.) was the subject of a hostile takeover.

The quality of earnings in the group also strengthened with AFUDC as a percentage of profits falling 16 percent. The large variance in this area reflects the inclusion of Eastern Utilities Associates (EUA) in the group. EUA is estimated to have AFUDC equal to 138 percent of profits in 1988 as a result of its Seabrook nuclear power plant situation.

The increased cash flows the group experienced during this period were used to strengthen the balance sheet. The times-earnings,
common equity, and long-term debt ratios for this group were comparable to that of the industry as a whole during 1988.

Strong Performing Electric Utilities The TRR for the 65 firms com-
prising this group (Table 5.4) ranged from 29.6 percent (Portland
General) to 20.2 percent (Interstate Power Co.) to average a substantial 25.6%.

This performance was driven by a 55 percent increase in share
price for firms in this group. Net profits were up only 11 percent
during this period on an average revenue gain of 13 percent. As a
group, these utilities were not quite as effective in converting revenue gains into profits compared to those utilities in the high performing group. The relevant financial characteristics of strong performing electric utilities are presented in Table 5.5.

While the increase in revenue among strong performing utilities
was comparable to that experienced by the stars, the stars were considerably more effective in translating increased revenues to increased profits. This generally reflected the stars' ability to control
costs under these circumstances. Although the flow of profits and
cash was not as abundant for this group as for the stars during this
period, both the level and quality of earnings increased for members of the strong performers. This solid performance enabled both
a significant increase in dividends and a substantial improvement
in balance sheet fundamentals.

Average Performing Electric Utilities The 24 utilities identified as
having average performance (Table 5.6) experienced TRRs ranging
from 19.9 percent for MDU Resources Group to 10.2 for Middle
South Utilities, Inc.

Although the increase in net profits (12 percent) for this group
was not significantly different from that of the strong performers,
utilities in this group generally failed to experience the appreciation
in share price experienced by groups with higher TRRs. This may
be seen in Table 5.7.

The failure of these stocks to appreciate as rapidly as others in
the industry generally tends to reflect a deterioration in the longer
term prospects for these utilities or a decline in the quality of earn-

Table 5.4   Strong Performing Electric Utilities (1984–1988)

Overall Rank	Rank in Group	Utility	Total Rate of Return
13	1	Portland General	29.64%
14	2	Wisconsin Energy Corp.	29.45%
15	3	SCANA Corporation	29.31%
16	4	Pacificorp	29.19%
17	5	Potomac Electric Power Co.	29.07%
18	6	Philadelphia Electric Co.	29.06%
19	7	N.E. Utilities	28.90%
20	8	Consolidated Edison	28.85%
21	9	Central Vermont Pub. Ser.	28.84%
22	10	Duke Power Co.	28.70%
23	11	American Elec. Power	28.59%
24	12	Minnesota Power & Light Co.	28.58%
25	13	Green Mountain Power	28.50%
26	14	TECO Energy Corp.	28.43%
27	15	Kansas City Power & Light Co.	28.26%
28	16	Public Service Enterprise Group	28.04%
29	17	Carolina Power	28.04%
30	18	Central La. Electric Co.	27.87%
31	19	IE Industries	27.76%
32	20	Empire District Electric	27.72%
33	21	Florida Progress Corp.	27.50%
34	22	No. States Power Co.	27.32%
35	23	SCE Corp.	26.94%
36	24	IPALCO Enterprises Inc.	26.79%
37	25	Washington Water Power Co.	26.61%
38	26	Iowa-Illinois Gas & Electric Co.	26.14%
39	27	Kentucky Utilities Co.	26.03%
40	28	Houston Industries, Inc.	25.94%
41	29	Central & South West's Corp.	25.61%
42	30	Sierra Pacific Resources	25.39%
43	31	Wisconsin Public Service Corp.	24.79%
44	32	Kansas Power & Light Co.	24.73%
45	33	TNP Enterprises	24.22%

(Table continues)

Table 5.4   Strong Performing Electric Utilities (1984–1988) (Continued)

Overall Rank	Rank in Group	Utility	Total Rate of Return
46	34	Duquesne Light Co.	24.01%
47	35	Southern Co.	23.80%
48	36	Oklahoma Gas & Electric Co.	23.64%
49	37	CILCORP	23.63%
50	38	FPL Group Inc.	23.41%
51	39	Puguet Sound P & L Co.	23.19%
52	40	Nevada Power	22.94%
53	41	Louisville Gas & Electric Co.	22.79%
54	42	Central Illinois Pub. Ser. Co.	22.54%
55	43	Atlantic Energy Inc.	22.54%
56	44	Utilicorp United Inc.	22.16%
57	45	Delmarva Power	21.80%
58	46	Idaho Power Co.	21.79%
59	47	Commonwealth Edison	21.73%
60	48	Allegheny Power	21.71%
61	49	Orange & Rockland Utilities Inc.	21.07%
62	50	Detroit Edison	20.99%
63	51	Pacific Gas & Electric Co.	20.32%
64	52	S.W. Public Service Co.	20.20%
65	53	Interstate Power Co.	20.18%

ings recorded. Earnings prospects declined because the fundamental demand for service in their areas was weak or the utilities were likely to experience difficulties in cost control in the future. The regulatory climate for this group tended to be more difficult than for any of the others—a particular concern for utilities that have a significant portion of their earnings tied up in AFUDC and can look forward to after-the-fact prudency reviews.

In the absence of good business fundamentals, future growth in profits can come about only through rate relief and that is difficult to see happening for the utilities in this group. The utilities in this

Table 5.5   Strong Performing Electric Utilities (65 Stocks)

Characteristic	Average	Standard Deviation
TRR 1984–1988	25.6%	5.6%
Change in Stock Price 1984–1988	55.7%	18.8%
Change in Dividend 1984–1988	16.0%	15.5%
Change in Sales 1984–1988	12.7%	29.6%
Change in Net Profits 1984–1988	10.6%	20.4%
Change in AFUDC Percentage of Net Profits, 1984–1988	–28.9%	101.1%
Times Earnings Ratio 1988	2.8	0.6
Common Equity Ratio 1988	0.46	0.08
Long-Term Debt Ratio 1988	0.46	0.05

group are generally struggling with cash flows that are barely adequate to undertake necessary capital expenditures. As a consequence, dividends in this period have been reduced (–6 percent) and the balance sheet fundamentals have not improved in a manner comparable to the industry as a whole.

Dogs Seven firms have been identified as being low performers between 1984 and 1988 (Table 5.8).

The common thread among these utilities is a failed effort to develop a cost effective nuclear power source.

Public Service of New Hampshire is currently in bankruptcy almost entirely a result of its experience with Seabrook 1. Gulf State Utilities Co. is struggling under the weight of its $4.5 billion River Bend Unit 1. Public Service of New Mexico has 50 percent excess capacity as a result of its 10.2 percent stake in the Palo Verde nuclear facility. NIPSCO Industries has been badly hurt by its aborted attempt to develop its Bailly nuclear plant. Long Island Lighting

Table 5.6   Average Performing Electric Utilities (1984–1988)

Overall Rank	Rank in Group	Utility	Total Rate of Return
66	1	MDU Resources Group	19.94%
67	2	Central Maine	19.58%
68	3	Boston Edison	19.52%
69	4	N.Y. State Electric & Gas Corp.	19.45%
70	5	Iowa Resources Inc.	19.44%
71	6	Utah P & L	19.14%
72	7	Texas Utilities Co.	18.99%
73	8	Midwest Energy Co.	18.92%
74	9	Commonwealth Energy System	18.68%
75	10	United Illuminating Co.	18.48%
76	11	Kansas Gas & Electric Co.	18.46%
77	12	Public Service of Colorado	18.29%
78	13	New England Electric System	17.17%
79	14	Tucson Electric Power Co.	16.84%
80	15	Illinois Power Co.	16.83%
81	16	Dominion Resources	16.66%
82	17	CMS Energy Corp.	15.76%
83	18	Rochester Gas & Electric Corp.	15.54%
84	19	Pinnacle West Capital Corp.	14.93%
85	20	Montana Power Co.	14.83%
86	21	Central Hudson	14.61%
87	22	WPL Holdings Inc.	14.33%
88	23	Niagra Mohawk Power Corp.	12.31%
89	24	Middle South Utilities Inc.	10.19%

will probably not be allowed to operate its Shoreham Plant in the near future and the hoped for sale of the plant to New York State has been derailed. In addition, L.I. Lighting faces potential liabilities in the billions of dollars as a result of class action suits related to its Shoreham plant. PSI Holdings has now abandoned its Marble Hill nuclear program, while Centerior Energy Corporation is in the midst of negotiating a partial inclusion of its Perry 1 and Beaver Valley 2 nuclear investments into its investment base.

Table 5.7   Average Performing Electric Utilities (24 Stocks)

Characteristic	Average	Standard Deviation
TRR 1984–1988	17.0%	3.5%
Change in Stock Price 1984–1988	18.1%	17.4%
Change in Dividend 1984–1988	–5.7%	34.7%
Change in Sales 1984–1988	9.1%	21.1%
Change in Net Profits 1984–1988	12.1%	24.0%
Change in AFUDC Percentage of Net Profits, 1984–1988	–49.2%	55.0%
Times Earnings Ratio 1988	2.33	0.45
Common Equity Ratio 1988	0.42	0.06
Long-Term Debt Ratio 1988	0.50	0.06

Table 5.8   Low Performing Electric Utilities (1984–1988)

Overall Rank	Rank in Group	Utility	Total Rate of Return
90	1	Centerior Energy	9.80%
91	2	PSI Holdings Inc.	8.66%
92	3	Long Island Lighting Co.	6.22%
93	4	NIPSCO Industries Inc.	6.16%
94	5	Public Ser. New Mexico	1.45%
95	6	Gulf States Utilities	–2.80%
96	7	Public Service Co. of New Hampshire	–16.31%

Table 5.9   Low Performing Electric Utilities (7 Stocks)

Characteristic	Average	Standard Deviation
TRR 1984–1988	1.9%	8.4%
Change in Stock Price 1984–1988	−19.4%	28.2%
Change in Dividend 1984–1988	−73.8%	31.8%
Change in Sales 1984–1988	21.4%	33.9%
Change in Net Profits 1984–1988	−5.1%	40.8%
Change in AFUDC Percentage of Net Profits, 1984–1988	−36.7%	171.0%
Times Earnings Ratio 1988	1.8	0.9%
Common Equity Ratio 1988	35.9	7.5
Long-Term Debt Ratio 1988	49.7%	5.0

The impact of these difficult situations can be seen in the dismal financials shown in Table 5.9.

The unfortunate experiences these utilities have had with the development of nuclear power have seriously impaired their present and future earnings; this impact has been reflected in a decline in the average share price of these utilities. The nuclear plants have proved such prodigious consumers of cash that dividends have been cut and the financial bases of the firms allowed to seriously erode. Presently, these firms are wallowing in a quagmire of litigation and negotiation that consumes the energies of management keeping the firms from directing their efforts towards more positive ends.

The jury is still out on nuclear power in the electric utility industry. The General Public Utilities turnaround appears to be an exception to the general trend. There is scant hope for these seven firms to extricate themselves from their present difficulties. Not that it can't happen, but it's a speculator's play.

The prospects for investment in nuclear utilities are considered in Chapter 9.

Future Trends in the Electric Utility Industry

The specific projections developed in Chapters 6 and 7 for the stock prices and dividends of individual electric utilities through 1999 incorporate a number of assumptions and insights concerning future trends in the industry over the coming decade. The nature of these trends needs to be understood in order to interpret the unfolding events of the 1990s. The trends that potentially affect future price and dividend levels in the electric utility sector are (1) deregulation, (2) capacity, (3) diversification, (4) oil prices, (5) environmental legislation and (6) merger activity.

The Regulatory Environment

The trend toward deregulation at the wholesale level will be the major driving force creating high returns throughout the industry during the 1990s. The reasons for this may be found in (1) the implications of the breakdown of the historic compact between the utilities and regulators at the state level and (2) the market's use of price and profit as a signaling mechanism.

The Compact Between Regulators and Utilities The traditional tendency in the industry to anticipate increasing demand by building capacity prior to the point it is needed has been severely penalized by after-the-fact prudency reviews. Electric utility executives are typically engineers who are quite sensitive to the technical difficulties and long lead times necessary to build additional capacity. Prior to the last few years, a "compact" was felt to exist between the utility executives and regulators that saw this behavior as in the public interest. This compact no longer exists. The regulatory process has become highly adversarial and politicized. Professional advocates for the public interest appear to have a bias against the addition of existing capacity, preferring to deal with this problem through energy conservation measures. Additional capacity can be entered into a rate base at the present time only after the most prolonged and grueling administrative and judicial procedures. This situation will not change as long as the supply of electricity is plentiful. As the future brings increasing degradation of service (as it inevitable will under the present circumstances) and increasing reliance on rationing existing power supplies, the public may well cry out for change.

It should be noted that state regulatory commissions see the implementation of this philosophy as intruding on their territory and usurping their rightful prerogatives and may be counted on to resist a loss of control over the price of electricity. This conflict will no doubt muddy the waters for some time to come. Nevertheless, the outcome of this conflict is most likely to be that the production and wholesaling of electricity become the effective province of the federal government and, by and large, this sector will rely on market mechanisms (price and profit) to determine the supply and allocation of electricity. State regulators will find their responsibilities increasingly related to the retailing of electric power with the cost of power becoming a "given" determined outside their control. As state regulators currently have a great deal to say about the cost of power, this transition will take at least a decade to complete.

Prices, Profits and Regulation Prices and profits have been influenced by a policy shift on energy at the federal level: a shift away from deciding demand-supply questions administratively and towards relying on such decisions to be made by a competitive market. This policy shift reflects a philosophy that the market is a more effective regulator than the government. This idea has been deeply embedded in the federal government during the Reagan years and appears likely to continue under President Bush. Indeed, this philosophy has a powerful political constituency and may well continue to dominate the thinking about the structure of all utilities for some time to come.

The current thrust of deregulation in this industry is to separate the distribution function from the production function. The impact of PURPA (Public Utilities Regulation Act of 1978), as interpreted by the FERC, is to eliminate any advantages a utility may have in producing its own power relative to purchasing it in an open market. The intention is to create a market of electric power wholesalers so that the public may benefit from whatever efficiencies are gained.

Many executives in the industry feel that this application of a competitive model is inappropriate for technological reasons and will result in a degradation of system reliability. Be this as it may, the advantage to this restructuring of utilities is that it tends to free them from the regulatory morass currently enveloping the construction of additional capacity.

Utilities generally purchase power at "avoided cost" (at one time this was the highest cost to a utility, but is presently interpreted as the hypothetical cost of power that regulators deem profitable to cogenerators). This approach clearly has a potential for regulatory abuse; i.e., the avoidable cost could be set artificially high or low by the regulators to accomplish other policy goals. However, at the very least, this approach is no worse than a system of fully administered prices.

In addition, the opportunities for this abuse may well be prohibited by the market function. That is, since utilities will be purchasing power in a competitive market, the only way to obtain the power is to pay for it. If a state regulatory agency deems "avoidable cost" to be less than market price—then they won't get the power. Under the present system, if the regulatory agency determines costs are too high, the utility has no choice but to accept this decision, unless they wish to appeal it to the courts, which is both a time-consuming and expensive process. In the market mechanism envisioned, there would be no appeal to price.

Given the press on capacity expected to develop in the next five to ten years and the long lead times necessary to add additional generating capacity, the next decade may be expected to see steadily rising electricity prices. It is a classic case of a short-run inelastic supply curve: if the demand for power is such that the higher price is proportionally larger than the fall in quantity demanded, the increase in price may well be of considerable magnitude.

This increase in the price of electricity will generate profits for those unregulated producers free to sell their output to the highest bidder. These profits will signal other potential suppliers to enter the market and thus increase supply and eventually bring down the price of electricity to cost. In the disequilibrium period, firms with productive capacity to sell can anticipate extraordinary profits. Many electric utilities are currently engaged in developing cogenerating subsidiaries that will qualify as independent power producers in a deregulated market.

Capacity

Currently, the real rate of growth in the demand for electricity has begun to increase following a number of years of unusually slow growth.

Sales growth is anticipated to be slower than the growth in the actual production of electricity as regulatory commissions push down tariffs to keep firms within their allowed rates of return.

Even with the increased use of purchased power from outside the United States (Canada and Mexico) and from independent power producers (IPPs) and other qualifying facilities (QFs), it is

Table 5.10   Electric Utility Sales Growth and Capacity Forecasts (1989–1998)

		Estimated Capacity	
Area[1]	Sales Growth	1987	1996
U.S	2.1%	24.8%	18.4%
East Central Area	1.8	28.0	22.0
Mid-Atlantic Area	1.6	22.0	20.0
Western Systems Area	2.0	30.0	23.0
Southeastern	2.4	23.0	17.0
Southwest	2.1	28.0	17.0
Texas	3.3	12.0	10.0
Mid-America	1.8	25.0	12.0
Mid-Continent	1.8	25.0	17.0
Northeast	1.6	20.0	16.0[2]

[1] Power pools and interconnecting networks. *North American Electric Reliability Council*, 1987.
[2] Assumes Seabrook and Shoreham nuclear power plants enter service.

clear from the estimates in Table 5.10 that the industry is moving from a period of excess supply to a period of excess demand.

Diversification

As many utilities are currently enjoying substantial flows of free cash (net profits after taxes + depreciation – dividends – necessary capital expenditures), the question becomes one of how to dispose of this cash.

Some utilities have apparently decided to sit on significant liquid assets. Other utilities have chosen to invest this cash in securing their fuel supplies—most notably coal mining. Montana Power Company, Pacific Corporation, and Florida Progress Corporation have all made substantial investments in coal mining operations. Still other utilities have chosen to diversify completely out of their present industry—for instance, Minnesota Power & Light Company in the paper mill business and IE Industries and Pacificorp in telecommunications.

Given that an electric utility company has a great deal of experience in the production and distribution of electric power, exactly how will this expertise enable them to achieve success in unrelated areas? While success is certainly possible, it seems that electric utilities would perform better by concentrating on areas in which their existing expertise provides them with a competitive advantage. A number of cases illustrate this point: Pinnacle West's experience in the banking industry has proved rather dismal. Public Service of New Mexico is selling off a variety of real estate development and manufacturing projects after achieving lackluster results. Florida Progress has found the competitive pressure too great in its building products subsidiaries.

A potentially profitable area of diversification for which electric utilities are admirably equipped would be power production in the unregulated sector. This could take the form of independent power producers under PURPA or cogeneration joint ventures. While the thrust of current FERC regulation is to deny existing utilities any unfair advantage in the wholesale power market, there is no presumption that utilities would not be able to take advantage of their inherent skills and expertise in this area.

While the power market in 1989 will be characterized by excess supply, this will not be the situation in five years. Given the three- to five-year lead necessary for the construction of new production facilities, now is an ideal time for utilities to be entering this market.

Oil Prices

The oil crises of 1973 and 1976 illustrated how vulnerable the United States was to interruptions in foreign oil supplies. As a result of nuclear power generation and a conversion to coal, the electric utility industry is less sensitive to foreign oil interruption than it was in the 1970s. Oil generated approximately 9.2 percent of all electric power in 1986—compared to 45.3 percent for coal and 12.6 percent for nuclear power. In 1976, oil was responsible for generating about 16 percent of electric power. The National Electric Research Council (NERC) estimates that by 1996 oil will generate 8.2 percent of all domestic power.

However, oil is still an important fuel source in the industry, while the Middle East situation remains unstable. The interests of the United States, the Soviet Union, Israel, and the various nationalities involved in that region are complex. It is difficult to see a mutually satisfactory solution to the present situation.

At the close of the 1980s, the price of oil was gradually declining as the OPEC Cartel continued to weaken as a result of internal strife and partisan politics. This may prove to be a temporary situation. Any number of scenarios can be imagined that would result in a serious interference to the present supply of oil. The impact of an oil shortage on electric utilities (particularly in the Northeast) could be disruptive, but will not be disastrous.

An interruption of oil supplies in the first half of the coming decade is not likely to seriously impede the production of electricity. As consumption moves closer to capacity levels of production in the latter half of the decade, any disturbance in the supply of oil may have a substantial impact on the cost of electricity.

Environmental Legislation

There is a growing public concern with the issues of acid rain and the greenhouse (global warming) effect. While these phenomena pose serious threats to the health of all human beings, the impact of these phenomena is diffused over both time and space. In contrast, the remedies for such problems are local, immediate and painfully expensive.

The cost of ameliorating the impact of fossil fuels (primarily coal) on the environment may be substantial. A great deal depends on the type and level of emissions covered by the legislation. Some hope is offered by promising new technologies that may reduce the cost of emissions control. However, a dominant satisfying technology has yet been developed.

Under present cost trade-offs, it is difficult to envision that utility regulators in Michigan (for example) would be so concerned about the acidification of lakes in Sweden or a slow rise in world atmospheric temperatures, that they would be willing to significantly increase the cost of electricity to either industry (the creator of jobs) or to residential customers (including the poor and elderly).

It has been proposed that the federal government support the necessary conservation measures out of the general tax revenues. In an era of concern over continuing budget deficits and an even larger cost to the savings and loan crisis, the response to this proposal has been lukewarm at best.

In the absence of a major health crisis where the electric utility industry's present environmental stance is clearly inadequate, it is unlikely that this issue will be seriously addressed during the 1990s.

Merger Activity

The merger between Pacificorp and Utah Power & Light at the close of the 1980s did not appear to significantly enhance the wealth of either firm's shareholders, in the short run. By 1990, these advantages in this merger for Pacificorp shareholders had become clear. The long term is clearly going to bring the new company net advantages from operating efficiencies and a reduced need for generating capacity (because the two companies' peak seasonal demands tend to be offsetting). In addition, concessions were made in the various service areas that ensured the largest winners from the merger would be the customers of the two companies.

While SCE Corp's hostile takeover attempt of San Diego Gas & Electric did have an immediate impact on the stock prices of both firms, the effect was not large and the uncertainties surrounding SCE's ability to actually complete the deal lessened the impact of the takeover on share value.

These two cases illustrate the inherent difficulty for acquisitions and mergers to take place in such a way as to benefit shareholders. The presumptive reason for a takeover is that the firm to be taken over has "hidden value" that can be somehow captured by the acquiring firm. However, it is unlikely that the regulatory agencies involved would permit such an acquisition unless the ratepayers were clearly going to benefit from any restructuring.

Assuming the regulators are acquiescent, there are a number of possible strategies for developing hidden value. Perhaps the most promising of these strategies would be to transfer assets from a less favorable regulatory environment to a more favorable regulatory environment. In particular, a utility may wish to restructure so that its assets come under FERC auspices rather than state regulations. It is generally thought that assets operated under FERC are more likely to earn a market rate of return than comparable assets operated in most state jurisdictions.

It is also possible that a utility could achieve a higher financial leverage, a more efficient capital structure or improved access to capital through a restructuring. Many takeovers and mergers in the industrial sector have become more highly leveraged as a result of this type of activity. While some stockholders may have benefited from such financial legerdemain, it is not clear that such activity is desirable from a social point of view.

It is possible that a takeover or merger situation could revitalize a moribund management. A new management could engage more aggressively in cost-cutting activities and be more active in improving productivity.

A merger or takeover could also be used to sustain or increase dividend payouts. The merger of a cash-poor company with a utility that has substantial free cash could benefit both sets of stockholders if the cash-poor company has superior opportunities for future earnings. In the industrial sector, marriages between "cash cows" and "stars" are considered mutually advantageous.

Chapter 6

THE FUTURE FOR INVESTMENT IN NONNUCLEAR ELECTRIC UTILITIES

Performance Overview

Investments in the nonnuclear segment of the electric utility industry will be solid gainers in the 1990s. Particularly worth looking at are Pacificorp, Central La. Electric Co., Pacific Gas and Electric, Utilicorp United, Inc., St. Joe Power & Light Co., and the Potomac Electric Power Co.

While stock prices in this area will experience occasional volatility, the trend in both dividends and stock prices will be generally upward. Stock price weakness in this sector should be seen as a buying opportunity.

In the early part of the decade, stock prices will be largely a function of dividends. Dividend growth will be strong during this period as a result of rising profits. Towards the end of this decade, the utilities are likely to lower dividend payout ratios to fund the construction of power generation facilities. Stock prices will then tend to be driven more by cash flow than dividends towards 1999.

Profitability will increase slowly in the early part of the decade as existing power-generating capacity is absorbed, then rise with increasing speed as capacity is pressed. Towards the end of the decade, profits will be tempered by additional power generating capacity coming on line and consumer resistance to higher electricity prices stemming from rising energy prices. Profits will increasingly result from the sale of wholesale power by unregulated IPP or cogeneration subsidiaries. The industry will largely be structured into unregulated power producers (which will provide almost all additions to power generation capacity throughout the decade), regulated power producers (the relative size of this sector of the industry will depend on the outcome of the power struggle between state regulatory agencies and FERC), long-distance transmission facilities (which will function as common carriers), and locally regulated distributors. The emerging energy shortage is expected to result in strong increases in the cost of electric power beginning in the middle of the decade. However, the resultant political pressures are unlikely to reverse the course of deregulation in the industry. The net effect of this scenario for investors is presented in Table 6.1.

In terms of mid-1989 prices, it is clear that four of these utilities may be considered as presenting outstanding opportunities for investment return—Hawaiian Electric Industries, Utilicorp United, Inc., St. Joe Light & Power Co., and the Potomac Electric Power Co.

Forecasting Stock Prices

The approach to forecasting stock prices used in this segment of the industry is the Dividend Discount Model (DDM). The specific formulation of this model relies on estimates of future dividend levels. Future dividend levels are in turn estimated by considering the future sales, earnings, cash flow, and payout ratios for each individual firm. These considerations are then used to specify the parameters of the DDM for each firm on an individual basis. Forecasting dividend payments is critical because the stock prices of electric utilities without nuclear exposure are largely determined by their level of dividends. The tight relationship between stock prices and dividends ($R^2 = .89$) in 1988 may be seen in Figure 6.1.

The consistency of this relationship may be contrasted with other performance attributes of the firm that do not have the same degree of explanatory power with respect to stock prices: net profit per share ($R^2 = .71$) and cash flow per share ($R^2 = .63$).

The dividend declared to common stockholders is indirectly related to earnings. The payout ratio (dividends paid out/earnings)

Table 6.1   Projected TRRs Nonnuclear Electric Utilities

TRR Rank 1989-1994		Projected TRRs	
		1989-93	*1989-99*
1	Utilicorp United Inc.	21.54%	16.01%
2	Potomac Electric Power Co.	20.48%	18.17%
3	TNP Enterprises	18.06%	15.65%
4	Central La. Electric Co.	17.91%	16.53%
5	IPALCO Enterprises Inc.	17.35%	14.57%
6	St. Joe Light & Power Co.	17.02%	15.31%
7	Allegheny Power	16.74%	14.64%
8	Oklahoma Gas & Electric Co.	15.93%	14.05%
9	Empire District Electric	15.76%	13.75%
10	CILCORP	15.74%	13.73%
11	Puget Sound P&L Co.	15.58%	13.44%
12	Minnesota Power & Light Co.	15.27%	13.33%
13	DPL Inc.	15.25%	13.15%
14	Sierra Pacific Resources	15.25%	13.15%
15	Hawaiian Electric Industries	15.20%	14.45%
16	Kansas Power & Light Co.	15.09%	13.02%
17	Cincinnati Gas & Electric Co.	15.05%	12.81%
18	S.W. Public Service Co.	14.76%	12.75%
19	Central Illinois Pub. Ser. Co.	14.45%	12.40%
20	Washington Water Power Co.	14.44%	12.30%
21	Midwest Energy Co.	14.40%	12.73%
22	Idaho Power Co.	14.11%	12.35%
23	Orange & Rockland Utilities	13.91%	11.99%
24	Interstate Power Co.	13.76%	11.74%
25	Louisville Gas & Electric Co.	13.71%	11.87%
26	Pacificorp	12.80%	18.78%
27	MDU Resources Group	12.75%	11.33%
28	Montana Power Co.	12.45%	10.66%
29	So. Indiana Gas & Electric Co.	12.19%	11.91%
30	Nevada Power	12.00%	10.29%
31	Kentucky Utilities Co.	11.87%	11.28%
32	TECO Energy Corp.	6.59%	10.11%
33	Tucson Electric Power Co.	6.43%	36.45%

**Figure 6.1   Nonnuclear Electric Utilities Price–Dividend
Relationship**

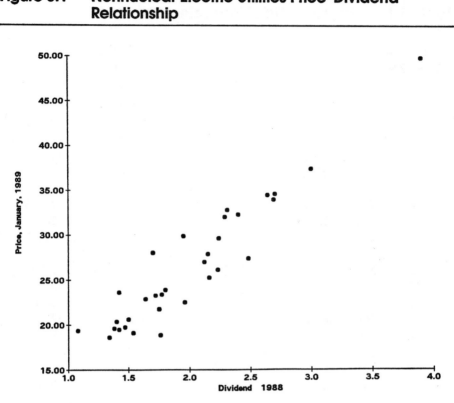

for the 33 utilities without nuclear exposure examined in this Chapter ranged from 130 percent (Idaho Power Company) to 57 percent (Cincinnati Gas & Electric Company). The determinants of the payout ratio include the size of the cash flow relative to earnings, present and future capital needs, the quality of earnings, the strength of the balance sheet, and management's proclivity to reinvest in the utility industry, invest in other areas (diversify), or return profits to the shareholders.

As discussed in Chapter 3, net profits are not necessarily a good measure of the firm's economic performance or its ability to sustain or increase dividends. The inclusion of AFUDC as earnings for electric utilities is of particular concern, especially in light of the tendency for regulatory agencies to conduct aggressive after-the-fact prudency reviews of new generating capacity. Aside from the distortions resulting from a variety of accounting conventions, the fundamental determinants of earnings include the level of demand in the service area, the cost of producing and distributing electric power, the allowable rate of return permitted by regulatory authorities, and the actual tariff structure in use.

Less certain, but even more important, is the utility's potential for increasing earnings and dividends. The factors determining future earnings and dividends are similar to those determining current earnings and dividends. Although the future is not known with certainty, it is possible to make an informed judgment concerning future earnings and dividends.

Insight into the future dividend levels of the 33 utilities examined may be gained through a reconciliation of the specific circumstances surrounding their present dividend payments, their market price, the price predicted directly by the DDM, and the price predicted by a model. The later three data series are presented in Table 6.2.

The DDM Estimate

The DDM model is $D/(r-g)$ where: D is the dividend in a given year; r the risk-adjusted rate of interest; and g the expected rate of growth of dividends. The sum of $(r-g)$ may be referred to as the net effective discount factor. (A more detailed explanation of this model is presented in Chapter 3.)

The DDM estimate in Table 6.2 was developed by dividing current year dividends by a net effective discount rate of .08. Market conditions in 1990 suggested the net effective discount rate which best described the stock prices of nonnuclear electric utilities was .08.

Note that within this model an increase in market risk will result in a fall in stock price. In contrast, increases in the expected rate of growth will cause an increase in stock prices. In the real world these offsetting effects are frequently found to be associated with the same event (e.g., an entry into a new market will increase both the firm's market risk and its potential future growth). Higher net

Table 6.2 Dividend Discount Model Estimate Analysis; Electric Utilities without Nuclear Exposure

Utility	Stock Price Jan 1989	DDM Estimate	Model Estimate	DDM Estimate Error	Model Estimate Error
Allegheny Power	37.25	37.50	37.30	-0.25	0.20
Central Illinois Pub. Ser. Co.	21.75	21.88	23.54	-0.13	-1.67
Central La. Electric Co.	32.00	28.63	32.64	3.38	-4.01
CILCORP	32.25	30.00	32.86	2.25	-2.86
Cincinnati Gas & Electric Co.	26.13	27.88	27.43	-1.75	0.45
DPL Inc.	25.25	27.00	26.65	-1.75	0.35
Empire District Electric	27.88	26.88	28.98	1.00	-2.10
Hawaiian Electric Industries	29.88	24.38	30.75	5.50	-6.38
Idaho Power Co.	23.88	22.50	25.43	1.38	-2.93
Interstate Power Co.	22.50	24.50	24.21	-2.00	0.29
IPALCO Enterprises Inc.	22.88	20.50	24.54	2.38	-4.04
Kansas Power & Light Co.	23.25	21.50	24.88	1.75	-3.38
Kentucky Utilities Co.	18.63	16.75	20.77	1.88	-4.02
Louisville Gas & Electric Co.	33.88	33.63	34.30	0.25	-0.68
MDU Resources Group	19.50	17.75	21.55	1.75	-3.80
Midwest Energy Co.	19.13	19.25	21.22	-0.13	-1.97
Minnesota Power & Light Co.	23.25	21.50	24.88	1.75	-3.38
Montana Power Co.	34.50	33.75	34.86	0.75	-1.11
Nevada Power	20.63	18.75	22.55	1.88	-3.80

(Table continues)

Utility	Stock Price Jan 1989	DDM Estimate	Model Estimate	DDM Estimate Error	Model Estimate Error
Oklahoma Gas & Electric Co.	32.75	28.88	33.30	3.88	-4.43
Orange & Rockland Utilities, Inc.	29.63	28.00	30.50	1.62	-2.53
Pacificorp	34.38	33.00	34.75	1.38	-1.75
Potomac Electric Power Co.	19.63	17.25	21.66	2.38	-4.41
Puget Sound P&L Co.	18.88	22.00	20.99	-3.13	1.01
S.W. Public Service Co.	27.00	26.50	28.20	0.50	-1.70
Sierra Pacific Resources	23.38	22.13	24.99	1.25	-2.86
So. Indiana Gas & Electric Co.	28.00	21.25	29.09	6.75	-7.84
St. Joe Light & Power Co.	20.38	17.50	22.32	2.88	-4.82
TECO Energy Corp.	23.63	17.75	25.21	5.88	-7.46
TNP Enterprises	19.75	18.38	21.77	1.38	-3.39
Tucson Electric Power Co.	49.50	48.75	48.17	0.75	0.58
Utilicorp United Inc.	19.38	13.50	21.44	5.88	-7.94
Washington Water Power Co.	27.38	31.00	28.54	-3.63	2.46

discount rates lower stock price, lower net discount rates raise stock prices.

The net effective discount rate which best described stock prices in this sector in 1984 was .10. This discount rate reflected both the significantly higher interest rate structure prevailing in 1984 and higher growth expectations for electric utilities. By 1990, both risk-adjusted interest rates and growth expectations had fallen for this segment of the industry. Since interest rates had fallen faster than growth rates, the net discount rate also fell. This effect brought about a substantial increase in stock prices between 1984 and 1989.

If constant risk adjusted interest rates in the 10 percent range are assumed to prevail throughout the 1989–1999 period, the current price structure has embedded within it only a 2 percent growth factor. This is probably an overly conservative assumption for many electric utilities and suggests the possibility of future price increases.

The sensitivity of the DDM to differing assumptions concerning the effective net discount rate is illustrated in Table 6.3 through the use of higher (.10) and lower (.06) base effective net discount rates.

The Model Estimate

The model estimate in Table 6.2 was developed by regressing the DDM estimate directly on the actual stock price. The model estimate is thus the value of the stock predicted by the DDM. The significance of the model estimate is that it isolates what would happen if the DDM model were perfectly accurate, i.e., if stock prices reflected nothing else but the relationship between dividends and the net discount rate. Since the DDM is conceptually based upon future dividend levels and the actual estimate is based on current dividend levels, the difference between this estimate and the DDM direct estimate isolates the market's perception of future dividend growth potential.

An example of this interpretation for Allegheny Power is that the DDM estimate is .25 higher than actual price, suggesting that for some reason the market is not according Allegheny Power's stock price the value suggested by its dividend. The model estimate error (.20) suggests that the bulk of the total DDM error does not come from a misspecification of growth (i.e., the effective discount

Table 6.3   1994 Stock Price Forecasts; Nonnuclear Electric Utilities Differing Net Discount Factors (r – g)

Utility	0.06	0.08	0.11
Allegheny Power	60.89	46.42	37.51
Central Illinois Pub. Ser. Co.	32.49	24.61	19.81
Central La. Electric Co.	57.28	42.96	34.37
CILCORP	50.61	37.96	30.37
Cincinnati Gas & Electric Co.	35.88	27.90	22.83
DPL Inc.	39.05	29.56	23.78
Empire District Electric	45.18	33.91	27.15
Hawaiian Electric Industries	62.33	42.71	32.49
Idaho Power Co.	40.20	28.78	22.41
Interstate Power Co.	33.57	26.08	21.33
IPALCO Enterprises Inc.	43.69	31.26	24.34
Kansas Power & Light Co.	1.74	1.30	1.03
Kentucky Utilities Co.	27.07	20.23	16.15
Louisville Gas & Electric Co.	53.53	40.15	32.12
MDU Resources Group	30.04	21.95	17.30
Midwest Energy Co.	29.22	22.17	17.86
Minnesota Power & Light Co.	38.22	28.29	22.45
Montana Power Co.	49.02	36.62	29.22
Nevada Power	32.99	23.73	18.52
Oklahoma Gas & Electric Co.	57.26	41.80	32.91
Orange & Rockland Utilities	47.11	34.48	27.19
Pacificorp	55.43	41.41	33.06
Potomac Electric Power Co.	41.40	30.04	23.57
Puget Sound P&L Co.	29.48	22.24	17.86
S.W. Public Service Co.	41.58	31.30	25.09
Sierra Pacific Resources	36.44	27.10	21.57
So. Indiana Gas & Electric	43.00	30.71	23.89
St. Joe Light & Power Co.	44.26	31.65	24.63
TECO Energy Corp.	35.90	26.07	20.46
TNP Enterprises	1.84	1.32	1.03
Tucson Electric Power Co.	120.07	86.94	68.15
Utilicorp United Inc.	57.46	34.00	24.15
Washington Water Power Co.	38.03	29.63	24.27

rate). Consequently, the reason for the underestimate of price must be sought elsewhere. However, in this case, the error is so small that for all practical purposes the DDM estimate may be considered accurate.

In contrast, in the case of Central Illinois PSC, the DDM only underestimates the value of the stock by a small amount (.13). However, the model estimate suggests that by virtue of its dividend, the actual price should be much lower (1.67). The reason for this difference could lie in the anticipation of unusual growth in earnings for Central Illinois PSC. Alternatively, the explanation could lie in an unusually low payout ratio or strong balance sheet—suggesting the possibility of a dividend increase.

The model estimate is described by the equation: $Y = 4.2458 + .8873 X$, where Y is the actual price of the stock and X the DDM estimate. The degree of variance (R^2) in stock prices explained by this model is .89.

The data in Table 6.2 may thus be used (and are used below) to interpret the specific circumstances of an individual utility in order to estimate its future dividends and to make any adjustment to the net effective discount factor necessary to forecast price.

Specific Utility Forecasts

Allegheny Power

The DDM suggests this stock was priced right in early 1989: it had a strong balance sheet and is well positioned to serve its area needs. Allegheny's service area is mature and its growth should be somewhat less than that of the industry throughout the 1990s. Consequently, its growth factor is reduced somewhat, resulting in an assumed net effective discount rate of 8.28 percent for this firm.

Allegheny's operations are seen as sufficiently strong to permit dividends to average a steady 4.5 percent annual increase throughout the forecast period.

Central Illinois Pub. Ser. Co. (CIPS)

A strong balance sheet is encouraging this utility to move to holding company status. At the beginning of 1989, the regulators were fighting this move. As it is confronted with few opportunities for growth in its service area, CIPS would like to diversify. In the absence of a successful diversification effort, growth is likely to be .25 percent below the industry average, yielding CIPS a net effective discount rate of 8.25 percent. Dividends are expected to increase at a 2.5 percent annual rate throughout this period.

Central La. Electric Co. (CLECO)

With good quality income, a balance sheet strengthened by a healthy cash flow, and a stable market, CLECO is likely to increase its dividend slightly below an average annual rate of 7 percent throughout the forecast period.

Even with the recovery of the region's oil economy, the utility's growth prospects do not warrant its current market premium. By 1991, Central's growth will parallel that of the industry as a whole with a net effective discount factor of 8 percent.

CILCORP

This utility's stock is somewhat overvalued relative to both the DDM and its growth prospects. The financials are solid at this company, but the prospects for the future unexciting.

Dividends are expected to increase 4 percent throughout the forecast period. No adjustment is needed for its effective discount rate.

Cincinnati Gas & Electric Co. (CG&E)

The DDM model suggests this stock was slightly undervalued at the beginning of 1989. This reflects the belief that the current rate of dividend growth will be hard to maintain as the utility struggles with its conversion of the Zimmer Nuclear power plant to coal. However, once this facility is factored into its rate base, its substantial cash flows can be used to increase its balance sheet fundamentals and increase dividends. The utility should find its regulatory authorities relatively favorably disposed to this as the utility is relatively short of generating power.

Provided CG&E does not undertake excessive investments in new generating facilities, an annual increase in dividends of 2 percent may be anticipated over the intermediate and long term. The need to increase generating capacity is expected to hold down its growth throughout the forecast period. As a result, a net effective discount factor of 9 percent is used to forecast this utility's stock price.

DPL Inc.

Share price for this utility is slightly undervalued by the DDM. Its circumstances are similar to those of Cincinnati Gas and Electric with whom it shares an interest in the Zimmer plant conversion. Problems with the quality of earnings limit DPL's capacity to increase its current dividends, and a relatively low rate of growth in its service sector limits its long-term earnings potential.

Dividends are anticipated to average a 2 percent increase throughout the forecast period. Growth at DPL is expected to approximate the industry average throughout the period.

Empire District Electric (EDE)

AFUDC credits will remain a substantial portion of this utility's profits through the early 1990s, as EDE attempts to match capacity to its growing market. EDE's relatively large cash flows should allow this utility to maintain a dividend increase of 4 percent throughout the forecast period. Its growth is expected to mirror that of the industry.

Hawaiian Electric Industries (HEI)

This stock is a market favorite and consequently trades at a significant premium to the DDM. HEI's long-term outlook is bolstered by solid growth prospects in its service area.

It has begun a strategy of using IPPs as an alternative to building its own generating capacity. In addition, HEI's substantial cash flows are being invested in other industries—savings and insurance so far. Management appears to be of sufficient quality to make the diversification effort successful.

Dividends are anticipated to increase 5 percent through 1992 and at 7 percent thereafter. HEI's growth premium is expected to increase throughout the period as Hawaii's position as the door to the Asian rim and as a desirable retirement area continue to bolster regional growth. HEI's net effective discount rate in 1999 is expected to be 5.5 percent.

Idaho Power Co. (IPC)

Idaho Power stock prices are slightly overvalued in the market at the beginning of 1989. This reflects some temporary loss of earnings consequent on drought conditions at the end of the 1980s (58 percent of IPC's power is derived from hydroelectric sources). With its slow growing market, this utility may well have excess capacity to sell in the 1990s. Given a return to normal weather patterns, this situation is expected to help Idaho Power rebound from its lackluster performance in the 1980s.

Idaho Power's growth factor is expected to be about 1 percent higher than the industry average, yielding a 7 percent net discount rate. Dividends are expected to increase an average of 2.9 percent annually throughout the forecast period.

Interstate Power Co. (IPC)

IPC stock is somewhat undervalued by the market relative to the DDM. This reflects some weakness in the balance sheet and to operations in a stagnant market.

Growth is expected be a full percentage point below the industry average. Dividend increases may be expected in the 2 percent range throughout the forecast period.

IPALCO Enterprises Inc.

IPALCO stock is overvalued relative to the DDM stock price estimates. This strong performance is based on its recent and potential growth along with a very strong balance sheet.

The earnings of this utility are particularly vulnerable to environmental legislation because of its reliance on high sulfur coal. President Bush's 1989 proposed acid rain legislation would require a major rate increase for IPALCO. However, even if such legislation emerges, the cost is likely to be passed on to its customers and its current finances are sufficiently strong to carry it through negotiations with its regulators without impairing its dividend.

Dividends are expected to increase between 4 and 5 percent throughout the forecast period. IPALCO is expected to maintain its current market premium (implying a 7 percent net effective discount rate) through the decade.

Kansas Power & Light Co.

This stock is slightly overvalued in the market relative to the DDM. Its service market is mature and no additions to capacity are planned until the regulatory climate changes so as to not penalize additions to base capacity.

Dividends are forecast to increase at a rate of 3 percent throughout this period. Its growth in earnings is expected to be slightly above that of the industry.

Kentucky Utilities Co. (KU)

Despite the location of a large Toyota plant in its service area, KU's growth prospects remain dim. The company has recently reformulated itself into a holding company and may well make nonutility acquisitions.

The stock is currently overvalued by the DDM. Dividends are forecast to increase at 3 percent throughout the forecast period. This stock may perform significantly better or worse, depending on how its acquisitions fare.

Dividends are seen to increase at an average 3 percent annual rate. The present growth premium embedded in its market price is expected to dissipate by the middle of the decade.

Louisville Gas & Electric Co. (LG&E)

LG&E's earnings will remain depressed as it absorbs the excess capacity of its Trimble 1 coal fired plant. The slow growth of its market may yield it some opportunities to sell excess power in the 1990s.

Dividends are anticipated to increase at a 3 percent annual rate. LG&E's growth factor is seen to increase a full point with the revival of the petroleum economy between 1993 and 1996.

MDU Resources Group (MDU)

MDU's stock was overvalued in the market at the beginning of 1989, despite the attribution of good growth prospects to its electric utility and nonutility businesses. It has had a difficult experience in its gas operations, which have depressed earnings at the end of the 1980s. Once these problems are overcome (early in the decade), the company should be better able to realize its growth potential.

Dividends are anticipated to increase at 2 percent per year until 1992 and 3 percent thereafter. A 1 percent positive adjustment to its growth factor is phased in between 1993 and 1996.

Midwest Energy Co. (MEC)

MEC currently has adequate generating capacity for serving its low-growth market. Its relatively high payout rate suggests that in the absence of rate relief, any adversity could imperil its dividend. MEC's heavy reliance on coal makes it particularly susceptible to any increasing costs resulting from changed environmental regulations. The 1989 proposed acid rain legislation could force a dividend cutback in the absence of immediate rate relief.

Barring such legislation, dividends are expected to increase 3 percent throughout the forecast period. MEC's earnings growth is expected to slightly lag that of the industry as a percent.

Minnesota Power & Light Co. (MPL)

As a result of growth consequent on diversification, MPL stock price was somewhat overvalued relative to the DDM in early 1989. Whether or not these diversification efforts will actually flow through to the bottom line is not clear.

Dividends are anticipated to increase at a 4 percent annual rate throughout the forecast period. No downward adjustment for growth is made on the assumption that its investments will yield market rates of return.

While this stock's performance is forecast to correspond to industry trends, it is a little riskier of an investment than many other electric utilities because of its diversification strategy.

Montana Power Co. (MPC)

MPC has significant excess capacity which it is currently in the process of obligating for long periods of time at prices below cost. While this strategy will boost earnings (because at least some of its fixed costs will be recovered) in the near term, it is mortgaging its potential for significant profits in the mid-1990s.

MPC has diversified into a variety of other businesses and derived 36 percent of its total revenues from its nonutility operations in 1988. This diversification is likely to yield MPC better returns than its electric operations. Whether or not the returns from these ventures exceed the opportunity cost of the capital invested is less certain.

Current dividend rates are expected to increase 2 percent throughout the forecast period. No adjustment to the DDM is necessary for MPC.

Nevada Power Co. (NPC)

Nevada Power Co. is overvalued relative to the DDM, reflecting the tendency of its regulatory commission to cut its rates as it approaches its allowed rate of return, thus limiting its ability to continue to increase dividends. However the stock is undervalued relative to its growth rate based on low operating costs, low cost of capital and a burgeoning market area.

Dividends are expected to increase 2 percent annually throughout the forecast period. NPC's favorable discount factor of 7 percent is expected to continue for the duration of the forecast period.

Oklahoma Gas & Electric Co. (OGE)

OGE stock is overvalued relative to both the DDM model estimate and the growth factor estimate. OGE is a well-run company with good finances trapped in a stagnant market. OGE is currently looking to diversify, but its prospects in this area are questionable.

Although the oil economy should pick up by the middle of the decade, the growth prospects for this firm will remain limited. Dividends are anticipated to increase at a steady 5 percent throughout the forecast period, but OGE's market premium will slowly erode as other utilities prove to be better growth vehicles.

Orange & Rockland Utilities, Inc. (ORU)

ORU is a financially solid utility whose earnings may be expected to edge up as the result of the conversion of some oil fueled plants to coal. ORU's stock price is somewhat overvalued by the market relative to the DDM, its service area growth is steady.

Dividends are expected to increase 2 percent annually until 1992 and 3 percent thereafter. Its growth factor will continue to give its stock a premium in the market.

Pacificorp

Pacificorp's acquisition of Utah P&L was to be finalized at the end of 1989 and a new utility to be created named Pacificorp Oregon. The gains of the merger will be split between customers and stockholders. A near-term reduction in per share earnings will hopefully translate into greater share earnings down the road. The market believes this and has accorded its shares a higher value than would be expected from its level of dividends.

Dividends are expected to increase 3 percent until 1992, 5 percent until 1995 and 8 percent thereafter. Growth at Pacificorp is expected to mirror industry averages.

Potomac Electric Power Co. (PEPCO)

PEPCO has had difficulty translating its rapidly growing sales in Washington, D.C., and its Maryland suburbs into profits. Its shares tend to be overvalued relative to its present level of dividends, but undervalued from the perspective of its long-term growth prospects. As its current construction plans are modest, PEPCO will be forced to either purchase additional power supplies in an unfavorable market in the mid-1990s or build additional base load capacity. In the latter case, dividend yields will have to rise sufficiently to attract the necessary capital.

Dividends are estimated to increase 8 percent throughout the forecast period. As a result of continued strong growth in its service area, PEPCO's already favorable growth factor is adjusted gradually upward in the middle of the decade. By the end of the decade, PEPCO stock will sport a 7 percent net effective discount rate.

Puget Sound P&L Co. (PSP&L)

PSP&L was hurt by its involvement in the unfinished WPPSS 3 nuclear plant, which has lowered the quality of its earnings and resulted in some balance sheet weaknesses. Even though the economy in its service area is robust, its dividend is not likely to be increased until the early 1990s. Dividends are expected to remain unchanged until 1992, when they will rise to a 3 percent annual increase throughout the forecast period.

The stock is undervalued relative to the DDM prediction. The low growth expectations attached to this stock reflect problems embedded in an increasingly distant past. We expect these negative attributions to largely dissipate by 1996 and the expected growth of PSP&L to mirror that of the rest of the industry.

S.W. Public Service Co.

The depressed oil economy in this service region continues to take its toll on this utility. With average strength in its balance sheet, there is little chance of a change in the modest prospects for this utility in the foreseeable future. Dividends are expected to increase at 3 percent throughout the forecast period and growth to parallel that of the rest of the industry.

Sierra Pacific Resources (SPR)

SPR's service area is showing above-average growth, but its stock is slightly overvalued by the DDM. Its plans to add to base load capacity by contracting with IPPs assures a steady, if slow, increase in earnings.

Dividends are anticipated to increase 3 percent throughout the forecast period. Growth at SPR is expected to track industry averages.

So. Indiana Gas & Electric Co. (SIG)

SIG is significantly overvalued by the DDM and this is not accounted for by potential growth. The utility's finances are strong and its need to add capacity nonexistent until the mid-1990s.

Dividends may be expected to increase 3 percent until 1992 and 6 percent thereafter. A negative adjustment of .75 percent in its growth factor is expected by 1994.

St. Joe Light & Power Co. (St. Joe)

St. Joe is located in a steadily growing market and is extremely well-positioned to take advantage of that. The utility has exceptionally high stockholders' equity (60 percent) and a relatively low payout rate. This excess capital can either be reinvested in nonutility operations or returned to its owners. In either case, although the stock is currently somewhat overvalued relative to the DDM estimate, the value of this stock is likely to rise faster than the industry as a whole.

On the assumption that management will not go the acquisition route, cash dividends are likely to increase at a hefty 7 percent average throughout the forecast period. St. Joe's is expected to improve its market premium slightly by the middle of the decade as the prospects in its home market continue to brighten.

TECO Energy Corp.

TECO's rapidly growing Tampa, Florida, market has caused its share price to be significantly overvalued relative to DDM expectations. The critical question with this utility is whether or not it will be able to translate the increased sales of electric power into increased earnings. In such a strongly growing market, increased earnings would be hard to avoid.

TECO also has significant nonutility sales in coal mining and transportation. There is no particular reason why these subsidiaries should outperform the market.

Dividends are expected to increase 5 percent throughout the forecast period with a negative adjustment to its growth factor in the mid-1990s.

TNP Enterprises

TNP Enterprises is undervalued by the DDM and overvalued by the growth factor estimate. TNP does not generate its own electricity and won't until its first plants come on line in the mid-1990s. This utility has very strong financials and may be able to finance some generating capacity from internal funds. Its demand prospects are poor as long as the petroleum industry remains moribund. However, TNP is well positioned to take advantage of oil's anticipated revival in the middle of the decade. Over the long haul, TNP's reliance on purchased power will hurt.

Dividends are anticipated to increase at an annual rate of 3 percent until 1993 and 6 percent thereafter. Its power generating capacity should come on line at a most opportune time, and this will translate into a market premium for TNP shareholders.

Tucson Electric Power Co. (TEP)

At the beginning of 1989, TEP's stock was slightly overvalued relative to its DDM predicted price and significantly overvalued relative to assumed industry growth. Subsequent events proved this situation was misleading.

TEP has currently suspended its dividend and faces the possibility of being forced into bankruptcy. Even if management is successful in renegotiating its debt, TEP's fundamental near-term market outlook is grim.

Continuing troubles will arise from its excess capacity in a market that is already awash with excess capacity. TEP has a reserve margin of 41% and the southwest suffers from a glut of electric power. It will be well into the 1990s before TEP is able to extradite itself from its current woes. A revival of the oil economy and a booming shortage of electricity in the mid-1990s will signal the light at the end of the tunnel.

Utilicorp United Inc. (UUI)

Utilicorp is engaged in an aggressive growth strategy based on the acquisition of other electric and gas utilities—five since 1985. The stock is significantly overvalued at current price levels relative to its DDM predicted price. This reflects the extremely high growth rate attributed by the market to this utility.

Buying other utilities in a market characterized by excess capacity is a fundamentally good long-term strategy. However as long as its markets are characterized by excess capacity, UUI will have difficulty sustaining an increasing dividend. As demand begins to press on supply, the unobligated portions of UUI's generating capacity should be able to make a powerful contribution to earnings.

In the absence of any dramatic large acquisitions or a significant downturn in the industrial portion of the midwest economy, dividends are anticipated to increase at 6.5 percent until 1992 and 9 percent after that. On the basis of its continued use of a selective acquisitions strategy, UUI's growth factor is expected to increase until 1995 and decline somewhat thereafter. UUI's current (1989) effective net discount rate is 6 percent; this is expected to fall to 5 percent by 1995 and rise back to 6 percent by the end of the forecast period.

Washington Water Power Co. (WWP)

Despite its name, this utility derives over 80 percent of its revenues from the sale of electric power. Its dividend did not increase between 1984 and 1988. This dividend was maintained with a relatively high payout ratio, which the utility was able to support thanks to its sizeable cash flow. Increased earnings are contingent on rate relief.

Dividends are not expected to increase until 1990 and thereafter at a 2 percent annual rate. WWP's growth rate is given a 1 percent positive adjustment in 1995 that reflects a "halo effect" from this sector of the industry. This is a reaction to the market attribution of an extraordinarily low growth rate in 1989.

Dividend Forecasts

The statistics set forth in Table 6.4 were used to generate the following set of dividend projections.

Forecasting Stock Prices

Future stock prices can be forecast from the dividends projected in Table 6.4 using the DDM. A critical assumption that must be made in this forecast is the effective net discount rate. At the beginning of 1989, it appears that a net discount rate of .08 would be most appropriate for this industry over the coming decade. This rate is used as an industry norm to develop the set of stock prices forecast (subject to the modifications noted above) in Chapter 2, Table 2.1.

If the industry were to grow at a faster or slower rate, this would have a significant impact on the future price of these utility stocks. As noted in Chapter 3, the perception of growth prospects and risk by the investment community is highly subjective, not entirely rational (i.e., market perceptions often have an emotional component), and may change with startling rapidity. To the extent that investors' fears come to dominate their perceptions of market prices, the net effective discount rate could be expected to rise. To the extent that the prospect of future increases in earnings becomes brighter, the net effective discount rate may be expected to fall.

Table 6.4 Dividend Forecasts; Electric Utilities without Nuclear Exposure

Utility	1989	1990	1991	1992	1993	1994	1995	1996	1997	1998	1999
Allegheny Power	3.14	3.28	3.42	3.58	3.74	3.91	4.08	4.27	4.46	4.66	4.87
Central Illinois Pub. Ser.	1.79	1.84	1.88	1.93	1.98	2.03	2.08	2.13	2.19	2.24	2.30
Central La. Electric Co.	2.45	2.62	2.81	3.00	3.21	3.44	3.68	3.93	4.21	4.50	4.82
CILCORP	2.50	2.60	2.70	2.81	2.92	3.04	3.16	3.28	3.42	3.55	3.69
Cincinnati Gas & Electric	2.27	2.32	2.37	2.41	2.46	2.51	2.56	2.61	2.67	2.72	2.77
DPL Inc.	2.20	2.25	2.29	2.34	2.38	2.43	2.48	2.53	2.58	2.63	2.69
Empire District Electric	2.24	2.33	2.42	2.52	2.62	2.72	2.83	2.94	3.06	3.18	3.31
Hawaiian Electric Industries	2.05	2.15	2.26	2.37	2.54	2.71	2.90	3.11	3.32	3.56	3.81
Idaho Power Co.	1.80	1.80	1.85	1.91	1.97	2.03	2.09	2.15	2.21	2.28	2.35
Interstate Power Co.	2.02	2.08	2.14	2.21	2.27	2.34	2.41	2.48	2.56	2.63	2.71
IPALCO Enterprises Inc.	1.72	1.81	1.90	1.99	2.09	2.20	2.31	2.42	2.54	2.67	2.80
Kansas Power & Light Co.	1.81	1.86	1.92	1.97	2.03	2.09	2.16	2.22	2.29	2.36	2.43
Kentucky Utilities Co.	1.38	1.42	1.46	1.51	1.55	1.60	1.65	1.70	1.75	1.80	1.85
Louisville Gas & Electric	2.77	2.85	2.94	3.03	3.12	3.21	3.31	3.47	3.65	3.83	4.02
MDU Resources Group	1.45	1.48	1.51	1.54	1.58	1.63	1.68	1.73	1.78	1.84	1.89
Midwest Energy Co.	1.59	1.63	1.68	1.73	1.79	1.84	1.89	1.95	2.01	2.07	2.13
Minnesota Power & Light Co.	1.79	1.86	1.93	2.01	2.09	2.18	2.26	2.35	2.45	2.55	2.65
Montana Power Co.	2.73	2.75	2.78	2.81	2.84	2.89	2.95	3.01	3.07	3.13	3.20
Nevada Power	1.53	1.56	1.59	1.62	1.66	1.69	1.72	1.76	1.79	1.83	1.87
Oklahoma Gas & Electric Co.	2.43	2.55	2.67	2.81	2.95	3.10	3.25	3.41	3.58	3.76	3.95
Orange & Rockland Utilities	2.28	2.33	2.38	2.42	2.50	2.57	2.65	2.73	2.81	2.90	2.98
Pacificorp	2.72	2.80	2.88	2.97	3.12	3.28	3.44	3.71	4.01	4.33	4.68
Potomac Electric Power Co.	1.49	1.61	1.74	1.88	2.03	2.19	2.37	2.55	2.76	2.98	3.22
Puget Sound P&L Co.	1.76	1.76	1.76	1.76	1.76	1.81	1.87	1.92	1.98	2.04	2.10
S.W. Public Service Co.	2.18	2.25	2.32	2.39	2.46	2.53	2.61	2.69	2.77	2.85	2.93

(Table continues)

Utility	1989	1990	1991	1992	1993	1994	1995	1996	1997	1998	1999
Sierra Pacific Resources	1.82	1.88	1.93	1.99	2.05	2.11	2.18	2.24	2.31	2.38	2.45
So. Indiana Gas & Electric	1.75	1.80	1.86	1.91	2.031	2.15	2.28	2.42	2.56	2.71	2.88
St. Joe Light & Power Co.	1.51	1.63	1.76	1.90	2.06	2.22	2.40	2.59	2.80	3.02	3.26
TECO Energy Corp.	1.49	1.57	1.64	1.73	1.81	1.90	2.00	2.10	2.20	2.31	2.43
TNP Enterprises	1.54	1.59	1.64	1.69	1.74	1.79	1.90	2.01	2.13	2.26	2.39
Tucson Electric Power Co.	4.21	4.55	4.91	5.31	5.73	6.30	6.93	7.63	8.39	9.23	10.15
Utilicorp United Inc.	1.16	1.24	1.32	1.42	1.51	1.67	1.83	2.02	2.22	2.44	2.68
Washington Water Power Co.	2.48	2.48	2.53	2.58	2.63	2.68	2.74	2.79	2.85	2.91	2.96

Evaluating Investment Return

The true success of an investment in utility stocks is not measured by either dividends or price appreciation. Rather, the best approach is to examine the discount factor, which equates positive and negative cash flows over time. As discussed in Chapter 3, this measure is called the total rate of return (TRR) and expresses itself as an annual percentage rate.

The estimated TRRs from the 33 electric utilities without nuclear exposure in 1994 and 1999 have been presented in Table 6.1. It should be noted that this table embeds an effective discount factor of .08 to make its predictions, as well as any firm-specific growth estimates noted above. Changes in market rates of growth, changes in the perceived "riskiness" of the industry, or changes in the time preference for money (i.e., the risk-free interest rate) will change this discount factor. As suggested in Table 6.3, even small changes in this factor can have a sizeable impact on price appreciation and, consequently, on the TRR to the investor.

In contrast to the troubled decade of the 1970s, the industry as a whole is likely to perform well throughout the 1990s. While the spectacular run-up in prices that occurred in the last half of the 1980s is not likely to repeat itself, the TRRs to investors from the major electric utilities without nuclear exposure are likely to be strong throughout the 1990s.

On the average, investments in nonnuclear electric utility stocks are likely to outperform investments in industrial stocks in the coming decade. Among the 33 utilities examined in this chapter, four (Hawaiian Electric Industries, Utilicorp United, St. Joe Light & Power Co., and Potomac Electric Power Co.) clearly represent an outstanding opportunity for investors.

How to Use These Forecasts

The projections developed in this chapter are not cast in stone. These projections are valid only to the extent they embody valid assumptions about the future. While these assumptions are reasonable in the light of current knowledge, unforeseen events will surely occur.

The material presented here provides the reader with sufficient information to modify these projections in the light of such unforeseen events. For example, If the oil industry becomes resurgent earlier in the decade, the low growth rates imputed to Central Louisiana Electric Co. and the Oklahoma Gas & Electric Co. would no longer be appropriate. The reader may then modify the price forecast in Table 6.1 based on this information. In turn, these new price projections, along with current prices, can be used in conjunction with the dividend forecasts in Table 6.4 to develop a new estimated TRR for an investment in these companies.

The stock price projections in Table 6.1 provide a handy guide for evaluating buying opportunities or selling situations. The projected stock prices can be compared with current prices to make an investment decision. These investment decisions should always consider current market conditions and the significance of unfolding events.

Aside from changes relevant to specific firms, the material in this chapter may be readily modified to reflect changed macroeconomic assumptions. For example, if there were an unanticipated rise in interest levels, the net effective discount factor used in Table 6.1 would have to be raised. As this would lower stock prices, these new price levels could be used to evaluate the attractiveness of possible investments in the industry.

Chapter 7

THE FUTURE FOR INVESTMENT IN ELECTRIC UTILITIES WITH NUCLEAR EXPOSURE

Performance Overview

Investments in the nuclear segment of the electric utility industry will carry high levels of risk throughout the 1990s. Two groups of utilities among the 63 firms that comprise this market segment have been identified: 23 firms whose future financial performance is primarily dependent on economic and market factors and 40 firms whose financial future lies almost entirely within the hands of politicians and regulators.

This segment of the industry was brought to the brink of destruction in the 1970s and early 1980s by its attempt to develop a nuclear source of electric power. The incredible unanticipated expenses of nuclear facility construction; resistance to such facilities in the community; the unforeseen slow-down in energy consumption; and *ad hoc* prudency reviews by regulatory agencies (which resulted in the exclusion of significant amounts of expended capital from the rate base) proved a deadly combination.

The mid-1980s saw a partial recovery for this segment of the industry as excess capacity began to be absorbed and the various nuclear facilities either entered service, were refitted to burn conventional fuels, or were abandoned. Investors reaped significant

121

gains during this period as stock prices recovered from unrealistically low levels.

The 23 utilities with relatively successful nuclear power development will not reap any gains proportionate to the risk they incurred. This power is in their regulated base and the lower costs of production will flow through to their customers. The legacy of this effort for all electric utilities with nuclear exposure is a severely weakened balance sheet and a reduced ability to fund potentially profitable unregulated power generation facilities.

Among the 23 utilities with a nuclear exposure judged to be able to influence their own financial outcomes, only modest gains can be expected during the 1990s. The prospective TRRs for this segment of the industry are presented in Table 7.1.

These modest returns are associated with significantly higher risk than were the electric utilities without nuclear exposure covered in Chapter 6. The higher risk arises from a number of sources: (1) a nuclear mishap at a particular firm would have a negative impact on earnings and share price at that firm; (2) a nuclear mishap at any firm could dampen investor enthusiasm for this segment of the industry—affecting the stock prices of all firms with nuclear power generating facilities; and (3) the market has currently (1990) attributed a very low net effective discount factor to these firms—it's unlikely this factor would become more favorable, but quite possible for it to become less favorable.

Prospective investors in a utility with nuclear exposure should take a very hard look at the risk-return combination in this investment. Better opportunities appear to be available among electric utilities without nuclear exposure.

The 40 utilities (listed in Table 7.2) with nuclear exposure judged to be highly risky present interesting speculative possibilities. Each of these utilities is a candidate for a significant turnaround, because the earnings of each are severely discounted by the market. Experience in this sector between 1984 and 1988 suggests that turnarounds can yield investors substantial rewards.

The question is whether stock prices of these utilities will remain depressed. A case can be made that by the mid 1990s the shortage of electrical capacity will be so critical and the need for a

Table 7.1   Projected TRR for Electric Utilities with Nuclear Exposure

TRR Rank 1990–93	Utility	Projected TRR 1990-94	Projected TRR 1989-99
1	Delmarva Power	19.37%	13.87%
2	Public Service of Colorado	17.65%	14.93%
3	Consolidated Edison	17.49%	14.50%
4	Baltimore Gas & Electric	17.02%	15.13%
5	Public Service Enterprise Group	15.86%	14.41%
6	FPL Group, Inc.	15.64%	12.06%
7	Iowa-Illinois Gas & Electric Co.	15.52%	13.55%
8	Atlantic Energy, Inc.	15.15%	14.59%
9	Pacific Gas & Electric Co.	15.11%	16.01%
10	Green Mountain Power	15.02%	12.95%
11	Florida Progress Corp.	14.53%	11.94%
12	SCANA Corporation	14.32%	12.38%
13	Central Vermont Pub. Ser.	14.20%	12.45%
14	Wisconsin Energy Corp.	14.16%	11.77%
15	No. States Power Co.	13.97%	11.93%
16	SCE Corp.	13.10%	12.91%
17	WPL Holdings Inc.	13.10%	11.89%
18	Pennsylvania Power & Light Co.	13.10%	11.37%
19	General Public Utilities	12.65%	11.18%
20	Carolina Power	12.49%	10.24%
21	Duke Power Co.	12.12%	11.62%
22	Wisconsin Public Service Corp.	10.90%	9.21%
23	PSI Holdings, Inc.	9.87%	9.34%

healthy utility industry so obvious, that these firms will be allowed by their regulators to repair their financial structures. It is unlikely that these utilities will return themselves to financial health by the middle of the 1990s. Certainly they will not do it on their own. The outcomes for these firms will be determined by political factors. Financial health is only a rate increase away.

Table 7.2   Speculative Electric Utilities with Nuclear Exposure

1   American Electric Power
2   Boston Edison
3   Centerior Energy
4   Central & South West's Corp.
5   Central Hudson
6   Central Maine
7   CMS Energy Corp.
8   Commonwealth Edison
9   Commonwealth Energy System
10   Detroit Edison Co.
11   Dominion Resources
12   Duquesne Light Co.
13   Eastern Utility Associates
14   Gulf States Utilities
15   Houston Industries, Inc.
16   IE Industries
17   Illinois Power Co.
18   Iowa Resources Inc.
19   Kansas City Power & Light Co.
20   Kansas Gas & Electric Co.
21   Long Island Lighting Co.
22   Middle South Utilities Inc.
23   Midwest Energy Co.
24   N.E. Utilities
25   N.Y. State Electric & Gas Corp.
26   New England Electric System
27   Niagra Mohawk Power Corp.
28   NIPSCO Industries Inc.
29   Ohio Edison Co.
30   Philadelphia Electric Co.
31   Pinnacle West Capital Corp.
32   Portland General
33   Public Service of New Mexico
34   Public Service Co. of New Hampshire
35   Rochester Gas & Electric Corp.
36   San Diego Gas & Electric Co.
37   Southern Co.
38   Texas Utilities Co.
39   Union Electric Co.
40   United Illuminating Co.

While investment in this sector may well prove profitable, it is not recommended for the investor concerned with the preservation of his or her capital.

Forecasting Share Prices

Investment outcomes among electric utilities with nuclear exposure are much riskier than the outcomes associated with utilities that do not have a nuclear exposure. The DDM does not explain stock price behavior with the same consistency in this sector as among electric utilities without nuclear exposure.

The relationship between dividends and share price for the 63 firms is weak. As can be seen in Figure 7.1, dividends are able to

Figure 7.1 Nuclear Electric Utilities Price–Dividend Relationship

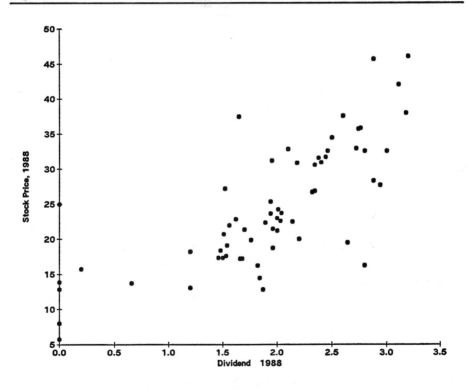

explain only slightly more than half ($R^2 = .54$) the variance in price in this sector.

The weakness in this relationship may be explained by considering the dependency of firms in this sector on the outcome of political and social factors beyond their control. Whatever the validity of the underlying rationale for nuclear power, the issue has become highly politicized and contentious. Forecasting performance is difficult because of the importance of noneconomic factors. Investors would do well to be wary in this area.

All investments in electric utilities owning nuclear generating capacity should be considered speculative. However, acquiring an equity interest in some firms in this area is less speculative than acquiring a similar interest in others. Discerning the more desirable utilities is a tricky business. Normal business and financial analytical tools do not lend themselves to discovering what is really going on in an individual firm. Figure 7.2 illustrates the general absence of a consistent relationship ($R^2 = .53$) between share price and net profits per share for the 63 firms.

Even adjusting for problems in the quality of earnings by examining cash flows does not yield insight into stock valuation fundamentals. This point is illustrated by the weak relationship ($R^2 = .68$) between share price and cash flow per share in Figure 7.3.

The Nuclear Background

An understanding of the present situation can be helped by considering the historical origins of the situation.

Investing in nuclear powered generating facilities looked very attractive in the early 1970s. In the context of an energy crisis in which fuel might not be available at any price, rapidly rising oil prices, a growing concern over the environmental impact of fossil fuels, and a general inflation which was badly hurting the utilities because of regulatory lag, nuclear power looked very desirable. Engineers assumed that it was "safe," capital costs looked moderate, operational costs appeared astonishingly low, fuel sources were virtually unlimited, and it did not appear to have an adverse environmental impact. Small wonder that 63 of the 96 major investor-

Figure 7.2   Nuclear Electric Utilities Price–Profit Relationship

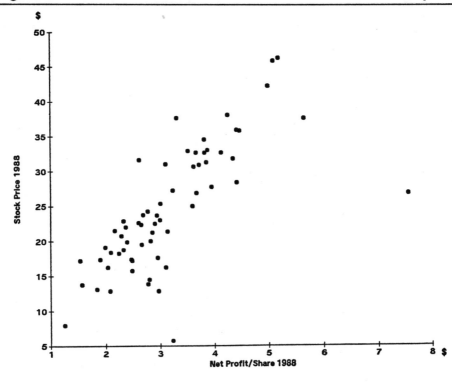

owned electric utilities in the United States made a foray into nuclear power.

How time has shown this course of action to be folly: capital construction costs escalated tremendously, significant environmental concerns were raised, and AFUDC accounting created a cash squeeze. The demand for electricity slowed and many companies were left with expensive capital investments that they were not allowed to bring into their rate base because the creation of excess capacity was deemed not to be prudent.

Even where nuclear facilities were brought on line within budget, there were no exceptional rewards given to investor-owned utilities.

**Figure 7.3   Nuclear Electric Utilities Price–Cash Flow
                Relationship**

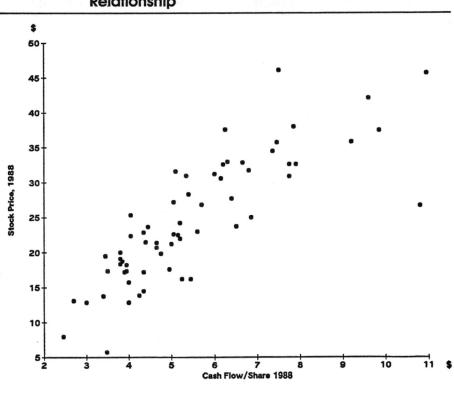

Nuclear Facilities and Risk

Under the best of circumstances, electric utilities with investments
in nuclear power are at risk. The reason for this lies not in the technology of nuclear power, but in the difficulty of sustaining human
performance levels.

Baltimore Gas & Electric Company was able to operate its twin
Calvert Cliffs nuclear plants in exemplary fashion for over a decade. By 1987, their operation had achieved an international reputa-

tion and was visited by delegations from all over the world seeking guidance on nuclear plant management. In 1988, they were placed on the Nuclear Regulatory Commission's (NRC) list of plants needing special supervision because of serious safety violations.

In the words of their vice president in charge of nuclear power, ". . . we have been a victim of our own success." Management and workers became complacent. If this can happen in a utility with excellent management, what is happening in utilities with average and poor management? The NRC was so concerned with the general quality of management at the Philadelphia Electric Company, which operates the notorious Peach Bottom nuclear facility, that they required a general housecleaning, forcing the Chairman of the Board and the CEO to retire.

As long as nuclear facilities depend on humans, they will not be safe. To have zero chance of a disaster requires perfect human beings. Of course, nuclear facilities can be operated within reasonable safety standards. However, it is all too clear that in the event of a disaster, the stockholders will suffer seriously. Existing insurance arrangements fail to protect utilities fully from a catastrophe. Even the temporary cessation of operations at a plant may cost the utilities substantial penalties (as decreed by the regulators). The exclusion of an inoperative nuclear facility from a firm's rate base would be disastrous in itself.

As an investor one must ask, why expose yourself to the risk? Investors in electric utilities with nuclear facilities are certainly not compensated for bearing such risks.

The experience of the electric utility industry with nuclear power has been expensive for investors. The legacy of this experience is revealed in the number of utilities which have been substantially disabled by the expense of constructing a nuclear facility and the difficulties of having these costs passed on to its customers. Even though an effective moratorium on new nuclear facilities exists, many utilities hover on the brink of financial disaster, awaiting the outcome of torturous regulatory and judicial processes.

Forecasting Returns for Electric Utilities with Nuclear Exposure

It is possible to earn a substantial return from speculating in electric utilities with nuclear exposure. The TRRs earned in this sector between 1984 and 1989 are illustrated in Table 7.3.

The tremendous returns accruing to General Public Utilities (GPU) reflect its recovery from the Three Mile Island disaster. As a consequence of the generosity of its regulatory agency and the general economic health of its service area, GPU has been able to strengthen its once decimated balance sheet and resume paying dividends to its investors. Eastern Utilities has shown strength on the basis of the improving prospects of putting Seabrook 1 into service. If this happens, Eastern Utilities will be in an excellent position both in its own market and to sell its low-cost excess capacity in the power-short New England area. Union Electric has proved able to recover from the difficulties of getting its Callaway 1 nuclear unit into service.

Will Public Service Company of New Hampshire (PSCNH) be able to emerge from bankruptcy in a fashion that will reward its long-suffering shareholders? Everything depends on getting Seabrook 1 into service. If this nuclear plant does come on line, is operated successfully, and receives favorable regulatory treatment, it may well be able to generate substantial profits for its owners. All together, it's a lot of "ifs." A contrarian might well believe that everything bad that can happen has already happened and that there is no place to go but up. It's not inconceivable that PSCNH could do a turnaround by 1995 just as GPU did a decade earlier.

Gulf States Utilities (GSU) continues to struggle with its regulators over its River Bend Unit 1 that came on line in 1986. GSU's situation is made more complex by the need to coordinate its two jurisdictional regulatory bodies (Texas and Louisiana) in a market that doesn't need the additional capacity. What will be the outcome of this process?

Public Service of New Mexico (PSNM) also is constrained by its regulators. Its 10 percent stake in the Palo Verde nuclear generating station has given it over 50 percent excess capacity. What portion of its expenses the regulators will ultimately allow into its rate base will determine PSNM's financial health.

Table 7.3   Returns to Investors in Electric Utilities with Nuclear Exposure (1984–1988)

Rank	Utility	TRR
1	General Public Utilities	49.37%
2	Eastern Utility Associates	35.73%
3	Union Electric Co.	32.96%
4	San Diego Gas & Electric Co.	31.85%
5	Pennsylvania Power & Light Co.	31.32%
6	Baltimore Gas & Electric	30.92%
7	Ohio Edison Co.	30.71%
8	Portland General	29.64%
9	Wisconsin Energy Corp.	29.45%
10	SCANA Corporation	29.31%
11	Philadelphia Electric Co.	29.06%
12	N.E. Utilities	28.90%
13	Consolidated Edison	28.85%
14	Central Vermont Pub. Ser.	28.84%
15	Duke Power Co.	28.70%
16	American Electric Power	28.59%
17	Green Mountain Power	28.50%
18	Kansas City Power & Light Co.	28.26%
19	Public Service Enterprise Group	28.04%
20	Carolina Power	28.04%
21	IE Industries	27.76%
22	Florida Progress Corp.	27.50%
23	No. States Power Co.	27.32%
24	SCE Corp.	26.94%
25	Iowa-Illinois Gas & Electric Co.	26.14%
26	Houston Industries, Inc.	25.94%
27	Central & South West's Corp.	25.61%
28	Wisconsin Public Service Corp.	24.79%
29	Duquesne Light Co.	24.01%
30	Southern Co.	23.80%
31	FPL Group Inc.	23.41%
32	Atlantic Energy Inc.	22.54%
33	Delmarva Power	21.80%
34	Commonwealth Edison	21.73%
35	Detroit Edison Co.	20.99%
36	Pacific Gas & Electric Co.	20.32%

(Table continues)

**Table 7.3   Returns to Investors in Electric Utilities with Nuclear
                  Exposure (1984–1988) (Continued)**

Rank	Utility	TRR
37	Central Maine	19.58%
38	Boston Edison	19.52%
39	N.Y. State Electric & Gas Corp.	19.45%
40	Iowa Resources Inc.	19.44%
41	Texas Utilities Co.	18.99%
42	Midwest Energy Co.	18.92%
43	Commonwealth Energy System	18.68%
44	United Illuminating Co.	18.48%
45	Kansas Gas & Electric Co.	18.46%
46	Public Service of Colorado	18.29%
47	New England Electric System	17.17%
48	Illinois Power Co.	16.83%
49	Dominion Resources	16.66%
50	CMS Energy Corp.	15.76%
51	Rochester Gas & Electric Corp.	15.54%
52	Pinnacle West Capital Corp.	14.93%
53	Central Hudson	14.61%
54	WPL Holdings Inc.	14.33%
55	Niagra Mohawk Power Corp.	12.31%
56	Middle South Utilities Inc.	10.19%
57	Centerior Energy	9.80%
58	PSI Holdings Inc.	8.66%
59	Long Island Lighting Co.	6.22%
60	NIPSCO Industries Inc.	6.16%
61	Public Service of New Mexico	1.45%
62	Gulf States Utilities	–2.80%
63	Public Service Co. of New Hampshire	–16.31%

The previous examples are suggestive of the fact that investor returns in this sector are unusually dependent on political forces that are impossible to forecast. While this is true to some extent, it would be unfair to argue that this situation characterizes the whole industry. There is a contingent of firms in this sector that are in a situation with a relatively predictable outcome.

Identifying Reliably Performing Electric Utilities with Nuclear Exposure

The 63 firms that compose this sector can be divided into those whose fate rests with regulators and politicians and those whose outcome is primarily dependent on economic factors.

Table 7.4 identifies the two groups of utilities. There is little doubt that significant profits can be made by speculating in the securities of the more speculative group. The potential greater return is also matched by greater risk. This area is for speculators who are good at divining the intentions of regulators and politicians.

Future returns with the less speculative group are more amenable to forecasting techniques. However, because the ever-present risk of nuclear disaster is not compensated for by higher returns, none of these utilities is recommended for investment purposes.

Those 23 utilities that have invested in nuclear powered generating facilities and are labeled "less" speculative are distinguished from other utilities in this sector by meeting the following criteria: (1) no more than 25 percent of net profit is AFUDC, (2) the dividend payout (of earnings) does not exceed 85 percent, (3) owners equity is 40 percent of total liabilities or greater, and (4) long-term debt as a percentage of liabilities does not exceed 50 percent.

Dividend Forecasts

Compared with the utilities that do not meet the above criteria, the performance of the 23 utilities is primarily dependent upon their ability to function as business entities. As a consequence, the DDM has greater relevance to determining share values. The relationship between share price and dividends depicted in Figure 7.4 is stronger ($R^2 = .68$) than for the larger group.

In contrast, the relationship between price and dividends was much more consistent ($R^2 = .89$) among electric utilities without nuclear exposure. This implies that the price forecasts for the 23 electric utilities with nuclear exposure will be less accurate than for the group of electric utilities without nuclear exposure.

Future dividend levels for these 23 utilities are estimated by considering the specific circumstances surrounding their present level of dividend payments, the market price, the price predicted

Table 7.4   Nuclear Electric Utilities

Number	*"More" Speculative Utilities*	Number	*"Less" Speculative Utilities*
1	American Electric Power	1	Atlantic Energy Inc.
2	Boston Edison	2	Baltimore Gas & Electric
3	Centerior Energy	3	Carolina Power
4	Central & South West's Corp.	4	Central Vermont Pub. Ser.
5	Central Hudson	5	Consolidated Edison
6	Central Maine	6	Delmarva Power
7	CMS Energy Corp.	7	Duke Power Co.
8	Commonwealth Edison	8	Florida Progress Corp.
9	Commonwealth Energy System	9	FPL Group Inc.
10	Detroit Edison Co.	10	General Public Utilities
11	Dominion Resources	11	Green Mountain Power
12	Duquesne Light Co.	12	Iowa-Illinois Gas & Electric
13	Eastern Utility Associates	13	No. States Power Co.
14	Gulf States Utilities	14	Pacific Gas & Electric Co.
15	Houston Industries, Inc.	15	Pennsylvannia Pwr. & Light Co.
16	IE Industries	16	PSI Holdings Inc.
17	Illinois Power Co.	17	Public Ser. Enterprise Group
18	Iowa Resources Inc.	18	Public Service of Colorado
19	Kansas City Power & Light Co.	19	SCANA Corporation
20	Kansas Gas & Electric Co.	20	SCE Corp.
21	Long Island Lighting Co.	21	Wisconsin Energy Corp.
22	Middle South Utilities Inc.	22	Wisconsin Public Ser. Corp.
23	Midwest Energy Co.	23	WPL Holdings Inc.
24	N.E. Utilities		
25	N.Y. State Electric & Gas Corp.		
26	New England Electric System		
27	Niagra Mohawk Power Corp.		
28	NIPSCO Industries Inc.		
29	Ohio Edison Co.		
30	Philadelphia Electric Co.		
31	Pinnacle West Capital Corp.		
32	Portland General		
33	Public Ser. N. Mexico		
34	Public Ser. Co. of New Hampshire		
35	Rochester Gas & Electric Corp.		
36	San Diego Gas & Electric Co.		
37	Southern Co.		
38	Texas Utilities Co.		
39	Union Electric Co.		
40	United Illuminating Co.		

Figure 7.4   Nuclear Electric Utilities Price–Dividend Relationship

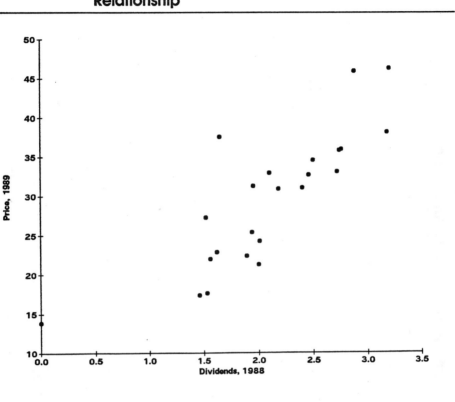

directly by the DDM and the price predicted by a model. Exactly the same framework is used as in Chapter 6. These DDM and model estimates are presented in Table 7.5.

The DDM estimate in Table 7.5 was developed by dividing current year dividends by a net effective discount rate of .07—a rate which best describes the current year market stock prices in this sector. (This process is fully described in Chapters 3 and 6.)

Although the .07 discount rate was used in developing the best estimate DDM stock price forecasts for nuclear exposed electric utilities in Table 7.5, a discount rate of .08 was found to best describe current nonnuclear stock prices in early 1989 (Table 6.1).

Table 7.5 Stock Price Data; Electric Utilities with Nuclear Exposure

Utility	Market Price	DDM Estimate	Model Estimate	DDM Estimate Error	Model Estimate Error
Atlantic Energy Inc.	33.00	38.86	31.67	-5.86	7.19
Baltimore Gas & Electric	31.25	27.86	30.44	3.39	-2.58
Carolina Power	35.88	39.43	33.69	-3.55	5.74
Central Vermont Pub. Ser.	25.38	27.71	26.31	-2.34	1.41
Consolidated Edison	46.13	45.71	40.90	0.41	4.81
Delmarva Power	17.38	20.86	20.68	-3.48	0.18
Duke Power Co.	45.75	41.14	40.64	4.61	0.51
Florida Progress Corp.	34.50	35.71	32.72	-1.21	2.99
FPL Group Inc.	30.88	31.14	30.18	-0.27	0.97
General Public Utilities	37.50	23.57	34.83	13.93	-11.26
Green Mountain Power	22.38	27.00	24.20	-4.62	2.80
Iowa-Illinois Gas & Electric	38.00	45.43	35.19	-7.43	10.24
No. States Power Co.	32.88	30.00	31.58	2.88	-1.58
Pacific Gas & Electric Co.	17.63	21.86	20.86	-4.23	1.00
Pennsylvania Power & Light Co.	35.75	39.14	33.60	-3.39	5.54
PSI Holdings Inc.	13.88	0.00	18.22	13.88	-18.22
Public Service Enterprise Group	24.25	28.71	25.52	-4.46	3.20
Public Service of Colorado	21.25	28.57	23.41	-7.32	5.17
SCANA Corp.	31.00	34.29	30.26	-3.29	4.02
SCE Corp.	32.63	35.14	31.41	-2.52	3.74
Wisconsin Energy Corp.	27.25	21.71	27.63	5.54	-5.91
Wisconsin Public Service Corp.	22.00	22.29	23.93	-0.29	-1.65
WPL Holdings Inc.	22.88	23.14	24.55	-0.27	-1.41

The lower net effective discount factor implies that dividend increases among these electric utilities with nuclear exposure will have a larger impact on stock prices than similar dividend increases for nonnuclear electric utilities. Despite higher risk, the market imputes a significantly higher growth rate to electric utilities with a nuclear exposure than conventional electric utilities. This imputation may well reflect the questionable assumption that ownership of low-cost nuclear power may well prove profitable as capacity is squeezed in the mid-1990s and utilities have the opportunity to sell this power on an unregulated wholesale market.

The model estimate in Table 7.5 was developed by regressing the DDM estimate directly on the actual stock price. The model estimate is thus the value of the stock predicted by the DDM. The significance of the model estimate is that it isolates what would happen if the DDM model were perfectly accurate, i.e., if stock prices reflected nothing else but the relationship between dividends and the net discount rate. Since the DDM is conceptually based upon future dividend levels and the actual estimate is based on current dividend levels, the difference between this estimate and the DDM direct estimate isolates the market's perception of future dividend growth potential.

The tendency for firms in this sector to have large, diverse error terms between the DDM estimate and the model estimate suggests that factors other than economic performance are important in determining the stock price level in this sector.

Specific Utility Forecasts

The data in Table 7.5 were used to make the following interpretations with respect to future dividends and growth rates for the 23 utilities.

Atlantic Energy Inc. (AE)

In the near term, the consequence of having its Peach Bottom units 2 and 3 out of service limits profitability and the potential for dividend increases. Assuming these facilities are back in service by the early 1990s, AE will be well positioned to service its dynamic southern New Jersey market. In addition, AE will have significant excess capacity to wholesale to the northeast power markets. A big question mark concerns the ability of Philadelphia Electric to manage these facilities effectively. If the additional assumption is made that effective management will indeed be forthcoming, the future for AE is quite rosy.

This situation is reflected in the large negative DDM estimate error (suggestive of its short-term troubles) and its large positive model estimate error (suggestive of long-term growth potential). As a result, dividends are anticipated to grow at 2 percent through 1991, 4 percent through 1994, and 6 percent thereafter. A small growth adjustment is made throughout the forecast period to yield a net effective discount factor of 8.14 percent.

Baltimore Gas & Electric (BG&E)

BG&E has been successfully operating its Calvert Cliff units since 1977. This has resulted in low prices to the consumer and solid record of earnings and dividends. If the operation of the Calvert Cliff plants continues successfully, the company should perform well as it meets the demands of strong growth in its service area. However, managerial and structural problems emerged with these twin plants in 1989. These problems suggest a much higher level of risk than is presently factored into the stock price. Continuing problems at Calvert Cliffs could seriously impact earnings at BG&E.

Assuming the Calvert Cliffs problems are effectively dealt with, a small upward adjustment is made to bring BG&E's net effective discount factor to 7.4 percent. Dividends are seen to grow at 6 percent throughout the forecast period.

Carolina Power (CP)

CP was badly hurt as a result of its investment in the Harris 1 nuclear plant and the abandonment of 3 additional Harris units. Growth in its service area is dependent on the health of the textile industry. New base load capacity will be needed in the early 1990s. Its balance sheet fundamentals may not have fully recovered from the Harris experience by then.

Dividends are forecast to increase 3 percent annually over the forecast period. A negative growth adjustment of .5 percent is made after 1994 for a net effective discount rate of .071 at that time and following.

Central Vermont Public Service (CVPS)

CVPS currently derives 42 percent of its generating power from nuclear fuel, giving it relatively low operating costs. These low costs have yet to be translated into higher operating profits and are not likely to be under the watchful eye of its regulatory commission. A write-off of its investment in Seabrook did it some harm but did not decimate its balance sheet. Future power requirements are likely to be met by importing cheap hydroelectric power from Quebec.

Dividends are estimated to grow at 4 percent throughout the coming period.

Consolidated Edison (Con Ed)

Con Ed has enjoyed continued growth in its service market, despite the highest cost per kwh in the country. Although the company has a solid balance sheet and a strong record of dividend growth since they were last cut in 1974, the specter of deregulation may cost it some customers.

Dividends are expected to grow at 6 percent annually until 1994 and 4 percent thereafter.

Delmarva Power (DP)

The out-of-service Peach Bottom nuclear plants continue to impair DP's earnings power. The long-run contribution of these facilities to the bottom line remains in doubt. Despite relatively strong growth in its service area, dividend growth of only 3 percent is forecast through 1999.

Duke Power Co. (Duke)

Duke's acknowledged expertise in nuclear power plant management serves it well. The company is aggressively positioning itself to take advantage of the coming deregulation. Almost two-thirds of its power is already derived from nuclear generating facilities and its Bad Creek nuclear plant is scheduled for completion in 1992.

Dividends are expected to increase 5 percent annually through-out the forecast period. A positive growth adjustment of 1 percent for Duke is made throughout the forecast period.

Florida Progress Corp.

This utility has experienced some setbacks in its attempts to diver-sify. However, the company is located in a strong growing market.
Dividends are anticipated to increase 3 percent annually.

FPL Group Inc. (FPL)

FPL is located in a market with good growth potential. However, they currently have no excess capacity or plans to add base load. Future power requirements are anticipated to be met by purchasing from other utilities and cogeneration. This strategic decision limits growth potential (and risk). FPL has a major insurance subsidiary (Colonial Penn).

Dividends are anticipated to grow 2.5 percent throughout the forecast period.

General Public Utilities (GPU)

GPU has recovered from the depths of its Three Mile Island catas-trophe in 1979. From 1984 through 1988 it rewarded its sharehold-ers handsomely, thanks to substantial price appreciation. Its dividend had been suspended from 1980 through 1986. Earnings are currently being driven by strong growth in its New Jersey and Philadelphia markets. In an effort to improve its balance sheet, it has planned significant common stock buybacks in the early 1990s.

Dividends are anticipated to increase at 6 percent through 1993 and 4 percent thereafter. Growth is adjusted up 1 percent for the entire forecast period as Three Mile Island returns to service early in the 1990s.

Green Mountain Power (GMP)

GMP is a solid conservative company that owns 18 percent of Ver-mont Yankee Nuclear Power Corporation. The company is begin-ning to diversify into Vermont's propane gas market. A weak market in the 1990s requires a small negative growth adjustment.

Dividend growth in the 3 percent range is expected throughout the forecast period.

Iowa-Illinois Gas & Electric Co. (IIGE)

IIGE enjoys steady, if slow, growth in a difficult regulatory climate. The model estimate in Table 9.3 suggests that this firm may experience substantial price appreciation as its stock is undervalued relative to income levels. The negative DDM estimate in 1989 reflects a "take or pay" problem with its gas operations.

Dividends are expected to increase 4 percent annually. A slight positive growth adjustment is made throughout the forecast period.

Northern States Power Co. (NSP)

NSP has a healthy balance sheet and strong earnings record thanks to its untroubled operation of two nuclear power plants since the early 1970s. NSP currently carries a very strong growth attribution by the market. This may be expected to fall by the mid-1990s.

Dividend growth of 5 percent may be expected throughout the forecast period.

Pacific Gas & Electric Co. (PG&E)

Dividend levels were cut at the end of the 1980s as a result of PG&Es involvement with the Diablo Canyon nuclear plant. A negotiated settlement has led to an outcome that depresses earnings near term and has the effect of increasing potential earnings in the future. As a result of the unusual terms of the agreement, if PG&E can find a ready market for its power, it will reap substantial benefits. In additional to the normal risks surrounding the operation of this plant, it happens to have been constructed on top of an active earthquake fault.

In the absence of a disaster, dividends are expected to increase at 3 percent until 1992 and average a healthy 9 percent thereafter.

Pennsylvania Power & Light Co. (PPL)

PPL is a low-cost power producer as a result of its exceptionally efficient Susquehanna nuclear units. As it is unlikely to need to add capacity until the mid-1990s, its cash flow will increase significantly. However, this will probably be used to strengthen its balance sheet rather than to reward stockholders.

Dividends are forecast to increase at 3 percent annually.

PSI Holdings Inc.

This utility is in the process of recovering from its losses surrounding the abandonment of its Marble Hill nuclear plant. The residual litigation will continue well into the 1990s. Dividends were suspended in 1986 and had not been reinstated as of the first quarter of 1989. The market expects this litigation to have a positive impact on earnings at PSI. If this favorable impact occurs, it is already built into the 1990 price. This stock may decline precipitously upon adverse news.

Dividends were reinstated at .80¢ per year in 1989 and are expected to grow at 3 percent through 1992 and 5 percent thereafter.

Public Service Enterprise Group, Inc. (PSEG)

PSEG's earnings have been hard hit by its 42.5 percent stake in the out-of-service Peach Bottom nuclear plants. In addition, the company has ownership in three other nuclear plants. Its service area is mature and PSEG is reacting with an aggressive diversification program. When Peach Bottom comes back on line, its earnings and cash flow picture will brighten considerably.

Dividends will increase at 2 percent until 1991 and 5 percent thereafter. No adjustment is made to its growth factor.

Public Service of Colorado

This utility is moving out of nuclear power with the decommissioning and conversion of its St. Vrain nuclear plant. Revenues in its mature market have been flat and profits uneven. Dividends are seen increasing 2 percent throughout the forecast period. The market currently attributes a large negative growth factor to this company. This negative attribution may be expected to moderate in the 1993–95 period, favorably impacting prices at that time.

SCANA Corporation (SCANA)

SCANA's market is stagnant and unlikely to change. Its balance sheet fundamentals are barely respectable, but the quality of its earnings is high. The absence of a need for new capacity should allow it to maintain a modest 3 percent annual increase in its dividend throughout the forecast period.

SCE Corp. (SCE)

As a result of its strong fundamentals, SCE has been looking for acquisitions in the utility industry. San Diego Gas and Electric looks like a good fit but has been resistant. Twenty percent of SCE's power is derived from nuclear plants. It has a sufficiently strong cash flow to fund whatever additional capacity is needed throughout the 1990s.

Dividends are likely to increase at a 3 percent rate until 1994 and 6 percent thereafter.

Wisconsin Energy Corp. (WEC)

WEC's performance is very much tied into the health of the midwestern heavy machinery industry. The successful operation of its nuclear plants has left it with a strong balance sheet and good quality earnings. Dividends are expected to move up at 6 percent through 1992 and 4 percent thereafter.

Wisconsin Public Service Corp. (WPS)

WPS has a single nuclear plant and it appears well managed. The fortunes of this company are heavily impacted by the industrial economy of the upper midwest (52 percent of its sales are industrial). Revenues have grown steadily throughout the 1980s, although profits have been uneven.

Dividends are anticipated to increase 1 percent annually throughout the forecast period.

WPL Holdings Inc. (WPL)

WPL has a 41 percent stake in the Kewaunee nuclear plant, which has been operating safely since 1974. Revenue and earnings growth have been flat throughout the 1980s as a consequence of slow growth in its service area. WPL has significant diversification activities outside the utility industry and these may contribute to earnings in the 1990s.

Dividends are forecast to increase at a 3 percent annual rate until 1994 and at 4 percent thereafter.

Dividend Forecasts
The following considerations were used to generate estimates of dividends between 1989 and 1999 for these 23 utilities.

Forecasting Stock Prices
Future stock prices can be forecast from the dividends projected in Table 7.5 using the DDM. These forecast prices are presented in Table 2.1 of Chapter 2. As was discussed in Chapter 6, this formulation of the model is highly sensitive to the assumption of a net effective discount rate.

Evaluating Investment Return
The true success of an investment in utility stocks is not measured by either dividends or price appreciation. Rather, the best approach is to examine the discount factor, which equates positive and negative cash flows over time. As discussed in Chapter 3, this measure is called the total rate of return (TRR) and is expressed as an annual percentage rate.

The estimated TRRs for 23 electric utilities with nuclear exposure in 1994 and 1999 are presented in Table 7.1. It should be noted that this table embeds an effective discount factor of .07 to make its predictions, as well as any firm-specific growth estimates noted above. Changes in market rates of growth, changes in the perceived "riskiness" of the industry, or changes in the time preference for money (i.e., the risk-free interest rate) will change this discount factor. As suggested in Chapter 6, Table 6.3, even small changes in this factor can have a sizeable impact on price appreciation and, consequently, on the TRR.

Risk Among Electric Utilities with Nuclear Exposure

In contrast to the disastrous decade of the 1970s for these firms, barring an unforeseen nuclear disaster, industry performance will be characterized by steady growth throughout the 1990s.

An unforeseen nuclear disaster would have a number of different effects. First, it would have a dramatic impact on the stock of the affected firm. Secondly, such a disaster would probably convince the investing public of the inherent dangers of investing in utilities with a nuclear exposure. This recognition would significantly depress the prices of all such utilities.

Even after Three Mile Island, utilities with nuclear exposure argued "it can't happen here." A second such disaster would make this argument less compelling.

In addition, considerable opposition would be generated to starting up any plants not currently in service. Increased scrutiny of and downtime for in-service nuclear plants is to be expected. This will reduce the potential supply of electricity and increase its price.

The higher price of electricity will make the generating capacity of utilities without nuclear exposure more valuable. Some of these utilities (such as Utilicorp United) will be well positioned to reap the benefits of this situation.

The returns shown in Table 7.1 (compared to the returns in Table 6.1) clearly indicate that the present market structure does not reward investors for investing in utilities with nuclear exposure. Those returns are less favorable than those anticipated for utilities without nuclear exposure in Chapter 6, even without considering the additional risk to be born.

Significant opportunities for profit may be found among the 40 utilities with nuclear exposure for which return forecasts were not developed. The experience of General Public Utilities between 1984 and 1989 clearly indicates the substantial rewards that can occur to prescience in this area. These rewards were so great precisely because few investors saw anything but a prolonged wake of losses in the aftermath of Three Mile Island.

It is within the realm of possibility that Public Service Co. of New Hampshire will be restructured in such a way that when it emerges from bankruptcy it will generate substantial earnings, repair its balance sheet, and begin paying generous dividends. Such a scenario would reward investors indeed.

A similar situation exists with Long Island Lighting. Will the Shoreham nuclear plant be sold to New York State? If so, on what terms? Will it actually enter operations? How will the regulatory agency treat it? This is as close to a soap opera as an investor can get.

How to Use These Forecasts

The projections developed in this chapter are highly dependent on an array of economic and noneconomic factors. These projections are valid only to the extent they embody valid assumptions about the future. While these assumptions are reasonable in the light of current knowledge, unforeseen events will surely occur.

The material in this chapter provides the reader with sufficient information to modify these projections in the light of such unexpected events. For example, if the industrial sector in Wisconsin benefits from unexpected growth, then the low rates of growth projected for the Wisconsin Energy Group and the Wisconsin Public Service Corporation will be inappropriate. The reader may then modify the price forecast in Table 2.1 based on this information. In turn, these new price projections, along with current prices, can be used in conjunction with the dividend forecasts in Table 7.5 to develop a new estimated TRR for an investment in these companies.

Aside from changes relevant to specific firms, the material in this chapter may be readily modified to reflect changed macroeconomic assumptions. For example, if there were a recession consequent on declining world trade in the early 1990s, the level of economic growth would slow and the expected shortage in generating capacity would not develop. Under these circumstances, earnings and dividends would not increase at expected rates and the dividend projections in Table 7.5 would need to be modified.

Chapter 8

NATURAL GAS INDUSTRY
FUNDAMENTALS

Organizational Overview of the Natural Gas Industry

Many firms explore for, produce, or transmit natural gas on a basis that is incidental to their main business interests. Chapters 8-10 are focused on those firms whose major business activity is the exploration, production, transmission, or distribution of natural gas. This chapter examines the past, present and future of the fundamental conditions influencing 49 large firms in the industry. Chapter 9 forecasts future stock prices and dividends among 19 diversified gas companies (defined as those companies who have a major interest in the production and/or transmission of natural gas). Chapter 12 forecasts the stock prices and dividends for 30 local distribution companies (defined as those companies whose primary economic activity is the local distribution of natural gas under a state regulatory authority).

Gas Industry Performance Overview

Tremendous opportunities await the informed investor in the natural gas industry today. Investors in this industry between 1984 and 1989 earned an average 23 percent annual return. The future for those firms heavily involved in the exploration, production, and transmission of natural gas may be even brighter.

The price of natural gas will not be any lower in the 1990s than it is in 1990. Conditions of excess supply at the end of the 1980s temporarily depressed the price of natural gas and the value of those firms that explore for it, produce it, or transmit it.

Natural gas is a premium fuel. Its environmental and handling characteristics will increasingly make it the fuel of choice in the future. These attributes will give it increasing penetration into the energy market despite the fact that its price tends to be tied to the price of its petroleum substitutes (Nos. 2, 4, and 6 oils). Greater penetration into the energy market results in higher sales and higher capacity utilization by the gas companies. Higher sales and capacity utilization will translate into higher earnings. Higher earnings means higher dividends and greater stock appreciation.

In addition, many gas companies own considerable in-ground natural gas reserves. In the face of increasingly tight oil supplies in the 1990s, their value is likely to rise considerably. This increase will not be a simple change in book value that finds difficulty in flowing through to shareholders. The increasingly valuable gas reserves can be readily converted to increased earnings by pumping it out and selling it to eager customers.

Industry Structure

WWII spurred the development of the natural gas industry. Vigorous economic expansion and abundant supplies kept prices low while volume expanded into the mid-1950s. The 1954 Supreme Court decision in *Phillips Petroleum* vs. *Wisconsin* introduced a two-tier pricing system in the industry, with interstate rates uncontrolled and intrastate rates controlled. This decision resulted in pipelines tending to assume a marketing function in providing the local distribution companies with supplies. This decision also created artificially low prices, which encouraged consumption but restricted production. By 1968, the United States began to consume more natural gas than it discovered. By the mid-1970s, gas shortages were the rule of the day.

In order to encourage production and rationalize consumption, gas prices at the wellhead entered a period of phased deregulation (where gas would be fully deregulated by 1991) with the passage of the National Gas Policy Act (NGPA) in 1978.

The NPGA effectively deregulated certain categories of new gas ("offshore" and "deep" gas), which were produced and purchased at very high prices. This price structure began to erode demand and encouraged exploration and production. Uncertain supplies in this era (when memories of the energy crisis were very recent) caused many local distribution and pipeline companies to lock in long-term gas supplies at these very high prices using "take or pay" contracts. By the mid-1980s, gas supplies exceeded gas demand creating what has been called a gas bubble. This situation was compounded by a dramatic fall in petroleum prices in the mid- and late-1980s.

In 1986, FERC issued Order 436 (later amended in Order 500), which began a gradual move towards deregulation of the interstate transmission function in the gas industry. While open access was not mandated, interstate carriers who granted any customer access to their transmission facilities had to do so on a nondiscriminatory basis for all potential customers. This allowed large customers to bypass the transmission company and purchase the now inexpensive gas directly from the producer.

Many transmission companies (who had assumed a marketing function) and local distribution companies who had purchased gas in the 1970s with high-priced "take or pay" contracts now found themselves in serious trouble. They were unable to recover the cost of their high-priced gas from their large customers. Shifting the burden of these costs to residential users was generally deemed unacceptable by the regulatory agencies.

Prior to deregulation, the energy crisis, and periods of price volatility, full vertical integration appeared to offer firms in the gas industry significant advantages. An integrated system in which a single company produced the fuel, transported the fuel, and distributed the fuel appeared to offer many opportunities for cost savings as well as a higher level of system reliability. While this conclusion may have been valid in a regulated environment characterized by stable fuel prices, an era of deregulation and gyrating gas prices has left integrated firms in a punishing situation. Results of this include a reduction in the degree of vertical integration by most firms in the industry and attempts at diversification outside the industry.

Industry Characteristics

In 1987, 75 percent of all natural gas produced came from 254,000 gas wells, 60 percent of which are located in Texas and Louisiana. The remaining gas came as a by-product from oil wells. In addition, 4 percent of the total natural gas consumed was imported from Canada. Proven reserves of natural gas have consistently declined every year since 1970. Current rates of consumption are about 10 percent of proven reserves.

Natural gas is but one of a number of sources of energy. Crude oil, coal, hydroelectric power, and nuclear electric power are good substitutes for natural gas. The cross-price elasticity among these sources of energy is high in both the short and long run. Thus, the demand for any given source of energy is quite sensitive to changes in price.

This situation has tended to produce feast or famine conditions in the industry.

In general, rising gas usage and falling prices tend to work to the benefit of the local distribution companies. Falling prices cause usage to increase. Rising volumes enable local distribution companies to approach or exceed their allowed rate of return. Falling gas prices make regulators more amenable to passing higher non-gas costs on through to the customers.

Falling gas prices impact adversely on exploration and production activities, as supply tends to be inelastic in the short run.

In contrast, a situation of rising prices tends to cut volume. Local distribution companies have fewer sales over which their fixed costs can be spread. Regulators are more resistant to passing cost increases through to customers when the client population is already sensitized to increasing gas costs.

As conditions deteriorate for the local distribution companies, firms engaged in gas production and exploration activities find that their assets become more valuable when gas prices are rising. Profits can advance dramatically under these circumstances.

Financial Performance

The five-year period covering 1984 to 1988 was characterized by a fall in the price of natural gas, increased natural gas usage, and excess gas supplies. This situation worked to the basic benefit of the

Table 8.1   Gas Industry Sales and Profits 1984–1988

	Distribution Companies			Diversified Companies		
	1988	*1984*	*Change*	*1988*	*1984*	*Change*
Sales	21,328	24,253	–12.1%	50,967	64,832	–21.4%
Profits	1,109	970	14.3%	1,219	2,553	–52.3%

Total sales and profits in $000,000. for 29 LDCs and 18 DGCs.

local distribution companies and to the detriment of the diversified gas companies.

The impact of this situation on the two different types of companies is revealed in Table 8.1

The diversified gas companies were hit by a double whammy: the burdensome take or pay contracts committed to by the pipelines in an earlier era of short supplies and deregulation also allowed their former customers to transport their own gas on these pipelines. Gas producers struggled through a period of falling prices as a result of the gas bubble and falling oil prices. The excess supplies of gas discouraged exploration activities. Diversified gas companies focusing on exploration, production and transmission encountered staggering losses as all sectors of their business were in trouble.

Local distributing companies who had entered into take or pay contracts or lost revenue through bypass or its threat were less hard hit as the falling price of gas allowed them to pass these losses on to their customers. Thus, even though revenues fell, profits increased.

Future Returns

The 1990s will see a reversal of the performance of distribution companies and diversified companies compared to their respective experiences in 1984–1988. Well positioned diversified gas companies will reap the rewards of increasing natural gas prices as they are able to sell their uncommitted stocks at ever higher prices. Increased fees for pipeline transportation and associated services in a deregulated environment will be experienced as gas consumption rises to the point where the capacity of existing distribution systems is taxed. Exploration activities will become increasingly valuable as the gas shortage intensifies.

In contrast, local distribution companies will find tough sledding in gaining rate relief as gas prices rise and the public becomes increasingly sensitized to rising energy costs. These increased energy costs will encourage larger customers to threaten or engage in bypass to minimize their own costs. In either case, there will be a loss of revenues from industrial customers which will place additional pressure on profit margins.

This effect may be partially offset by the distribution companies aggressively developing new markets for their natural gas supplies. In an era of rising petroleum prices, potential threats to the supply of petroleum products, and increasing environmental sensitivities, this will not be an impossible task.

Supply-Demand Fundamentals

While the demand for any given source of energy is price elastic, the demand for energy itself, in the short run, is highly inelastic. This means that sudden shifts in the supply of crude oil will shift the whole complex of energy prices up or down.

The importance of imported crude oil as a source of energy produced in the United States is indicated in Table 8.2. At the close of the 1980s, imported crude accounted for more than one-sixth of all energy produced. A 20 percent reduction in imported crude would be equivalent to losing all hydroelectric power produced in the United States. Uncertainties in the international political situation impacting the ability of the United States to import oil, are consequently capable of having an immediate and dramatic effect on domestic energy prices. The past three decades have clearly shown that the most volatile component in this mix of energy sources is crude oil.

Demand

Coal, natural gas, hydroelectric power and nuclear electric power compete with each other as preferable sources of energy. The mix of

Table 8.2   Sources of Energy

Year	Coal	Natural Gas	Domestic Crude Oil	Net Imported Crude Oil	Hydro-Power	Nuclear Power
1970	22.0%	32.6%	30.7%	10.4%	4.0%	0.4%
1971	19.7%	33.4%	30.0%	12.1%	4.2%	0.6%
1972	20.2%	31.9%	28.8%	14.1%	4.1%	0.8%
1973	19.3%	30.6%	26.9%	17.9%	3.9%	1.3%
1974	19.8%	29.9%	26.2%	17.8%	4.5%	1.8%
1975	21.4%	28.1%	25.4%	17.9%	4.5%	2.7%
1976	21.5%	26.8%	23.7%	20.9%	4.1%	2.9%
1977	20.7%	25.7%	22.9%	24.0%	3.1%	3.6%
1978	19.7%	25.7%	24.3%	22.5%	3.9%	4.0%
1979	22.4%	25.6%	23.1%	21.6%	3.7%	3.5%
1980	24.5%	26.2%	24.0%	17.8%	3.8%	3.6%
1981	25.0%	26.8%	24.7%	15.5%	3.8%	4.1%
1982	26.4%	25.8%	25.9%	12.8%	4.6%	4.4%
1983	25.4%	24.3%	27.1%	13.4%	5.2%	4.7%
1984	26.9%	24.5%	25.7%	13.5%	4.5%	4.8%
1985	27.1%	23.7%	26.6%	12.6%	4.1%	5.8%
1986	26.6%	22.4%	25.0%	15.7%	4.1%	6.1%
1987	27.1%	22.7%	23.7%	16.4%	3.5%	6.6%

power sources that are the most at any given time is sensitive to the relative price of each energy source. Considerable variation may occur in the relative price of the different energy sources depending on industry conditions, the international situation, the rate of growth in the demand for energy, and government intervention in the market. The historical trends in fuel prices are exhibited in Table 8.3.

Natural gas and Nos. 2, 4 and 6 oil are excellent substitutes for each other and are in active, direct competition with each other in most markets. The price of natural gas is particularly responsive to changes in the price of crude oil. This is primarily because large fuel consumers in the industrial sector design into their plants the

Table 8.3   Fuel Prices (Cents per Million Btu)

Year	Crude Oil	Natural Gas	Coal
1970	54.8	15.4	26.2
1971	58.4	16.3	30.1
1972	58.4	17.3	32.7
1973	67.1	20.1	36.5
1974	118.4	27.3	68.2
1975	132.2	41.1	83.9
1976	141.2	53.1	85.0
1977	147.8	72.3	87.7
1978	155.2	83.6	97.9
1979	217.9	108.1	105.3
1980	372.2	144.8	109.4
1981	547.8	179.5	117.9
1982	491.7	222.2	122.1
1983	451.6	232.3	117.2
1984	446.2	239.9	115.9
1985	415.3	225.7	114.8
1986	215.7	174.8	108.2
1987	265.7	154.1	104.8

Note: Price is cost at point of production.
Source: Annual Energy Review, 1987.

ability to switch between fuel oil and natural gas at a moment's notice. Such industrial customers monitor the relative costs of each fuel continuously and are not hesitant to switch back and forth.

While they cannot act as quickly as industrial consumers, residential users are also capable of responding to cost differentials between the two fuels. Additions to the housing stock may be set up for the use of either fuel as a heating source (54 percent of all new single-family homes used gas as a heating source in 1988). Consumers selecting replacement appliances can also significantly impact demand over time. In 1989, it was estimated that 8.1 million homes served by gas used fuel oil or electricity to heat water. There is a clear potential for consumers to respond to price signals in this area.

New sources of demand are emerging in the natural gas market. The commercial market for gas cooling has tremendous potential. The use of gas to enhance the recovery of oil may well be the single largest new market for gas—particularly as the price of oil strengthens.

The repeal of the Power Plant and Industrial Fuel Use Act in 1987 has eliminated the restrictions on using gas in new industrial and power generation facilities. This is quite significant as combined cycle power generation (the use of waste heat from a gas turbine to generate heat for a steam turbine) appears to be emerging as a dominant technology in electric power generation. In addition, electric utilities with a shortage of capacity can cut down on long lead times (as well as environmental problems) by constructing more baseload generating capacity using gas-fired combustion or combined-cycle technologies. As co-firing both enhances efficiency and reduces nitrous oxide and sulfur dioxide emissions, this technology may see wide use in the 1990s.

The demand for natural gas is not uniformly distributed. Price may vary significantly between regions as a result of cost of production difference, access to transport, government regulation, and the degree of competition from competing fuels. Table 8.4 suggests the magnitude of the changing pattern of consumption of natural gas in the residential sector. It is clear that location may very much be a factor in determining the degree of success of a firm in this industry.

Table 8.4   Natural Gas Consumed by Households

	1978	1984
Northeast	20.4%	18.7%
North Central	45.3%	40.0%
South	17.2%	23.1%
West	17.0%	18.3%

Figure 8.1   Natural Gas Relative Price–Market Share Ratio

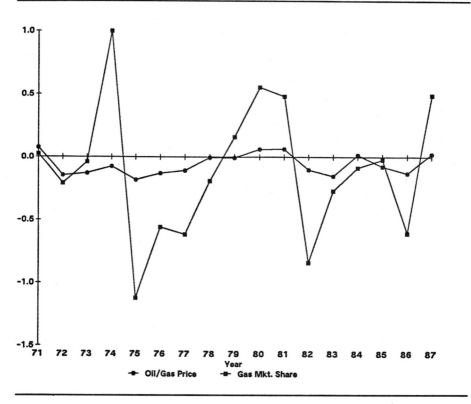

The relationship between the relative price of crude oil and the share of the energy market that natural gas takes is depicted in Figure 8.1.

Figure 8.1 illustrates that as the ratio of oil to gas prices rises (cents per mm btu), the market share of natural gas will rise. Similarly, as the ratio of oil to gas prices fall, so too does gas market share. For example, the fall in this ratio from 1985 to 1986 and its subsequent rise from 1986 to 1987 produced a full percentage point swing in market share, a change in unit volume of 4.4 percent, or 739 billion cubic feet. This significant change in volume can easily spell the difference between depression and prosperity in the industry.

Supply

Considerable confusion exists in the mind of the public over the fact that natural gas is in some sense not a renewable resource. While this is true in the sense that the potential supply of gas is finite, it obscures the larger truth that gas supplies are abundant given appropriate economic incentives. For all practical purposes, the available supply of gas is inexhaustible in the sense that sufficiently high prices will bring about innovative extractive technologies that will result in the production of new gas.

Potential sources for new gas supplies include not only drilling in existing exploratory dry land and offshore basins as well as recovering gas from oil wells now vented off, but new sources of gas (e.g., extraction of gas from coal seams, in-plant or underground gasification of coal, and exploitation of tight sands and gas shale formations) and imports.

Mexico currently has larger proven gas reserves than the U.S., but imports were suspended in 1984 when the negotiating parties were unable to reach an agreement on price. Future agreements depend on the political situation in both countries and the level of world energy prices. Low prices might force Mexico to sell in order to earn foreign exchange. High prices might encourage the U.S. to import to hold down the domestic price of energy.

Canadian imports of natural gas will become increasingly important to the U.S. The passage of the Agreement on Natural Gas Prices and Markets, which became effective in 1985, effectively deregulated Canadian gas for export. The Free Trade Act passed in 1989 effectively removes trade barriers. Canadian producers are moving rapidly to take advantage of the situation. Local distribution and transmission companies are eager for this source of low cost gas.

Recent levels of proven domestic reserves of natural gas and oil are presented in Table 8.5.

Price

The impact of the existing system of production and distribution on natural gas consumers is uneven. In particular, changes in the wellhead price of natural gas are not passed along to consumers proportionally, nor are the changes in price evenly distributed among

Table 8.5   Proven Reserves

Year	Crude Oil (bil brls)	Natural Gas (tcf)
1970	39.0	290.7
1971	38.1	278.8
1972	36.3	266.1
1973	35.3	250.0
1974	34.2	237.1
1975	32.7	228.2
1976	30.9	216.0
1977	31.8	207.4
1978	31.4	208.0
1979	29.8	201.0
1980	29.8	199.0
1981	29.4	201.7
1982	27.9	201.5
1983	27.7	200.2
1984	28.4	197.5
1985	28.4	193.4
1986	26.9	191.6

consumers. This effect partially reflects the differing elasticities of demand characterizing different consuming groups and partially the pursuit of noneconomic goals by regulatory authorities. For example, in 1986 wellhead prices fell 26 percent, while the price to electric utilities fell 32 percent, to industrial customers 18 percent, but the price to residential customers fell only 5 percent.

The price relationships among the different consuming sectors are presented in Table 8.6.

The Natural Gas Industry: 1990–1999

Two assumptions are critical to the future of the natural gas industry in this decade. The first assumption concerns the price of crude

Table 8.6   Average Price of Natural Gas

Year	Wellhead Price	Residential Price	Commercial Price	Industrial Price
1970	0.17	1.09	0.77	0.34
1971	0.18	1.15	0.82	0.38
1972	0.19	1.21	0.88	0.41
1973	0.22	1.29	0.94	0.46
1974	0.30	1.43	1.07	0.65
1975	0.45	1.71	1.35	0.88
1976	0.58	1.98	1.64	1.11
1977	0.79	2.35	2.04	1.34
1978	0.91	2.56	2.23	1.52
1979	1.18	2.98	2.73	1.82
1980	1.59	3.68	3.39	2.42
1981	1.98	4.29	4.00	3.00
1982	2.46	5.17	4.82	3.61
1983	2.59	6.06	5.59	3.94
1984	2.66	6.12	5.55	3.99
1985	2.51	6.12	5.50	3.73
1986	1.94	5.83	5.08	3.06
1987	1.71	5.56	4.76	2.57

Note: All prices expressed in dollars per thousand cubic feet.
Source: Annual Energy Review, 1987.

oil. The second concerns the responsiveness of gas supply to changing price.

Although there is considerable potential upside and downside variance in the following estimate, the following analysis of firms in this industry presupposes that world price of crude oil will be moving toward $21.00-$22.00 per barrel in 1990. Furthermore, according to that estimate, the world price will increment steadily through the middle of the decade at a rate of about 10 percent, but then moderate towards the end of the decade. This will produce a price per barrel (in 1989 prices) of $31.00-$32.00 in 1994 and $42.00-$45.00 in 1999.

This assumption is based on a scenario of an increasingly rationalized and stable Middle East political situation, which will permit the Middle Eastern OPEC players to act with greater cohesiveness. It is assumed that as they acquire greater power this power will be manifested in a slowing of the rate of increase in world production sufficient to bring about rising prices in the 10 percent range. An important element in this scenario is that the OPEC players have learned from the experiences of the 1970s that too rapid a rise in the price of oil can be counterproductive. Equally important is the notion that ideological differences will eventually give way to mutual self-interest.

The impact of this scenario in the United States will be energy prices that escalate at a slightly higher rate than 10 percent through the middle of the 1990s and then ease significantly as increased domestic supplies of oil and gas come to the market and world prices soften.

Natural gas prices in the U.S. will respond to this scenario by rising in rough concordance with oil prices, but maintain a significant competitive price advantage into 1995 that will increase unit volume consumed to the point of straining existing transportation and distribution facilities. Following 1995, gas prices will tend to lose market share to oil as oil prices decline relative to gas prices.

This scenario suggests that the short-run supply elasticity of gas is greater than that of oil, but less elastic in the long run. Gas supplies are seen to be more elastic in the short run because of the possible importation of gas from Canada and Mexico, the activation of currently unused LNG facilities, and new gas supplies available from coal seam extraction. Longer term supplies of gas can be forthcoming through the development of the Alaskan gas fields, offshore drilling, development of frontier Canadian gas fields, and the development of tight sand gas resources. However, such development may be quite expensive relative to long-term incremental oil supplies. In the absence of an energy crisis and a significantly higher price structure than that envisioned above, these supplies of natural gas will not be developed in the twentieth century.

Analysis of Diversified Gas Company Performance: 1984–1988

Diversified gas companies are characterized by disparate portfolios. Some diversified companies are primarily gas production companies (such as Burlington Resources), some are primarily pipeline companies (such as The Williams Companies) and some own a significant number of local (regulated) distribution companies (such as Consolidated Natural Gas) in addition to their other business interests. In addition, diversified gas companies frequently have significant business activities outside the gas industry (e.g., Burlington Resources in forestry products, Coastal Corporation in oil refining, Hadson Corporation in defense technology, and Tenneco in shipbuilding).

Table 8.7 identifies 19 diversified gas companies and the return they would have generated to an investor purchasing their stock at the beginning of 1984 and selling at the end of 1988.

The generally poor performance found in this group reflects the effects of excess supplies, moribund demand, and fierce competition from competing fuels. The amazing aspect of this situation is not that the TRR generated for investors was so low during this period, it's amazing that the TRR was positive at all!

A "gas bubble" (a condition where production exceeds consumption) was created by the combination of decontrol of natural gas prices at the wellhead in the late 1970s (at a time of scarce supplies and high prices) and a fall in petroleum prices as the OPEC cartel faltered in the early 1980s (resulting in a loss of revenue when customers switched to the now cheaper fuel oil). These events led to falling natural gas prices and a decrease in actual production for many producers.

At the same time, pipelines had, in the context of the natural gas shortages of the late 1970s, committed to purchasing long-term supplies of gas at the then prevailing high prices (take or pay contracts) and then found themselves unable to pass this high-priced gas on to industrial customers or local distribution companies because of competitive or regulatory constraints. Industrial customers and local distribution companies were encouraged by the deregulations embedded in FERC Order 436 to shop the spot gas market for cheap supplies and use the pipelines as open access carriers to transport their gas. This situation was intensified by the pressure regulators put on the local distribution companies to pass the reduced fuel costs on to residential customers and not segregate or earmark low-cost supplies for price-sensitive industrial customers.

If the diversified companies were fully integrated and perfectly hedged (i.e., if they produced, transported and sold the same amounts of gas through their own subsidiaries), it would have been possible to maintain profit margins in the face of falling revenues. Unfortunately, as a group, the diversified companies were long on

Table 8.7   Diversified Gas Companies

Rank by TRR	Diversified Gas Co.	TRR 1984–1988
1	Burlington Resources	64.07%
2	Coastal Corp.	29.89%
3	Consolidated Natural Gas	25.46%
4	KN Energy	23.40%
5	Enron Corporation	18.87%
6	Panhandle Eastern Corp.	16.96%
7	Tenneco Inc.	13.93%
8	Columbia Gas System, Inc.	11.61%
9	Williams Companies	10.19%
10	Texas Eastern Corporation	7.90%
11	Equitable Resources	7.51%
12	Transco Energy Company	6.22%
13	Sonat Inc.	4.99%
14	Enserch Corporation	3.36%
15	Oneok Inc.	0.71%
16	Seagull Energy Corp.	−6.82%
17	Mitchell Energy and Development	−13.78%
18	Hadson Corp.	−20.51%
19	Valero Energy Corporation	−53.15%

Table 8.8   Diversified Gas Company Fundamentals 1984–1988

Characteristic	Average	Standard Deviation
Internal Rate of Return 1984–1988	4.8%	18.9%
Change in Stock Price 1984–1988	13.6%	52.8%
Dividend Yield, 1988	3.7%	2.3%
Sales (billions)		
1988	$2.831	$3.416
1984	$3.602	$3.480
Net Profits (billions)		
1988	$ 67.7	$ 66.0
1984	$141.9	$143.5
Cash Flow/Share		
1988	$4.88	$2.49
1984	$6.82	$4.37
Long–Term Debt (billions)		
1988	$1.291	$1.396
1984	$1.065	$1.170

Note: Excludes Burlington Resources which was created as a spin-off from Burlington Northern, Inc. in July, 1988 for $22.50 a share.

production and exposed as pipelines, with relatively little coverage in the distribution function (with the notable exceptions of Consolidated Natural Gas, KN Energy, and Columbia, whose TRR's were quite respectable).

The effect of this environment on the diversified companies is indicated in Table 8.8.

As shown in Table 8.8, sales declined 26 percent, profits plunged 52 percent and cash flow per share fell 28 percent. Consequently, the balance sheet weakened as owners' equity declined and long-term debt increased 21 percent. Dividends were cut to conserve cash as earnings proved barely able to cover interest obligations.

Revenues declined as natural gas prices were driven downward by falling crude oil prices. Producers were unable to recover the cost of production from recently developed high-cost gas wells. Existing low-cost gas production became less profitable.

Pipeline operations lost volume as natural gas as an energy source lost market share to fuel oil—reducing revenues and increasing average costs. Some pipelines were locked into take or pay contracts; i.e., they had committed to purchase natural gas at prices considerably (typically 90 percent) above prevailing levels. Some pipelines were able to buy their way out of this situation. For others, the contracts were so onerous that they were effectively unenforceable. As might be expected, the lawyers and consultants profited from this situation.

Uncertainty surrounding this situation increased when FERC Order 436 failed to deal effectively with this situation. Subsequently, FERC Order 500 provided a mechanism for pipelines to recover buydown or buyout take or pay liabilities. Most contracts were being settled for 15 to 20 cents on the dollar, and the losses and gains were, for the most part, fully factored into the diversified companies' stock price structures by the end of 1989.

Diversified companies with exploration and drilling subsidiaries sustained heavy losses from this activity as the presence of significant excess supplies was a powerful disincentive to bringing new supplies to market.

A common reaction to this situation was an attempt by many firms to lessen their degree of vertical integration. Depending on the initial situation, firms spun off their production and exploration subsidiaries into independent companies. For those firms positioned to do so, there was also an attempt to diversify into new fields.

The experience of this group between 1984 and 1988 is actually suggestive of significant upside potential in the 1990s. The fundamental conditions determining performance will change dramatically.

Even at current low gas price levels, the gas bubble is dissipating. Demand for natural gas as a fuel with little adverse environmental impact has been increasing steadily. Exploration activities which would bring new supplies into the market have been curtailed. Even with the currently depressed level of petroleum prices, it is anticipated that excess gas supplies will disappear by 1990.

If instability in the Middle East led to an increase in petroleum prices, the high cross-price elasticity between natural gas and fuel oil would create conditions of excess demand and rising natural gas prices almost immediately.

In addition, increasing residential demand for natural gas cannot be supplied in all sections of the country because of limited pipeline capacity. This situation will worsen as rising electricity costs spur the demand for natural gas as a heating fuel. The pipelines have seen the downside of deregulation. A situation in which increasing pipeline capacity was seen as an important social goal and an excess demand for transportation services existed would bring about increasing prices for these services. Given that pipelines have extremely high operating leverage (almost all fixed costs), profits may be expected to escalate rapidly for pipelines whose services are in demand.

Nine of these diversified companies have significant proven reserves (in gas and oil combined). These companies are listed in Table 8.9.

These companies may be particularly well positioned to benefit from an increase in gas prices. Allowances must necessarily be made for the amount of reserves under contract at existing price levels. In addition, these firms, as well as other diversified gas companies, may own substantial unproven reserves and have drilling or exploration subsidiaries that are currently idle or not employed at competitive rates of return. Were the petroleum situation to tighten, these subsidiaries would benefit from greater use and higher prices.

Panhandle Eastern Corporation has a $514,000,000 unused LNG facility. Higher natural gas prices could make this facility viable and substantially enhance the earnings of this company.

In general, this sector has weathered the worst that could possibly have happened to it. Recovery may be slow or fast, but the potential is there to reward investors not dismayed by this sector's recent performance.

Analysis of Distribution Company Performance: 1984–1988

Local distribution companies generally performed quite well between 1984 and 1986—returning annual gains of 23 percent over this period. This outstanding performance compares favorably with the performance of both utility and industrial stocks (TRR = .18) as measured by the Dow Jones Indexes (refer to Chapter 4 for more details) during this period. These 29 distribution companies and their individual performance during this period are listed in Table 8.10.

In contrast to the diversified activities among diversified companies, distribution companies typically have a strong focus on just

Table 8.9   Proven Reserves*
**   Diversified Gas Companies**

Rank in Reserves/share		Reserves per Share	Total Reserves ($ billion)
1	Enron Corporation	33.47	1.59
2	Columbia Gas System, Inc.	30.70	1.40
3	Texas Eastern Corporation	24.32	1.35
4	Equitable Resources	22.56	0.49
5	Transco Energy Company	21.54	0.66
6	Mitchell Energy	20.66	0.97
7	Enserch Corporation	17.24	1.00
8	Consolidated Natural Gas Co.	14.55	1.20
9	Coastal Corp.	11.35	0.63
10	Burlington Resources	9.83	1.47
11	Seagull Energy Corp.	4.43	0.03

* Reserves valued at pretax income.

Table 8.10   Local Distribution Companies

Rank by TRR		TRR 1984–1988
1	Atlanta Gas Light Company	42.23%
2	Bay State Gas Company	41.55%
3	National Fuel Gas Co.	37.93%
4	Michigan Energy Resources Co.	36.13%
5	Peoples Energy Corporation	34.21%
6	Providence Energy Corporation	33.54%
7	Indiana Energy, Inc.	32.30%
8	Laclede Gas Company	31.42%
9	Wicor, Inc.	31.21%
10	Piedmont Natural Gas Co.	28.32%
11	UGI Corporation	28.00%
12	Connecticut Natural Gas Corp.	27.77%
13	South Jersey Industries, Inc.	26.84%
14	Cascade Natural Gas Company	26.58%
15	Washington Gas Light Co.	26.43%
16	New Jersey Resources Corp.	23.65%
17	Southwest Gas Corporation	22.22%
18	Washington Energy Co.	22.05%
19	Brooklyn Union Gas Company	21.73%
20	Diversified Energies, Inc.	21.71%
21	Nicor Incorporated	15.15%
22	Questar Corporation	14.92%
23	NUI Corporation	11.98%
24	Pacific Enterprises Corp.	11.97%
25	Energen Corporation	11.38%
26	Louisiana General Services Inc.	7.76%
27	Eastern Gas & Fuel Associates	7.05%
28	Arkla, Inc.	4.95%
29	Southern Union Company	−7.08%

one activity—providing natural gas service in a regulated environment. The distribution companies that have performed poorly over this period have generally suffered as a result of (1) poor market conditions, (2) take or pay contract costs which they were not allowed to pass on to their customers, or (3) unfortunate attempts at diversification

In the environment that prevailed between 1984 and 1988, distribution companies proved very solid performers. This may be seen in the performance data of Table 8.11.

Although firms in this group experienced falling revenues as gas prices plunged during this period, the fall was only 12 percent (compared with 26 percent for the diversified gas companies). Furthermore, these companies were successful in translating the new revenue structure into increased profits—net profits increased 14 percent over the period. These net profits were used both to increase dividends and increase the strength of their balance sheets.

Deregulation in the industry has primarily impacted producers and pipelines. While deregulation potentially affects the distribution companies by allowing bypass, most distribution companies have met this threat with aggressive rate cutting. Regulators have allowed the distribution companies to be responsive to this threat because of the similarity of this situation to that of competition arising from the substitution of fuel oil for gas. Large (primarily industrial) customers in this market have long maintained the capability to switch between fuels to minimize their own cost. Consequently, distribution companies historically have been responsive to fluctuations in the price of fuel oil.

This situation has generated what used to be called a block tariff structure, in which larger volumes were sold at lower prices. The resultant cost structure winds up charging higher prices for gas to residential users; however, since the industrial users are paying rates above marginal cost they are making a contribution to distribution companies overhead, and the residential users thus pay less than if no gas at all were sold to industrial users. It should be noted that this is exactly the opposite of what has happened to basic operating companies in the telecommunications industry.

In addition, in an environment where overall rates are falling, regulators find it easier to be more responsive to a utility's need to

Table 8.11   Local Distribution Company Fundamentals 1984–1988

Characteristic	Average	Standard Deviation
Internal Rate of Return 1984–1988	23.2%	11.6%
Change in Stock Price 1984–1988	59.5%	49.8%
Dividend Yield, 1988	6.7%	1.2%
Sales (millions)		
1988	$735.5	$1,071.4
1984	$836.3	$ 902.0
Net Profits (millions)		
1988	$38.2	$41.4
1984	$33.4	$36.8
Cash Flow/Share		
1988	$4.31	$1.80
1984	$4.36	$1.85
Long-Term Debt Ratio		
1988	44.9%	7.7%
1984	44.9%	7.7%
Common Equity Ratio		
1988	49.7%	8.1%
1984	50.2%	7.3%
Dividend Payout Ratio		
1988	75.4%	16.5%
1984	65.3%	20.5%

earn a competitive rate of return. Thus, between 1984 and 1985, falling natural gas prices yielded both lower gross costs for gas users and higher profits for the gas distributor.

The late 1970s were characterized by the opposite situation, i.e., natural gas prices were rising and gross prices to gas users were rising even more rapidly as industrial users switched to alternative fuels. At this time, distribution companies' profits were squeezed and stock prices suffered accordingly. As demand and supply conditions changed in the early 1980s, stock prices were poised to rebound. Thus the superior performance indicated in Table 8.11.

Distribution companies will be hard pressed to extend the strong performance of 1984–1988 into the 1990s. However, significant variance among firms will occur as a result of their specific market conditions, access to supplies, and regulatory environment.

The basic threat to distribution companies will come from the fact that the 1990s will be an era of rising natural gas prices. For most utilities, demand will be strong into the mid-1990s, as natural gas prices lag the increase in fuel oil prices. This will increase capacity utilization and lower unit costs. For many utilities, a reduction in costs from this source will be sufficient to offset any reluctance regulators have to pass through increasing costs (e.g., from the capital costs of additional plant and equipment) in a period of rising energy prices.

However, as price increases continue to build up the relative cost of energy, regulators may be expected to be increasingly deferential to the political forces resisting price increases. In addition, after the midpoint of this decade, natural gas will lose some of its competitive advantage to fuel oil as oil prices begin to rise less rapidly than natural gas prices. This effect will reduce capacity utilization and slow growth thus raising unit costs and squeezing profits.

Consequently, many distribution companies will be unable to offer the returns through the 1990s that they were able to offer investors between 1984 and 1988.

Chapter 9

THE FUTURE FOR INVESTMENT IN DIVERSIFIED GAS COMPANIES

Performance Overview

Diversified gas companies offer superb opportunities for investors in the 1990s. The forces underlying this sector of the utilities market will generate very favorable risk-return combinations throughout the decade. While some volatility may be encountered because of uncertainties inherent in the world energy situation, these same uncertainties will create additional opportunities for informed buyers.

The diversified companies' general lackluster performance during the last half of the 1980s has set the stage for superior returns for the undaunted investor able to envision the future. These returns, in fact, will be subject to greater uncertainty than those found in most utility situations.

This uncertainty arises from the diversified companies' dependency on the general complex of petroleum prices in the 1990s and whether or not the deregulatory initiatives begun under FERC in the 1980s will be continued. In spite of the reliance on what are largely political outcomes, the evolving conditions in this industry appear to have generated sufficient momentum to create an outcome that has a high probability of yielding investors exceptional returns. The fundamentals influencing diversified companies' per-

Table 9.1   TRR Forecasts; Diversified Gas Companies

Rank by TRR 1990-94		TRR 1990-94	TRR 1990-99
1	Enron Corporation	43.3%	21.6%
2	Equitable Resources	33.0%	19.9%
3	Columbia Gas System, Inc.	30.6%	13.9%
4	Mitchell Energy and Devel.	28.8%	12.4%
5	Consolidated Natural Gas Co.	28.6%	18.3%
6	Enserch Corporation	27.4%	11.8%
7	Panhandle Eastern Corp.	24.6%	15.7%
8	Williams Companies	24.0%	15.8%
9	KN Energy	23.9%	8.6%
10	Transco Energy Company	23.0%	10.8%
11	Oneok Inc.	22.1%	13.4%
12	Burlington Resources	20.8%	18.2%
13	Coastal Corp.	20.3%	20.3%
14	Valero Energy Corp.	18.9%	8.5%
15	Sonat Inc.	17.1%	6.2%
16	Tenneco Inc.	16.4%	9.0%
17	Seagull Energy Corp.	13.4%	7.1%

formance limit the downside risk and offer tremendous possibilities on the upside.

The price and dividend forecasts presented in Table 2.3 and 2.4 for the 17 diversified companies suggest the likelihood of exceptional returns for most firms in this sector of the industry.

As these TRRs represent annual returns throughout the forecast period, this forecast is clearly ahead of the conventional perception of developments among this group of firms.

The accuracy of these forecasts is contingent upon the validity of the model used to predict stock prices and dividends and the accuracy of the assumptions incorporated in the forecast. These are discussed below and followed by a specific application of the model and assumptions to each of the 17 diversified companies.

Future Energy Prices

The absolute price of natural gas and the price of natural gas relative to competing fuels (primarily Nos. 2, 4 and 6 fuel oil) are critical in estimating the future earnings of diversified gas companies.

Analysis of the determinants of future energy prices (discussed at length in Chapter 8) suggests that world price of crude oil will be $20.00–22.00 a barrel in 1990 and that the world price of crude oil will increase steadily through the middle of the decade at a rate of about 10 percent. This will produce a price per barrel of $31.00–$32.00 in 1994. As new supplies of oil hit the market, or demand abates, the increases in price will moderate towards the end of the decade with an ultimate price range of $42.00–$45.00 per barrel in 1999.

The impact of this scenario will be evidenced in the United States by energy prices that escalate at a rate slightly higher than 10 percent through the middle of the 1990s and then ease significantly as increased domestic supplies of oil and gas come to the market and world prices soften.

Natural gas prices in the U.S. will respond by rising in rough concordance with oil prices, but maintain a significant competitive price advantage into 1995 that will increase unit volume consumed to the point of straining existing transportation and distribution facilities. Following 1995, gas prices will tend to lose market share to oil as oil prices decline relative to gas prices.

Many diversified companies will benefit from this situation. Natural gas prices at the wellhead are deregulated and subject to a market determination of value. An increase in the price of fuel oil will cause an increase in the demand for natural gas and a lower, but comparable, increase in natural gas prices. The increase will be less than proportionate because the short-run elasticity of supply is greater for natural gas than oil.

The long-run elasticity of the gas supply may also be greater than that of liquid petroleum, at least in the context of domestic supply. The reason for this lies in the ability of industry to locate new gas fields, to use enhanced recovery techniques in existing gas fields, to produce gas (methane) from waste, or in the application of new technologies to the production of gas (e.g., the nuclear gasification of coal).

However, high oil prices are likely to bring forth a veritable flood of new international supplies of oil by the end of the decade and the most likely impact of this on domestic energy prices is that the rise in oil prices will slow relative to the rise in natural gas prices.

In addition, natural gas is a premium fuel. From an industrial standpoint, its use requires less labor and variable cost than competing fuels. From an environmental standpoint, compared to alternative fuels natural gas is virtually pollution-free. While large industrial users generally have the capability of switching between gas and fuel oil, most residential gas consumers do not. These factors contribute to the relative inelasticity of demand for natural gas.

The long-run demand for gas is sensitive to the price of competing petroleum fuels and the infrastructure that exists to transport and distribute gas to potential customers.

The result of relatively inelastic short-run supply and demand in combination with more elastic long-run supply and demand produces a situation where prices may be expected to experience long cycles of rising and falling prices. Given the assumptions concerning petroleum prices above and the recent completion of an era of low prices, natural gas prices may be expected to begin a rising cycle which will extend throughout most of the 1990s. The rise in gas prices will begin slowly, but be rapidly rising by the mid-1990s to slow again towards the end of the decade. This price behavior suggests a potential bonanza for firms owning uncommitted gas supplies.

The situation in the electric industry (Chapters 5-7) will impact the demand for natural gas in two ways. A large portion of existing coal-fired power-generating facilities will be refitted to be co-fired with natural gas to increase operational efficiency and reduce unfavorable environmental impacts. The movement in this direction has been encouraged by the low gas prices of the late 1980s, but discouraged by uncertainties over the form of forthcoming clean air legislation. When this uncertainty is reduced, there will be a shift towards co-firing.

As a result of deregulation and recent unsatisfactory experiences utilities have had in attempting to build additional generating capacity, much of the additional base load capacity in the future will be built by independent third parties operating as cogenerators. Moreover, this capacity will be brought on line in response to power shortages that creates economic incentives, i.e., increasing prices.

Cogenerators will demand increasing quantities of natural gas because of its superiority to fuel oil in matters of handling and environmental impact. The relatively low prices for natural gas in the early part of the decade will encourage this preference.

As electricity becomes an increasingly expensive and less reliable source of power, homeowners will express an increasing preference for natural gas. This situation may create considerable pressure on gas supplies and transportation and distribution capacity. In the absence of direct political intervention and regulation, all segments of the industry except the regulated distribution companies are likely to experience enhanced profitability.

One factor that might keep potential profits from natural gas transmission would be the conversion of oil pipelines to gas transmission. Such conversion can be accomplished quickly and with relatively little expense. Some conversion should occur as there is a relative paucity of gas pipelines and deregulation in gas transmission makes this conversion attractive.

As the demand for natural gas rises, bottlenecks in transportation will become increasingly common. The Northeast already suffers from a shortage of pipeline capacity and the east central region is close to capacity. As pipeline services have been deregulated and unbundled, these circumstances should lead to an increase in the value of pipeline transport and traffic management services. Those companies providing such services to areas where the demand for natural gas will grow should benefit accordingly.

In addition to the ownership of gas wells and pipelines, many diversified gas companies own substantial gas and oil exploration facilities. As a result of excess supplies in the latter part of the 1980s, these assets have been quite unprofitable. As oil prices rise steadily throughout the 1990s, the pace of exploration activities may be expected to quicken. For diversified gas companies with exploration subsidiaries, this will bring about the return to profitability for this activity.

Political instability could once again create concern with America's energy self-sufficiency. The pressures for self-sufficiency in the late 1970s created a tremendous boom in oil and gas exploration activities. A resurgence of concern in this area could transform what were nonearning assets for diversified gas companies at the end of the 1980s into extremely profitable assets.

Returns, Earnings, and Stock Prices Among the Diversified Gas Companies

An understanding of the DDM as it applies to diversified companies can be obtained by examining the pattern of relationships that exists between dividends, stock price, cash flow and returns between 1984 and 1988.

Figure 9.1 clearly indicates that dividend yields were not related to the returns accruing to investors in these companies during this period. Diversified gas companies typically have low payout ratios (1.1 percent in 1988). The absence of a relationship between the TRR and dividends over the short-run reflects a number of factors, including a history of earnings volatility and an image that the diversified companies have of themselves as growth companies. This image requires that they reinvest earnings back in the company itself.

The dispersion of the scatter in Figure 9.2 suggests that even price changes did not have a consistent impact on TRR in this sector between 1984 and 1988. However, the lack of an apparent pattern between price change and TRR reflects the fact that the market does not treat positive and negative returns symmetrically.

Abstracting from those firms that returned a negative TRR to investors during this period, a very consistent relationship ($R^2 = .82$) is found (Figure 9.3) between the TRR and stock price changes between 1984 and 1988 among the 15 remaining firms.

It would be fair to conclude from this analysis that the future returns to investors in diversified gas companies will depend primarily on any future appreciation (or depreciation) in stock prices.

**Figure 9.1   Diversified Gas Companies TRR–
                Divided Yield Relationship**

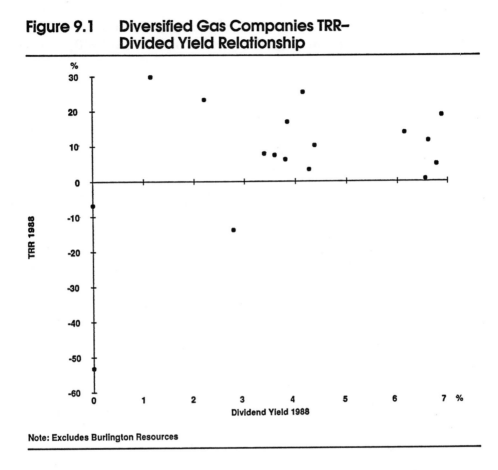

Note: Excludes Burlington Resources

Stock Prices

A very weak (R^2 = .49) relationship is found between dividends and stock prices among diversified gas companies. This may be seen in Figure 9.4

The absence of a significant relationship between dividends and stock prices in this sector does not invalidate the DDM. Stock prices are still a function of future earnings. However, among diversified companies, dividends are not suggestive of future earnings.

Figure 9.2   **Diversified Gas Companies Total Return–
Stock Price Change Relationship 1984–1988**

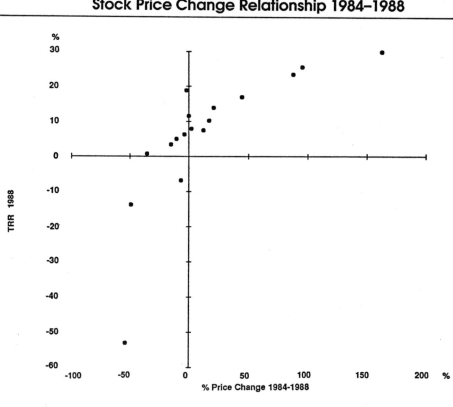

Neither is the current cash flow suggestive of earnings potential among firms in this sector. As can be seen in Figure 9.5, stock prices and cash flow among these firms were not closely (R^2 = .31) related between 1984 and 1988.

It is quite common to speak of low-growth firms with low price-earnings multiples and high-growth firms with high price-earnings multiples.

But this is not the case for diversified gas companies. As a result of the potential earnings volatility in this sector, the market does not confuse current and future cash flows. What is important

Figure 9.3   Selected Diversified Gas Companies

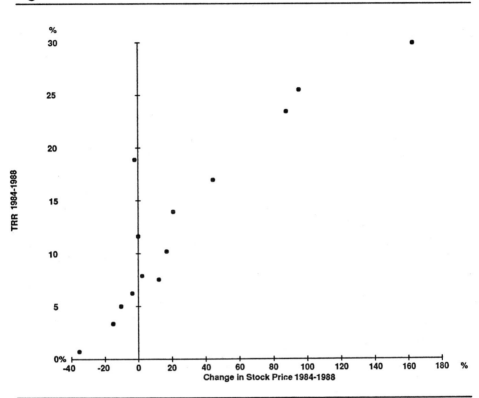

among diversified gas companies is not current earnings, but future earnings.

This consistent pattern observed between current growth and share price among industrial companies is not found among diversified gas companies. The reason for this is that recent and current earnings are not closely related to future earnings in this sector. Potential earnings may only be revealed by future circumstances.

Even the relationship between changes in cash flow and changes in stock price was not consistent (R^2 = .63) among these firms between 1984 and 1988, as seen in Figure 9.6.

Figure 9.4   19 Diversified Gas Companies

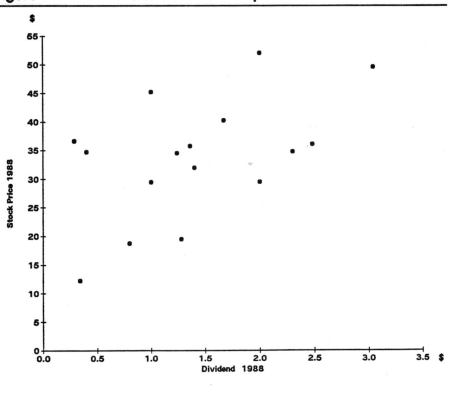

The market clearly gives little credence to momentum in this sector. The ability of gas reserves, pipelines and exploration subsidiaries to contribute to earnings might be one thing under conditions of an excess supply of natural gas, but quite another under conditions of an excess demand for natural gas. As a consequence of this very anticipatory mode, investors in this sector can expect significant firm-specific stock price volatility.

Figure 9.5   Diversified Gas Companies Price–
Cash Flow Relationship

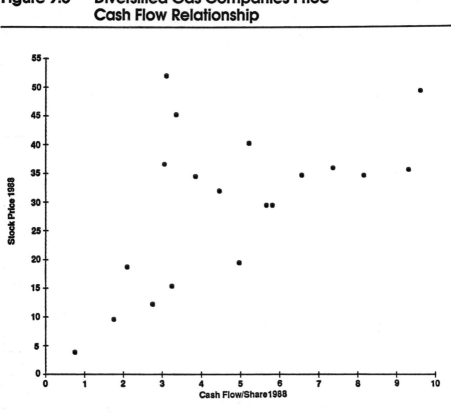

Forecasting Diversified Gas Company Stock Prices

Forecasting returns among diversified gas companies is more difficult than forecasting returns among electric utilities because stock
prices among diversified gas companies are not related to dividend
yields. While the DDM retains its basic validity, the market focuses
on a causal chain in determining stock prices among diversified gas
companies that emphasizes potential cash flow as the force that
drives future dividends.

**Figure 9.6   Diversified Gas Companies Price Change–
              Cash Flow Change Relationship**

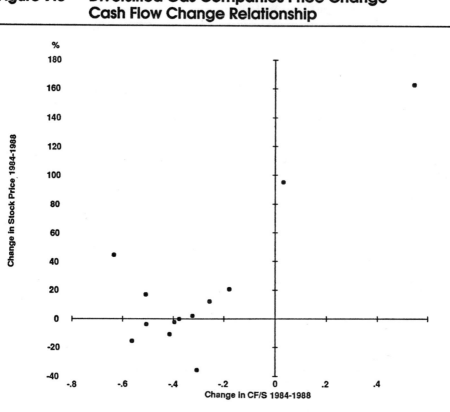

This is analogous to what occurs in the industrial sector, where a strong consistent relationship may be observed between stock prices and cash flow. However, earnings in most industrial firms are characterized by a relatively stable relationship between current cash flow and future cash flow. Thus, in the industrial sector, current cash flow can be used as a good proxy for future cash flow.

In the more volatile environment of diversified gas companies, precious little consistency is found in the relationship between current cash flow and future cash flow. Therefore, future cash flows must be estimated directly from sales projections and assumptions about operating leverage for each specific diversified gas company. These projections are made on a firm-by-firm basis below.

These projections can then be used in the DDM to forecast stock prices. The estimate of future earnings developed is embedded in the P/E ratio, as discussed in Chapter 3. These P/E ratios can then be directly applied to the earnings estimates in a given year to estimate the stock price for that year. The use of net profit is preferred to cash flow in this case because earnings are more volatile than cash flow and it is the volatility of earnings that is driving stock prices among the diversified gas companies.

Given additional assumptions about payout ratios, dividends may also be forecast. With stock prices and dividends known, annual rates of return can be estimated.

This is the basic framework for the TRR estimates presented in Table 9.1.

Specific Diversified Gas Company Forecasts

Burlington Resources (BR)

Burlington resources was created in 1988 as a holding company for the energy and resources businesses of Burlington Northern, Inc. The company has a rich asset base, with 2.8 billion cubic feet in proven gas reserves. Its El Paso Natural Gas Company subsidiary owns more than 60 percent of the interstate pipeline transmission capacity going to California. The company also has substantial forest products and real estate development interests. BR is investing heavily to extract more gas from its existing properties in the San Juan Basin and to develop coal seam gas wells.

This situation is expected to result in accelerating sales to a maximum annual increase of 20 percent between 1995 and 1997. Operating leverage is also expected to increase dramatically as sales become increasingly profitable up until 1996. The effect of these considerations leads to the forecast presented in Table 9.2. The assumptions upon which this forecast is based are presented in Table 9.3.

This forecast yields a TRR for an investor purchasing Burlington Resources in 1990 an annual return of 20.8 percent at the end of

Table 9.2   Burlington Resources Return Forecast

Year	Sales (000,000)	Profits (000,000)	Dividends Per Share	Stock Price
1990	$1,715	$175.00	$0.70	$42.25
1991	$1,801	$186.38	$0.72	$45.68
1992	$1,981	$212.47	$0.80	$51.05
1993	$2,278	$260.27	$0.88	$64.82
1994	$2,734	$343.56	$1.13	$83.88
1995	$3,280	$460.37	$1.49	$119.13
1996	$3,936	$621.50	$2.37	$145.85
1997	$4,527	$784.64	$2.93	$180.53
1998	$4,753	$851.34	$3.11	$181.65
1999	$4,848	$876.88	$3.14	$183.43

1995 and 18.2 percent at the end of 1999. It is interesting to note that the prospective returns for BR are less than those of gas companies with heavy resource concentrations (e.g., Enron and Columbia Gas System) because the events of the late 1980s did not have the opportunity to unduly depress earnings at BR.

It should be noted that this analysis is quite sensitive to the anticipated rate of sales growth. If some unforeseen international crisis created a domestic energy shortage that had the effect of causing an average annual increase of revenues of 25 percent at Burlington Resources throughout the period, the TRR to the investor in 1995 would approach 40 percent (given the remaining assumptions embodied in Table 9.3).

Coastal Corporation

Coastal Corporation is principally engaged in the interstate transmission of natural gas with a major pipeline in the Midwest and one in the Rocky Mountains. The company also has considerable capital tied up in six oil refineries. In addition, the company engages in exploration activities and owned proved reserves of $11.35 per share in 1989.

Table 9.3   Burlington Resources Forecast Assumptions

Year	Annual Sales Change	Operating Leverage	Dividend Payout	P/E Ratio	Shares Out (000,000)
1990	5%	1.30	0.35	25	140.00
1991	5%	1.30	0.55	35	142.80
1992	10%	1.40	0.55	35	145.66
1993	15%	1.50	0.50	37	148.57
1994	20%	1.60	0.50	37	151.54
1995	20%	1.70	0.50	40	154.57
1996	20%	1.75	0.60	37	157.66
1997	15%	1.75	0.60	37	160.82
1998	5%	1.70	0.60	35	164.03
1999	2%	1.50	0.60	35	167.31

The strategic direction of the company is to deemphasize its refinery activity and move into new pipeline ventures. As the markets its pipelines presently serve are not positioned to benefit from the coming shortages in gas transportation facilities, Coastal's future earnings prospects are not as bright as for other pipeline companies.

Revenues are expected to increase throughout the forecast period as improving supply and demand conditions allow Coastal to exploit the value of its reserves and exploration activities. Its pipelines will make a contribution to earnings as volume transported increases, even though it serves slower growing markets.

Previous earnings' volatility and operating leverage are expected to decline as the refinery operations diminish in relative importance. As energy costs rise toward mid-decade, refinery margins will come under increasing pressure as consumer resistance is encountered at the retail level.

This forecast does not make allowance for undertaking a substantial new pipeline. If such a project is undertaken in the ortheast, the earnings prospects for Coastal would brighten considerably. The sale of some or all of its refinery capacity is anticipated to re-

Table 9.4   Coastal Corporation Return Forecast

Year	Sales (000,000)	Profits (000,000)	Dividends Per Share	Stock Price
1990	$ 8,500	$210.00	$0.40	$32.13
1991	$ 9,265	$238.35	$0.45	$34.11
1992	$10,284	$277.68	$0.52	$38.96
1993	$11,827	$329.74	$0.60	$51.41
1994	$13,601	$391.57	$0.70	$63.37
1995	$15,913	$474.78	$0.84	$75.33
1996	$17,504	$527.00	$0.91	$68.32
1997	$18,905	$569.16	$1.21	$57.87
1998	$19,472	$528.82	$1.21	$48.41
1999	$19,666	$585.74	$1.19	$47.70

Table 9.5   Coastal Corporation Forecast Assumptions

Year	Annual Sales Change	Operating Leverage	Dividend Payout	P/E Ratio	Shares Out (000,000)
1990	7%	2.00	0.15	13	102.75
1991	9%	1.50	0.20	15	104.81
1992	11%	1.50	0.20	15	106.90
1993	12%	1.25	0.20	17	109.04
1994	12%	1.25	0.20	18	111.22
1995	15%	1.25	0.20	18	113.44
1996	10%	1.10	0.20	15	115.71
1997	8%	1.00	0.25	12	118.03
1998	3%	0.80	0.25	10	120.39
1999	1%	0.50	0.25	10	122.80

sult in a loss of earnings that will be offset by the retirement of debt consequent on revenues generated by such sales.

The resultant forecast is contained in Table 9.4. The specific assumptions used in these forecasts are presented in Table 9.5.

The annual return to an investor purchasing in 1989 and selling at the end of 1994 would be a 20.2 percent on the basis of the performance described in Table 9.3. An investor who holds the stock to 1999 will earn a TRR of 20.3 percent even though deteriorating supply and demand conditions cause the stock price to fall towards the end of the decade.

Columbia Gas System (CGS)

CGS is a major integrated gas transmission and distribution company that owned gas and oil reserves valued at $30.70 per share in 1989. Earnings had been significantly depressed in the late 1980s as the firm sought to extricate itself from heavy "take or pay" commitments. A global settlement was reached with transmission company customers in late 1989. It cost CGS about $1 billion to buy out of its take or pay commitments. The net result was to leave CGS with

Table 9.6   Columbia Gas System Return Forecast

Year	Sales (000,000)	Profits (000,000)	Dividends Per Share	Stock Price
1990	$3,175	$125.00	$2.20	$44.13
1991	$3,366	$135.50	$2.23	$50.23
1992	$3,702	$154.47	$2.34	$56.14
1993	$4,257	$191.54	$2.65	$75.84
1994	$5,002	$248.53	$3.38	$106.12
1995	$6,003	$335.51	$4.79	$146.83
1996	$6,603	$389.19	$5.45	$137.95
1997	$6,933	$416.44	$5.71	$114.24
1998	$7,072	$423.93	$5.70	$91.22
1999	$7,213	$428.17	$5.65	$75.27

Table 9.7   Columbia Gas System Forecast Assumptions

Year	Annual Sales Change	Operating Leverage	Dividend Payout	P/E Ratio	Shares Out (000,000)
1990	6%	1.50	0.80	14	47.60
1991	6%	1.40	0.80	18	48.55
1992	10%	1.40	0.75	18	49.52
1993	15%	1.60	0.70	20	50.51
1994	18%	1.70	0.70	22	51.52
1995	20%	1.75	0.75	23	52.55
1996	10%	1.60	0.75	19	53.61
1997	5%	1.40	0.75	15	54.68
1998	2%	0.90	0.75	12	55.77
1999	2%	0.50	0.75	10	56.89

very market-responsive contracts that will have the effect of increasing pipeline usage.

Nevertheless, CGS is well positioned to take advantage of its valuable gas reserves and pipeline services as the demand and supply conditions in the industry improve into the 1990s.

As can be seen in Table 9.6, revenues are expected to grow throughout the period—more slowly at first and then with increasing speed as the company is able to capitalize on the value of its reserves. Its pipeline operations are also expected to contribute handsomely to earnings. Sales of gas and pipeline activities are expected to become increasingly profitable throughout the period, but their impact is muted by CGS's eight local distribution companies, which become a drag on earnings by the middle of the decade. The assumptions embodied in this forecast are presented in Table 9.7.

Investing in CGS brings an outstanding return by 1994—a TRR of 30.6 percent—primarily as a result of its being able to capitalize on its ample gas reserves in a period of excess demand. This return is expected to fall to 13.9 percent by 1999 as a result of a fall in stock price as conditions of excess demand for natural gas yield to conditions of excess supply and as the price of gas falls.

Table 9.8   Consolidated Natural Gas System Return Forecast

Year	Sales (000,000)	Profits (000,000)	Dividends Per Share	Stock Price
1990	$3,000	$210.00	$1.84	$45.00
1991	$3,210	$235.73	$2.02	$48.37
1992	$3,531	$276.98	$2.17	$55.72
1993	$3,972	$337.57	$2.59	$73.98
1994	$4,568	$438.84	$3.30	$103.71
1995	$5,368	$592.43	$4.37	$137.26
1996	$6,173	$747.94	$5.41	$139.01
1997	$6,790	$860.13	$6.09	$139.31
1998	$7,130	$907.44	$6.30	$126.08
1999	$7,272	$925.59	$6.30	$126.08

Table 9.9   Consolidated Natural Gas System Forecast Assumptions

Year	Annual Sales Change	Operating Leverage	Dividend Payout	P/E Ratio	Shares Out (000,000)
1990	4%	1.85	0.75	16	86.00
1991	7%	1.75	0.75	18	87.72
1992	10%	1.75	0.70	18	89.47
1993	13%	1.75	0.70	20	91.26
1994	15%	2.00	0.70	22	93.09
1995	18%	2.00	0.70	22	94.95
1996	15%	1.75	0.70	18	96.85
1997	10%	1.50	0.70	16	98.79
1998	5%	1.10	0.70	14	100.76
1999	2%	1.00	0.70	14	102.78

Consolidated Natural Gas Company (CNG)

CNG is a fully integrated natural gas system with five LDCs, an interstate gas pipeline, an exploration business unit and proven oil and gas reserves valued at $14.55 in 1989. This company has avoided the "take or pay" debacle and enters the 1990s with considerable financial strength.

This company is structured to have considerable operating leverage which, in combination with strong sales growth, will result in significant advances in profits throughout the forecast period. Share price will be supported by healthy dividend payouts in addition to potential growth. Share price will also be favorably influenced by some stock buyback activity in the early part of the forecast period. This forecast is presented in Table 9.8. The assumptions for this forecast are expressed in Table 9.9.

Operating leverage is so high at CNG because of a combination of the favorable location of its pipelines (e.g., serving the Washington, D.C., area), its proven reserves, and the maintenance of its exploration capabilities through lean times.

It is expected that CNG will yield an investor buying in 1990 a TRR of 28.64 percent in 1994 and a TRR of 18.26 percent in 1999. The decline in stock prices towards the end of the decade reflects diminished growth prospects for its reserves (as increasing gas supplies begin to drive prices down), its transmission activities (as additional pipelines are brought on stream), and its exploration activities. An additional factor reducing earnings will be difficulty in obtaining rate relief for its local distribution companies in an environment of escalating fuel costs.

Enron Corporation

Enron operates five major pipelines (Northern Natural Gas, Transwestern, Florida Gas, Houston Pipeline and Northern Border) and is heavily involved in exploration, liquid fuels and cogeneration projects. The fall in gas prices during the last half of the 1980s badly hurt Enron's earnings (operating income declined from $5.15 per share in 1984 to zero in 1988). Nevertheless, its pipelines are well positioned to take advantage of an increasing demand for natural gas.

Table 9.10   Enron Corporation Return Forecast

Year	Sales (000,000)	Profits (000,000)	Dividends Per Share	Stock Price
1990	$10,600	$95.00	$2.48	$55.88
1991	$12,720	$190.00	$2.48	$91.31
1992	$15,900	$285.00	$2.90	$134.28
1993	$19,875	$409.69	$3.25	$158.96
1994	$26,831	$624.77	$3.50	$203.72
1995	$33,539	$827.82	$8.09	$264.63
1996	$40,247	$1,026.50	$9.83	$268.09
1997	$44,272	$1,118.89	$10.50	$267.39
1998	$46,485	$1,160.85	$10.68	$233.12
1999	$47,415	$1,172.45	$10.58	$192.36

In 1989, at the prevailing depressed price levels, the value of its proven reserves stood at $30.47 per share. It exploration and liquid gas operations will also benefit enormously from any increase in energy prices. Given the depressed state of its stock in 1989 as a consequence of past conditions of excess supply, this company is situated to offer astute investors tremendous returns. Enron's forecast is presented in Table 9.10. The assumption used to make this forecast may be found in Table 9.11.

The exceptional earnings gains indicated early in the forecast period reflects the impact of some cost containment programs begun as a result of earlier severe pressure on earnings and the position of most of its operations at their break-even point. These increases in sales will translate into large earning gains. A relatively high degree of operating leverage is maintained until 1996, when supply will begin to catch up with demand. The substantial increase in earnings will come from all sectors of the company: production, pipelines and exploration. Investors, under these circumstances, can anticipate an amazing annual return of 43.3 percent through 1994 and 21.6 percent through 1999.

Table 9.11   Enron Corporation Forecast Assumptions

Year	Annual Sales Change	Operating Leverage	Dividend Payout	P/E Ratio	Shares Out (000,000)
1990	8%	15.00	nmf	30	51.00
1991	20%	5.00	nmf	25	52.02
1992	25%	2.00	nmf	25	53.06
1993	25%	1.75	nmf	21	54.12
1994	35%	1.50	nmf	18	55.20
1995	25%	1.30	0.55	18	56.31
1996	20%	1.20	0.55	15	57.43
1997	10%	0.90	0.55	14	58.58
1998	5%	0.75	0.55	12	59.75
1999	2%	0.50	0.55	10	60.95

Enserch Corporation

Enserch is a pipeline company with diversification in exploration, power plant construction and cogeneration. In 1989, Enserch had proven reserves valued at $17.24 per share. This company's weak performance throughout the last half of the 1980s reflected losses in its now discontinued oilfield services division and the moribund economy of its service area—Texas and southern Oklahoma.

These events have depressed the price of Enserch's stock. Although the rise in petroleum prices anticipated in the 1990s will bring its service area back to life and improving supply and demand fundamentals will fill its pipeline and increase the value of its reserves, the return to former levels of profitability will be slow.

The forecasted returns for Enserch are presented in Table 9.12. The assumptions in this forecast are listed in Table 9.13.

As the price of Enserch at the close of the 1980s has been adjusted to reflect prior losses and modest current earnings levels, investors in this company can expect significant near-term rewards from the coming turnaround. The expected TRR through 1994 is 27.4 percent. This return is anticipated to fall to 11.8 percent by 1999.

Table 9.12   Enserch Corporation Return Forecast

Year	Sales (000,000)	Profits (000,000)	Dividends Per Share	Stock Price
1990	$2,800	$92.50	$0.80	$25.52
1991	$3,080	$106.38	$0.81	$30.57
1992	$3,450	$125.52	$0.94	$37.44
1993	$3,967	$153.77	$1.12	$44.97
1994	$4,681	$195.28	$1.40	$59.10
1995	$5,617	$253.87	$1.78	$79.29
1996	$6,179	$285.60	$1.97	$65.59
1997	$6,488	$299.88	$2.03	$63.02
1998	$6,683	$308.88	$2.05	$59.09
1999	$6,749	$311.66	$2.02	$53.95

Table 9.13   Enserch Corporation Forecast Assumptions

Year	Annual Sales Change	Operating Leverage	Dividend Payout	P/E Ratio	Shares Out (000,000)
1990	6%	2.00	0.50	16	58.00
1991	10%	1.50	0.45	17	59.16
1992	12%	1.50	0.45	18	60.34
1993	15%	1.50	0.45	18	61.55
1994	18%	1.50	0.45	19	62.78
1995	20%	1.50	0.45	20	64.04
1996	10%	1.25	0.45	15	65.32
1997	5%	1.00	0.45	14	66.62
1998	3%	1.00	0.45	13	67.96
1999	1%	0.90	0.45	12	69.32

Equitable Resources (ER)

Equitable Resources is a natural gas distribution company that owns significant proven gas and oil reserves. The distribution company's service area includes Pittsburgh and parts of West Virginia and Kentucky. Its gas and oil reserves (amounting to $22.56 per share in 1989) are located in the low-cost Appalachian field and are well located to supply the large Northeast markets. This combination of low-cost resources and proximity to a large growing market gives this firm great potential for appreciation as an investment.

The anticipated performance of ER during the forecast period is presented in Table 9.14. The assumptions upon which this forecast is based are contained in Table 9.15.

Moderate sales growth characterizes ER at the beginning of this period while profits increase steadily as the market for natural gas moves towards equilibrium and earnings from distribution activities stabilize. In 1992, this company is expected to sell increasing amounts of gas to the northeast market on very favorable terms as that market begins to experience an increasing shortfall in supply. Sales and profits then grow rapidly, until major new gas supplies enter the market. Earnings towards the end of the decade are re-

Table 9.14   Equitable Resources Return Forecast

Year	Sales (000,000)	Profits (000,000)	Dividends Per Share	Stock Price
1990	$550	$55.00	$1.34	$34.79
1991	$589	$60.78	$1.48	$40.59
1992	$647	$69.89	$1.70	$49.03
1993	$712	$82.12	$1.96	$64.02
1994	$819	$103.68	$2.42	$93.22
1995	$983	$139.97	$3.21	$123.38
1996	$1,130	$171.46	$3.85	$133.36
1997	$1,243	$192.89	$4.49	$130.74
1998	$1,305	$202.54	$4.63	$117.77
1999	$1,331	$205.98	$4.61	$117.42

Table 9.15   Equitable Resources Forecast Assumptions

Year	Annual Sales Change	Operating Leverage	Dividend Payout	P/E Ratio	Shares Out (000,000)
1990	5%	1.75	0.50	13	20.55
1991	7%	1.50	0.51	14	20.96
1992	10%	1.50	0.52	15	21.38
1993	10%	1.75	0.52	17	21.81
1994	15%	1.75	0.52	20	22.24
1995	20%	1.75	0.52	20	22.69
1996	15%	1.50	0.52	18	23.14
1997	10%	1.25	0.55	16	23.61
1998	5%	1.00	0.55	14	24.08
1999	2%	0.85	0.55	14	24.56

duced as a result of difficulties associated with distribution activities in an era of rising prices.

The resultant price appreciation and dividend payouts are expected to yield investors a TRR of 33 percent in 1994 and a TRR of 19.9 percent to investors who hold throughout the entire forecast period.

Hadson Corporation

Hadson Corporation is a conglomerate whose activities include producing and supplying energy, electric cogeneration, signal processing and defense products. The acquisition of Ultrasystems in April 1988 and HRB Singer in August 1988 had not been fully digested in 1989, resulting in a significant drop in share price.

Management appears to be aggressively into expansion, and additional acquisitions during the forecast period are quite likely.

As the bulk of the company's activities are not related to natural gas production, transmission, or distribution, no forecast is developed for Hadson Corporation. While its energy activities may prosper during this period, their contribution to returns during this period are likely to be overwhelmed by the firm's other activities.

Table 9.16   KN Energy Return Forecast

Year	Sales (000,000)	Profits (000,000)	Dividends Per Share	Stock Price
1990	$390	$14.50	$1.13	$25.68
1991	$429	$17.04	$1.22	$29.58
1992	$472	$19.76	$1.29	$35.62
1993	$529	$23.56	$1.50	$41.62
1994	$581	$27.33	$1.71	$49.97
1995	$610	$29.51	$1.81	$52.91
1996	$629	$30.84	$1.85	$45.64
1997	$641	$31.46	$1.85	$39.94
1998	$629	$30.96	$1.93	$33.02
1999	$566	$29.41	$1.92	$30.76

With a beta of 1.35, the future for this firm appears highly speculative.

KN Energy (KN)

KN Energy is a natural gas transmission and distribution company. It serves markets from Kansas to the Rocky Mountains. KN's future growth prospects are tied primarily to the use of natural gas in enhanced oil recovery operations. Its pipelines have significant excess capacity. As the price of oil rises, enhanced recovery operation will intensify and KN will benefit.

Investors in KN Energy may expect to do well in the forecast period, but KN's performance will not be as strong as those firms holding significant natural gas reserves or those firms serving rapidly growing markets. The forecasts for KN Energy are presented in Table 9.16. The assumptions underlying these forecasts may be found in Table 9.17.

Annual returns of 23.9 percent to investors in KN Energy who purchased at the beginning of 1989 and hold through 1994 may be expected. The forecast TRR for 1989–1999 is 8.6 percent.

Table 9.17   KN Energy Forecast Assumptions

Year	Annual Sales Change	Operating Leverage	Dividend Payout	P/E Ratio	Shares Out (000,000)
1990	7%	1.75	0.75	17	9.60
1991	10%	1.75	0.70	17	9.79
1992	10%	1.60	0.65	18	9.99
1993	12%	1.60	0.65	18	10.19
1994	10%	1.60	0.65	19	10.39
1995	5%	1.60	0.65	19	10.60
1996	3%	1.50	0.65	16	10.81
1997	2%	1.00	0.65	14	11.03
1998	–2%	0.80	0.70	12	11.25
1999	–10%	0.50	0.75	12	11.47

Mitchell Energy and Development Corporation (ME)

ME is an exploration, production and transmission company in the natural gas industry that also holds substantial real estate in the Houston, Texas, area. Per share reserves owned in 1989 were $20.66 and the real estate holdings on the books were carried at cost rather than market value. As the oil economy recovers, ME will reap significant benefits in both areas.

Growth in sales and profits will be slow during the early part of the decade, but will rapidly pick up steam as the price of oil rises. This scenario is evident in Table 9.18. The assumptions on which this forecast is based may be found in Table 9.19.

This forecast assumes that a major expansion of development activities will not take place during the forecast period. An increase in this activity in a recovering Houston economy would significantly enhance profits.

A wild card in this situation is George P. Mitchell, who owns 62 percent of the stock. It is unlikely he could be forced into selling or restructuring the organization. However, ME would be an extremely attractive acquisition for a major integrated oil company or foreign investors under conditions likely to prevail by the mid-1990s. It may be that a price could be found that would induce Mr.

Table 9.18   Mitchell Energy and Development Corporation Return Forecast

Year	Sales (000,000)	Profits (000,000)	Dividends Per Share	Stock Price
1990	$690	$43.00	$0.32	$17.48
1991	$759	$49.45	$0.37	$21.99
1992	$835	$56.87	$0.48	$27.43
1993	$960	$70.52	$0.66	$35.14
1994	$1,133	$92.73	$0.95	$43.84
1995	$1,360	$122.40	$1.37	$49.82
1996	$1,563	$145.35	$1.61	$52.72
1997	$1,720	$159.89	$1.75	$44.66
1998	$1,806	$167.88	$1.82	$39.80
1999	$1,842	$170.90	$1.84	$33.43

Table 9.19   Mitchell Energy and Development Corporation Forecast Assumptions

Year	Annual Sales Change	Operating Leverage	Dividend Payout	P/E Ratio	Shares Out (000,000)
1990	8%	1.75	0.35	19	46.75
1991	10%	1.50	0.35	21	47.22
1992	10%	1.50	0.40	23	47.69
1993	15%	1.60	0.45	24	48.17
1994	18%	1.75	0.50	23	48.65
1995	20%	1.60	0.55	20	49.13
1996	15%	1.25	0.55	18	49.63
1997	10%	1.00	0.55	14	50.12
1998	5%	1.00	0.55	12	50.62
1999	2%	0.90	0.55	10	51.13

Mitchell to sell or restructure. This possibility could bring extraordinary gains in addition to those forecast.

In the absence of such dramatic events, a TRR of 28.8 percent is anticipated as of 1994 and 12.4 percent as of 1999.

Oneok Inc.

Oneok is a gas transmission and distribution company in Oklahoma. The fall in energy prices at the end of the 1980s gave Oneok a double whammy: (1) it depressed its basic service market, and (2) it left itself exposed to considerable take or pay liabilities. Subsequent litigation caused its directors to temporarily suspend its dividend payment in 1989.

Oneok may be expected to work through its troubles and perform modestly throughout the 1990s as its service area recovers.

The forecast for Oneok is contained in Table 9.20. The assumptions upon which this forecast is based may be found in Table 9.21.

Oneok may be expected to generate an annual solid return to investors of 22.1 percent by 1994 and 13.4 percent by 1999. This rather substantial return reflects more of the recovery of Oneok

Table 9.20   Oneok, Inc. Return Forecast

Year	Sales (000,000)	Profits (000,000)	Dividends Per Share	Stock Price
1990	$640	$36.00	$0.74	$13.48
1991	$659	$37.62	$0.77	$15.35
1992	$686	$39.88	$0.88	$17.57
1993	$720	$43.07	$0.94	$18.79
1994	$756	$46.51	$1.00	$23.44
1995	$809	$51.72	$1.11	$25.80
1996	$865	$57.15	$1.21	$26.21
1997	$909	$60.01	$1.26	$25.16
1998	$927	$61.09	$1.27	$25.36
1999	$945	$62.19	$1.28	$23.43

Table 9.21   Oneok, Inc. Forecast Assumptions

Year	Annual Sales Change	Operating Leverage	Dividend Payout	P/E Ratio	Shares Out (000,000)
1990	3%	1.50	0.55	10	26.70
1991	3%	1.50	0.55	11	26.97
1992	4%	1.50	0.60	12	27.24
1993	5%	1.60	0.60	12	27.51
1994	5%	1.60	0.60	14	27.78
1995	7%	1.60	0.60	14	28.06
1996	7%	1.50	0.60	13	28.34
1997	5%	1.00	0.60	12	28.63
1998	2%	0.90	0.60	12	28.91
1999	2%	0.90	0.60	11	29.20

from its currently depressed condition in the stock market than from any spectacular improvement in operating performance.

Panhandle Eastern (PE)

PE is primarily engaged in the transmission of interstate natural gas from Texas to the upper Midwest since it spun off its oil and gas producing activities as Anadarko Petroleum Corporation in October 1986. Earnings performance lagged towards the end of the 1980s as the firm became embroiled in a variety of lawsuits and continued to hold onto its unutilized LNG facilities.

The performance of PE in the 1990s will depend on the continued resurgence of economic conditions in the upper Midwest. If the net effect of deregulation in the gas industry is to make natural gas pricing more flexible and responsive to competitive conditions, natural gas consumption will increase and PE will be able to make use of its excess capacity.

The anticipated improvement in natural gas supply and demand fundamentals will probably make PE's LNG facilities economically viable by 1991–92. By the middle of the decade, assuming low cost supplies of LNG can be obtained, these facilities should be contributing heavily to earnings.

Table 9.22   Panhandle Eastern Corporation Return Forecast

Year	Sales (000,000)	Profits (000,000)	Dividends Per Share	Stock Price
1990	$3,500	$130.00	$2.00	$25.32
1991	$3,745	$120.00	$2.00	$28.30
1992	$4,120	$141.00	$2.00	$31.05
1993	$5,767	$239.70	$2.00	$36.22
1994	$6,344	$281.65	$2.00	$41.73
1995	$6,978	$330.94	$2.06	$51.50
1996	$7,676	$388.85	$2.37	$59.33
1997	$8,060	$413.15	$2.47	$53.56
1998	$8,221	$423.48	$2.48	$49.68
1999	$8,386	$431.95	$2.48	$41.40

Table 9.23   Panhandle Eastern Corporation Forecast Assumptions

Year	Annual Sales Change	Operating Leverage	Dividend Payout	P/E Ratio	Shares Out (000,000)
1990	7%	4.00	nmf	17	87.30
1991	7%	2.00	nmf	21	89.05
1992	10%	1.75	nmf	20	90.83
1993	40%	1.75	nmf	14	92.64
1994	10%	1.75	nmf	14	94.50
1995	10%	1.75	0.60	15	96.39
1996	10%	1.75	0.60	15	98.31
1997	5%	1.25	0.60	13	100.28
1998	2%	1.25	0.60	12	102.29
1999	2%	1.00	0.60	10	104.33

This scenario is embodied in the forecast presented in Table 9.22. The assumptions behind this forecast may be examined in Table 9.23.

It should be noted that this is an optimistic appraisal of the situation of PE. If the demand for natural gas is depressed through 1993 by excess supplies of oil, PE would be forced to cut its substantial dividend. The market may interpret this adversely and cut PE's P/E ratio. This stock has considerable downside potential if this occurs.

As PE recovers from the erosion of its earning power, investors may expect a 22.7 percent annual return through 1994 an annual return of 14 percent through 1999. It should be noted that this forecast presumes the LNG plant will fully come on stream in 1993 and contribute almost $600 million to sales.

Seagull Energy Corp. (SE)

Seagull Energy is engaged in pipeline transmission of natural gas in the Gulf of Mexico and Alaska as well as in the exploration and production of natural gas and oil. The company appears to be engaged in an active program to add to its current (1989) proven reserves of $4.43 per share. Seagull Energy was created from a Tenneco spinoff in 1981 and has yet to pay any dividends to its common stockholders.

In the absence of a major acquisition, this company may be expected to benefit moderately from the coming changes in gas demand-supply fundamentals. SE's Alaskan utility operations will not contribute significantly to increased profits during this period, although a cold 1990 winter gave profits a temporary boost.

The forecast for Seagull Energy is contained in Table 9.24. The assumptions used to make this forecast are presented in Table 9.25.

Investors in this firm may anticipate a TRR of 13.4 in 1994 and a TRR of 4.1 percent by the end of 1999.

Sonat, Inc.

Sonat is a pipeline company transporting gas from the Gulf Coast to the Southeast with some diversification into exploration, contract drilling, and production. Serious losses were incurred as a result of unmet gas purchase commitments at the end of the 1980s. Fierce

Table 9.24   Seagull Energy Corporation Return Forecast

Year	Sales (000,000)	Profits (000,000)	Dividends Per Share	Stock Price
1990	$190	$13.20	$0.00	$25.60
1991	$205	$14.78	$0.00	$28.11
1992	$224	$16.78	$0.00	$33.23
1993	$248	$19.09	$0.00	$37.06
1994	$276	$21.71	$0.97	$41.33
1995	$309	$24.71	$1.09	$43.40
1996	$333	$26.88	$1.16	$40.51
1997	$350	$28.09	$1.19	$35.57
1998	$361	$28.77	$1.19	$32.74
1999	$364	$28.91	$1.20	$29.32

Table 9.25   Seagull Energy Corporation Forecast Assumptions

Year	Annual Sales Change	Operating Leverage	Dividend Payout	P/E Ratio	Shares Out (000,000)
1990	7%	1.25	0.00	16	8.25
1991	8%	1.50	0.00	16	8.42
1992	9%	1.50	0.00	17	8.58
1993	11%	1.25	0.00	17	8.75
1994	11%	1.25	0.40	17	8.93
1995	12%	1.15	0.40	16	9.31
1996	8%	1.10	0.40	14	9.29
1997	5%	0.90	0.40	12	9.48
1998	3%	0.80	0.40	11	9.67
1999	1%	0.50	0.41	10	9.86

competition from competing fuels and customers threatening bypass will keep profits depressed in the early part of the 1990s.

As the fundamental supply and demand situation for natural
gas improves, Sonat will begin a slow return to previous levels of
profitability. As oil prices rise throughout the decade, Sonat's exploration and drilling activities will also once again contribute to earnings. Sonat's profits may be helped by an aggressive acquisition
plan in the early 1990s.

The anticipated performance for this firm is presented in Table
9.26. The assumptions embedded in this forecast are contained in
Table 9.27.

The TRR of 17.2 percent accruing to the investor purchasing at
the beginning of 1989 and holding till the end of 1994 results from
taking advantage of the sharp drop in profits in 1989. The anticipated TRR between 1989 and 1999 is 6.2 percent.

Tenneco, Inc.

Tenneco is a holding company with interests in widely diversified
businesses. Its natural gas pipelines accounted for 25 percent of assets and 33 percent of operating income in 1989. The company was

Table 9.26   Sonat, Inc. Return Forecast

Year	Sales (000,000)	Profits (000,000)	Dividends Per Share	Stock Price
1990	$1,850	$107.00	$2.02	$49.77
1991	$1,943	$113.15	$2.08	$52.11
1992	$2,137	$127.30	$2.30	$57.47
1993	$2,457	$151.16	$2.51	$73.60
1994	$2,826	$179.51	$2.73	$77.90
1995	$3,250	$210.47	$3.13	$89.54
1996	$3,575	$233.63	$3.26	$73.08
1997	$3,753	$244.14	$3.29	$64.89
1998	$3,829	$248.04	$3.28	$54.69
1999	$3,905	$250.53	$3.35	$49.23

Table 9.27   Sonat Inc. Forecast Assumptions

Year	Annual Sales Change	Operating Leverage	Dividend Payout	P/E Ratio	Shares Out (000,000)
1990	3%	1.15	0.81	20	43.00
1991	5%	1.15	0.80	20	43.43
1992	10%	1.25	0.80	20	44.30
1993	15%	1.25	0.75	22	45.18
1994	15%	1.25	0.70	20	46.09
1995	15%	1.15	0.70	20	47.01
1996	10%	1.10	0.67	15	47.95
1997	5%	0.90	0.66	13	48.91
1998	2%	0.80	0.66	11	49.89
1999	2%	0.50	0.68	10	50.89

in the midst of a substantial restructuring at the end of the 1980s. It sold its production and refinery businesses in 1988 and used the proceeds to reduce debt and buy back stock. It may spinoff the perennially unprofitable Case IH farm equipment unit. Other businesses include shipbuilding, chemicals, packaging, and auto parts. The pipelines serve New England and the upper Midwest from Texas.

It may be anticipated that Tenneco's pipeline units will become increasingly profitable as gas fundamentals improve in the 1990s. The forecast for Tenneco assumes that its non-pipeline businesses will average 5 percent sales growth with current levels of profitability throughout the forecast period. This forecast is presented in Table 9.28. The assumptions made in this forecast are stated in Table 9.29.

On this basis, an investment in Tenneco may be expected to yield 16.4 percent annually between 1989 and 1994 and 9 percent between 1989 and 1999.

Transco Energy

Transco Energy is engaged in the interstate transmission of gas among the Gulf Coast states, up the Mississippi-Ohio River Basin

Table 9.28   Tenneco, Inc. Return Forecast

Year	Sales (000,000)	Profits (000,000)	Dividends Per Share	Stock Price
1990	$15,000	$650.00	$3.12	$66.54
1991	$15,750	$685.75	$3.38	$69.85
1992	$16,695	$733.07	$3.60	$80.01
1993	$17,697	$783.65	$3.65	$91.18
1994	$18,935	$846.73	$3.92	$98.03
1995	$20,261	$914.89	$4.22	$105.40
1996	$21,477	$975.28	$4.47	$96.89
1997	$22,550	$1,028.92	$4.69	$86.06
1998	$23,452	$1,073.78	$4.87	$89.37
1999	$24,391	$1,120.17	$5.06	$84.33

Table 9.29   Tenneco, Inc. Forecast Assumptions

Year	Annual Sales Change	Operating Leverage	Dividend Payout	P/E Ratio	Shares Out (000,000)
1990	4%	1.10	0.61	13	127.00
1991	5%	1.10	0.63	13	127.64
1992	6%	1.15	0.63	14	128.27
1993	6%	1.15	0.60	15	128.91
1994	7%	1.15	0.60	15	129.56
1995	7%	1.15	0.60	15	130.21
1996	6%	1.10	0.60	13	130.86
1997	5%	1.10	0.60	11	131.51
1998	4%	1.09	0.60	11	132.17
1999	4%	1.08	0.60	10	132.83

and to the East Coast. Its performance in the last half of the 1980s was compromised by take or pay contracts that were entered into under different conditions. While resolving these problems will take through the early 1990s, the depressed stock price appears to offer investors good potential as industry fundamentals improve. Transco is well positioned to reap the benefits of surging gas volume.

The forecasted performance for Transco is presented in Table 9.30. The assumptions on which this forecast is based are presented in Table 9.31.

The results of this forecast are that an investor purchasing Transco stock at the beginning of 1989 and selling at the end of 1994 would reap an annual return of 23 percent. The comparable TRR for 1989–1999 would be 10.8 percent.

Valero Energy

Valero Energy retains a 49 percent interest in a Master Limited Partnership to which it sold five Texas pipelines. The pipelines may be expected to benefit from the improvement in supply-demand fundamentals. Valero continues to operate a refinery. The near-term

Table 9.30   Transco Energy Company Return Forecast

Year	Sales (000,000)	Profits (000,000)	Dividends Per Share	Stock Price
1990	$3,150	$90.00	$1.35	$41.18
1991	$3,371	$97.88	$1.46	$47.50
1992	$3,708	$110.11	$1.76	$56.44
1993	$4,078	$126.63	$2.21	$68.28
1994	$4,588	$150.37	$2.83	$80.28
1995	$5,162	$173.86	$3.24	$86.50
1996	$5,678	$192.99	$3.56	$71.30
1997	$5,962	$202.64	$3.71	$67.94
1998	$6,141	$207.20	$3.75	$62.53
1999	$6,202	$207.71	$3.72	$62.07

Table 9.31   Transco Energy Company Forecast Assumptions

Year	Annual Sales Change	Operating Leverage	Dividend Payout	P/E Ratio	Shares Out (000,000)
1990	15%	1.75	0.46	14	30.60
1991	7%	1.25	0.46	15	30.91
1992	10%	1.25	0.50	16	31.22
1993	10%	1.50	0.55	17	31.53
1994	13%	1.50	0.60	17	31.84
1995	13%	1.25	0.60	16	32.16
1996	10%	1.10	0.60	12	32.48
1997	5%	1.00	0.60	11	32.81
1998	3%	0.75	0.60	10	33.14
1999	1%	0.25	0.60	10	33.47

prospects for the refinery operation look good into the 1990s, when additional refinery capacity will likely come on stream.

The forecast presented in Table 9.32 reflects the assumption that the petroleum industry will not enter into a period of excess refinery capacity in the 1990s. In addition, it is assumed that Valero will not seek a major acquisition or be sought. The emerging economics of deregulation in the gas industry suggests that Valero's MLP would be a desirable acquisition for a pipeline system that could use its lines to increase its efficiency. Additional assumptions are indicated in Table 9.33.

The results of this forecast suggest that investors in Valero Energy could look forward to a TRR of 18.9 percent between 1989 and 1994 and a TRR of 8.5 percent between 1989 and 1999.

The Williams Companies, Inc. (WC)

The Williams Companies completed a restructuring at the end of the 1980s, selling off a number of businesses unrelated to pipeline transmission of natural gas. The company also took a beating in its take or pay contracts, but will have put that behind it by 1990.

Table 9.32   Valero Energy Return Forecast

Year	Sales (000,000)	Profits (000,000)	Dividends Per Share	Stock Price
1990	$1,002	$65.00	$0.20	$16.25
1991	$1,062	$69.88	$0.29	$17.30
1992	$1,136	$76.23	$0.42	$20.76
1993	$1,227	$84.16	$0.57	$27.23
1994	$1,326	$92.91	$0.62	$29.76
1995	$1,392	$98.49	$0.91	$36.44
1996	$1,461	$103.41	$0.95	$29.77
1997	$1,535	$108.58	$0.70	$28.13
1998	$1,581	$111.19	$0.71	$25.67
1999	$1,596	$111.75	$0.71	$25.54

Table 9.33   Valero Energy Forecast Assumptions

Year	Annual Sales Change	Operating Leverage	Dividend Payout	P/E Ratio	Shares Out (000,000)
1990	6%	1.25	0.11	9	36.00
1991	6%	1.25	0.15	9	36.36
1992	7%	1.30	0.20	10	36.72
1993	8%	1.30	0.25	12	37.09
1994	8%	1.30	0.25	12	37.46
1995	5%	1.20	0.35	14	37.84
1996	5%	1.00	0.35	11	38.21
1997	5%	1.00	0.25	10	38.60
1998	3%	0.80	0.25	9	38.98
1999	1%	0.50	0.25	9	39.37

WC enters the 1990s as a pipeline company serving Louisiana, the Midwest and the Northwest. It has a small subsidiary (4 percent of revenues in 1989), which owns a fibre optics telecommunication system linking the Midwest and the West Coast. This subsidiary is likely to become a valuable income-producing asset by the mid 1990s.

The forecasts for WC are presented in Table 9.34. The assumptions used to make this forecast are presented in Table 9.35.

Investors in the Williams Companies may expect an annual yield of 24 percent for holding the stock between 1989 and 1994. The comparable yield between 1989 and 1999 would be 15.8 percent.

Summary

The rankings for the 18 diversified gas companies by expected TRR may be found in Table 9.1. As a group, diversified gas companies currently appear to offer excellent opportunities to the investor, particularly into the mid-1990s.

Table 9.34   The Williams Companies, Inc. Return Forecast

Year	Sales (000,000)	Profits (000,000)	Dividends Per Share	Stock Price
1990	$1,770	$75.00	$1.40	$30.91
1991	$1,894	$82.88	$1.41	$35.81
1992	$2,064	$94.06	$1.59	$40.24
1993	$2,312	$110.99	$1.88	$49.62
1994	$2,590	$128.98	$2.25	$60.09
1995	$2,900	$149.87	$2.59	$69.14
1996	$3,190	$168.60	$2.89	$69.31
1997	$3,382	$179.73	$3.05	$65.02
1998	$3,585	$190.52	$3.20	$68.24
1999	$3,800	$201.95	$3.36	$71.62

Table 9.35   The Williams Companies, Inc. Forecast Assumptions

Year	Annual Sales Change	Operating Leverage	Dividend Payout	P/E Ratio	Shares Out (000,000)
1990	7%	2.00	0.77	17	41.25
1991	7%	1.50	0.71	18	41.66
1992	9%	1.50	0.71	18	42.08
1993	12%	1.50	0.72	19	42.50
1994	12%	1.35	0.75	20	42.92
1995	12%	1.35	0.75	20	43.35
1996	10%	1.25	0.75	18	43.79
1997	6%	1.10	0.75	16	44.23
1998	6%	1.00	0.75	16	44.67
1999	6%	1.00	0.75	16	45.11

The critical factors influencing their performance were: (1) the presence of significant natural gas reserves (refer to Table 8.3), (2) their position in a service market that is characterized by good growth potential, (3) their possession of underutilized exploration and drilling subsidiaries, and (4) the extent to which the debilitating environment of the last half of the 1980s depressed their stock price in 1990.

Chapter 10

THE FUTURE FOR INVESTMENT IN LOCAL DISTRIBUTION COMPANIES

Performance Overview

Although a number of these utilities will be squeezed by higher energy prices in the 1990s, some local distribution companies will provide an investor good returns where the investor's desire to preserve capital is paramount. The industry's two high performers (Washington Energy Company and Louisiana General Services) are in comeback situations. Their performances will mirror the excellent recovery the rest of the firms in this sector made between 1984 and 1989. Generally, however, returns in this sector during the 1990s will be well below those experienced between 1984 and 1989. The potential returns available in this sector of the gas industry during the 1990s will be inferior to those found among the diversified companies.

As suggested in Chapter 8, the superior performance of the local distribution companies between 1984–1988 was in great contrast to their depressed states at the beginning of that period. The present stock prices of local distribution companies now (1990) fully incorporate their return to health.

Earnings gains for this group will be strongest in the early 1990s when the price of natural gas is rising moderately, but at a lower rate than competing fuels. (Refer to Chapter 8 for a discussion of energy prices in the 1990s.) This situation will encourage the demand for natural gas. As a result of this rising demand: capacity utilization will grow as penetration in existing markets increases, growth into new markets will be stimulated, and regulatory agencies will be relatively amenable to passing through increased costs. This environment will produce a modest, but steady, growth in earnings and dividends.

As the economy moves past 1995, significant political pressure will be generated in an adverse reaction to the prolonged rise in energy costs. Even though the rate of increases in costs will be moderate, rate relief will become more difficult to secure.

Even more damaging to the distribution companies will be the eventual fall in the price of fuel oil relative to that of natural gas. This will tend to cause a loss of market share and reduce capacity utilization. Great pressure will be brought on earnings under these circumstances and rates of return in this sector of the industry will fall.

These negative trends will be partially offset by increasing demands for nonpolluting sources of energy: natural gas alone burns cleaner than coal. In addition, new co-firing technologies significantly reduce the discharge of contaminants into the atmosphere.

The expected annual rates of return on an investment made in the 29 distribution companies covered in this study for 1989–1994 and 1989–1999 are presented in Table 10.1.

Returns Among Local Distribution Companies

In many ways, the stock of distribution companies and electric utilities perform in a similar fashion. Stock prices in both sectors depend largely on dividends, companies in both sectors pay out the bulk of their earnings in the form of dividends and companies in both sectors have a policy of maintaining dividends in the face of adversity.

Yet there are significant differences in the two sectors. Earnings among distribution companies are more volatile than earnings among electric utilities. There is a constant threat of competition from fuel oil to distribution companies and this competition can quickly erode earnings and reduce revenues. Deregulation has in-

Table 10.1   Local Gas Distribution Company Returns

Rank by 1994 TRR		TRR 1994	TRR 1998
1	South Jersey Industries, Inc.	26.0%	16.3%
2	UGI Corporation	18.1%	11.8%
3	Atlanta Gas Light Company	18.0%	12.2%
4	Southwest Gas Corporation	17.8%	13.3%
5	Providence Energy	17.6%	11.6%
6	Diversified Energies, Inc.	16.2%	10.0%
7	MCN Corporation	16.1%	11.9%
8	Bay State Gas Company	15.8%	11.1%
9	Questar Corporation	15.2%	10.0%
10	Pacific Enterprises Corp.	15.2%	11.6%
11	Washington Energy Company	14.7%	11.2%
12	Arkla, Inc.	14.5%	9.5%
13	Washington Gas Light Company	14.5%	10.5%
14	Cascade Natural Gas Company	13.9%	11.3%
15	Piedmont Natural Gas Company	13.6%	10.1%
16	National Fuel Gas Company	13.3%	9.5%
17	Connecticut Natural Gas Corp.	12.5%	10.9%
18	New Jersey Resources Corp.	12.2%	9.9%
19	NUI Corporation	12.1%	10.7%
20	Peoples Energy Corporation	11.1%	9.2%
21	Louisiana General Services, Inc.	11.1%	7.3%
22	Energen Corporation	10.8%	7.8%
23	Wicor, Inc.	10.8%	8.8%
24	Laclede Gas Company	10.7%	9.6%
25	Indiana Energy, Inc.	10.3%	11.7%
26	N.W. Natural Gas	9.3%	7.9%
27	Brooklyn Union Gas Company	8.5%	8.0%
28	Eastern Gas & Fuel Associates	7.8%	6.7%
29	Nicor Incorporated	7.4%	6.6%

creased the sensitivity of distribution companies to competition, not only from fuel oil but also from supplies of gas shipped directly from producers or pipelines as large customers "bypass" the distribution company.

Local distribution companies are also quite sensitive to uncertainty in supplies. Aside from the social necessity incumbent on the gas utility to supply its "noninterruptible" customers on demand, inadequate supplies of gas reduce capacity utilization and thus lose potential revenues and increase unit costs. With the hindsight of the "gas bubble" it is clear that local distribution companies entering into "take or pay" contracts were too cautious. However, the reason that the utilities entered into such onerous contracts in the first place was because they desperately wanted to guarantee adequate supplies of natural gas.

In the recovery period of 1984–1988, stock price appreciation played a much more important role in generating returns to investors than did dividends. This may be clearly seen from the absence of a significant relationship between IRR and dividends (Figure 10.1) and a strong relationship between IRR and price appreciation (Figure 10.2).

While the return forecasts generated for local distribution companies (Figure 10.3) do not anticipate that price appreciation will play a comparably important role in generating returns in the 1990s, the potential is clearly there to influence returns and, consequently, must be considered. As shown in Figure 10.3, a strong (R^2 = .74) relationship exists between stock price and dividends among local distribution companies.

However, an even stronger (R^2 =.81) relationship was found between cash flow and stock price, as demonstrated by Figure 10.4.

It is important to note that cash flow has more explanatory power over stock price than earnings (R^2 = .71), reflecting the artificiality of earnings in a regulated environment.

Forecasting Stock Prices and Returns

Future anticipated increases in the volatility of distribution company earnings will slowly diminish the importance of dividends in determining stock price while, at the same time, increasing the importance of cash flow as an influence on stock price. Investors will increasingly look past dividends to the ability of a company to maintain or increase such payments out of earnings in the future. As a consequence, forecasts of future stock prices among local dis-

**Figure 10.1   Gas Distribution Companies Total Return–
                Dividend Relationship**

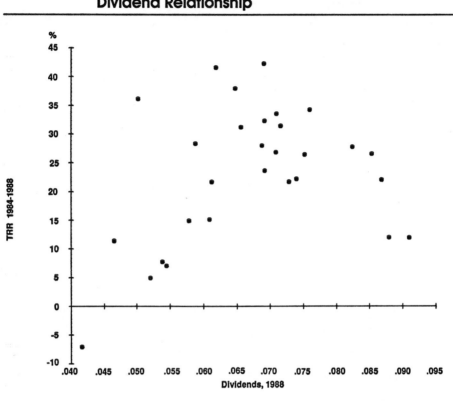

tribution companies will need to look at cash flow as well as dividends.

The DDM is used to forecast stock prices in this sector consistent with the methodology developed in Chapter 3. The specific formulation of the model used is P = 8.16 + 3.589 (CFS): where P = the price of the stock; 8.16 a constant; 3.589 a growth factor the market sets; and CFS is the estimate of cash flow per share in any given year.

In the regression format above, the growth factor is actually the reciprocal of the net effective discount rate (r–g) discussed in Chap-

Figure 10.2   Local Distribution Companies Total Return–
Stock Price Relationship

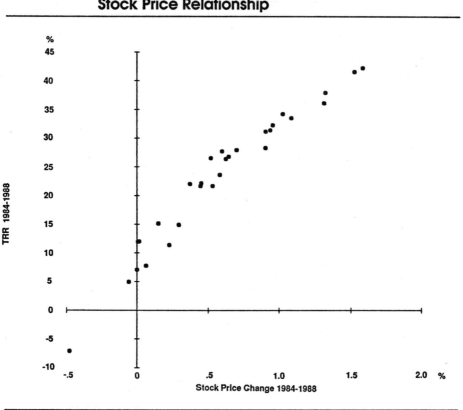

ter 3. This format merely provides a convenient way of expressing the DDM.

The growth factor (referred to as "b" below) of 3.589 in the above equation may or may not be appropriate for a particular firm. This factor is adjusted on a firm-by-firm basis below.

As earnings among distribution companies are less volatile than among diversified companies, CFS can be estimated directly from sales and operating leverage estimates. As earnings are not as volatile in this sector, it is not necessary to forecast the detail of financial performance among distribution companies as it was among diversified companies.

**Figure 10.3   Gas Distribution Companies Stock Price–
Dividend Relationship**

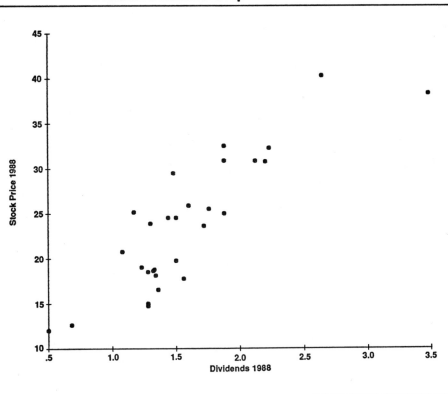

This methodology requires separate forecasts of dividends to de-termine future returns to investors. This approach allows a distinc-tion to be made between changes in the ability of the firm to sustain a particular dividend level and the dividend itself. The selection of this methodology to forecast returns in the distribution company sector is a particularly critical one, as the 1990s are likely to bring about a deterioration of the ability of firms in this sector to pay a given dividend before the dividend itself changes.

Table 10.2 presents the DDM forecast and error terms obtained for 1988 using the methodology described above. These results sug-

**Figure 10.4   Gas Distribution Companies Price–
                 Cash Flow Relationship**

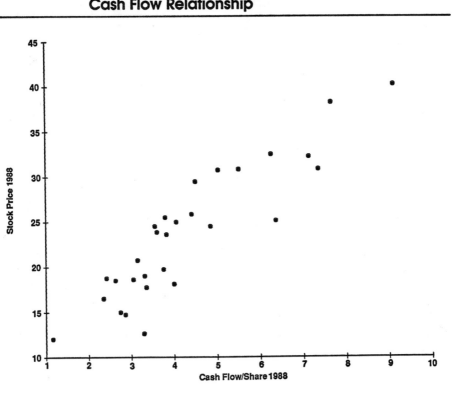

gest a relatively high degree of predictive power from this approach.

Specific Local Distribution Company Forecasts

Arkla, Inc.

Arkla distributes natural gas to over a thousand communities in Arkansas, Louisiana, Texas, Oklahoma, and Kansas. Pipeline acqui-

Table 10.2   DDM Forecast

Local Distribution Company	Stock Price 1988	DDM Predicted Price	DDM Error
Arkla, Inc.	20.75	19.47	−1.28
Atlanta Gas Light Company	25.50	21.76	−3.74
Bay State Gas Company	25.88	23.99	−1.89
Brooklyn Union Gas Company	23.63	21.87	−1.76
Cascade Natural Gas Company	15.00	18.03	3.03
Connecticut Natural Gas Corp.	16.50	16.59	0.09
Diversified Energies, Inc.	24.50	25.57	1.07
Eastern Gas & Fuel Associates	23.88	21.08	−2.79
Energen Corporation	25.13	30.99	5.86
Indiana Energy, Inc.	32.25	33.75	1.50
Laclede Gas Company	30.75	26.21	−4.54
Louisiana General Services, Inc.	12.63	19.97	7.34
Michigan Energy Resources Co.	29.50	24.31	−5.19
NUI Corporation	17.75	20.18	2.43
National Fuel Gas Company	19.00	20.04	1.04
New Jersey Resources Corp.	18.50	17.60	−0.90
Nicor Incorporated	30.88	34.36	3.48
N.W. Natural Gas	21.38	22.87	1.50
Pacific Enterprises Corp.	38.25	35.62	−2.63
Peoples Energy Corporation	19.75	21.62	1.87
Piedmont Natural Gas Company	24.50	20.90	−3.60
Providence Energy	18.75	16.85	−1.90
Questar Corporation	32.50	30.59	−1.91
Southern Union Company	12.00	12.29	0.29
South Jersey Industries, Inc.	18.63	19.11	0.48
Southwest Gas Corporation	18.13	22.52	4.39
UGI Corporation	30.83	27.90	−2.93
Washington Gas Light Company	14.75	18.42	3.67
Washington Energy Company	25.00	22.70	−2.30
Wicor, Inc.	40.25	40.82	0.57

sitions at the end of the 1980s have given Arkla access to new markets in the Midwest, East Coast and New England. As a result of these acquisitions and the recovery of much of its service area, CFS growth is expected to average 9 percent through 1995 and 2 percent thereafter. The DDM model has not factored in this new growth, so "b" is given a positive adjustment of .5.

Atlanta Gas Light

Atlanta Gas Light provides natural gas service in over 200 Georgia communities including Atlanta. Sales growth will be strong throughout the forecast period as a result of continued growth in its booming markets. However, the need for more facilities will require the issuance of additional stock diluting advances in CFS. CFS is expected to increase 6 percent on the average throughout the forecast period. The comparable increase for dividends will be 5 percent.

The DDM factor "b" is corrected .75 to allow the market to recognize this growth potential in the future. A further adjustment of $3.00 is made to the stock price to reflect market conditions prevailing in 1990.

Bay State Gas

Bay State distributes natural gas in Massachusetts, New Hampshire and Maine. Bay State has access to huge Canadian gas fields, which should enable it to meet increasing demand as oil prices rise in the 1990s. CFS is expected to rise 3 percent annually until 1992, 5 percent through 1996, and 2 percent thereafter. Dividends are expected to rise 6 percent annually through 1992, and 4 percent subsequently.

No correction is made for the DDM error. It is assumed the market overestimates the growth possibilities at Bay State. An additional negative adjustment of $5.00 is made to reflect current market conditions in 1990.

Brooklyn Union Gas Company (BUG)

BUG supplies natural gas to the mature markets in the Brooklyn, Queens, and Staten Island boroughs of New York City. Future growth in earnings is dependent on continued favorable treatment from the NYPSC. Such treatment is unlikely to be forthcoming in an era of rising energy costs.

CFS is anticipated to increase an average of 3 percent until 1993, 1 percent to 1996, and –2 percent for the remainder of the forecast period. Dividends are expected to increase at a 2.5 percent annual rate until 1999.

Although the DDM underestimates market price, no adjustment is made to the growth factor because the market premium existing in 1989 reflects the favorable treatment this stock has had in the press at this time. This factor is accounted for in a $6.00 adjustment to "a" in the 1990–99 forecast.

Cascade National Gas Company (CNGC)

CNGC retails natural gas to 86 communities in Washington and Oregon. While its residential market can be anticipated to grow steadily throughout the forecast period, the strength of competitive forces in its industrial market will keep earnings uneven. Whenever natural gas enjoys a price advantage over oil, it has a direct positive impact on earnings at CNG and vice versa.

CNGC's CFS is expected to increase 4 percent annually through 1993 and 2 percent thereafter. Dividends are expected to increase 2.5 percent throughout the entire period.

The DDM overestimates the market price. A reduction in the growth factor of .5 and a negative adjustment in its constant of $.50 is made to reflect the pressures of this competitive environment.

Connecticut Natural Gas (CNG)

This firm distributes gas to 135,000 customers in Connecticut. Its service area is prosperous and growing, but this does not necessarily impact its bottom line favorably. A great deal depends on the relative price of petroleum products. The company is beginning to diversify in order to enhance its growth prospects.

This effort appears to be focused around some cogeneration projects. If these efforts are successful (they are not factored into the model), the growth prospects at CNG could improve significantly.

Anticipated growth at CFS is estimated at 5 percent annually through 1993, 1 percent until 1996 and –2 percent thereafter. Dividends are anticipated to grow 2 percent per year until 1997 and then remain constant. A negative adjestment is made to the forecasts model of $1.00 to reflect 1990 market conditions.

Diversified Energies, Inc. (DEI)

DEI is a holding company with 82 percent of its revenues derived from Minnegasco as of 1989. Minnegasco is a regulated utility serving the upper Midwest. DEI's diversification activities tend to depress current yields but offer greater potential price appreciation. Minnegasco's basic service area is low growth and suffers from strong competitive pressure for industrial business from petroleum suppliers.

CFS is expected to maintain a steady 6 percent annual increase throughout the forecast period as rising income from DSI's diversification efforts offsets falling income from its utility operations. Dividends are expected to grow at 3 percent throughout the forecast period.

Although the DDM overestimates stock price in 1988, it is felt that the growth potential in the unregulated subsidiaries of this firm is not adequately recognized in the market. Consequently, an addition of .25 is made to the growth factor and $2.50 to the forecasting base.

Eastern Gas and Fuel Associates (EGFA)

EGFA is a holding company which distributes natural gas through its Boston Gas Company and has minor interests in barge and coal mining. Although Boston Gas tends to have an advantage over competing fuels in its service area, future growth of the bottom line is dependent on regulatory favor. While this may be forthcoming in an era of falling energy prices, such treatment is not likely to continue in an environment like the one anticipated by the mid-1990s.

Bolstered by its rebounding barge and coal mining interests, CFS is likely to increase at a 7 percent annual rate through 1992. However, growth will fall to 2 percent from that point until 1996 when CFS will decline 3 percent a year. Dividend increases are anticipated to average 3.5 percent until 1994 and 1 percent thereafter. The basic earnings power of this company is recognized by a positive $6.00 adjustment to the forecasting model to recognize 1990 market conditions.

Energen Corporation

Energen is a holding company whose principal subsidiary is the Alabama Gas Company, which distributes natural gas in central Alabama. An exploration subsidiary is heavily involved in coal seam methane extraction to help lower its cost of natural gas. The company has also invested in new incinerator technology.

CFS is expected to grow at 4 percent through 1992, 3 percent until 1997 and fall 1 percent thereafter. Dividends are expected to grow at 2 percent to 1993 and average 3 percent for the remainder of the forecast period.

While Energen's CFS is not characterized by strong growth potential, it is not as weak as suggested by the growth model. Therefore, the growth factor is adjusted downward by only .5. A reduction in anticipated 1990 earnings leads to a further negative adjustment in the forecasting model of $8.00.

Indiana Energy, Inc. (IE)

IE distributes gas through the Indiana Gas Company in 47 counties in Indiana. IE fared well between 1984 and 1988 because it is served by five pipelines and was able to play one off against the other to secure low-cost supplies. Tightening supply conditions during the 1990s will lessen the advantage of this situation. The downward impact of this situation on earnings will be exacerbated by IE's heavy reliance on industrial customers.

CFS is expected to rise 2 percent until 1992 as new large customers come on line, but will increase only 1 percent from then until 1995. Thereafter CFS is likely to average a 2 percent fall throughout the remainder of the forecast period. Dividends may be expected to increase 3 percent to 1994 and remain flat for the rest of the forecast period. Acquisition activity in 1990 results in a positive per share adjustment of $2.00 to IE's forecasting base.

Laclede Gas Company (LG)

LG is a regulated utility distributing gas in the St. Louis area of Missouri. Its strength is a largely residential (61 percent) residential customer base. Its weakness tends to be low growth potential. The company has minor real estate development and exploration subsidiaries, but these are not positioned to substantially impact its growth rate.

CFS is seen to grow at 1 percent through 1992, remain flat through 1995 and decline 2 percent thereafter as higher gas prices erode its customer base and rate increases become more difficult to secure. Dividends may be expected to rise 4 percent in 1989 and 1990. However, they are likely to increase 1 percent annually for the following three years and remain unchanged for the balance of the forecast period.

The DDM price prediction is significantly below the actual stock price in early 1989, accurately reflecting the LG's low growth potential. Consequently, a downward adjustment of one is made to the firm's growth factor in predicting future price levels while an additional $7.50 is added to the model's constant to reflect 1990 market conditions..

Louisiana General Services, Inc. (LGS)

LGS distributes natural gas in southeastern and northern Louisiana. The health of the market it serves is tied into conditions in the petroleum market. LGS has been positioning itself for future growth in the weak market of the late 1980s by acquiring low-cost gas reserves (valued at $4.19 per share in 1989). Steady improvement is seen for this utility as conditions in its region improve throughout the forecast period.

CFS is expected to average an increase of 5 percent annually through 1995 and 3 percent thereafter. Dividends are also expected to increase at 5 percent through 1995 and 3 percent thereafter.

The CFS growth model suggests this stock is undervalued at current (1989) price levels. This is reflected in a $.50 per share negative adjustment to the model.

MCN Corporation (MCN)

MCN is a holding company that owns Michigan Gas Utilities, with significant diversification in communication and cablevision. In 1988 a merger was proposed with Utilicorp. As of early 1989 this merger had not been successfully consummated, although the prospects for the merger appeared favorable. In the absence of a merger, relatively slow growth can be expected for the gas utility operations in its mature market. In contrast, the communications and cablevision subsidiaries may be presumed to grow rapidly in the future based on past experience and industry conditions.

CFS per share is estimated to grow at an annual rate of 3 percent throughout the forecast period as earnings from the communications and cablevision subsidiary increasingly replace revenues from the gas utility. Dividends may be anticipated to increase at an annual rate of 2.5 percent.

As a result of anticipated favorable merger terms, MCN stock bore a significant premium to the price estimated by the CFS growth model in 1988. If this merger does not go through, the future price of MCN stock will fall as merger speculation dissipates. This factor in 1990 has been reflected in a $5.00 downward adjustment in the forecasting model.

National Fuel Gas Company (NFG)

NFG is a public utilities holding company distributing natural gas in and around Buffalo, New York. The company has good access to Canadian gas through its own pipeline supply network and engages in minor exploration activities.

The successful adoption of the U.S.-Canadian free trade pact should add a strong boost to the economic resurgence of NFG's service area. NFG is well positioned to benefit from this growth.

CFS is likely to grow at an annual rate of 4 percent through 1995 and 3 percent thereafter. Prior to 1989, the company had recorded 17 years of increased dividends. This pattern may be expected to continue with an average 3 percent increment over the forecast period.

In 1989, this company was slightly undervalued relative to the predictions of the CFS growth model. An adjustment of one is made to the model's growth factor for future price estimates as a consequence of the increased growth expected from increased U.S.-Canada trade. A negative adjustment of $1.25 is made to the model's forecasting base.

New Jersey Resources Corporation (NJRC)

NJRC is the holding company for New Jersey Natural Gas, a regulated utility supplying natural gas to rapidly growing mideastern

New Jersey. NJRC is attempting to develop access to low-cost supplies through an equity position in a Canadian pipeline.

Heavy capital spending will be necessary to accommodate the expected rapid growth of the early 1990s. As earnings fall off in the face of rising gas prices in the mid-1990s, CFS should remain strong supporting the dividend payment.

CFS is anticipated to increase 3.5 percent through 1994 and 1 percent annually thereafter. Dividends are expected to grow at an annual rate of 2 percent through 1992 and 3 percent thereafter.

NICOR, Inc.

NICOR owns the large regulated Northern Illinois Gas Company as well as having diversified into oil and gas exploration and the offshore containerized shipping business. Profits in its mature service area are dependent on regulatory favor. The subsidiaries are likely to experience good growth, but their operations are small relative to regulated gas sales. Good regional prospects for gas fired cogeneration operations resulted in a $10.00 adjustment to the forecasting model in 1990.

CFS is expected to increase at an annual rate of 2 percent until 1993, 1 percent between 1993 and 1995, and to fall 1 percent throughout the balance of the forecast period. Dividends may be expected to average an increase of 1 percent throughout the forecast period as a result of NICOR's exceptionally solid financial condition in 1989.

As a result of NICOR's limited growth prospects, its CFS growth model's growth factor is given an adjustment of –1 in predicting future stock price.

NUI Corporation (NUI)

NUI owns two regulated gas utilities: Elizabethtown Gas Company (73 percent of its customers) serving east central New Jersey and City Gas Company serving the east coast of Florida.

The acquisition of City Gas will dilute per-share earnings because both service areas offer limited growth prospects. The Elizabethtown area in New Jersey is mature, while the demand for gas in South Florida is weak and will become weaker in the face of rising energy costs.

CFS is expected to rise at an annual rate of 3 percent until 1993, remain unchanged for the following two years, and then fall at an average rate of 2 percent for the remainder of the forecast period. Dividends are likely to stay flat at $1.56 through 1991 as the City Gas acquisition is integrated into existing operations, then a token increase to $1.60 will occur. Dividends will stay at that level through 1999, although the high payout rate toward the end of the period will increase the likelihood of a dividend cut.

As a result of the premium carried by the DDM relative to the NUI stock price in 1989, a downward adjustment of $1.50 is made for the price of this firm's stock in the future.

Northwest Natural Gas Co. (NNG)

NNG is a regulated utility distributing natural gas to communities in Oregon and Washington. Moderate growth in the residential sector (40 percent) of its service area may be expected through 1999, but its dependence on a cost-conscious industrial sector will lend a high degree of uncertainty to its earning power. Bypass will remain a serious problem for NNG and probably limit its earnings potential. Profitability will be chiefly a function of how willing the regulatory commission is to raise the residential tariff. Favorable tariff decisions in 1990 resulted in an addition of $3.00 to the company's base forecast.

CFS is anticipated to increase at a rate of 3 percent through 1992, 2 percent through 1995, and decline at an annual rate of 1 percent following that point. Dividends may be expected to average a 2 percent increase through 1994 and 1 percent thereafter.

Pacific Enterprises Corporation (PEC)

PEC is a diversified holding company owning the nation's largest gas utility (Southern California Gas Company) and having exploration and production and specialty retailing subsidiaries. Continued growth may be expected in its service area and the exploration and production subsidiary should make a nice contribution to earnings over the forecast period. These bright prospects resulted in an addition of $4.50 to share price in 1990.

CFS may be expected to grow at a rate of 4.5 percent until 1994, a 3 percent rate through 1996, and 1 percent thereafter. Dividends will probably be flat through 1992 (with the utility under some pressure for a dividend cut owing to share dilution consequent on the acquisition of Sabine Corporation—its exploration and production subsidiary—in 1988). Investors may then look forward to an increase in dividends at a 3 percent rate to 1995 and a 2 percent rate thereafter.

Peoples Energy Corporation

Peoples Energy is a holding company for two regulated utilities: Peoples Gas Light & Coke and North Shore Gas. These utilities provide gas in the relatively mature Chicago and eastern Illinois areas. Competition is heavy in its areas. A cold winter in 1990 boosted earnings and resulted in an addition of $1.50 to PE's forecasted share price. More than 20 percent of its business in 1989 was transport for industrial customers who purchased the gas elsewhere. The fight to preserve market share will keep pressure on this firm's profit margins throughout the 1990s.

Prospective increases in CFS are anticipated to average 4 percent through 1994, 2 percent to 1996 and to decline 1 percent on average until 1999. The increases in cash flow will be accompanied by an average dividend increase of 3 percent. When CFS begins to decline, dividends will be held constant.

Piedmont Natural Gas Company

Piedmont is a regulated utility that distributes natural gas to 65 communities in the Carolinas and Tennessee. The company's service area shows good long-term growth potential. A favorable regulatory environment should allow Piedmont to register significant bottom-line growth through the early 1990s. This was reflected in a market performance in 1990 which resulted in a $4.50 addition to the model forecast base. Increased gas prices in the mid-1990s will bring about a rapid deterioration of earnings.

CFS should average a 7 percent gain through 1993, a 4 percent gain through 1995, and a 2 percent annual increase for the remainder of the forecast period. Investors may expect dividends to move along at a 5 percent pace through 1995, but to fall to the 2 percent level for the remainder of the decade.

Piedmont stock is currently (1989) overvalued relative to its existing cash flow. This represents an acknowledgment by the market of its growth outlook. No change is necessary for the CFS growth model.

Providence Energy Corporation (PEC)

PEC is a regulated utility distributing natural gas to 22 communities in Rhode Island and Massachusetts. Its service area has moderately good growth prospects throughout the 1990s and its revenue base is stable with 63 percent of its revenues derived from residential business. PEC is becoming involved in cogeneration projects that will prove quite profitable by the mid-1990s when the energy shortage in New England is in full force.

As a result of a surge in capital spending at the end of the 1980s, PEC will enjoy an 11 percent increase in CFS through 1993, an 8 percent increase through 1995, and a 4 percent increase for the remainder of the forecast period. Dividend growth averaging 7 percent through 1995 is anticipated. Dividends are then expected to grow at 5 percent throughout the 1990s. A positive $3.00 adjustment is made to PEC's forecast base to relfect these favorable prospects.

Questar Corporation

Questar is a holding company whose subsidiaries include Mountain Fuel Supply Company (a regulated utility distributing natural gas in Utah and Wyoming) and Questar Pipeline Company (which owns and operates gas transmission lines in Utah, Colorado and Wyoming). Questar's revenues and profitability are sensitive to industry conditions in the steel manufacturing and mining industries. Increased growth is dependent on Questar's ability to extend its service lines to new areas.

CFS will grow 6 percent through 1992 as gas fundamentals improve and industrial customers switch to gas. Contributions to the bottom line from its exploration and production subsidiaries will maintain CFS growth at the 5 percent level through 1996. CFS growth will slow to 2 percent for the remainder of the forecast period. Dividends will grow at 6 percent through 1992, 4 percent between 1992 and 1996, and 3 percent thereafter. A $1.00 adjustment is made to the model base to reflect 1990 market conditions.

South Jersey Industries (SJI)

SJI is a holding whose principle subsidiary is South Jersey Gas Company, a regulated utility distributing natural gas to Atlantic City and its environs. The spread of suburban Philadelphia across the Delaware River and the resurgent Atlantic City economy will give SJC strong earnings momentum well into the 1990s.

CFS is expected to increase at a 9 percent annual rate through 1995 and 7 percent thereafter. Dividend growth will be slowed by the need to finance expansion. Dividends are expected to average a 5 percent increase throughout the forecast period. Disappointing earnings in 1990 resulted in a negative $4.00 adjustment to share prices.

The depressed stock price for SJI in 1990 combined with its strong prospects for growth offers investors an exceptional opportunity. An annual return from 1990 prices through 1994 will yield investors expected annual returns of 26 percent.

Southwest Gas Corporation (SGC)

SGC is a diversified company with subsidiaries that are regulated distributors of natural gas in Nevada, Arizona and California. SGC also operates small gas production companies and pipelines, as well as Primerit—a federal savings bank. The market served by the utility is exceptionally stable (82 percent of revenues are derived from residential customers) but has limited growth prospects.

CFS is expected to increase 5 percent annually through 1993, 4 percent until 1996 and 2 percent thereafter. Dividends are expected to grow 4 percent annually through 1996 and 3 percent thereafter.

The growth factor in the DDM is given a negative adjustment of .5 and the model constant is reduced $4.75 to correct for the excessive model error in 1989. The error may reflect SGC's involvement with its financial subsidiary, which only converted from S & L status in 1989, at a time when all S & L's were suspect.

UGI Corporation (UGI)

UGI Corporation has two principal subsidiaries: a regulated utility which distributes natural gas in eastern Pennsylvania and Cal Gas, the fourth largest marketer of propane gas.

Its utility operations suffer from the competition of alternative fuels and the threat of bypass as only 25 percent of its revenues are derived from residential sales. Aggresive marketing has helped UGI maintain market share through 1990 resulting in a positive $6.75 adjustment to its forecast base in 1990. The forces of competition will keep even rising oil prices from making significant increases to the bottom line.

In contrast, the propane market is likely to boom throughout the 1990s. This business can be quite profitable and UGI appears well positioned to take advantage of coming events.

CFS is anticipated to increase at 5 percent through 1992 and 7 percent thereafter. Dividends are expected to average an annual increase of 5 percent throughout the forecast period.

Washington Energy Company (WEC)

WEC is a holding company whose principal subsidiary is the Washington Natural Gas Company, a regulated utility distributing natural gas in the Puget Sound area. WEC is also involved in coal mining, transportation, exploration and production.

Although its financial performance in the last part of the 1980s was poor, the utility subsidiary has gained considerable penetration in a market that shows good growth potential. However, higher gas prices in the 1990s may slow the growth in the bottom line as customers are attracted to competing fuels or cheap hydroelectric power. As a result the model forecast was lowered by a constant $2.50 throughout the forecast period.

CFS is expected to rebound to $3.65 in 1989 and increase at a rate of 5 percent until 1994. Thereafter, CFS is expected to grow at 2.5 percent per year for the remainder of the forecast period. Dividends of $1.30 are expected in 1989 and will increase at an annual rate of 3 percent until 1995 and 2 percent until 1999.

Washington Gas Light Company (WGL)

WGL is a regulated utility distributing natural gas in the metropolitan Washington, D.C., area; it also owns a small exploration and production subsidiary.

WGL's future in the 1990s will be characterized by rapid sales growth from new customers and heavy capital expenditures to finance the necessary expansion of facilities. This potential added $5.50 to share prices throughout the forecast period.

Estimated CFS in 1989 of $2.40 is expected to grow at an annual rate of 6 percent through 1994 and 3 percent thereafter. Dividends will grow at an average rate of 2.5 percent through 1995 and 3 percent thereafter.

WICOR Inc.

Wicor is a holding company whose largest subsidiary is Wisconsin Gas Company, a regulated Wisconsin gas utility. Wicor also owns a pump manufacturing subsidiary and an oil and gas exploration company.

The utility subsidiary faces the doubly tough task of growing in a low-growth economy while facing excessive competition from fuel oil for its industrial customers. Success in 1990, however, raised its forecast base $1.00 per share.

CFS is anticipated to rise at a rate of 4 percent through 1992, 2 percent through 1996 and decline 1 percent a year thereafter. Dividends are expected to rise at a 2 percent rate until 1997 and then remain flat.

Summary

The rankings for the 29 distribution companies by expected TRR may be found in Table 10.1. As a group, distribution companies offer cautious investors an average combination of risk and return into the mid-1990s.

These expected returns were based upon a direct application of the DDM to anticipated cash flows and to forecast dividends. With the exception of a major energy crisis resulting in exploding energy prices (an unlikely event in the 1990s), little downside risk is found in this sector.

Chapter 11

TELECOMMUNICATION INDUSTRY FUNDAMENTALS

Organizational Overview of the Telecommunications Industry

Past, present, and future conditions in the telecommunications industry are examined in Chapters 11-14. Chapter 11 identifies technology as the driving force in the industry and scrutinizes the implications of this for investors. Chapter 12 explores the factors influencing the financial performance of the 10 largest independent telephone companies. Specific consideration is given to the impact of mergers and acquisitions on these firms. Returns are forecast for this group through 1999. Chapter 13 examines those factors bearing on the potential return on investment in the seven bell regional holding companies in the coming decade. Chapter 14 investigates the financial performance of the four major common carriers during the 1990s.

Telecommunications Industry Performance Overview

Exceptional gains are anticipated for investors in the telecommunications industry throughout the 1990s, though these potential returns will not be without considerable risk.

A major source of gains will come from the tremendous profits accruing to those firms able to convert new technologies into marketable successes. It is, however, difficult to pinpoint the degree of success that any given firm will experience in this highly competitive and fast-moving market. Even the more established firms in this industry have yet to prove their ability in this type of market.

A second major source of profits will arise because of the possibilities for friendly or unfriendly takeovers. The telecommunications industry is characterized by a relatively few large cash-rich established firms who have trouble being innovative and a plethora of aggressive capital-short firms with strong desires to open new markets and exploit new technologies. The disparity between these two types of firms creates a situation ripe for acquisitions.

Industry Structure

When dated from the Simplex Telegraph wire, the telecommunication industry is about 150 years old and its evolution throughout suggests powerful interrelationships between employment patterns, economic prosperity and information services. These interrelationships indicate that economic prosperity results from a substitution of capital for labor and that information services are a necessary catalyst to this process. The telecommunications industry is sometimes spoken of as mature—nothing could be further from the truth.

Continued economic growth will require increasing telecommunications services. The use of the market mechanism of profit (and loss) to spur the implementation of these new technologies is suggestive of a promising situation emerging for investor gains.

Telecommunications activities are still beginning an exponential growth curve. Even prior to 1990, it was not uncommon for workers to work at home on computers and then download such work to their office. Insurance companies in California and New York commonly use a computer to scan claim forms and then transmit them to Ireland for processing and receive them back during the course of one working day. Managers of automobile plants located in Michigan, California, New Jersey and Mexico regularly teleconference to coordinate production schedules. The Eastern Management Group estimates that in 1989 8 percent of the budget of Fortune 1,000 firms was spent on communication. This figure is expected to rise to 10 percent by 1993.

The future will bring integrated global data networks, a global financial community, increasingly automated and decentralized factories, the increasingly widespread use of artificial intelligence (made possible by advances in computer technology) to supplant human thought and the increasing use of robotics to replace human brawn.

All this will require a tremendous increase in information exchange. The demand for telecommunications services will continue to increase dramatically into the foreseeable future.

Industry Environment

The overwhelming characteristic of the industry today is dynamic change, fueled by technological advances, driven by fierce competition, and made possible by an administratively contrived competitive environment. Although the industry is still dominated by the legacy of the old AT&T system, strong competitive behaviors are emerging in all sectors of the industry.

Technological change has made competition possible in many of the telecommunication market segments that have traditionally been thought of as natural monopolies. This competition has been carefully fostered by the FCC and the Judge (Greene) charged with the responsibility of supervising the 1982 consent decree that resulted in the divestiture of AT&T's operating companies. Where competition is not possible, regulations have been designed to cause the types of behavior that would occur if competition were present.

The combination of competition and technological advances has brought about a significant increase in the array of telecommunication products and services available. Many of these new products are being developed in unregulated portions of the industry, prompting considerable diversification into these areas by almost all firms in the industry. In addition, there exists a veritable swarm of small new market entrants with ambitious plans for exploiting the new technologies. The existence of capital-hungry firms in the proximity of cash-rich firms (the larger, established telecommunications firms) suggests possibilities for mutually beneficial mergers and consolidations.

The results of this situation have benefitted the consumer. While the costs of local service rose 35 percent between 1984 and 1989, it did not deter an increase in the percentage of U.S. households with phones from 91 percent in 1984 to 93 percent in 1989. It may be that the consumer perceives that the extraordinary range of options now available with phone service has increased its value despite the rise in price. Long distance rates have fallen considerable since divestiture and promise to fall even further in the 1990s. Overall phone costs increased about 16 percent between 1984 and 1989.

Returns to investors in this industry have been generally excellent since divestiture, and offer much promise for the future. While it is hard to find a telecommunications firm that has performed poorly in the post-divestiture period, the dynamics of competition ensure greater variability of performance in the future.

Financial Performance 1984–1988

Returns to investors during this period ranged from extraordinary to unsatisfactory. For the most part, investors in the telecommunication service industry reaped above average returns between 1984 and 1989. The annual returns accruing to investors who bought at the beginning of 1984 and sold at the end of 1989 are listed in Table 11.1.

The strongest performances were turned in by those independent telephone companies who aggressively sought emerging opportunities in the midst of deregulation and technological change. The market rewarded those telecommunications companies perceived as having proven their growth potential with significant stock price appreciation.

Investors in the seven baby bells during this period also received a handsome return, well above that provided by fixed income securities. These strong returns were especially significant given that the RHCs were in a transitional stage, adjusting to new found freedoms in an era of structured deregulation.

Less aggressive independent telecommunications companies and the diversified carriers tended to show a weaker performance between 1984 and 1989 as the market judged them to have significantly less proven growth potential than the other firms in this in-

Table 11.1   Telecommunication Companies

TRR Rank 1984-88		TRR 1984-89
1	Century Telephone Enterprises	60.26%
2	Cincinnati Bell Inc.	52.90%
3	C-Tec Corporation	51.84%
4	Citizens Utilities "B"	37.29%
5	Pacific Telesis Group	33.44%
6	NYNEX Corporation	32.68%
7	Bell Atlantic Corporation	32.63%
8	American Information Technologies	32.50%
9	United Telecommunications, Inc.	31.47%
10	Bellsouth Corporation	31.43%
11	U.S. West Inc.	31.00%
12	Centel Corporation	30.93%
13	Southwestern Bell Corp.	30.53%
14	Alltel Corporation	30.07%
15	Contel Corporation	27.66%
16	Rochester Telephone Corporation	24.22%
17	MCI Communications Corp.	21.66%
18	Southern New England Telephone	21.48%
19	American Telephone (AT&T)	20.82%
20	GTE Corporation	20.62%
21	Communications Satellite Corp. (COMSAT)	–1.18%

dustry. These firms may well have significant growth potential, however as of 1989, the market has judged this potential to be speculative.

Although the conventional long distance carriers performed well, returns in this area were significantly below those of the RHCs and many of the ITCs. That profits were less robust for these carriers is eloquent testimony to the vitiating effects of price competition as AT&T struggled to hold market share in the face of aggressive new competitors. COMSAT, with a singularly poor performance, stands apart from the group as the new technologies effectively permitted invasion of its territorial monopoly.

Future Returns

Independent operating companies Anticipated returns to investors from the independent telephone companies in the 1990s will range from outstanding to mediocre. The forecast returns are presented in Table 11.2. The general rational for these forecasts and individual company prospects in this period are fully discussed in Chapter 12.

Alltel appears to have significant potential for growth in earnings that is not factored into its 1990 price. Century, Centel and C-Tec are poised for significant gains and their price has not run up sufficiently to diminish the incentive to invest. Cincinnati Bell's 1990 price has full discounted almost all possible future earnings gains. Contel, GTE and SNET have yet to prove they have the ability to exploit the opportunities presently in their markets.

Regional Operating Companies (RHCs) The RHCs are expected to turn in a generally strong performance during the forecast period. However, this return will be significantly below that obtained in the 1984–1988 period.

The returns will not be as high as in the earlier period because of the emerging forces of competition and the threat of bypass. Southwestern Bell turns in a leading performance based on the assumed recovery of the southwest oil economy. NYNEX lags the pact because of unsuccessful diversification efforts and tremendous pressure on margins from the threat of bypass. The forecasted returns for the RHCs are presented in Table 11.2. The rationale for these forecasts are developed in Chapter 13.

Common Carriers The market for long distance and enhanced telecommunication services is seen to grow at a 15 percent rate throughout the forecast period. Translating this growth into profits will be difficult since the firms in this sector will experience price competition as they struggle for market share. Profit performance will nevertheless be strong as these firms benefit from having great operating leverage in an environment of real growth.

Table 11.2   Forecast Returns
Telecommunications

1990-94 TRR Rank		TRR 1990-94	TRR 1990-99
1	Alltel Corporation	32.5%	20.2%
2	Contel Corporation	24.0%	18.8%
3	United Telecommunications	23.2%	23.6%
4	Southwestern Bell Corp.	21.6%	21.6%
5	Rochester Telephone Corporation	21.1%	17.3%
6	Century Telephone Enterprises	19.8%	17.4%
7	MCI	18.4%	18.7%
8	Centel Corporation	18.4%	15.3%
9	GTE Corporation	17.1%	18.5%
10	Pacific Telesis Group	16.8%	16.8%
11	Bell Atlantic Corporation	16.4%	15.4%
12	Citizens Utilities "B"	15.8%	10.3%
13	Bellsouth Corporation	14.2%	15.2%
14	C-Tec Corporation	13.2%	10.8%
15	U.S. West Inc.	12.7%	12.6%
16	Ameritech	12.3%	11.6%
17	AT&T	11.6%	11.6%
18	Cincinnati Bell Inc.	10.8%	10.8%
19	Southern New England Telephone	10.6%	14.1%
20	NYNEX Corporation	8.5%	8.3%
21	COMSAT	5.4%	5.4%

COMSAT will continue to lose business to fibre optics transmission. Industry conditions and the assumptions behind these forecasts are discussed in Chapter 14.

Industry Structure

Regulatory Policy Understanding current regulatory policy in the telecommunications industry is of critical importance in evaluating the prospects of individual firms in the industry. The late 1980s saw the birth of a new regulatory philosophy that prefers to induce competitive behavior through administrative force. Depending on how this philosophy unfolds on a practical level, this change creates great opportunities and threats for all firms in the industry.

Competition by regulation implies opportunities for both extraordinary profits and for potential losses. The investor can no longer use the guaranteed rate of return mentality that allowed a focus on dividend yield. The inherent volatility in the present industry structure requires a realistic consideration of each firm's present and future market position to determine future earnings.

Regulation will determine the character of the playing field for a given market. AT&T cries out for a "level playing field." MCI desires "fair" competition. Regulators want a rational environment that yields a competitive outcome.

Whatever characteristics evolve in the market as a result of regulatory intervention, profit outcomes will depend on the strengths of a given firm relative to those of existing and potential competitors. The situation is further complicated by the possibility that if the regulators (primarily Judge Greene and the FCC) do not like the outcome, they may well change the characteristics of the playing field. Therefore, attention must be paid to both existing regulatory policies and to philosophical trends that will shape future regulatory policy.

Regulation in the telecommunications industry has been, and remains, quite dynamic. In general, the basic policy thrust has been to adapt the regulatory environment to major economic, technological, and political changes rather than to refine traditional regulatory tools developed at some prior point in time.

The justification for regulation in the industry is found in (1) the existence of natural monopoly conditions, (2) the potential for competition to interfere with accepted social norms and (3) the "essential" nature of communications. As a result, Congress created the Federal Communications Commission (FCC) with the passage of the Communications Act of 1934 to consolidate communications jurisdiction into a single agency and provide central guidance for communications policy.

The FCC has interpreted its underlying statutory objectives (in a 1976 Docket No. 18128 decision) to be

(1) equitable treatment of system services;
(2) carrier operational efficiency and innovation;
(3) managerial accountability for its rate structure, investment, and other actions;
(4) fair competition; and
(5) clarity in operating rules for planning purposes.

For all effective purposes, it may be said that these goals translate into a desire for equity, efficiency and universal telephone service (UTS).

The goal of equity is both an appealing moral value and a necessary complement to the new regulatory philosophy. Equity implies an equal footing for all participants in a market, large and small, established and newcomer, alike. An equal footing is suggestive of an ability to successfully compete in a given market. Where competition does not meet the classic test of the inability of an individual firm to effect equilibrium price, competition should be "workable." Workable competition becomes kind of an artificially fostered substitute for classic competition, which brings about socially desirable outputs and an efficient allocation of resources. Achieving equity in this sense creates the necessary conditions for workable competition.

Efficiency is sought after in two senses: (1) to encourage the development and utilization of new communications technologies and (2) to eliminate waste and inefficiency from conventional utility organizations. The experiences of the 1970s strongly suggested that the bureaucratic inertia and organizational resistance to change inherent in an administered regulatory system had a chilling impact on the introduction of new technologies into the telecommunications field. It is felt that firms in a workable competitive environment will aggressively seek to develop and deploy new technologies to achieve "first mover" advantages. A corollary expectation is that the uninhibited introduction of technological innovation will drive user costs down.

Universal Telephone Service (UTS) is the concept that all individuals should have access to the telecommunications system. This concept has moral validity as an egalitarian ideal (telephone service is a right that is not influenced by income, location or personal circumstances) and desirability as a social goal (the telephone system is more valuable to each individual in society as more individuals are connected with the system). UTS may be interpreted to mean that everyone should simply have access to the system or that everyone should be able to afford system usage. There exists considerable political pressure for the latter interpretation. Past practices have funded this interpretation by charging in excess of costs for more inelastic telephone services, e.g., long distance. The effect of the structured deregulation now being implemented is to eliminate this kind of cross-subsidization. The justification for this situation is that competition will promote efficiency and technological innovation and ultimately bring about lower costs.

Prior to deregulation, the political appeal of providing lifeline telephone services and telephone service to the economically disadvantaged at nominal cost led to the widespread situation in which long distance rates were effectively set so as to subsidize flat rate (unlimited local calling) telephone service. The separation of long distance services from local services consequent on deregulation has set the stage for this subsidization to end. The forces of competition (including the threat of bypass) for long distance service is reducing long distance rates to cost of service.

As a result, their has been a tremendous shift in the cost structure of telephone service. Costs of long distance service have fallen dramatically (and will continue to fall into the mid-1990s) since deregulation. Lower rates for long distance services have prompted increased usage and net revenue gains for the carriers. In contrast, since deregulation established common carriers (ECCs) have filed for massive rate increases to cover the cost of providing UTS. Rate increases for this service, which has a relatively inelastic demand, has led to increased net revenues for this service.

The demands of equity in this context have resulted in an unbundling of local telephone services. The pricing of individual services (e.g., operator assistance and information) has created an increased interest in local measured service (LMS). LMS basically requires the individual to pay for services actually used as contrasted to flat rate service, which allows an individual an unlimited amount of local calling for one fee.

This situation has been made more palatable by technological advances resulting in a proliferation of attractive services (e.g., call forwarding and conference calling) that are characterized by relatively inelastic demand. Since the marginal cost of these services is quite low (relative to average costs), it is possible in the absence of significant competitive pressure to set tariffs so that the these new attractive products can subsidize the basic (lifeline) telephone service, at least in the short run. As the environment becomes increasingly competitive, or if the rate of new product development slows, the ability of the BOCs to continue this practice will be diminished.

Regulation and Deregulation The primary method the FCC used to regulate AT&T's interstate services between 1934 and 1965 was called "continuing surveillance." This constituted a process of informal negotiation between AT&T and the FCC over system revenue requirements. During this period of time the market for telephone services closely resembled the conditions necessary for a natural monopoly (i.e., an absence of competitive products). The self-serving implications of this arrangement were mitigated by continuous decreases in the effective cost of system services resulting from technological advances. The focus of the FCC was on deterring monopoly pricing, i.e., pricing above cost.

In the late 1950s, AT&T's concern over emerging competition from private microwave systems led to tariff requests that began to shift the focus of the FCC's attention to the below-cost pricing of certain services by AT&T in order to prevent the introduction of competing services and technologies. This led to an era of service specific rate-of-return regulation (ROR) with selective open entry for competitors between 1965 and 1979.

ROR regulation sets the revenue required by the firm equal to its cost of service. Cost of service is equal to the total of its operating expenses, depreciation, taxes, and an allowed rate of return on the depreciated value of the assets used to produce the public utility service. ROR regulation is a simple task for a single product monopoly. ROR regulation for a multiproduct firm in a variety of markets with varying levels of competition is quite another story.

Effectively implementing ROR regulation requires correctly allocating costs among the different services provided by the carriers. The FCC attempt to develop a specific fully distributed costing methodology (Method 7) was never completely effective as the pace of technological change began to snowball in the 1970s. By the late 1970s, considerable evidence had accumulated that not only was ROR regulation difficult to implement, but that it inherently produced an array of economic distortions and inefficiencies.

At this time there also developed a growing disenchantment with the purpose and value of market intervention by federal authorities. While the reasons for this dissatisfaction were complex, the central concern was that regulation provided few consumer benefits relative to its cost and contributed substantially to the inflationary pressures of the era.

With the arrival of Charles Ferris as FCC Chairman in 1977, the philosophy of the FCC shifted from that of regulating a monopoly market structure to ensuring the presence of a workable competitive market structure. The basic view shifted from the notion that competition could be an effective complement to regulation, to the idea that competition could be a substitute for regulation.

This situation led to the current philosophy, which may be called selective competition or structured regulation. Structured regulation has two major components. First, where telecommunications firms possess little or no market power, they should be deregulated. The assumption being market forces will bring about a socially optimal allocation of resources. Second, in those sectors of the industry where firms retain sufficient market power so that regulation is necessary to avoid abuses of monopoly power, the traditional command tools of the regulators should not be used. Rather, command tools should be replaced with structural separation requirements (e.g., tariff restructuring, requiring shared use of services, or suppressing anticompetitive behaviors) which cause these firms to behave as if they were being regulated by competitive forces.

The application of ROR regulation by the beginning of the 1980s was no longer popular with the general public, the regulators, or many politicians. ROR regulation increasingly resembled a Rube Goldberg contraption. The attempts to achieve equity and efficiency in the context of exploding technological change became increasing tortureous for all concerned. Finally, AT&T capitulated to the forces pressing for structured deregulation.

On January 8, 1982, a consent agreement was reached between AT&T and the Department of Justice to settle a 1974 antitrust complaint and replace a 1956 consent decree. This agreement was approved by Judge Greene of the United States District Court for the District of Columbia who retained the right to administer and review the decree. Subsequent modifications of the decree were embodied in a modified final judgement (MFJ) and implemented on January 1, 1984. As subsequently amended, the MFJ basically provided that:

(1) AT&T must divest itself of its 22 local telephone companies (referred to as BOCs-basic operating companies) which were permitted to organize into seven consolidated entities (RHCs-regional holding companies).

(2) AT&T was allowed to retain its long distance network (long lines), Western Electric, and Bell Labs.

(3) The BOCs were not allowed to offer telephone services outside of their specifically designated areas (LATAs-Local Access Transport Areas).

(4) The BOCs were required to provide equal and nondiscriminatory access to all carriers on a tariffed and unbundled basis.

(5) The RHCs were not allowed to manufacture customer premises equipment (CPE).

(6) AT&T cellular phone, directory and CPE operations were transferred to the RHCs.

(7) Each RHC owns a regional service company (RSC) and one seventh of a Central Services Organization (CSO) that provides technical and administrative functions to the 22 BOCs and the minority owned Cincinnati Bell and Southern New England Telephone companies.

AT&T's manufacturing activities, Bell Labs and its information system were organized into AT&T Technologies. Long lines, along with former BOC long distance functions and facilities, were organized into AT&T Communications.

Diversification The effect of deregulation was to liberate the RHCs from their traditional role of providing local telephone service. The RHCs quickly demonstrated a significant desire for diversification into the many new and highly profitable emerging markets in the telecommunications industry. Consequently, Judge Greene issued an opinion that these diversification efforts were harmful to the RHC's obligations under the MFJ to provide equal access and high quality local telephone service. In addition, diversification was seen to raise a problem in detecting cross-subsidization activities.

The outcome of this opinion was that future requests to waive line of business restrictions contained in the MFJ would require four conditions:

(1) All non-regulated operations must be conducted through separate subsidiaries,

(2) These subsidiaries must obtain credit on their own account and may not obligate the assets of a BOC.

(3) No proposed activity may have estimated revenues that exceeds 10 percent of the total estimated revenues for an RHC.

(4) The Department of Justice was to review all such waiver requests.

Point (3) above has since been eliminated. While these restrictions have not impeded a successful performance by the RHCs to the present time, these restriction do limit the opportunities of these companies for major diversification efforts. Judge Greene apparently has strong concerns that extensive diversification efforts by the RHCs may detract from their ability to optimize the delivery of local telephone service. The significance of these limitations is further discussed in Chapter 15.

Bypass The bypass issue is important because of its implications for the strength of competition in the telecommunications industry. Bypass occurs when an existing franchised telecommunications service (i.e., an established common carrier) is circumvented by an alternative means of communication. Bypass may effect a long distance carrier (e.g., when AT&T lays an underwater fibre optics cable between the U.S. and Europe bypassing COMSAT) or a BOC (e.g., where a large brokerage firm located in New York City replaces its interoffice communication by public telephone with a private telecommunication system.) The greatest threat of bypass appears to be to the BOCs, particularly to those in metropolitan areas where a high concentration of access lines make bypass economically feasible.

Bypass may be economic if the cost of the alternative is lower or the quality of the service is higher. As a result of technological advances a wide spectrum of alternative communication means are now available. Prompted by a host of new market entrants, BOCs are scrambling to remain a dominant provider of telecommunication services in their markets. However, they are likely to loose dominance in a number of important segments. This may severely impact earnings and growth opportunities over the long run.

Bypass may be non-economic if the ECC rates are set above cost of service and the user benefits from the avoidance of this premium. The potential for non-economic bypass will continue to force a rationalization of the tariff structure at BOCs through the mid-1990s.

Bypass may be user initiated and may be aided by the ECC (established common carrier) if it is economic or if the local regulatory agency will not permit a fall in rates sufficient to deter bypass. In either case, there is a loss of revenue to the ECC that in the long run will reduce profits for the ECC and raise costs to the remaining consumers served.

Cellular Mobile Telephones Cellular mobile telephones (CMT) constitute the fastest growing segment of the telecommunications industry. The market for this service is likely to hit $3 billion in 1990 and has the potential to reach $10 billion by 1999. In the late 1980s and early 1990s the thrust of diversification in the telecommunications industry will be towards CMT. Developed by Bell Labs in the 1960s, this form of communication is comparable in quality to landline service and offers the American public what it wants most in any product—convenience. The bright future for this service ensures that many of the small independent companies now developing this market will eventually be absorbed by larger established telecommunication companies who will be glad to pay a premium price for a growth opportunity.

CMT is an unregulated industry on the basis of price or profits. However, the FCC has the authority to allocate frequency spectrum for this purpose and to determine the extent and number of operators in a given cellular geographic service area (CGSA). As of 1986, the FCC had allocated 59 MHz of spectrum to CMT communication, allowing for a total of 832 two-way channels. In 1981, each of the 305 Standard Metropolitan Statistical Areas (SMSAs) was designated a CGSA and provided for the licensing of two CMT operators in each SMSA. One operator was to be the local BOC and the other license was granted to the highest bidder (other than the local BOC). In 1988, the FCC began accepting applications for licenses in rural service areas (RSAs).

CMT derives its name from the small regions (cells) into which a CGSA or RSA is divided. Each cell is equipped with a transmitting/receiving base station. Each base station is connected to a switching facility, which then uses a computer to coordinate transmission calls to the transmitting/receiving units traveling through the different cells of the CGSA or RSA.

Instead of transmitting its signal throughout the service area, a given base station only transmits throughout the cell. This means the same channel can be used simultaneously for several calls (frequency reuse) as cells adjacent to one another can use the same frequency without interference from each other. This effectively increases system capacity far above that suggested by the absolute number of available channels.

As of 1988, 1.5 million CMTs were in actual operation, a figure expected to increase to 2.5 million in 1990. This rapid growth requires extensive capital to finance it, a situation that has tended to attract the large cash-rich RHCs into the field (e.g., Pacific Telesis's acquisition of Communications Industries, Southwestern Bell's acquisitions from Metromedia and Bellsouth's purchase of Mobile Communication's CMT operations). This tendency may be expected to be observed throughout the forecast period. The extraordinary rise in the costs of acquiring a CMT franchise that took place in the late 1980s suggests that the costs of acquiring an established CMT company will rise to astounding heights by the end of the forecast period.

Financial Performance: 1984–1988

Independent Telephone Companies Returns to investors from ITCs during this period ranged from above average to absolutely outstanding. That 1984–1990 was a period of prosperity for the investor in this sector may be seen in Table 11.3.

The 11 firms in this sector share many similarities during this period. The primary activity in each of these firms is providing regulated telephone service (with the exception of Citizens Utilities) and each of the firms were actively diversifying into the unregulated sectors of the telecommunications industry. Cellular phones, paging services, long distance fibre optics transmission, data processing and information services proved popular directions for these firms.

An analysis of the financial performance of these firms during this period suggests that the market distinguished between six (Century, Cincinnati Bell, C-Tec, Citizens, United Telecommunications, and Rochester Telephone) of these firms that appeared to have proven their growth potential and a group of five (Alltel, Centel, Contel, SNET, and GTE) in which the potential for growth was treated as uncertain. This distinction does not refer to the potential for growth in earnings and revenues among these firms, but rather a difference in the manner in which the market has factored their growth potential into their stock price.

The distinction between these two groups of independent telephone companies is detailed in Table 11.4. GTE is considered separately because it is so large compared to the other ten firms and because of its association with Sprint.

Profits among all eleven firms increased as technological advancements permitted both profitable enhancements to the basic telephone service and reductions in costs. Profits were also helped during this period by a booming economy, the changing structure of telephone charges and a favorable regulatory environment.

Paradoxically, sales and profit gains were stronger among the uncertain growth firms and weaker among the proven growth

Table 11.3   Independent Telephone Companies

TRR Rank 1984-89		TRR 1984–89
1	Century Telephone Enterprises	60.26%
2	Cincinnati Bell Inc.	52.90%
3	C-Tec Corporation	51.84%
4	Citizens Utilities "B"	37.29%
5	United Telecommunications, Inc.	31.47%
6	Centel Corporation	30.93%
7	Alltel Corporation	30.07%
8	Contel Corporation	27.66%
9	Rochester Telephone Corporation	24.22%
10	Southern New England Telephone	21.48%
11	GTE Corporation	20.62%

firms. It would seem that the proven growth firms were more willing to sacrifice short-run profitability in order to strengthen long-run prospects. The bulk of the investment taking place among the proven growth firms was in cellular phone systems.

All firms in this sector responded to the presence of profitable opportunities in the telecommunications industry. All firms sought additional capital by increasing their common stock outstanding and cutting their dividends (as a percentage of earnings). However, those uncertain growth firms used their increased cash flow to strengthen their balance sheets while the proven growth firms aggressively expanded their long-term borrowings and reduced their common equity ratio.

This is not to suggest that the unproven growth firms have been moribund. Both Alltel and SNET have moved significantly into the cellular telephone market. Contel had a number of sizeable acquisitions during this period. GTE and United Telecommunications certainly made a major commitment to the future with their investment in the Sprint network. Rochester Telephone embarked on an aggressive local telephone company acquisition strategy.

Table 11.4   Performance Fundamentals
Independent Telephone Companies 1984–1988

Characteristic	Proven Growth	Uncertain Growth Little 4*	GTE
Average TRR			
1984–1988	36.3%	24.8%	20.6%
Average Sales ($000,000)			
1988	1,007.	1,471.	15,500.
1984	859.	1,148.	14,547
Change	17.2%	28.1%	6.5%
Profits			
1988	84.	139.	1,210.
1984	76.	106.	1,073.
Change	10.5%	31.1%	12.8%
Cash Flow/Share			
1988	5.94	9.43	11.25
Change from 1984	24.8%	27.4%	9.7%
Long-Term Debt Ratio			
1988	48.4	43.4	52.5
Change from 1984	2.1%	–4.8%	7.6%
Shares Outstanding			
Change 1984–1988	8.1%	9.7%	7.4%
Common Equity Ratio			
1988	50.0	52.5	43.5
Change from 1984	–1.0%	5.5%	3.1%
Percent of Revenues from Basic Telephone Operations	72.0%	75.0%	77.0%
Common Stock Dividend Yield			
1988	3.1%	5.0%	5.8%
Change from 1984	–59.8	–34.2	–18.3

* Little 4 include Alltel, Centel, Contel, and Southern New England Telephone.

Rather, the distinction between proven growth and uncertain growth is a matter of direction and degree. Sprint had yet to prove it had a commercial potential similar to that of the cellular telephone, particularly in a situation where operating control was shared by GTE and UTI. Contel's acquisitions have not proved successful. Alltel and SNET have not pursued the cellular phone market and/or other new markets with the zest of C-Tec, Centel, Century, and Cincinnati Bell.

This distinction between proven and uncertain growth firms among independent operating companies is confirmed by an analysis of the DDM in Chapter 12.

The relationship between price and cash flow among the proven growth firms suggests that the market has embedded these future growth prospects in their stock price. In contrast, the market had not factored significant future growth into the share price of uncertain growth firms by 1989. For uncertain growth firms, the market is awaiting confirmation that their potential can be converted to reality.

Regional Holding Companies The breakup of AT&T in 1984 created seven RBOCs with a total market value of over 45 billion dollars. The succeeding five years have seen the RHCs uniformly perform well. The returns to investors between 1984 and 1989 were substantial.

These gains primarily reflect rate increases by the BOCs for providing local telephone service and access. Rate increases have been facilitated by an environment in which the general fall in toll charges and the unbundling of services resulted in net lower rates for many consumers. The sustained economic expansion throughout the period also had a positive impact on this performance.

In the aftermath of deregulation, the RHCs have successfully negotiated new relationships with their state regulators, the FCC, Judge Greene, and the common carriers (primarily AT&T) that have allowed them to convert substantial increases in sales to even more substantial increases in profits in an environment characterized by the threat of competition, rapid technological change, and the proliferation of new products and services. This performance is detailed in Table 11.6.

Table 11.5   Regional Holding Companies

Rank 1984-89		TRR 1984-1989
1	Pacific Telesis Group	33.4%
2	NYNEX Corporation	32.7%
3	Bell Atlantic Corporation	32.6%
4	American Information Technologies	32.5%
5	Bellsouth Corporation	31.4%
6	U.S. West Inc.	31.0%
7	Southwestern Bell Corp.	30.5%

The excellent returns generated for investors during this period amply demonstrate that within the existing telecommunications industry and regulatory structure the RHCs are able to stand alone as independent companies. The opportunities they confronted were aggressively converted to substantial increases in revenues and profits. Their internal financial structures were strengthened. As a group, they appeared well positioned to offer investors attractive returns in the future.

The significant flows of free cash created from high earnings, depreciation and an effective cut in the dividend are being used to invest in new technologies and new sectors of the telecommunications market. Some of the RHCs have used a smaller portion of these cash flows to strengthen their balance sheets and increase the common equity ratio, while others have taken a more aggressive approach to the use of this cash. Some RHCs have reduced their common shares outstanding while Pacific Telesis and Bell South have increased their outstanding shares.

While investors in the different RHCs enjoyed similarly high returns, the differential in the increase in profits among the RHCs between 1984 and 1989 has been significant. Profit margins have increased for all RHCs except U.S. West and Bell South. Differing patterns in the financial performance among the RHCs should be expected to emerge as a result of differing economic environments,

Table 11.6   Performance Fundamentals Regional Holding Companies 1984–1988

Characteristic	Average	Standard Deviation
TRR, 1984–1988	32.0%	1.0%
Sales		
1988	10,419.	1,672.
1984	8,277.	920.
Change	25.3%	6.6%
Profits		
1988	1,269.	207.
1984	972.	135.
Change	30.2%	10.7%
Profit Margins		
1988	12.1	0.9
1984	11.8	0.9
Cash Flow/Share		
1988	12.51	4.02
1984	8.26	2.29
Change	50.2%	10.7%
Long-Term Debt Ratio		
1988	38.6	1.6
1984	41.2	1.5
Shares Outstanding		
1988	292.	108.
1984	290.	95.
Common Equity Ratio		
1988	61.6	1.7
1984	58.3	2.7
Percent of Revenues from basic telephone operations	85.6%	3.6%
Common Stock Dividend Yield		
1988	5.9%	0.2%
1984	9.3%	0.2%
Change from 1984	–36.2%	2.7%

disparate regulatory situations, and different business strategies. It is to be expected that these differentials will be increased in the future. This implies that the future will not bring such homogeneous returns to the investors in this group of firms.

Common Carriers The divestiture of its BOCs was the price AT&T paid for the freedom to compete to retain its hegemony in long-distance communications. While AT&T has not been able to halt the erosion in its market share, subsequent events have bought new vitality to the old warhorse. As can be seen from Table 11.7, AT&T's investors have fared well during this period.

Common Carriers (CCs) provide linkages between LATAs and other telecommunication systems. The three firms in this sector (AT&T, MCI, and COMSAT) all differ significantly in terms of history and market position. (As Sprint was jointly owned by UTI and GTE during this period, it is treated in the section examining the performance of ITCs.)

In 1984, AT&T was restructured into an entity that included the long distance phone lines and seven separate RHCs. AT&T retained its manufacturing activities, Bell Labs, and its information system as well. AT&T remains by far the largest telecommunications company in the United States. The period 1984 to 1988 was an era of transition for AT&T. There has been a continuing dialogue with Judge Greene, who retained the power to administer the consent decree which authorized the divestiture, the relationships to be negotiated with the RHCs and other carriers seeking equal access, and an adjustment to an environment characterized by rapid technological change and emerging competition. As can be seen from the data in Table 11.8, while total revenues have been stable, profits have increased significantly.

In this transitional period, AT&T has moved aggressively into new markets while struggling to retain its preeminence as a long distance carrier. AT&T has become a leaner, more responsive company. The dividend yield has been allowed to decline and long-term debt to creep up to finance entry into new market positions. The changing price structure for telecommunication services (particularly the fall in long distance rates) has had the effect of generat-

Table 11.7   Common Carriers

TRR Rank		TRR 1984-1989
1	MCI Communications Corp.	21.7%
2	American Telephone (AT&T)	20.8%
3	Communications Satellite Corp. (COMSAT)	−1.2%

ing sufficient volume to more than counteract the effect of falling prices and lower market share.

MCI is the new kid on the block in long distance services. More than any other single firm, MCI has served as a catalyst for the divestiture and reaped the benefit from equal access to the BOCs. While this period has seen MCI encounter some quality problems in providing its service, and it is handicapped by higher costs than AT&T, these difficulties have not impeded its explosive growth in revenues and profits. Since its appearance as a serious competitor for long distance communications in 1974, MCI has created a 700 million capacity circuit mile microwave and fibre network.

The financial fundamentals for MCI presented in Table 11.8 bear eloquent testimony to its success in the market place. The returns to investors during this period have been only slightly less than spectacular. The lack of stronger gains to investors reflects (1) the fact that a great deal of MCI's future growth was already factored into its stock price in 1984 and (2) MCI is on a roller coaster ride that remains to a considerable extent in the hands of its regulators (Judge Greene and the FCC) and the competitive stance of AT&T.

Sprint was jointly owned by UTI and GTE and its financial performance between 1984 and 1989 is treated above in the ITC analysis.

COMSAT is the sole U.S. carrier authorized to operate international satellite communication facilities. The international satellite system is owned by an international consortium in which COMSAT has a 26.5 percent interest. COMSAT leases satellite circuits to U.S. carriers, provides an array of specialized communication services and through COMSAT VIDEO provides in-room TV services.

Table 11.8   Performance Fundamentals
Common Carriers 1984–1988

Characteristic	AT&T	MCI	COMSAT
TRR, 1984–1988	20.8%	21.7%	−1.2%
Sales			
1988	34,675.	5,130.	345.
1984	33,188.	1,959.	442.
Change	4.5%	162%	−22%
Profits			
1988	2,255.	335.	59.
1984	1,370.	109.	59.
Change	65%	207%	0%
Profit Margins			
1988	6.5%	6.5%	17%
1984	4.1%	5.6%	13%
Cash Flow/Share			
1988	5.45	3.60	7.25
1984	3.89	1.64	6.53
Change	40%	120%	11%
Shares Outstanding			
1988	1,074.	242.	18.
1984	1,038.	235.	18.
Common Stock Dividend Yield			
1988	4.2%	0.	4.8%
1984	6.8%	0.	3.6%
Change from 1984	−38.2%		33.3%

The erosion of its market share between 1984 and 1988 reflects a loss to competing transmission technologies, particularly fibre optic cable. As depicted in Table 11.8, lost revenues during this era have been offset by rising profit margins to keep profits from falling. While COMSAT is far from an investor's nightmare at this point, serious questions must be addressed concerning this firm's long-run viability in the face of the continuing development of alternative transmission technologies.

Chapter 12

THE FUTURE FOR INVESTMENT IN INDEPENDENT TELEPHONE COMPANIES

Performance Overview

Local independent telephone companies (ITCs) will provide investors with significant opportunities for profit in the early 1990s as they work hard to outmaneuver larger competitors and develop profitable market niches. These returns will be accompanied by greater risk than those found among traditional utilities. The potential returns to be found in this sector are illustrated in Table 12.1.

Long in the shadow of Ma Bell, the ITCs face unprecedented opportunities to position themselves strongly as society becomes ever more dependent on the telecommunication industry to facilitate information exchange. The market for telecommunication services will become broader and deeper. Driven by continual technological innovation, these firms will have the chance to enter new market niches and establish profitable market positions. Not only will new firms enter the market, but old firms will reposition themselves as the telecommunications market enters a period of dynamic evolution.

The greatest asset these more established firms possess is the ability to move more swiftly to emerging markets than the competition and to react more quickly to changing technologies. The need to be nimble is acute, as the ITC's competitors will often be the

Table 12.1   Forecast Returns
             Independent Telephone Companies

1990-94 TRR Rank		TRR	
		1990-94	1990-99
1	Alltel Corporation	32.50%	20.20%
2	Contel Corporation	24.00%	18.80%
3	Rochester Telephone Corp.	21.10%	17.30%
4	Century Telephone Enterprises	19.80%	17.40%
5	Centel Corporation	18.40%	15.30%
6	GTE Corporation	17.10%	18.50%
7	Citizens Utilities "B"	15.80%	10.30%
8	C-Tec Corporation	13.20%	10.80%
9	Cincinnati Bell Inc.	10.80%	10.80%
10	Southern New England Telephone	10.60%	14.10%

large, savy, powerful, cash-rich RHCs. Effective exploitation of the opportunities they do have presupposes that the ITCs have a strong strategic focus on those opportunities.

Of great interest to investors is the potential for acquisitions or mergers in this sector of the industry. Merger with an RHC would provide the combined entity with many opportunities for cost reductions and service enhancement. If properly managed, these independent telephone companies will become obvious growth vehicles making them doubly attractive to RHCs who have taken a more conservative approach to exploiting the new growth areas.

Takeover from outside the industry is also a distinct possibility. A mature diversified giant with high tech capabilities (e.g., G.E., N. V. Phillips, or IBM) might find attractive growth possibilities present in such an acquisition.

With the opportunities for profits suggested in Table 12.1 comes increased risk heightened by the continuing movement towards deregulation. Policy at both the federal and state levels will move haltingly towards allowing market processes to determine outcomes of services and profits. Unfavorable regulatory decisions could result in the ITCs being squeezed out by their much larger

competitors. With their superior marketing muscle and greater stay-
ing power, the RHCs could successfully challenge the independents
in many of their most promising new markets.

Returns Among ITCs

The range of returns for investors in this sector between 1984 and
1988 was presented in Table 11.5. The relationship between the TRR
and stock price during this period is illustrated in Figure 12.1.

It is clear that returns to investors during this period reflected
the impact of stock price appreciation rather than dividend yield.
Local independent telephone companies have slashed the effective
dividend yield of their stocks from an average of 7.6 percent in 1984

**Figure 12.1 Independent Telephone Companies Total Return–
Stock Price Relationship**

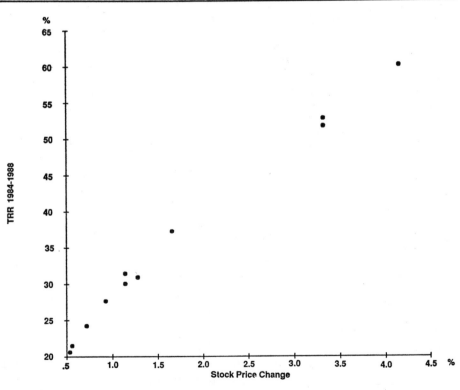

to 4.0 percent in 1988. Returns to investors among these firms are now almost entirely (R^2 = .99) a function of price change.

Stock Prices

The DDM suggests that the most important determinant of stock prices is future earnings. Future earnings in this sector are difficult to predict because earnings are dependent on the implementation of new technologies, the development of new products and the form in which federal and state regulators implement structured deregulation. Profits will also be sensitive to the aggressiveness with which the management in individual firms moves to aggressively pursue opportunities that will quickly emerge and just as quickly fade away.

Insight into the relationship between changes in CFS and changes in stock price may be developed by disaggregating the data incorporated in Figure 12.2 into the proven and uncertain growth sectors discussed in Chapter 11.

Figures 12.2 and 12.3 distinguish between this relationship for proven growth and uncertain growth firms. This approach generates an extraordinarily consistent relationship between the change in stock price and the change in CFS, considering the likelihood that future changes in CFS may not be highly correlated with current changes in CFS because of the unstable environment of the ITCs.

The relationship between the change in stock price and the change in cash flow for uncertain growth firms depicted in Figure 12.2 (R^2 = .79) has a low intercept and a high slope compared to the relationship for firms with established growth in Figure 12.3 (R^2 = .79) where the intercept is high and the slope is low. This implies that gains from new technologies, products and industry relationships are already embedded in the established growth companies, while the others have yet to prove themselves. The market clearly attributes a different price earnings multiple to firms based on the extent to which they have aggressively pursued the profitable opportunities in the present environment.

These relationships mean that increases in CFS in the established growth stocks will have a smaller impact on stock price than will similar increases for unproven growth stocks. The market has al-

Figure 12.2 Independent Telephone Companies with Uncertain Growth

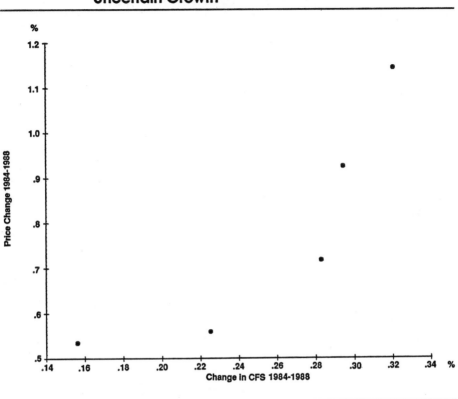

ready rewarded the proven growth stocks. A 10 percent increase in CFS for Cincinnati Bell is already in its price, a comparable gain for Century is quite another story. In contrast, potential gains will be greater for the uncertain growth stocks, if and when they are able to convert their potential to actual increases in CFS.

A corollary to this relationship is that the investment risks are higher in proven growth stocks. The failure of earnings to increase at anticipated rates could have a dramatic impact on stock price. What the market has built in, the market can take out. The proven growth stocks have greater downside potential than upside potential at current price levels.

**Figure 12.3   Independent Telephone Companies with
                 Proven Growth Price–Cash Flow Relationship**

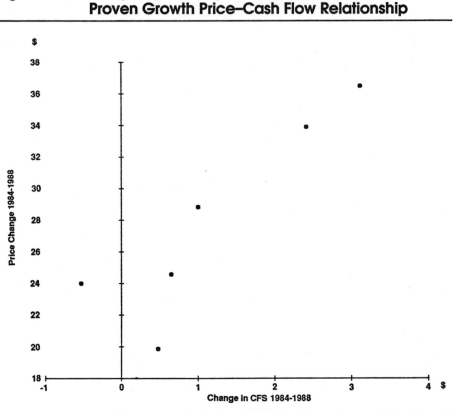

Similarly, there is considerable upside potential for the uncertain growth stocks. Precisely because future growth in earnings are not assured, increases in earnings will have a significant impact on stock prices. The environment for these firms is so potentially rewarding, it would probably not take much in the way of actual increases in earnings to cause the market to embed these firms with higher rates of growth.

Uncertain Growth Companies

The actual prices in early 1989 and the DDM estimates of these prices are presented in Table 12.2.

Table 12.2   Potential Growth
Independent Telephone Companies

	Stock Price	DDM Estimate	
	1988	1988	Error
Alltel Corporation	35.00	33.84	–1.16
Contel Corporation	41.88	41.98	0.10
GTE Corporation	44.00	44.79	0.79
Southern New England Telephone	54.00	55.36	1.36
Rochester Telephone Corporation	52.38	51.31	–1.06

The accuracy of the estimates obtained by this approach is impressive and suggests the validity of the predictions made below.

Specific Company Forecasts

Alltel Corporation Alltel has committed itself to a high efficiency, high growth scenario. Throughout the 1980s, Alltel has modernized and upgraded its facilities while at the same time positioning itself in high growth unregulated telecommunications market niches. In the environment of the 1970s, this led to a situation where capital spending per share always exceeded earnings per share. That Alltel's investment in itself is finally starting to pay off can be seen by comparing the size of its per share capital spending relative to cash flow per share in Figure 12.4.

It is highly significant that cash flow per share exceeded capital spending per share at Alltel for the first time in 1983. This trend is anticipated to continue throughout the 1990s. Note also the burgeoning impact of this expenditure on eps. This trend is expected to accelerate during the forecast period.

Alltel's highly efficient telephone operations provided the bulk of its revenues (78 percent) in 1989. Half of its telephone operations are in high growth suburban areas, which provide for steady increases in new high margined services (e.g., custom calling features). As a result some of these subsidiaries are earning close to

Figure 12.4   Alltel Corporation

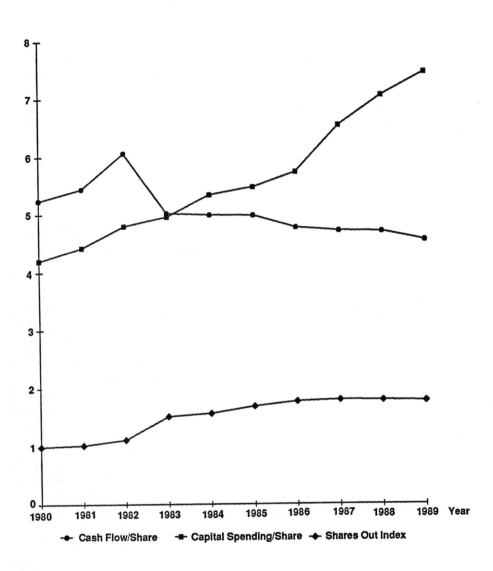

- ◆ Cash Flow/Share   ▪ Capital Spending/Share   ◆ Shares Out Index

their allowed rate of return, mitigating the possibility of continued increases in profitability from this source of activity.

The unregulated side of its business will continue to grow throughout the 1990s. Alltel is heavily into a number of cellular partnerships that will soon turn the corner. Its cellular operations are generally located in smaller sunbelt cities where it did not have to pay a premium price for the franchise. As these partnerships increase in sales and profits, Alltel will be in a position to increase its ownership. Alltel has also had a number of successful small acquisitions in telecommunications equipment in the late 1980s and owns a 32 percent stake in a regional long distance carrier.

Consequently, cash flow per share is expected to grow from its current levels into the 15 percent range (refer to Table 12.3) by the mid-1990s. Commensurate increases in earnings are anticipated. Additional capital spending (unless a large acquisition is undertaken) will be financed from internally generated funds. Dividends will decline as a percentage of earnings to the 45 percent level by the end of the forecast period.

The changing fundamentals at Alltel are presented in Table 12.3.

The resultant increases in cash flow can be used in the DDM to project stock prices through the 1990s. The stock price forecasts for Alltel are contained in Table 12.4.

An important determinant of the actual stock price at Alltel is the likelihood to which investors in the market perceive Alltel to be a takeover target and the extent to which Alltel is likely to be absorbed in a merger.

As a rapidly growing company with a strong balance sheet and growing cash flow, Alltel would be a desirable candidate for a larger firm stuck in mature markets. Alltel would also be a very attractive asset for one of the RHCs, who might well imagine that they are better prepared to exploit Alltel's different markets and could gain additional profits from increased operational efficiencies.

The slight premium the market bares to the DDM prediction (Table 12.1) in 1989 may reflect the existence of this type of pressure. As Alltel's profit potentialities become increasingly evident, the possibility of a takeover will increase. Towards the end of the forecast period Alltel's value as an acquisition is likely to drop as

Table 12.3   Fundamentals Forecast
Alltel Corporation

Year	CFS	EPS	Dividends
1990	4.45	2.40	1.20
1991	4.98	2.69	1.34
1992	5.73	3.09	1.55
1993	6.59	3.55	1.96
1994	7.58	4.09	2.25
1995	8.72	4.70	2.59
1996	10.02	5.41	2.97
1997	11.23	6.06	3.33
1998	12.57	6.78	4.07
1999	14.08	7.60	4.56

Table 12.4   Stock Price Forecast
Alltel Corporation

Year	No Takeover DDM Stock Price Estimate	Takeover Pressure Premium Price	Expected Value of Price
1990	24.48	48.00	31.53
1991	18.70	53.76	36.23
1992	24.18	77.28	56.04
1993	30.48	88.87	71.36
1994	37.73	102.20	82.86
1995	46.06	117.53	96.09
1996	55.65	106.01	90.90
1997	64.47	118.10	96.65
1998	74.34	131.40	102.87
1999	85.40	136.72	111.06

growth slows in the industry and increasing competition begins to press on profit margins.

The assumptions embodied in these stock price forecasts are presented in Table 12.5.

These forecasts generate a TRR of 32.5 percent between 1990 and 1994 and a TRR of 20.2 percent between 1990 and 1999. If a merger is actually undertaken during this period, significantly higher returns would actually be experienced. In the event of a bidding war (a real possibility), returns to investors would be gargantuan.

Contel Corporation The growth in Contel's earnings will come largely from its regulated and cellular telephone operations. These operations are its strength and can be expected to at least track industry averages. Contel has operations in 75 of the leading 100 cellular markets. Contributions from its federal systems division will remain uneven during the forecast period. However, it may sell off this division as it did its low-profit business systems division in 1989.

The probable rate of earnings growth at Contel is anticipated to rise slowly to the middle teens by the mid-1990s (Table 12.6). Cash flow and earnings are expected to run in tandem, while capital

Table 12.5 Forecast Assumptions; Alltel Corporation

Year	Probability of Takeover	DDM Implied PE Multiple	Full Premium Multiple	Assumed Growth Rate	Dividend Payout
1990	0.3	10	20	10%	0.50
1991	0.5	7	20	12%	0.50
1992	0.6	8	25	15%	0.50
1993	0.7	9	25	15%	0.55
1994	0.7	9	25	15%	0.55
1995	0.7	10	25	15%	0.55
1996	0.7	10	25	15%	0.55
1997	0.6	11	18	12%	0.55
1998	0.5	11	18	12%	0.60
1999	0.5	11	18	12%	0.60

Table 12.6   Fundamentals Forecast; Contel Corporation

Year	CFS	EPS	Dividends
1990	4.75	1.30	1.11
1991	5.18	1.42	1.19
1992	5.70	1.56	1.29
1993	6.38	1.75	1.43
1994	7.34	2.01	1.63
1995	8.44	2.31	1.85
1996	9.45	2.59	2.04
1997	10.39	2.84	2.25
1998	11.43	3.13	2.47
1999	12.58	3.44	2.72

spending will slowly decline. Small reductions in the percentage of earnings paid out as dividends will be used to lessen the need for outside capital.

Contel's stock price may well benefit from takeover fever in the industry as telecommunications attracts increasing attention throughout the 1990s. However, an actual merger or takeover by a larger firm remains a remote possibility. Prospective stock price levels for Contel are indicated in Table 12.7.

The assumption upon which these forecasts are based are presented in Table 12.8.

Annual returns to an investor holding Contel stock between 1990 and 1994 are expected to be 24 percent, in contrast with the expected value of 18.8 percent for the full forecast period.

GTE Corporation GTE provides regulated telephone service in 31 states and manufactures Sylvania lighting products. The bulk (77 percent) of GTE's revenues are derived from telephone service. A major strategy shift occurred in 1989 when GTE effectively sold off its half of the Sprint fibre optics network to United Telecommunications. This allows GTE to better focus on the opportunities it has in providing local telephone service.

**Table 12.7   Stock Price Forecast
                Contel Corporation**

Year	No Takeover DDM Stock Price Estimate	Takeover Pressure Premium Price	Expected Value of Price
1990	24.21	39.00	25.69
1991	27.35	42.51	28.86
1992	31.14	46.76	34.27
1993	36.15	52.37	39.40
1994	43.17	60.23	49.99
1995	51.23	69.26	58.44
1996	58.65	77.57	66.22
1997	65.58	85.33	69.53
1998	73.19	78.22	73.70
1999	81.57	86.04	82.02

**Table 12.8   Forecast Assumptions
                Contel Corporation**

Year	Probability of Takeover	DDM Implied Price Earnings Multiple	Full Premium Multiple	Assumed Growth Rate
1990	0.1	19	30	9%
1991	0.1	19	30	9%
1992	0.2	20	30	10%
1993	0.2	21	30	12%
1994	0.4	22	30	15%
1995	0.4	22	30	15%
1996	0.4	23	30	12%
1997	0.2	23	30	10%
1998	0.1	23	25	10%
1999	0.1	20	25	10%

The sharpening of its strategic focus is a good move; the margins obtainable at GTE from implementing new services and technologies in local regulated and unregulated services probably exceeds those obtainable from providing long-distance telecommunication service. The latter market will feature fierce price competition in the forecast period. Sprint (discussed in Chapter 16) will probably benefit from the undivided attention of UTI than it would with two hands at the helm.

Earnings increases from the existing local telephone operations will rise to the 10 percent level in the 1990s as the company aggressively reduces costs. A new era of cooperation with AT&T seems to be dawning which will give it quick access to advanced technology. GTE's rising cash flows may possibly signal a series of small or large acquisitions. A significant increase in profitability is possible if local regulators move swiftly (an unlikely event) to a price cap system of regulation.

In its manufacturing domain, GTE's Sylvania lighting division is confronted by larger competitors in a mature market. Profits in this sector are likely to remain stagnant.

As GTE itself is unlikely to be a takeover candidate, no premium over the value of its earnings is expected for these shares. The eventual impact of its refocused efforts in local telephone operations on stock price are presented in Table 12.9.

The impact of these events at GTE would result in investors earning an annual return of 17.1 percent between 1990 and 1994 and a return of 18.5 percent between 1990 and 1999.

Southern New England Telephone SNET provides regulated and cellular telephone services in Connecticut. Its regulated activities accounted for 81 percent of revenues in 1989, and this proportion may be expected to increase moderately in the forecast period as the cellular services rise rapidly. Strong growth is anticipated in cellular operations because Connecticut is such an affluent state and because SNET sits astride the bust Boston-N.Y.C. highway corridor.

SNET would be a desirable acquisition for NYNEX. NYNEX could pay a premium for SNET because of potential gains in operating efficiency and increased profits resulting from the consolida-

Table 12.9   Fundamentals Forecast; GTE Corporation

Year	CFS	EPS	Dividends	DDM Stock Price Estimate
1990	6.50	2.35	1.48	31.33
1991	6.96	2.51	1.58	34.66
1992	7.51	2.72	1.68	38.74
1993	8.19	2.96	1.84	43.69
1994	9.01	3.26	1.99	49.70
1995	9.91	3.58	2.18	56.30
1996	10.90	3.94	2.36	63.56
1997	11.88	4.29	2.58	70.75
1998	12.95	4.68	2.81	78.58
1999	13.98	5.06	3.03	86.18

tion of services. However, without an overwhelming economic incentive, it is unlikely that either SNET or its regulator would be amenable to a merger.

Earnings growth is seen to increase slowly from 8 percent at the turn of the decade to the 10 percent range by the mid 1990s. Capital spending is likely to increase the first half of the decade as SNET gears up for a belated modernization program. These assumptions yield the forecast presented in Table 12.10.

An investor in SNET may expect a TRR of 19.5 percent between 1989 and 1994 and a TRR of 17.4 percent between 1989 and 1999.

Rochester Telephone Corporation RTC is engaged in a strategy of expanding by acquiring small local telephones through an exchange of stock that does not dilute the earnings of the parent company. The hope is to provide enough size to achieve economies of scale.

It is quite possible that RTC itself will be acquired during the 1990s: the advantages accruing to a GTE or RHC would be substantial.

A continuation of its present policy of small acquisitions is likely to bring growth into the 12 percent range by the middle of the de-

**Table 12.10   Fundamentals Forecast
                Southern New England Telecommunications Corp.**

Year	CFS	EPS	Dividends	DDM Stock Price Estimate
1990	6.90	2.85	1.71	32.26
1991	7.45	3.08	1.85	36.31
1992	8.05	3.32	1.93	40.68
1993	8.77	3.62	1.99	45.99
1994	9.56	3.95	2.17	51.77
1995	10.52	4.34	2.39	58.78
1996	11.57	4.78	2.63	66.49
1997	12.50	5.16	2.99	73.28
1998	13.37	5.52	3.20	79.69
1999	14.31	5.91	3.43	86.55

cade. This assumption yields the solid performance indicated in Table 12.11.

The relative impact of RTC itself being a takeover candidate is estimated in Table 12.12.

The assumptions on which this forecast is based are presented in Table 12.13.

Investors purchasing RTC stock at the beginning of 1989 and selling at the end of 1994 may look forward to annual returns of 20.8 percent; comparable returns for the 1989-1999 period would be 17.6 percent.

Proven Growth Companies

As can be seen from the DDM generating the stock price estimates in Table 12.14, the ITCs that have demonstrated their viability in the high growth sector of the telecommunications industry already have significant future growth built into their current stock prices.

The implications of this model are that future price increases will only occur if growth opportunities are uncovered that are not

Table 12.11 Fundamentals Forecast
            Rochester Telephone Corporation

Year	CFS	EPS	Dividends
1990	4.95	2.19	1.45
1991	5.40	2.39	1.53
1992	5.94	2.63	1.65
1993	6.65	2.94	1.82
1994	7.44	3.29	2.04
1995	8.34	3.69	2.29
1996	9.34	4.13	2.56
1997	10.27	4.54	2.82
1998	11.30	5.00	3.00
1999	12.43	5.50	3.30

Table 12.12 Stock Price Forecast
            Rochester Telephone Corporation

Year	No Takeover DDM Stock Price Estimate	Takeover Pressure Premium Price	Expected Value of Price
1990	29.29	39.42	31.32
1991	32.56	42.97	34.64
1992	36.51	52.52	41.31
1993	41.73	58.82	46.86
1994	47.58	65.88	54.90
1995	54.13	73.78	61.99
1996	61.46	82.64	69.93
1997	68.31	90.90	72.83
1998	75.84	99.99	78.25
1999	84.12	109.99	86.71

Table 12.13 Forecast Assumptions
Rochester Telephone Corporation

Year	Probability of Takeover	DDM Implied Price Earnings Multiple	Full Premium Multiple	Assumed Growth Rate
1990	0.2	13	18	8%
1991	0.2	14	18	9%
1992	0.3	14	20	10%
1993	0.3	14	20	12%
1994	0.4	14	20	12%
1995	0.4	15	20	12%
1996	0.4	15	20	12%
1997	0.2	15	20	10%
1998	0.1	15	20	10%
1999	0.1	15	20	10%

already embedded in stock prices. In addition, any failure to achieve the expectations of strong upward growth in earnings may have a disproportionately large impact on stock prices as the market reevaluates the growth prospects of the company.

An important consideration in this sector would be the desirability of these companies as acquisitions. In general, the companies in this sector have strong balance sheets, excellent cash flow and superior earnings prospects. All of these attributes make them desirable takeover candidates. Despite their lofty price levels, its quite likely that at least some of them will be absorbed into larger telecommunications companies by the end of the 1990s.

Specific Company Forecasts

C-Tec C-Tec is a holding company that provides regulated telephone service in N.E. Pennsylvania and cable TV services to the Mercer County area in New Jersey; it is developing a cellular phone network. The telephone operations have been used as a cash cow to fund the development of the cable TV and cellular

Table 12.14   Proven Growth
Independent Telephone Companies

	Stock Price 1988	DDM Estimate 1988	Error
C-Tec Corporation	47.50	48.40	0.90
Centel Corporation	51.38	48.39	–2.98
Century Telephone Enterprises	30.50	29.84	–0.66
Cincinnati Bell Inc.	44.13	43.79	–0.34
Citizens Utilities "B"	31.88	34.99	3.12
United Telecommunications, Inc.	45.00	41.72	–3.28

phone businesses. Cable TV provided the impetus for growth in the last half of the 1980s and the cellular phone systems should enable C-Tec to continue this growth through the 1990s.

An acquisition of a Michigan Cable TV business in 1989 resulted in a 1990 per share loss and will severely impact earnings in the first half of the decade. Moderate earnings gains are forecasted throughout this period. These gains will increase stock prices somewhat, but current high earnings multiples will hold down this increase. Assuming that the most C-Tec could be worth to an acquiring firm is 40 times earnings, even significant takeover pressure will not have much of an impact on stock prices.

The anticipated increases in earnings are presented in Table 12.15. This increase is expected to bring about the stock prices projected in Table 12.16. The assumptions upon which these forecasts are based are presented in Table 12.17.

These assumptions will generate only moderate returns for investors in C-Tec. A TRR of 13.2 percent is projected for the 1990-94 period with a corresponding return of 10.8 percent for 1990-1994. In addition, an outside possibility exists that C-Tec could become the prize in a bidding contest between two of the RHCs. Such a situation would provide significant upside potential.

Centel Corporation Centel restructured itself late in the 1980s and substantially enhanced its growth potential throughout the 1990s

Table 12.15   Fundamentals Forecast
C-Tec Corporation

Year	CFS	EPS	Dividends
1990	3.20	−0.10	0.00
1991	3.52	0.40	0.12
1992	3.91	0.60	0.24
1993	4.34	0.67	0.27
1994	4.99	0.77	0.34
1995	5.84	0.90	0.40
1996	6.83	1.05	0.47
1997	7.85	1.21	0.60
1998	8.79	1.35	0.68
1999	9.85	1.51	0.76

Table 12.16   Stock Price Forecast
C-Tec Corporation

Year	No Takeover DDM Stock Price Estimate	Takeover Pressure Premium Price	Expected Value of Price
1990	16.58	28.00	20.00
1991	18.33	30.00	21.83
1992	20.45	28.00	22.72
1993	22.81	30.00	25.68
1994	26.37	33.00	29.02
1995	31.02	35.84	32.95
1996	36.45	41.94	39.20
1997	42.07	48.23	45.15
1998	47.23	54.02	49.27
1999	53.01	60.50	55.26

Table 12.17 Forecast Assumptions
             C-Tec Corporation

Year	Probability of Takeover	DDM Implied Price Earnings Multiple	Full Premium Multiple	Assumed Growth Rate
1990	0.3	nmf	nmf	8%
1991	0.3	nmf	nmf	10%
1992	0.3	nmf	nmf	11%
1993	0.4	nmf	nmf	11%
1994	0.4	nmf	nmf	15%
1995	0.4	35	40	17%
1996	0.5	35	40	17%
1997	0.5	35	40	15%
1998	0.3	35	40	12%
1999	0.3	35	40	12%

by selling off its lucrative cable TV operations for an excellent price and purchasing United Telecom's cellular properties. This allows Centel to use its regulated telephone operations as a cash cow while it is extremely well-positioned to develop these cash hungry cable properties. As many of the United Telecom properties are contiguous to Centel's existing properties, there will be significant opportunities to reduce unit costs.

The high price paid for these properties together with their development costs will retard earnings growth in the early years of the 1990s. The runup of Centel's stock price in 1990 will limit near-term gains. The fundamentals forecast in Table 12.18 suggests that earnings will rise strongly in the latter part of the decade as the cellular properties begin to contribute profits.

The stock price forecasts in Table 12.19 hypothesize the presence of considerable takeover pressure. The successful development of its cellular operations would make Centel a very attractive takeover target.

The assumptions upon which this forecast is based are presented in Table 12.20.

Table 12.18 Fundamentals Forecast
Centel Corporation

Year	CFS	EPS	Dividends
1990	3.18	0.46	0.85
1991	3.56	0.80	0.85
1992	3.99	1.00	0.85
1993	4.59	1.20	0.96
1994	5.28	1.38	1.04
1995	6.33	1.66	1.24
1996	7.60	1.99	1.49
1997	9.12	2.38	1.79
1998	10.67	2.79	2.09
1999	12.27	3.21	2.41

Table 12.19 Stock Price Forecast
Centel Corporation

Year	No Takeover DDM Stock Price Estimate	Takeover Pressure Premium Price	Expected Value of Price
1990	29.48	45.00	34.13
1991	31.57	48.00	36.50
1992	33.91	50.00	38.74
1993	37.19	51.00	42.71
1994	40.96	52.50	45.58
1995	46.74	57.96	51.23
1996	53.68	69.55	61.62
1997	62.01	83.46	72.73
1998	70.50	97.65	78.64
1999	79.27	112.30	89.18

**Table 12.20   Forecast Assumptions
              Centel Corporation**

Year	Probability of Takeover	DDM Implied Price Earnings Multiple	Full Premium Multiple	Assumed Growth Rate
1990	0.3	nmf	nmf	10%
1991	0.3	nmf	nmf	12%
1992	0.3	nmf	nmf	12%
1993	0.4	31	35	15%
1994	0.4	30	35	15%
1995	0.4	28	35	20%
1996	0.5	27	35	20%
1997	0.5	26	35	20%
1998	0.3	25	35	17%
1999	0.3	25	35	15%

After all is said and done, the investors in Centel will receive adequate returns on investments in this dynamic company. A modest TRR of 10.6 percent between 1990 and 1994 and 14.1 percent for the entire forecast period. Returns would be stronger, but the clear potential of its strategy had resulted in a run-up in the price of Centel stock in 1990.

Century Telephone Enterprises CTE is a diversified holding company with interests in regulated telephone operations, cellular phone operations, and paging services. Starting up the latter two business held earnings flat during the last half of the 1980s. However, CTE is now positioned to enjoy strong growth in earnings.

Aggressive growth assumptions are used to generate the fundamentals presented in Table 12.21. These assumptions are felt to be warranted by the operating leverage inherent in the CTE's cellular telephone and paging businesses in the affluent and growing markets served.

As CTE would be a highly desirable acquisition once its new business operations are established, a possible PE multiple of up to

Table 12.21   Fundamentals Forecast
Century Telephone Enterprises

Year	CFS	EPS	Dividends
1990	2.50	0.68	0.42
1991	2.88	0.78	0.47
1992	3.31	0.90	0.54
1993	3.80	1.03	0.62
1994	4.37	1.19	0.69
1995	5.03	1.37	0.75
1996	5.78	1.57	0.87
1997	6.65	1.81	0.99
1998	7.65	2.08	1.14
1999	8.79	2.39	1.32

35 is envisioned as a distinct possibility. Thus, the stock price forecast presented in Table 12.22.

The investor should consider that even with the highly aggressive assumptions (Table 12.23) used to develop the above forecast, CTE stock does not offer unusual returns for this sector of the telecommunications industry.

If everything does not work out as envisioned, CTE may prove disappointing to its investors. This stock has considerable downside potential from its current lofty level of expectations. On the basis of the above assumptions, investors may expect annual returns from CTE approaching 20 percent between 1990 and 1994 and returns of 17.4 percent between 1990 and 1999.

Cincinnati Bell Inc. Cincinnati Bell supplies regulated telephone services to the metropolitan Cincinnati area, but is fast diversifying into information and computer software services. Its regulated telephone operations have prospered from modernization and strong growth in the local economy. Further growth must come from elsewhere. While CB's ventures in these new areas look promising, the software and information services markets it is attempting to penetrate are both volatile and highly competitive.

Table 12.22 Stock Price Forecast
Century Telephone Enterprises

Year	No Takeover DDM Stock Price Estimate	Takeover Pressure Premium Price	Expected Value of Price
1990	17.74	21.76	18.14
1991	19.80	27.37	21.31
1992	22.16	31.48	24.95
1993	24.88	36.20	29.40
1994	28.00	41.63	33.45
1995	31.60	47.87	38.11
1996	35.73	55.05	45.39
1997	40.48	63.31	51.90
1998	45.95	72.80	54.01
1999	52.23	83.73	61.68

Table 12.23 Forecast Assumptions
Century Telephone Enterprises

Year	Probability of Takeover	DDM Implied Price Earnings Multiple	Full Premium Multiple	Assumed Growth Rate
1990	0.1	26	32	12%
1991	0.2	25	35	15%
1992	0.3	25	35	15%
1993	0.4	24	35	15%
1994	0.4	24	35	15%
1995	0.4	23	35	15%
1996	0.5	23	35	15%
1997	0.5	22	35	15%
1998	0.3	22	35	15%
1999	0.3	16	35	15%

The market already has factored a significant amount of the anticipated success into CB's stock price. This is a situation that makes for some downside volatility.

Prior to the AT&T breakup, AT&T had a significant minority interest in CB. Since that time, CB has maintained good relations with AT&T. This makes CB an unlikely willing partner in a merger with a RHC—although it would certainly be a highly desirable acquisition from an RHC's perspective. The political difficulties in a hostile takeover of CB for an RHC would be considerable. As a result, a takeover of CB is highly unlikely and not considered in the following forecasts.

Earnings growth in the seven to eight percent range throughout the forecast period is thought to be the most likely outcome for CB. This assumption generates the forecast presented in Table 12.24.

The forecast share price for CB ranges a PE multiple of 16-18. In the context of the market of the late 1980s, this would seem to effectively capture CB's growth prospects.

The outcome of this for the investor is a weak return. A TRR of 10.8 percent is anticipated for both the five- and eleven-year investment horizons. This small return reflects the fact that the market has already embedded the potential profits from its information services activities in CB's stock price. When the PE ratio is above 15 at CB, investors would do well to look elsewhere.

Citizens Utilities "B" CU has two classes of common stock: "A" receives only stock dividends, and "B" receives an equal value of cash.

CU provides a diversity of utility services, primarily to rural communities in the mid- and far-west. Electric power provided its primary source of revenues until 1985 when telecommunication services took the lead. Its location in rural areas and its ownership of desirable radio paging frequencies in the western states make it a tempting acquisition target for a larger telecommunication company.

Overall growth in earnings will be hard to come by in its slow-growth markets. If management focuses on developing its telecommunications businesses, modest growth should be forthcoming throughout the forecast period. As the anticipated rise in energy

Table 12.24   Fundamentals Forecast
Cincinnati Bell Inc.

Year	CFS	EPS	Dividends	DDM Stock Price Estimate
1990	3.62	1.60	0.77	23.88
1991	3.87	1.71	0.82	25.27
1992	4.14	1.83	0.92	26.75
1993	4.43	1.96	1.08	28.34
1994	4.79	2.12	1.16	30.29
1995	5.17	2.29	1.26	32.39
1996	5.59	2.47	1.36	34.65
1997	6.03	2.67	1.47	37.10
1998	6.46	2.85	1.57	39.42
1999	6.84	3.02	1.66	41.54

prices moves towards its climax in the mid 1990s, CU's other divisions are likely to have a difficult time contributing to corporate profit.

The fundamentals forecast in Table 12.25 assumes earnings growth in the 5-6 percent range throughout the decade.

The modest growth at CU results in a significant divergence between its value based on its earnings and its value to a larger telecommunications company. The magnitude of this difference may be clearly seen in the stock price forecast in Table 12.26. The assumptions on which this forecast is based are presented in Table 12.27.

The annual yield to an investor purchasing this stock at the beginning of 1990 and selling at the end of 1994 would be 15.8 percent. A comparable yield for 1990-99 would be 10.3 percent.

United Telecommunications Inc. With its purchase of a majority interest in Sprint and the sale of its cellular properties, UTI is more properly analyzed as a common carrier. This analysis can be found in Chapter 16.

Table 12.25   Fundamentals Forecast
Citizens Utilities Company

Year	CFS	EPS	Dividends
1990	3.00	2.17	1.74
1991	3.15	2.28	1.82
1992	3.31	2.39	1.91
1993	3.51	2.54	2.03
1994	3.72	2.69	2.15
1995	3.94	2.85	2.28
1996	4.18	3.02	2.42
1997	4.43	3.20	2.56
1998	4.69	3.39	2.71
1999	4.97	3.60	2.88

Table 12.26   Stock Price Forecast
Citizens Utilities Company

Year	No Takeover DDM Stock Price Estimate	Takeover Pressure Premium Price	Expected Value of Price
1990	32.94	54.25	35.07
1991	33.76	56.96	38.40
1992	34.62	71.77	42.05
1993	35.71	76.08	43.78
1994	36.86	80.64	49.99
1995	38.08	85.48	52.30
1996	39.37	90.61	54.74
1997	40.74	96.05	51.80
1998	42.19	101.81	54.12
1999	43.73	107.92	50.15

Table 12.27 Forecast Assumptions
Citizens Utilities Company

Year	Probability of Takeover	DDM Implied Price Earnings Multiple	Full Premium Multiple	Assumed Growth Rate
1990	0.10	15	25	5%
1991	0.10	15	25	5%
1992	0.25	14	30	5%
1993	0.25	14	30	6%
1994	0.25	14	30	6%
1995	0.20	13	30	6%
1996	0.20	13	30	6%
1997	0.20	13	30	6%
1998	0.10	12	30	6%
1999	0.10	12	30	6%

Summary

Many excellent investment opportunities will present themselves among the ITCs in the 1990s. The market for telecommunication services will become broader and deeper. Driven by continual technological innovation, these firms will have the chance to enter new market niches and establish profitable market positions. While new firms enter the market, old firms will reposition themselves as the telecommunications market enters a period of dynamic evolution.

The greatest asset the ITCs possess is the ability to move more swiftly to emerging markets than the competition and to react more quickly to changing technologies. The need to be nimble is acute, as the ITC's competitors will often be the large, savvy, powerful, cash-rich RHCs. Effective exploitation of the opportunities they do have presupposes that the ITCs have a strong strategic focus on those opportunities.

Potential profits from merger or acquisition activity among the ITCs increases the attractiveness of investments in this sector. Merger with an RHC would provide the combined entity with many opportunities for cost reduction and service enhancement. If properly managed, these independent telephone companies will become obvious growth vehicles. This would certainly make them doubly attractive to RHCs, which have taken a more conservative approach to exploiting the new growth areas in telecommunications.

Chapter 13

THE FUTURE FOR INVESTMENT IN REGIONAL HOLDING COMPANIES

Performance Overview

While the immediate post-divestiture period uniformly brought the RHCs unprecedented prosperity, the unfamiliar competitive milieu into which they have been thrust will begin to take its toll in the 1990s. As may be seen in Table 13.1, the forecast returns for the RHCs are consistently lower throughout the forecast period that they were in the immediate post-divestiture period. Moreover, returns among the RHCs will no longer be as uniform as in the past.

Returns to investors from will depend upon the performance of each RHC in the rough and tumble of the telecommunications market, the specifics of deregulation policies, and the success of their diversification, merger, and acquisition activities. Each RHC will adopt its own unique style in adjusting to the new conditions.

Significant earnings growth in the coming decade will be difficult to realize internally because of the present dominance of regulated operating companies in their business mix. Future earnings growth among the RHCs in the 1990s will result primarily from mergers and acquisitions.

The implications of this situation for investors is that returns in this area will be a function of stock price changes rather than dividends. Stock prices will be sensitive to current operating results

291

Table 13.1   Forecast Returns
Regional Holding Companies

1990 TRR Rank		TRR		
		1984-89	1990-94	1990-99
1	Southwestern Bell	30.5%	21.6%	21.6%
2	Pacific Telesis	33.4%	16.8%	16.8%
3	Bell Atlantic	32.6%	16.4%	15.4%
4	Bellsouth	31.4%	14.2%	15.2%
5	U.S. West	31.0%	12.7%	12.6%
6	Ameritech	32.5%	12.3%	11.6%
7	NYNEX	32.7%	8.5%	8.3%

and, more importantly, anticipated changes in future operating performance. The linkage of returns to stock prices adds an element of risk to this type of investment that did not exist prior to divestiture.

Industry Driving Forces

There are four major factors which will have a significant impact on the operating performance of the RHCs over the next decade: (1) management quality, (2) regulatory reform, (3) regional growth and development, and (4) the level and effectiveness of capital spending.

Management Quality

Relative to the spectrum of all industrial firms, the RHCs are conservatively managed. Their response to the prosperity of the period following divestiture has been to use a significant portion of available funds to reduce long-term debt and increase the common equity ratio. Yet within this general framework differences in strategies among the RHCs are apparent: e.g., U.S. West and Bell Atlantic are notably diversification minded, while Ameritech has retained a distinctively traditional view of its function.

The RHCs finds themselves in an environment that abounds with opportunities and threats. Each RHC has responded to avail ifself of the potential benefits from entering new markets and developing new products and each has moved to protect existing market shares in its traditional markets and to be a strong player in emerging markets. Yet the degree of diversity in this response among the different RHCs is striking.

Conservative management is not necessarily good or bad management. Progressive management is not necessarily good or bad management. Aside from the issue of formulating an appropriate strategy, the quality of management is measured by its ability to implement a given strategy in such a way as to favorably impact operating performance and shareholder wealth.

At the time of divestiture, the RHCs inherited a large inflexible bureaucratic management structure. While this type of management structure was perfectly appropriate for a regulated natural monopoly, it is no longer appropriate for the highly fluid market conditions which will prevail in the telecommunications market of the 1990s. Operating success will require the RHCs effectively compete with a host a smaller and larger competitors. While the RHCs have considerable strength (technological capabilities, marketing muscle, experience, and prior customer relationships), the race more often goes to the fleet-footed than the strong.

Even in those areas where the RHCs are effectively managed, fierce price competition may well limit profitability. The movement from ROR regulation to structured regulation (see below) will change the requirements of effective management. There is a world of difference between arguing the merits of a given expenditure in front of a regulatory body and passing the merciless market test. Talking "lean and hard" is one thing, doing it another. The burden of proof rests upon the management of the RHCs.

Even with the most able managers, the RHCs may be hard put to meet the test of operating performance in many markets. Given the attractiveness of many new and existing telecommunication markets to outside firms, there may well be an influx of competitors sufficient to drive profitability out of the market completely. At least in the first decade and a half of structured deregulation, there is a significant possibility of the type of excess capacity disequilibrium that characterized deregulation in the airline passenger industry in its first decade.

Regulatory Reform

The use of competition as a substitute for regulation in the telecommunications industry, in those areas where workable competition is present and the development of administrative rules to create competitive behavior where competition is absent, is referred to as structured deregulation. This approach to regulation in the industry creates a dynamic tension among market participants. They are free to compete. They are not necessarily free to win. Where the regulators have the perception that success was due to unfair advantages (rather than good management or just plain luck), the rules of the game can be altered to bring about an outcome that is more in accord with the desires of the regulators.

As a result of their high profile, size and many advantages, the RHCs may often find themselves is situations where they will be handicapped to ensure an outcome that does not result in their dominance of a particular market. This situation and its inherent uncertainties are likely to lower the profit potential of the RHCs. The performance of the RHCs may also be restrained by service and other social goals mandated for the BOCs by local regulatory bodies. Insofar as their restraints are not imposed on their competitors, the RHCs necessarily suffer a competitive disadvantage.

Direct competition is the primary method of regulating behavior under structural deregulation. Under equal access other firms may use the BOC's own lines to offer the consumer an array of telecommunication services that are direct substitutes for those offered by the BOC. In addition, competitors are free to develop alternative telecommunication systems that compete directly with the basic hard wire service provided by the BOC.

This potential form of competition raises the possibility of bypass. Bypass, or its threat, will be a major force holding down earnings at the RHCs during the 1990s.

Certainly, bypass will occur where their is economic reason. The extent to which this occurs is dependent on future technological developments, the extent to which these developments are seized upon by firms other than RHC entities, and the extent which the

RHC are willing to use the new technologies themselves. Where workable competition is not possible, the market will be structured administratively by the regulatory authorities to facilitate those behaviors which would occur if competition were present. Administrative intervention in this context takes a variety of forms. An important administrative remedy effecting RHCs is equal access. This concept effectively makes the RHC a common carrier of access to the telephone consumer and puts the RHC on an equal footing with all its competitors in the provisioning of other telecommunication products and services. RHC's are also subject to an array of other limitations with respect to businesses they are prohibited from entering, e.g., manufacturing telecommunications equipment and providing long-distance services.

A significant danger will arise to the RHC from the threat of uneconomic bypass. In their pursuit of service and social goals, local regulatory agencies may lag in allowing the BOCs to price their products and services at cost. The effect of uneconomic bypass will normally represent a loss to both the RHC and the public and should be avoided. However, existing tariff structures, which encourage bypass, are only moving to a cost basis slowly. At the end of the 1980s, many situations exist where significant amounts of uneconomic bypass are a distinct possibility.

Regional Growth and Development

The demand for traditional telephone services is dependent on the health and rate of growth in the area served. A stable economy means consumers can afford the service and there will be an absence of resistance to rate hikes to maintain profit margins. A growing economy means more access lines, which in spreading fixed costs further reduces the unit cost of service.

The demand for residential service has traditionally not been as sensitive to economic fluctuations as commercial services. Expansions or contractions in the business sector, particularly in the services industry which is highly telecommunications dependent, can have a disproportionate impact on BOC revenues.

The plethora of new telephone services becoming available (gateways, mobile phones, marine, air-to-ground, foreign exchange circuits, custom calling, touch calling, call waiting, speed calling, conference calling, paging, etc.) are transforming the nature of the telecommunication services market. The demand for these products tends to be more price inelastic and income elastic than the basic telephone services. This situation provides the RHCs with many opportunities to develop profitable market niches. In these markets, the first mover will gain a significant competitive advantage. If these opportunities are not developed quickly by the RHCs, competing suppliers will enter the market and will be difficult to dislodge.

Capital Spending

The situation at the time of the breakup left the RHCs with a high level of capital spending relative to their cash flow. As revenues and profits have increased, the RHCs have moved to lower this ratio and increase the discretion they have with respect to allocating this free cash.

Pacific Telesis and Southwest Bell have driven the ratio of capital spending to cash flow on a per share basis to historically low levels. Southwest Bell may feel its investment opportunities constrained by the region's poor economic condition between 1984 and 1988. Pacific Telesis may have felt this was an appropriate response to prior years in a very difficult regulatory environment. The surfeit of cash at these firms may be used to increase their dividends or (more likely) be held in a liquid form awaiting future opportunities. Their success in driving down this ratio is depicted in Figure 13.1.

Ameritech, Bell Atlantic, Bell South, NYNEX, and U.S. West have chosen a middle road, balancing off present opportunities, future opportunities and financial security with a ratio of capital spending to cash flow in the mid 60 percent range. Their pattern of capital spending to cash flow is presented in Figure 13.2.

The net effect of this pattern is an accumulation of liquid assets at the RHCs. With the exception of NYNEX, this cash hoard clearly exceeds the need for modernization or extending existing business lines. Consequently, this cash will be used to acquire other firms, which will either compliment the firm's present activities or add

**Figure 13.1   Regional Holding Companies
             Conservative CSS/CFS Ratio**

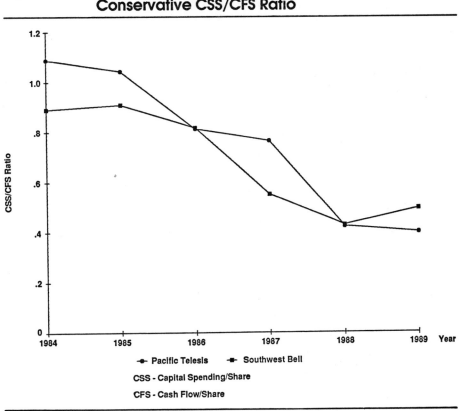

significantly to its growth. The real question in this area is not if these acquisitions will occur, but what form will they take.

The most likely direction for acquisition activities would seem to be the unregulated sector of the telecommunications industry. Given the conservative orientation of RHC management, these acquisitions are likely to be small- to moderately-sized entrepreneurial organizations that have developed a strong position in a very small segment of the market. The RHCs are likely to be willing to pay top dollar for such acquisitions.

Figure 13.2   Regional Holding Companies
Moderate CSS/CFS Ratio

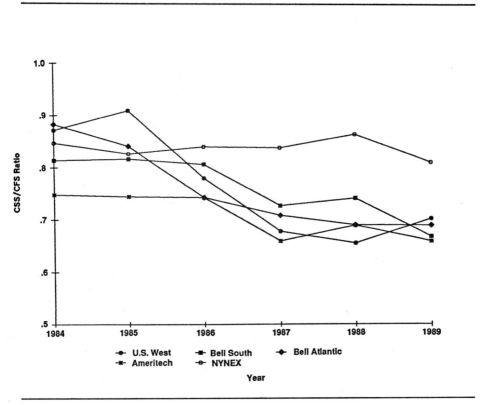

RHC Return Forecasts

The breakup and subsequent deregulation of AT&T has created a situation where its BOCs, by being grouped into RHCs in the manner described in Chapter 13, have been transformed into growth companies. This transformation is being driven by the forces of technological change and competition. Telephone utilities in the past may well have connated to the investor safety and stability of return. This is no longer an appropriate perspective.

Shareholder wealth at the RHCs will be determined by future earnings power rather than dividend yield. This may be seen from

**Figure 13.3   Regional Holding Companies Total Return–
Stock Price Relationship**

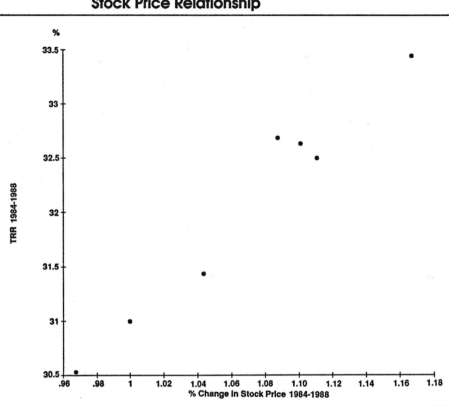

the fact that the price of RHC stock bore no systematic relationship
to its dividend yield between 1984 and 1988. Since their divestiture,
the RHCs have cut their effective dividend yield by more than one-
third.

As growth companies, investor return among the RHCs between
1984 and 1988 was almost entirely (R^2 = .97) a function of the
change in share price. This may be seen in Figure 13.3.

While the RHCs may be thought of as growth companies, their
growth is constrained by a number of factors. Their primary business activity by far remains providing basic telephone services.

While returns from these services may increase as a result of alternative regulatory methods, the change will be slow in coming.

Even though some of the RHCs have aggressively sought out emerging opportunities, their concentration in providing regulated telephone service will inhibit their growth. Earnings momentum can be expected to increase slowly and steadily. The RHCs are large firms, severely constrained by environmental, regulatory, and organizational factors. The activities and performance of an RHC is not going to change abruptly. For forecasting purposes, where change is an incremental process, small variations in present performance can be a good guide to likely changes in future performance.

The application of the DDM to forecasting would suggest that future stock prices are likely to be related to future cash flows. It is particularly important to distinguish between cash flows and earnings in this context because, as of 1988, the FCC has mandated the use of the Uniform Systems of Accounts Rewrite (USOAR) for the RHCs. This change represents a shift away from the treatment of capitalized items common in unregulated industrial enterprises. Significant items (certain types of plant capitalization, pensions leases, compensated absences, and income taxes) will now be expensed rather than capitalized. Thus USOAR will decrease net earnings by increasing expenses, but improve the timing of cash flows.

The inherent stability of the RHCs suggests that existing trends in cash flows can be expected to drive stock prices throughout the forecast period. In particular, between 1984 and 1988 the change in stock prices among these firms was highly correlated ($R^2 = .88$) with their change in CFS. This relationship is depicted in Figure 13.4.

The consistency of this relationship allows its use as a method for forecasting the future stock prices of the RHCs. An application of this model to stock prices in 1988 is presented in Table 13.2.

The model appears to have good predictive ability with the exception of an underestimate for Ameritech. This may reflect a market premium for the stability perceived in this, the most utility-like, of the RHCs. Understanding the future risks and returns offered by the different RHCs requires considering the specific factors that will impact their success in the coming decade. This is done in the following section.

Figure 13.4   Regional Holding Companies Stock Price–
EPS Relationship

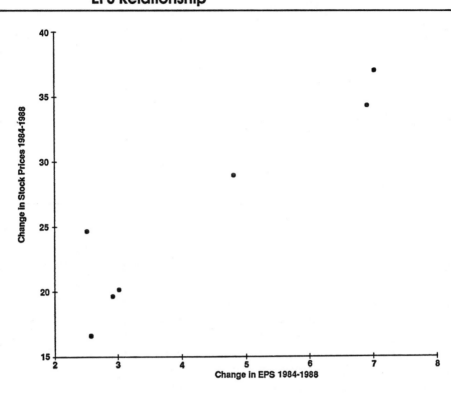

Specific RHC Forecasts

Ameritech (American Information Technologies)

Ameritech's BOCs are Illinois Bell, Indiana Bell, Michigan Bell, and Wisconsin Bell. Ameritech sits astride America's industrial heartland. Therein lies both its strength and weakness.

The region's economy is highly dependent on the old smokestack industries related to automobile production. These industries have been retrenching since the late 1970s. Their future success will

**Table 13.2   Regional Holding Companies
             DDM Estimates**

	Price 1988	DDM Estimate	DDM Error
Pacific Telesis Group	30.88	34.06	3.19
NYNEX Corporation	65.75	67.02	1.27
Bell Atlantic Corporation	70.50	69.48	−1.02
American Information Technologies	46.88	41.81	−5.07
Bellsouth Corporation	39.50	40.77	1.27
U.S. West Inc.	57.88	56.86	−1.01
Southwestern Bell	40.00	41.41	1.41

depend on the ability of American automobile manufacturers to compete in world markets using America's industrial plant.

If the area's manufacturing industries recover, a significant restructuring will have taken place. Manufacturing will no longer be so concentrated geographically. This bodes well for Ameritech, for these far-flung organizations will become increasingly avaricious consumers of telecommunications services.

In the late 1980s these industries began a resurgence based upon a stronger international dollar and productivity improvements. In addition, service industries (with high telecommunication requirements) attracted by low costs and an ample labor force began to increase their presence in the area served by Ameritech. The continuance of these two factors throughout the forecast period is expected to produce sustained growth for Ameritech.

This region contains the Detroit, Cleveland and Chicago SMSAs. The concentration of financial services in these SMSAs will probably work to hold down profits as such concentration presents great opportunities for bypass.

Although productivity is high at Ameritech, there is considerable potential for increasing efficiency. As regulatory reform seeps to the state level, Ameritech will have the opportunity to depart from traditional rate of return controls and enter into agreements

Figure 13.5 Ameritech

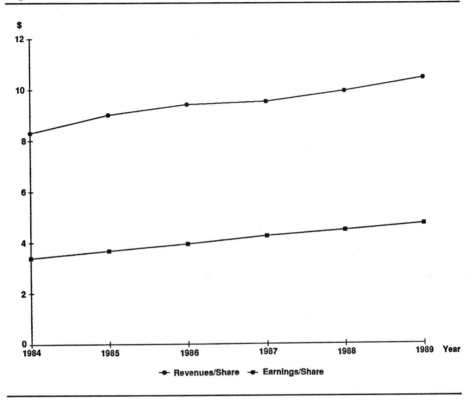

where, within a rate cap and subject to certain constraints, increased profits will be shared by the firm and consumer. This factor is seen to increase Ameritech's profit margin from the 12 percent level to 15 percent by 1994

As of the late 1980s, the prime focus of management appeared to maintain its traditional utility business as best it could and enhance shareholder wealth by using the current flow of profits to strengthen its balance sheet and repurchase its stock. Revenues in this era have grown steadily but slowly at Ameritech. These Trends can be seen in Figure 13.5

Despite some bright spots, overall growth is seen as remaining sluggish at Ameritech throughout the forecast period—unless the firm undertakes significant diversification efforts. Profit margins will be under severe pressure from bypass competition. A myriad of small firms will invade many of the minor market niches where Ameritech is currently reaping high profits.

These considerations lead to the stock forecast for Ameritech presented in Table 13.3. The assumptions on which this forecast is based may be found in Table 13.4.

This forecast leads to an annual return of 12.3 percent between 1990 and 1994 and 11.6 percent between 1990 and 1999.

The stock price forecast in Table 13.3 bears a $5.00 premium to what its earnings suggested by the general formulation of the DDM in this sector. This premium reflects investor sentiment with respect to the great stability evidenced by this firm in an era of tumult. If this stability is perceived as a liability at a time when other firms in the industry are performing better, investors may become disenchanted and the stock price suffers accordingly. This would depress the expected moderate rate of return even further.

It should be noted that the expected returns to investors in Ameritech are subpar for the industry and may bring shareholder pressure for more aggressive diversification. Ameritech has the capital and ability to enter a number of growth areas. Internal growth at significantly higher rates is unlikely to occur. Internal growth will be difficult to achieve because of the relatively large size of regulated activities (marginal improvements will be proportionately small) and because the entrenched bureaucracy at Ameritech is clearly risk adverse.

Such diversification is not built into the forecast above. Growth through acquisition could offer an opportunity to significantly enhance investor returns and could create a significant advance in shareholder wealth.

Bell Atlantic Corporation

Bell Atlantic is located in the middle Atlantic area with its major subsidiaries being the four Chesapeake and Potomac BOCs, Pennsylvania Bell, New Jersey Bell, and the Diamond State Telephone Company.

Table 13.3 Forecast; Ameritech

Year	DDM Stock Price Estimate	Revenues	Net Profit	EPS	CFS	Dividends
1990	60.40	10,150	1,218	3.12	7.68	2.06
1991	63.12	10,759	1,291	3.34	8.22	2.17
1992	66.02	11,405	1,369	3.58	8.80	2.33
1993	71.10	12,089	1,511	3.99	9.82	2.60
1994	80.88	12,814	1,794	4.79	11.78	3.11
1995	89.55	13,583	2,037	5.49	13.51	3.57
1996	94.32	14,398	2,160	5.88	14.46	3.82
1997	99.43	15,262	2,289	6.30	15.49	4.09
1998	104.91	16,178	2,427	6.74	16.58	4.38
1999	110.77	17,148	2,572	7.22	17.75	4.69

Table 13.4   Forecast Assumption; Ameritech

Year	Shares Outstanding	Profit Margin	Revenue Growth	Payout Ratio
1990	390.0	0.120	0.060	0.66
1991	386.1	0.120	0.060	0.65
1992	382.2	0.120	0.060	0.65
1993	378.4	0.125	0.060	0.65
1994	374.6	0.140	0.060	0.65
1995	370.9	0.150	0.060	0.65
1996	367.2	0.150	0.060	0.65
1997	363.5	0.150	0.060	0.65
1998	359.9	0.150	0.060	0.65
1999	356.3	0.150	0.060	0.65

The Bell Atlantic region includes the heart of the communications intensive federal government civilian and military operation and the major Philadelphia, Baltimore, Pittsburgh, and Washington D.C. SMSAs. The density of its territory has resulted in a low investment and wage cost per access line.

Although growth in the mid-Atlantic region has been relatively slow in the last half of the 1980s, it is an affluent area with high levels of household disposable income. The area is ripe for developing the many new telecommunication products and services available and Bell Atlantic is pursuing these opportunities with considerable vigor.

Although costs per access line are low at Bell Atlantic, there are opportunities to increase earnings through regulatory reform. Bell Atlantic has aggressively sought, and is likely to continue to seek these opportunities from its various regulatory bodies. By 1990, Bell Atlantic will be operating under alternative regulatory plan in almost three quarters of its service area. Bell Atlantic was the petitioner in the historic New Jersey rate case that exempted competitive service from ROR regulation in exchange for rate caps on basic

Figure 13.6   Bell Atlantic

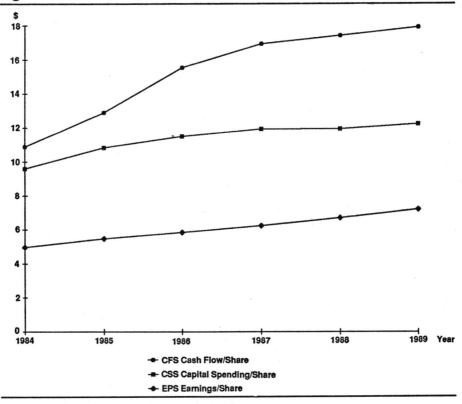

services. This aggressive approach to pricing its services will allow Bell Atlantic to react swiftly to bypass threats.

Bell Atlantic is an aggressive growth company. It has moved energetically to enter potentially profitable emerging market niches. This can be seen by examining its trends in cash flow (CFS), capital spending (CSS), and earnings (EPS) on a per share basis. These trends are presented in Figure 13.6.

Bell Atlantic is clearly converting its rising earnings into future growth by aggressive capital spending to occupy emerging highly profitable market niches. Although bypass and the need to protect market share in these new market will exert a downward force on profit margins, this trend will mitigate as its marketing efforts take hold and its efforts to fortify strategically sound positions bears fruit. In the interim, cost reduction activities under the new regulatory provisions will exert a steady upward force on profit margins through the early part of the decade.

These trends produce the forecasts presented in Tables 13.5 and 13.6 below.

The combination of steady growth propelled by its success in finding and developing unregulated lines of business and cost reduction activities in its regulated operations is seen to create regular increases in earnings.

These earnings translate into both an increase in the absolute level of dividends and stock price appreciation. The resultant TRR for investors between 1990–1994 is 16.4 percent and 15.4 percent between 1990–1999.

Bellsouth Corporation

Bellsouth's territory encompasses 38 LATA's spread over Florida, Georgia, North Carolina, South Carolina, Kentucky, Alabama, Mississippi, and Louisiana. Bellsouth has two principle operating subsidiaries: Southern Bell Telephone and South Central Bell Telephone.

Its location in the rapidly growing sunbelt has given Bellsouth the benefits of steady growth in access lines and continuous construction projects that have left it a modern and efficient plant. The relative absence of industrial and urban concentration confers both benefits and disadvantages. The principle benefit is the relative absence of bypass threat. The disadvantage lies in the relatively high number of assets and employees necessary to maintain such a dispersed system. Bellsouth's generally high cost structure and low marginal profit per access line will function to retard earnings growth throughout this period barring a major acquisition.

Bellsouth has aggressively deployed its assets in unregulated businesses while simultaneously seeking regulatory reform, which would exchange rate reductions and lower revenue requirements for profit sharing agreements. Despite a good position in the cellular phone market, continued population growth will provide the

Table 13.5   Forecast; Bell Atlantic

Year	DDM Stock Price Estimate	Revenues	Net Profit	EPS	CFS	Dividends
1990	50.00	12,150	1,397	3.58	10.00	2.33
1991	54.05	12,758	1,531	3.95	11.01	2.52
1992	58.88	13,523	1,690	4.38	12.22	2.71
1993	65.18	14,605	1,899	4.94	13.79	3.06
1994	72.77	15,919	2,149	5.62	15.69	3.49
1995	78.76	17,352	2,343	6.16	17.19	3.82
1996	86.02	19,087	2,577	6.81	19.00	4.22
1997	94.04	20,996	2,834	7.53	21.01	4.67
1998	102.91	23,095	3,118	8.32	23.23	5.16
1999	112.71	25,405	3,430	9.20	25.68	5.70

Table 13.6   Forecast Assumption; Bell Atlantic

Year	Shares Outstanding	Profit Margin	Revenue Growth	Payout Ratio
1990	390.0	0.115	0.050	0.65
1991	388.1	0.120	0.050	0.64
1992	386.1	0.125	0.060	0.62
1993	384.2	0.130	0.080	0.62
1994	382.3	0.135	0.090	0.62
1995	380.3	0.135	0.090	0.62
1996	378.4	0.135	0.100	0.62
1997	376.6	0.135	0.100	0.62
1998	374.7	0.135	0.100	0.62
1999	372.8	0.135	0.100	0.62

wellspring for profit advancement at Bellsouth. This will translate into steady, but slow, increases in earnings. Bellsouth's ample cash flow will serve to fund a generous dividend, but this will not be sufficient to offset the negative impact of slow earnings growth.

The relationship between CFS, CSS and EPS can be seen in Figure 13.7.

The trend toward increasing free cash at Bellsouth is likely to continue throughout the forecast period, in the absence of a major acquisition. Increasing cash flow reflects depreciation from significant expenditures on plant and equipment in recent years. How management deploys this cash in the coming years will determine the future prospects for investment in Bellsouth.

The available cash can be used to increase the dividend payout, strengthen the balance sheet, buy back common stock, or acquire new business ventures. The acquisition of MCAA in 1989 for stock suggests that management will be relatively conservative in the expenditure of cash for new business ventures.

An assumption is made that only a small amount of this cash will be directed towards stockholders in the form of dividends. A moderate amount of cash will be used to buy stock back and in-

Figure 13.7   Bellsouth

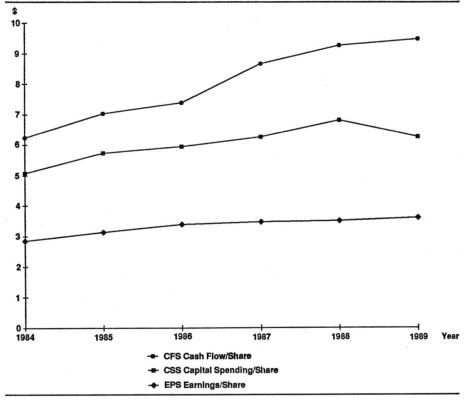

crease owners' equity early in the forecast period. An equally moderate amount of this cash will be directed towards acquisitions, but its effect on earnings growth in the forecast period will be small. The bulk of the excess cash will be used to upgrade existing businesses or it will be held in liquid form. These trends can be seen in the forecasts presented in Tables 13.7 and 13.8.

This pattern of earnings is expected to yields an investor holding Bellsouth between 1990 and 1994 an annual return of 14.2 percent. The comparable return for 1990–1999 would be 15.2 percent.

While not factored into the above forecast, there is a good chance that management will aggressively seek a large acquisition

Table 13.7   Forecast; Bellsouth

Year	DDM Stock Price Estimate	Revenues	Net Profit	EPS	CFS	Dividends
1990	52.50	15,000	1,875	3.92	10.50	2.75
1991	56.83	15,750	2,048	4.33	11.58	3.07
1992	59.63	16,538	2,150	4.59	12.28	3.26
1993	65.13	17,530	2,367	5.10	13.66	3.67
1994	67.84	18,582	2,509	5.36	14.33	3.86
1995	73.49	19,882	2,784	5.88	15.75	4.24
1996	82.67	21,473	3,221	6.74	18.04	4.85
1997	92.82	23,191	3,711	7.69	20.58	5.54
1998	99.34	25,278	4,044	8.30	22.21	5.97
1999	107.25	27,806	4,449	9.04	24.19	6.51

Table 13.8   Forecast Assumption; Bellsouth

Year	Shares Outstanding	Profit Margin	Revenue Growth	Payout Ratio
1990	478.0	0.125	0.050	0.70
1991	473.2	0.130	0.050	0.71
1992	468.5	0.130	0.050	0.71
1993	463.8	0.135	0.060	0.72
1994	468.4	0.135	0.060	0.72
1995	473.1	0.140	0.070	0.72
1996	477.9	0.150	0.080	0.72
1997	482.6	0.160	0.080	0.72
1998	487.5	0.160	0.090	0.72
1999	492.3	0.160	0.100	0.72

early in the forecast period. The acquisition would likely be financed with a combination of cash and stock. From an investor's point of view, Bellsouth is a company that should be leveraged up. Using currently free cash to service a large increase in debt to finance a significant increase in earnings growth makes a lot of sense for this company. While such a scenario may temporarily depress the price of Bellsouth stock, this weakness will provide excellent buying opportunities for the astute investor.

NYNEX Corporation

NYNEX encompasses the New York Telephone Company and the New England Telephone and Telegraph Company. Business revenues are highly concentrated in the New York and Boston SMSAs. Two-thirds of NYNEX's access lines are located in New York State. The density of its area served results in a high proportion of revenues from local service and a relatively low investment cost per access line.

The area's population base is affluent, but grows very slowly. The concentration of service center activity in New York City and

Boston raises the specter of bypass. The regulatory agencies have been very progressive in allowing NYNEX the rate flexibility to hold market share, preventing uneconomic bypass.

However, NYNEX has lagged in implementing digital switching and has a relatively high ratio of employees per access line, raising the possibility of economic bypass. In the late 1980s, Merrill Lynch built fibre optic networks in the New York and Boston metropolitan areas. The potential loss of revenue from economic bypass will result in a further increase in unit costs at NYNEX. Because of its unusual susceptibility to economic bypass, NYNEX may well be forced to offer telecommunication services below its costs to forestall additional revenue loss.

As technological innovation continues, economic bypass is likely to become an option for an increasing number of large firms in the region. Additionally, new competitors attracted by the potential profits from economic bypass might enter the market for telephone service. In either case, NYNEX will suffer loss of revenues and earnings. Whatever form bypass takes, it will be a major threat to NYNEX throughout the forecast period and exert continuous downward pressure on profit margins.

It may be that this rather grim scenario has prompted management to undertake major diversification efforts into the retail side of the information management business (computers and computer systems). Unfortunately, these acquisitions had not contributed to earnings by 1990 and were not expected to by most observers until at least the mid-1990s. The probability of this business ever contributing to earnings is remote. Retailing computers and computer systems is a competitive, mature business in which NYNEX holds no discernible competitive advantage.

If management is wise, this line of business will be sold or spun-off by the mid-1990s. NYNEX has to great a need for capital to modernize and upgrade its core business activities to continue to squander it into what has proved to be a black hole. This eventuality is not built into the forecast below.

Effective deployment of available capital will be critical in determining this firm's future earnings. NYNEX needs to get out of numerous low profit businesses it is currently enmeshed in and focus on the profitable telecommunication opportunities surrounding it.

Figure 13.8   NYNEX

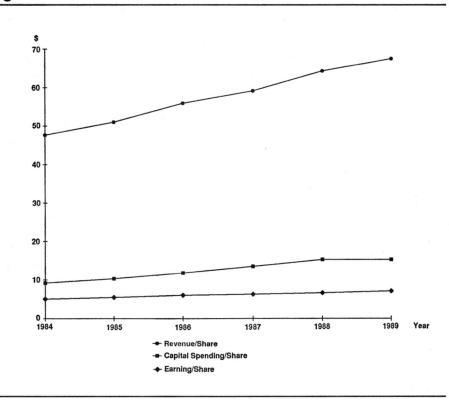

In the last half of the 1980s, NYNEX had relatively low profit margins. It does not appear to be positioning itself to improve this situation. Between 1984 and 1988, revenues per share grew 42 percent while capital spending per share increased 65 percent and earnings per share increased only 39 percent. These trends are depicted in Figure 13.8.

This would not be a bad situation if NYNEX were expending this capital to secure itself strong positions in emerging new markets, but this does not appear to be the case. NYNEX's capital expenditures appear primarily defensive and, in effect NYNEX appears to be running harder to stay in place. It is unlikely that

NYNEX will receive significant additions to capital through increased profits in its present business environment.

The outcome of this analysis is presented in Tables 13.9 and 13.10.

Revenue growth is expected to trail industry averages as the threat or reality of bypass exerts pressure on NYNEX to maintain market share. Profit margins are similarly expected to show a slight deterioration throughout the forecast period. Consequently investors in NYNEX can expect only a mediocre 8.5 percent TRR between 1990 and 1994 and a comparable return of 8.3 percent for the entire forecast period.

Pacific Telesis Group

Pacific Bell is the main operating subsidiary of Pacific Telesis, providing 97 percent of the rate base from 10 LATAs in California. These LATAs encompass the affluent SMSAs of San Francisco and Los Angelos. PT also owns Nevada Bell, which services Las Vegas and Reno.

Pacific Telesis has historically been a high cost company measured in terms of numbers of employees and investment per access line. To some extent this may be due to the need to service large, sparsely populated areas. Another reason might arise from the traditionally adversarial relationship between PT and the California Public Utilities Commission (CPUC).

California's population continues to grow rapidly and to increase in affluence, providing a good economic base for PT's operation. Access lines averaged 4 percent annual growth through the 1980s. The affluent and trendy California market will surely desire the full array of advanced telecommunication services as they become available.

Historically, PT has been burdened by relatively high levels of capital spending necessitated by its basic regulated telephone operation and a high level of debt service. The company used the prosperity following deregulation to reduce capital spending to manageable levels and strengthen its balance sheet. These trends may be seen in Figure 13.9.

As of the late 1980s, PT has begun to move more aggressively into unregulated lines of business in the telecommunications busi-

Table 13.9   Forecast: NYNEX

Year	DDM Stock Price Estimate	Revenues	Net Profit	EPS	CFS	Dividends
1990	82.20	13,800	1,256	6.34	18.50	4.50
1991	83.66	14,352	1,306	6.50	18.96	4.55
1992	84.47	14,926	1,343	6.59	19.21	4.61
1993	85.58	15,598	1,388	6.70	19.56	4.69
1994	86.71	16,300	1,434	6.83	19.91	4.78
1995	88.59	17,033	1,499	7.03	20.50	4.92
1996	90.53	17,800	1,566	7.23	21.10	5.06
1997	92.53	18,601	1,637	7.45	21.73	5.21
1998	94.92	19,531	1,719	7.71	22.48	5.39
1999	97.40	20,507	1,805	7.97	23.25	5.58

Table 13.10 Forecast Assumptions; NYNEX

Year	Shares Outstanding	Profit Margin	Revenue Growth	Payout Ratio
1990	198.0	0.091	0.040	0.71
1991	201.0	0.091	0.040	0.70
1992	204.0	0.090	0.040	0.70
1993	207.0	0.089	0.045	0.70
1994	210.1	0.088	0.045	0.70
1995	213.3	0.088	0.045	0.70
1996	216.5	0.088	0.045	0.70
1997	219.7	0.088	0.045	0.70
1998	223.0	0.088	0.050	0.70
1999	226.4	0.088	0.050	0.70

ness. Given the lucrative California market, these investments will bear fruit down the road. Short- and intermediate-term performance will increasingly depend upon the nature of the regulatory accords reached with the CPUC.

The late 1980s were characterized by a series of rate rollbacks that seriously impaired PT's ability to generate adequate returns for its shareholders. The dip in profits in 1987, illustrated in Figure 13.9, reflects the impact of a mandated rate cut. In an environment where PT has consistently earned below its allowable rate, the company and the CPUC will attempt to change the regulatory framework from an ROR orientation to an incentive orientation. The outcome of these negotiations will have a significant effect on PT's performance throughout the forecast period.

A forecast for stock prices and earnings is presented in Tables 13.11 and 13.12. The basic assumption is that the incentive regulatory schemata worked out between PC and the CPUC will be less favorable than those common in other parts of the country. Revenue growth will be held down early in this period as part of this agreement. Subsequently, revenues will increase moderately as unregulated business activities come on stream. Profit margins will in-

Figure 13.9   Pacific Telesis

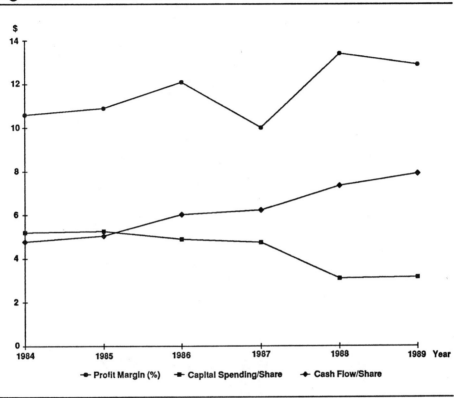

- ◆ Profit Margin (%)   ■ Capital Spending/Share   ◆ Cash Flow/Share

crease throughout the period as PT fully exploits its cost reduction opportunities.

This performance generates an annual return for investors of 16.8 percent in the 1990–94 and 1990–99 holding periods.

Southwestern Bell Corporation (S.W. Bell)

S.W. Bell operates 25 LATAs. Fifteen of these are located in Texas and the 10 remaining LATAs are distributed evenly throughout Arkansas, Kansas, Oklahoma, and Missouri. This region contains the Dallas-Ft Worth, Houston, and St. Louis SMSAs.

Table 13.11   Forecast; Pacific Telesis

Year	DDM Stock Price Estimate	Revenues	Net Profit	EPS	CFS	Dividends
1990	44.54	9,800	1,176	3.02	7.85	2.05
1991	48.55	10,290	1,286	3.37	8.76	2.15
1992	54.18	11,113	1,445	3.86	10.04	2.47
1993	58.84	12,225	1,589	4.26	11.10	2.64
1994	66.08	13,447	1,815	4.90	12.74	3.04
1995	72.18	15,061	2,033	5.43	14.13	3.37
1996	81.51	16,868	2,362	6.24	16.25	3.87
1997	92.13	18,892	2,739	7.17	18.67	4.45
1998	101.07	21,159	3,068	7.95	20.70	4.93
1999	110.99	23,698	3,436	8.82	22.95	5.47

Table 13.12   Forecast Assumptions; Pacific Telesis

Year	Shares Outstanding	Profit Margin	Revenue Growth	Payout Ratio
1990	390.0	0.120	0.040	0.68
1991	382.2	0.125	0.050	0.64
1992	374.6	0.130	0.080	0.64
1993	372.7	0.130	0.100	0.62
1994	370.8	0.135	0.100	0.62
1995	374.5	0.135	0.120	0.62
1996	378.3	0.140	0.120	0.62
1997	382.1	0.145	0.120	0.62
1998	385.9	0.145	0.120	0.62
1999	389.7	0.145	0.120	0.62

While the 1970s and early 1980s saw population and industry flourish in this sunbelt area, the fall in oil prices by the mid-1980s brought population growth and industrial expansion to a halt. Access line growth which had averaged 4.5 percent throughout the 1970s had barely climbed back to 2 percent by 1990.

The economic downturn in its region allowed S.W. Bell to slow its torrid capital spending pace. Despite slow revenue growth, the acceleration of cash flow as recent capital was depreciated created a healthy flow of free cash in the last half of the 1980s.

These trends may be seen in Figure 13.10.

This cash was used to reduce long-term debt and enter appropriate market niches in the unregulated sector of the telecommunications industry (e.g., cellular phones and paging). S.W. Bell should emerge from this period as a leaner and stronger company. With appropriate incentive regulation in place, by the time the oil economy picks up in the mid-1990s, S.W. Bell should be well positioned to take advantage of increased levels of business activity.

These assumptions lead to the forecast presented in Tables 13.13 and 13.14.

Figure 13.10 Southwestern Bell

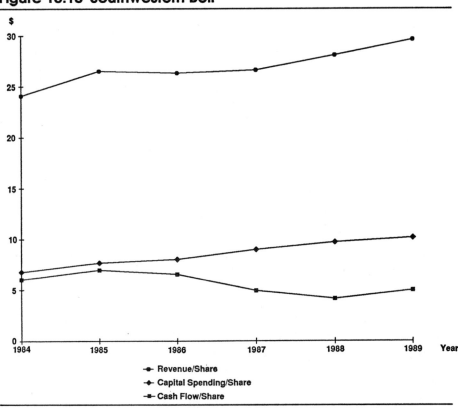

On the critical assumption that the oil economy will rebound strongly by the mid-1990s, investors in S.W. Bell can anticipate a handsome annual return of 21.6 percent if they buy at the beginning of 1990 and sell at the end of 1994. The return for 1990–99 would be the same.

U. S. West, Inc.

USW is a holding company operating in 14 states whose main subsidiaries include Mountain States Telephone Company, Northwestern Bell, and Pacific Northwest Bell.

Table 13.13 Forecast; Southwestern Bell

Year	DDM Stock Price Estimate	Revenues	Net Profit	EPS	CFS	Dividends
1990	54.00	9,125	1,186	3.95	10.00	2.77
1991	60.35	9,855	1,330	4.53	11.44	3.17
1992	69.20	10,841	1,572	5.32	13.45	3.62
1993	82.80	12,141	1,943	6.54	16.54	4.25
1994	91.13	13,598	2,176	7.29	18.44	4.74
1995	101.12	15,502	2,480	8.19	20.71	5.32
1996	119.69	17,827	3,031	9.86	24.93	6.41
1997	134.28	20,502	3,485	11.17	28.24	7.26
1998	142.52	23,577	3,772	11.91	30.12	7.74
1999	160.15	27,113	4,338	13.49	34.12	8.77

Table 13.14 Forecast Assumptions; Southwestern Bell

Year	Shares Outstanding	Profit Margin	Revenue Growth	Payout Ratio
1990	300.0	0.130	0.060	0.70
1991	294.0	0.135	0.080	0.70
1992	295.5	0.145	0.100	0.68
1993	296.9	0.160	0.120	0.65
1994	298.4	0.160	0.120	0.65
1995	302.9	0.160	0.140	0.65
1996	307.5	0.170	0.150	0.65
1997	312.1	0.170	0.150	0.65
1998	316.7	0.160	0.150	0.65
1999	321.5	0.160	0.150	0.65

Its service area is largely rural requiring a high capital investment per service line. Within its service area are a number of rapidly growing SMSAs—Minneapolis-St. Paul, Denver, Phoenix, Albuquerque, Tucson, and St. Lake City. To the extent that future population growth is concentrated in these urban areas, unit costs will tend to fall. To the extent that population growth occurs in less densely populated areas, units costs will rise.

A consequence of its high investment cost per line is a high overall level of capital spending (CSS) relative to cash flow (CFS) and earnings (EPS). While USW has made considerable progress in ameliorating these ratios since divestiture, the company does not throw off enough free cash to finance the desired level of diversification internally. Also, the relatively low return on investment from regulated operations exerts a downward pressure on stock price. This overall situation will remain throughout the forecast period, as seen in the trends presented in Figure 13.11.

Growth in the region's population and industry has been weak during the last half of the 1980s and the urban-rural balance has not altered significantly. USW has reacted to this by organizing its regulated telephone activities into a single corporate structure covering

Figure 13.11 U.S. West

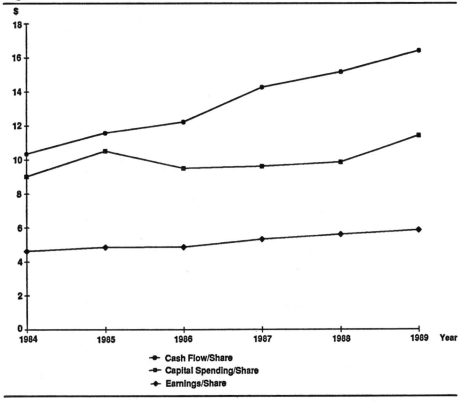

- Cash Flow/Share
- Capital Spending/Share
- Earnings/Share

all 14 states. The attempt is to better focus marketing efforts, achieve cost reduction through the centralization of facilities and present a united front to its many regulators. USW has historically been an efficient provider of telephone service and the coming (however haltingly) move to incentive regulation is not expected to significantly impact profits.

USW has an aggressive management that has sought to enhance stockholder wealth by very strong diversification efforts into unregulated sectors of the telecommunications industry. It is the major provider of cellular telephone services in its region.

Table 13.15 Forecast; U.S. West

Year	DDM Stock Price Estimate	Revenues	Net Profit	EPS	CFS	Dividends
1990	37.07	10,100	1,172	3.00	7.65	1.98
1991	38.88	10,706	1,263	3.19	8.13	2.04
1992	40.80	11,348	1,362	3.39	8.63	2.17
1993	42.58	12,143	1,457	3.57	9.10	2.29
1994	45.97	12,993	1,624	3.92	9.99	2.43
1995	48.02	13,902	1,738	4.14	10.53	2.56
1996	52.73	15,014	1,952	4.62	11.77	2.87
1997	56.07	16,216	2,108	4.97	12.65	3.08
1998	59.66	17,513	2,277	5.34	13.59	3.31
1999	63.51	18,914	2,459	5.74	14.61	3.56

Table 13.16   Forecast Assumptions; U.S. West

Year	Shares Outstanding	Profit Margin	Revenue Growth	Payout Ratio
1990	390.0	0.116	0.060	0.66
1991	395.9	0.118	0.060	0.64
1992	401.8	0.120	0.060	0.64
1993	407.8	0.120	0.070	0.64
1994	413.9	0.125	0.070	0.62
1995	420.1	0.125	0.070	0.62
1996	422.2	0.130	0.080	0.62
1997	424.4	0.130	0.080	0.62
1998	426.5	0.130	0.080	0.62
1999	428.6	0.130	0.080	0.62

The net results of these circumstances are incorporated in the following forecasts.

Given the anticipated steady growth in the region's economy during the forecast period and improvement in profit margins consequent on the success of the unregulated businesses, investors in USW may look forward to annual returns of 12.7 percent between 1990 and 1994 and 12.6 percent over the entire forecast period.

Summary

The seven Baby Bells are unlikely to duplicate their spectacular performance of 1984–1989 in the 1990s. However, potential returns to investors are solid with the exception of NYNEX, because of its cash flow problems and difficult, competitive environment. Potential returns are greatest at Southwestern Bell as a result of the anticipated recovery of the oil economy.

The upside or downside potential for the RHCs will increase as the acquisition of smaller high-tech telecommunications companies occurs. These acquisitions will be absolutely necessary to ensure satisfactory rates of growth in earnings. The ultimate impact on

RHC shareholders will depend upon the prices paid for these acquisitions and the ability of the RHCs to accommodate the more
adaptive and responsive management styles of the smaller companies.

Chapter 14

THE FUTURE FOR INVESTMENT IN COMMON CARRIERS

Performance Overview

The common carriers will offer investors excellent risk-return combinations during the 1990s. Fierce competition among AT&T, MCI, and Sprint will appear to threaten the well-being of one or more of these firms during this period. But it is in the interests of the regulators and consumers alike to have three viable firms striving to provide the best long-distance service. As a result, industry conditions will allow each firm to prosper.

The forecasted returns to investors are presented in Table 14.1.

MCI is likely to outperform its immediate post-divestiture accomplishments from an investors perspective. AT&T's performance is expected to slip somewhat—and rather badly towards the end of the forecast period. UT's relative fall in performance reflects a strong run up in price prior to the beginning of the forecast period as it became increasingly apparent that Sprint would become a commercial success.

With the exception of COMSAT, these firms will perform better than most RHCs in the decade of the 1990s. While some of the ITCs offer returns superior to the common carriers', these particular firms are associated with significantly higher risk.

AT&T appears to offer an especially attractive combination of risk and return during the forecast period. Despite the impending loss of its market share, AT&T is rock solid in its core markets and

Table 14.1   Forecast Returns; Common Carriers

1989-94 TRR Rank		TRR		
		1984-88	*1989-94*	*1989-99*
1	United Telecommunications	31.5%	23.2%	23.6%
2	MCI	21.7%	18.4%	18.7%
3	AT&T	20.8%	11.6%	11.6%
4	COMSAT	–1.2%	5.4%	5.4%

financially able to withstand the coming struggle. The decade of the 1990s will see AT&T lose its hegemony in the telecommunications industry, but its stockholders will be rewarded for their loyalty.

Industry Structure

The market for long distance telecommunication services is a battle-field. AT&T, MCI and Sprint are the combatants locked in a deadly struggle for market share. AT&T, the dominant player, is like a stag beginning to tire in the chase by the hounds. AT&T has many strengths, but the hounds are relentless in their quest.

The FCC and Judge Greene are aggressively pursuing a policy of encouraging workable competition by fettering the dominant firm. This creates a situation where AT&T is continually defending its receding share of the market.

The loss of market share for AT&T seems inexorable. The current (1988) long-distance carrier's market shares are illustrated in Figure 14.1

An anticipated market growth rate of 15 percent throughout the forecast period will sustain an increase in the absolute sales and profits of the three market participants. However, AT&T's share of the market will slip badly by 1999. This can be seen in Figure 14.2.

This deterioration in market share will be accompanied by steady pressure on margins as each participant strives to capture as

Figure 14.1   Common Carrier Market Share 1989

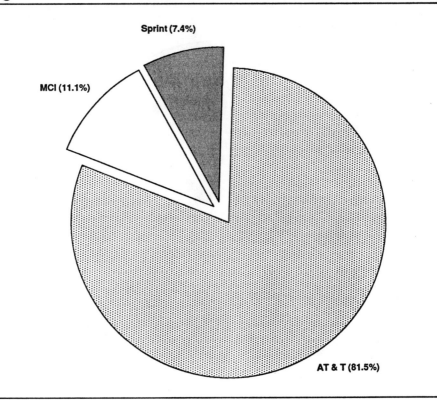

Sprint (7.4%)

MCI (11.1%)

AT & T (81.5%)

much of the emerging new business as possible while still holding onto past business. In an environment characterized by a ceaseless outpouring of new technology and a proliferation of new demands, each firm will need to exert great effort just to hold its position in existing markets, while at the same time moving aggressively to gain a strong foothold in the emerging new markets.

This creates an uncertain situation for investors. Promise and risk coexist. The market is rich and rapidly growing. Which firms are likely to succeed in the competition? Which are likely to fail? Will competition become so fierce that they each effectively kill each other off?

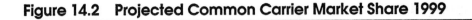

Figure 14.2   Projected Common Carrier Market Share 1999

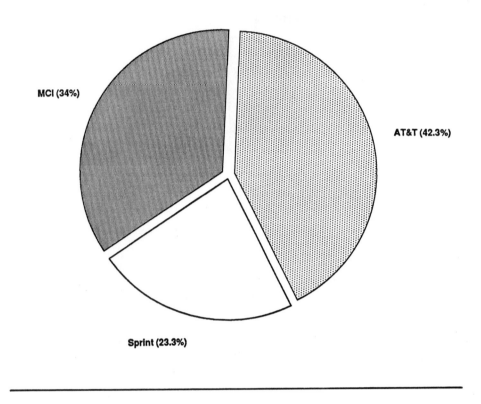

In developing the financial forecasts for these firms, a scenario emerges in which AT&T, Sprint, and MCI each prosper throughout the forecast period. Moreover, investors are rewarded with generous returns. However the likelihood of this scenario unfolding is based on the assumption that exceptionally strong market growth and exceptionally able management will continue for each of these three firms. The situation is analogous to that of a high wire act, mistakes by the performers are very difficult to correct. One slip and a great deal changes.

Returns Among Common Carriers

The small number of common carriers prohibits the application of statistical techniques in applying the DDM to forecasting stock prices in this sector. It would seem logical that the same forces that drive stock prices in other sections of the telecommunications industry would drive the stock prices of common carriers. As with other firms in the telecommunications industry, the common carriers have curtailed their dividend payout ratios to develop the many profitable opportunities they face. Stock prices would be expected to be a function of future cash flows.

The use of cash flows relative to net income in this sector is particularly important because, as of 1988, the FCC has mandated the use of the Uniform Systems of Accounts Rewrite (USOAR). This change represents a shift away from the treatment of capitalized items common in unregulated industrial enterprises. Significant items (certain types of plant capitalization, pensions leases, compensated absences, and income taxes) will now be expensed rather than capitalized. Thus, USOAR will decrease net earnings by increasing expenses, but improve the timing of cash flows. These changes will have a significant impact on common carrier net income throughout the forecast period.

By inspection it appears that a formulation of the DDM can be developed that has good predictive power during the 1984–1989 period. This formulation is presented in Table 14.2.

An attempt to apply this model suggests a lack of predictive validity. The problem is that 1984-1989 was a transition period and the market had treated the growth potential of the common carriers as unproven. This may have reflected the uncertainties of a situation in which the implications of competition, ongoing technological change, and a new regulatory approach were unknown. Therefore, the market was not automatically embedding any significant growth potential into theses stock prices, but was awaiting actual increases in cash flow. Thus, the sizable multiplier effect characterizing the model used in Table 14.2.

By 1989, it was apparent that the potential for increased profitability among firms in this sector had gained credibility in the mar-

Table 14.2   Diversified Common Carrier; DDM Estimates

	Price 1988	DDM Estimate	DDM Error
MCI Communications Corp.	23.00	25.16	2.16
American Telephone (AT&T)	28.75	25.62	−3.13
Communications Satellite Corp. (COMSAT)	26.38	27.42	1.04

DDM Estimator: Price Change (1984–88) = −18.6 + 16.97 × CFS Change (1984–88)

ket. At this point, the market had embedded a higher degree of growth in these stock prices than it had been willing to embed the immediate post-divestiture period. Thus it was necessary to alter the DDM from that suggested in Table 14.2.

The DDM used to develop the following forecasts has an intercept higher than that indicated in Table 14.2, but lower than that used for the RHCs. This reflects the market perception that future earnings are not as dependable among these firms as among the RHCs, but that they have become more dependable over the past five years. The slope of the DDM estimator is less than that used in Table 14.2, but higher than that applied to the RHC forecasts. This reflects strength of the linkage (in the mind of the market) between current performance and future performance among these firms. There is little doubt that quarter-to-quarter results among these firms will be thoroughly scrutinized to detect changing prospects among these firms. This situation may add a degree of volatility to stock prices in this sector that is not warranted by the underlying fundamentals.

AT&T Forecast

Although the signs are promising, the post-divestiture AT&T is not yet the lean and fast scion of the dowager Ma Bell it would like to be. The firm confronts an exceptional array of extraordinarily profitable opportunities. These opportunities will be reasonably well exploited in its long-distance communications business, albeit constrained by the legacy of the MFJ. AT&T's performance in its business, data, and consumer products area will be less than satisfactory. In this area, AT&T competes with both a set of large well-entrenched firms and a set of fast-moving, nimble and hungry market entrants. AT&T does not have sufficient firepower to blast out its larger opponents and is not mobile enough to compete with its smaller rivals. AT&T has many strengths, but they will not necessarily lead to success in this sector of the telecommunications market.

Divestiture has not freed AT&T from regulatory constraints in its core long-distance business. Continuing oversight by Judge Greene raises the possibility that the basic framework laid out under the MFJ could be altered. However, Judge Greene has taken a consistent and balanced approach to the needs of individual firms and the general public. It is quite likely that the trends established at the end of the 1980s will continue throughout the forecast period.

AT&T's strategic thrust is towards information management and movement. Despite its trendy high-tech sound, this is a potentially powerful concept that will allow AT&T to unify and focus its many strengths (technological expertise, solid customer relationships, excellent reputation, and superior research capabilities) into a host of potentially high profit market segments that are highly competitive, service intensive and driven by rapid technological change.

The question investors need to address is: Will this strategic thrust be implemented in a manner to allow AT&T to achieve the degree of responsiveness and adaptability necessary to success in such a context?

AT&T is beginning to prove itself in the new environment of structured deregulation. Its 1984-1988 IRR of 20.8 percent (see Chapter 13) is thought by many analysts to be a relatively strong performance, especially in light of asset write-offs of $1.6 billion in 1986 and $7.7 billion in 1988 (largely consequent on the conversion to digital switching). However, these returns to investors were significantly below those of the RHCs during this period.

An examination of its underlying business activities suggests the opportunities and threats confronting AT&T. AT&T is still primarily a long-distance communications carrier, as can be seen in Figure 14.3.

Between 1984 and 1989, telecommunication revenues were the only source of rising revenues for AT&T. Revenues from its busi-

Figure 14.3   AT&T Revenue Sources by Business Line

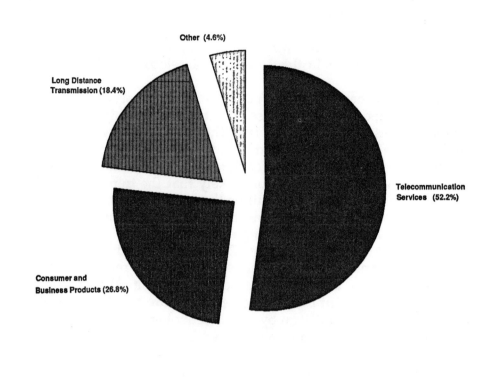

Other (4.6%)

Long Distance
Transmission (18.4%)

Telecommunication
Services (52.2%)

Consumer and
Business Products (26.8%)

ness, data, and consumer products held constant. Rental revenues fell throughout this period, as seen in Figure 14.4.

The net effect of the differing revenue streams was to leave total revenues essentially unchanged between 1984 and 1989. Net profits (excluding the very large adjustments from asset write-offs in 1986 and 1988) were up slightly during this period. These trends are illustrated in Figure 14.5.

This increase in net profits was made possible because of increasing margins in telecommunications services and business, data and consumer products. The increasing margins in telecommunications were largely the effect of falling access charges (Figure 14.4).

Figure 14.4   AT&T Revenue Components

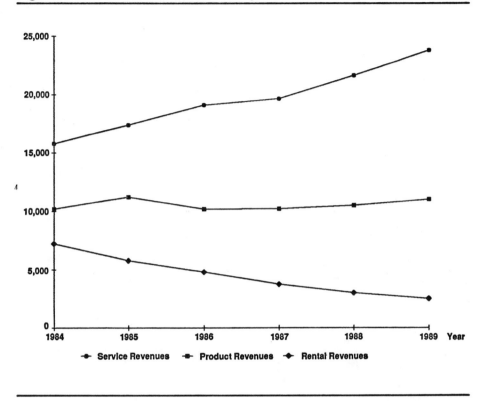

Increasing margins in the products area reflected strenuous cost reduction efforts. Operating margins shrank in the rental market as
increased competition severely pushed down sales (Figure 14.6).
The trends in margins are presented in Figure 14.6.

Telecommunication Services

Long-distance telecommunications services are provided through
public and private switched networks throughout the world. The
charge for these services generally includes an access charge which
is paid by AT&T to the BOC providing phone lines in the destina-

Figure 14.5   AT&T Income Statement Trends 1984–1989

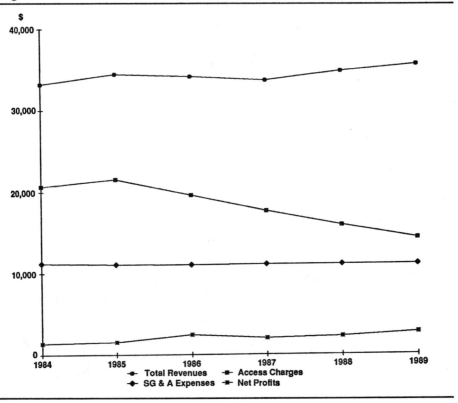

tion area of the call. As can be seen from Figure 14.4, these access charges are significant and their fall between 1984 and 1988 has been largely responsible for AT&T's net profits during this period.

As discussed in Chapters 13 and 14, this fall in access charges represents a rationalization of phone tariffs. Prior to divestiture, long-distance rates were set to subsidize local service rates. In the present competitive context, long-distance rates are being forced down toward cost (by competition and threat of bypass) and local service rates are rising. The direct consequence of this is falling access charges by the BOCs.

Figure 14.6   AT&T Profit Margins 1984–1989

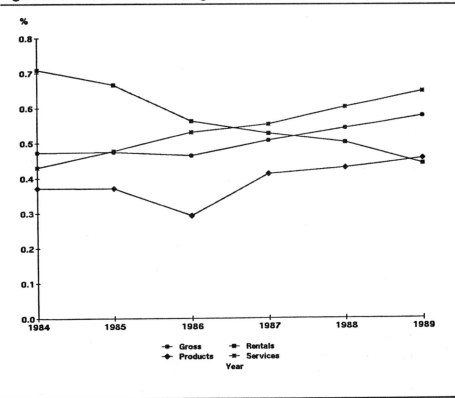

This fall in access charges will not continue indefinitely. The question then becomes where will future profits come from at AT&T.

The fall in long distance rates combined with technological advances that increase the value of long-distance telecommunications service and changes in business structure is estimated to propel the demand for this service upwards at an average annual rate of 15 percent. With private carriers providing 5 percent of long-distance telecommunication services by 1999, MCI will reach 35 percent, Sprint 23 percent, and AT&T the remaining 42 percent of the market for common long-distance carriers (refer to figure 14.2). Even with a dramatic fall in market share, AT&T's absolute telecommunication sales will rise strongly through the forecast period (Table 14.4).

Increasingly sophisticated communication needs on the part of business will bring forth a wide array of new telecommunication services. With the increasingly sophisticated needs of business, these service enhancements will move away from the category of luxuries to the category of necessities. These product lines will consequently carry higher profit margins. AT&T's technological capabilities guarantee it a large portion of this new business. Consequently, despite the severe price competition that is expected to characterize the forecast period, gross operating margins are expected to increase for AT&T in its telecommunications sector.

The movement from ROR to some form of price cap regulation at AT&T is also likely to enhance the bottom line at AT&T. The extent to which profits will be impacted depends upon (1) the exact form of price cap regulation and (2) the extent to which cost reductions are theoretically possible.

The exact form of rate regulation will be determined by political negotiations between AT&T, its competitors, Judge Greene, the FCC, and the Department of Justice—with rumblings from Congress thrown in. The prominence of AT&T as the epitome of "big business" will keep it under public scrutiny. Its size, large constituencies, and historically uneven relations with the Congress suggest that a resurgence of profits at AT&T is more likely to be interpreted as evidence of monopolistic behavior and consumer exploitation than the reward for a job well done. The price cap agreement reached in 1989 seems to have achieved an appropriate political balance, although this may change with experience.

The ability of AT&T to reduce costs sufficiently to increase profits under the 1989 price cap agreement is uncertain. Technological change may be reasonably expected to reduce absolute costs and increase the operating margins for long-distance telecommunications at AT&T. There is certainly room for the application of modern management practices at AT&T that could increase productivity. In addition, AT&T's $11 billion in selling, general, and administrative expenses would appear to have considerable potential for reduction.

Perhaps more important to the future of AT&T is its cost structure relative to that of its competitors. Changing technology appears to be reducing the importance of economies of scale in long-distance communication. As a result of the increasing size of its rivals, AT&T is likely not to have any inherent cost advantage over MCI and Sprint by 1999.

The net effect of these potentialities is likely to be a very modest rise in net operating margins to the 8 percent level in the telecommunications services area by the mid-1990s (Table 14.5). This assumes that the gain from the higher-margined new products will be largely offset by the loss of margins in presently established business lines to increasing competition. An assumption is also made that, as a result of political constraints, the gains from price cap regulation will be relatively small.

Business, Data and Consumer Products Business activity in this area includes the sale, installation, maintenance, and rental of communications and computer products for home and office use. (Administratively, AT&T differentiates between these products and telecommunication network systems—switching and communications equipment used by large communication companies. In this analysis, the two categories are grouped together.) This sector is characterized by constant product innovation and fierce competition. Performance to date has been mixed. Gains in new products and services have been largely offset by losses in existing products and services. This is an area where you have to run like heck just to stay even!

AT&T's potential in this area would be outstanding if it could effectively link the research innovations at Bell Labs with commercially successful products. As of 1990, AT&T was still too bureaucratic to accomplish this. Small aggressive companies in this market sector are able to move more quickly to new opportunities than is AT&T. This market sector also contains a number of larger well-entrenched competitors (e.g., IBM) whom AT&T will not be able to outmuscle.

AT&T's current limited success in this area is the result of tre-mendous cost-cutting. This is only a short-term palliative however, AT&T needs to become a more adaptive and responsive competitor. As price cap regulation may encourage it to downsize its bureau-cratic structure, the movement towards more decentralized man-agement may increase AT&T's effectiveness as a competitor.

Other Revenues This relatively small sector of the company will produce its most rapid growth in the forecast period (Table 14.4). This is a catchall category for a variety of specialized products and market niches where AT&T has achieved success, these in-clude the manufacture and sale of silicon chips, computer power supply devices, custom electronic components, special design products, and Federal Government sales. It is anticipated that AT&T will allocate increasing resources to these promising areas.

Overall Forecast The net effect of moderately increasing profits from the telecommunications area, stagnation in business prod-ucts, and rapid growth in miscellaneous markets is presented in Table 14.3 and supported by the assumptions developed in Tables 14.4-6.

For investors, the implication of this forecast is a good potential return subject to some degree of risk related to AT&T's ability to effectively implement its information management and movement strategy. On the basis of the assumptions presented, investors may expect an annual return of 11.6 percent between 1990 and 1994 and 11.6 percent in the full 10-year period.

It should be noted that the IRRs developed above reflect very aggressive growth assumptions concerning the telecommunications market. An economic downturn during this period could lead to considerably lower growth.

Also this forecast is quite sensitive to regulatory changes. A sig-nificant unfavorable change in the regulatory schemata could have a substantial negative impact on AT&T's fortunes.

In addition, the assumption is made that AT&Ts share of the long distance telecommunications market will stabilize at 42 per-cent. MCI and Sprint may not be willing to cede this. Private carri-ers may also become more active than presently assumed. Either case could reduce revenue growth and/or profitability at AT&T.

Table 14.3   Forecast; AT&T

Year	DDM Stock Price Estimate	Revenues	Net Profit	EPS	CFS	Dividends
1990	39.60	28,416	2,787	2.59	6.15	1.29
1991	43.58	29,831	3,254	3.01	7.14	1.44
1992	45.36	31,413	3,474	3.19	7.59	1.47
1993	46.78	32,642	3,644	3.34	7.94	1.50
1994	52.21	34,254	4,265	3.91	9.30	1.76
1995	53.98	35,739	4,465	4.10	9.74	1.85
1996	59.57	38,209	5,104	4.69	11.14	2.11
1997	67.50	41,022	6,008	5.52	13.12	2.49
1998	75.24	44,237	6,891	6.34	15.06	2.85
1999	82.85	47,736	7,757	7.14	16.96	3.21

Table 14.4   Forecast Assumptions; AT&T

Year	Shares Outstanding	Revenue Growth	Payout Ratio	PE Ratio	Access Charge Percentage
1990	1,077	4.50%	50%	15	47.5%
1991	1,082	4.74%	48%	14	47.5%
1992	1,088	5.04%	46%	14	47.5%
1993	1,090	3.77%	45%	14	47.5%
1994	1,089	4.70%	45%	13	47.5%
1995	1,089	4.16%	45%	13	47.5%
1996	1,088	6.46%	45%	13	47.5%
1997	1,088	6.86%	45%	12	47.5%
1998	1,087	7.27%	45%	12	47.5%
1999	1,087	7.33%	45%	12	47.5%

Table 14.5   Profitability Assumptions; AT&T

Year	Total Profit Margin	Profit Margins Telecommunications Services	Products	Other Services
1990	10%	8.00%	1.00%	11.00%
1991	11%	8.25%	2.00%	12.00%
1992	11%	8.25%	2.50%	12.00%
1993	11%	8.25%	3.00%	12.00%
1994	12%	8.50%	3.50%	14.00%
1995	12%	8.50%	4.00%	14.00%
1996	13%	8.50%	6.00%	14.00%
1997	15%	8.50%	8.00%	15.00%
1998	16%	9.00%	10.00%	15.00%
1999	16%	9.00%	12.00%	15.00%

An assumption that is particularly uncertain is the eventual (minimal) success in the business, data, and consumer products area. Computer production and sales activities have run several billion dollars in the red through the 1980s. Although this may reflect

Table 14.6   AT&T Revenue Forecast

Year	Total Revenues	Telecommunication Revenues			Product Revenues	Other Revenues
		Gross	Access Charges	Net of Access Charges		
1990	28,416	19,650	9,334	10,316	16,350	1,750
1991	29,831	21,222	10,080	11,142	16,677	2,013
1992	31,413	22,708	10,786	11,921	17,177	2,314
1993	32,642	24,070	11,433	12,637	17,344	2,662
1994	34,254	25,514	12,119	13,395	17,864	2,994
1995	35,739	27,300	12,968	14,333	18,038	3,369
1996	38,209	29,484	14,005	15,479	18,940	3,790
1997	41,022	32,138	15,265	16,872	19,887	4,263
1998	44,237	35,352	16,792	18,560	20,881	4,796
1999	47,736	38,887	18,471	20,416	21,925	5,396

entry costs that are now largely behind it, AT&T certainly has yet to prove itself in this area.

MCI Forecast

MCI is the second largest long-distance carrier, operating a 700 million capacity circuit mile microwave and fiber optics network. The driving force for improved profitability at MCI throughout the forecast period is the anticipated 15 percent annual growth expected in long-distance communication. MCI is expected to increase its market share to 32–36 percent of what will be a $186 billion market in 1999.

By 1990, MCI's capital needs will have stabilized. As can be seen from Figure 14.7, CFS exceeded CSS for the first time in 1988. This trend may be expected to continue throughout the forecast period, somewhat reducing MCI's stock price sensitivity to small fluctuations in operating results. MCI's efficient telecommunications network has significant operating leverage. This trend is evident in the rate rise in EPS in Figure 14.7.

MCI will be at the forefront of price-cutting tactics to increase its volume. However, its real thrust in expanding its market share will be powered by its speed and creativity in identifying and developing a wide array of specialized market niches in the telecommunications industry. It will lose some markets to AT&T's marketing muscle, existing customer relationships, and technological expertise, but it will win many more. AT&T can't be everywhere at the same time.

In addition, it is to the advantage of large business organizations (who generate a disproportionately large amount of long-distance business) to cultivate multiple vendors. By 1989, all Fortune 500 companies used some services from each of the common carriers. Long-distance telecommunications services in the 1990s will be characterized by rapidly rising demand, rapidly falling prices, and technological change. Under these conditions, it is both easy and profitable for large firms to retain the capability to shift their business among competing carriers.

While this depends on the warp and woof of competitive position and regulatory caprice, MCI is likely to enjoy continuous

Figure 14.7   MCI Financial Ratios 1984–1989

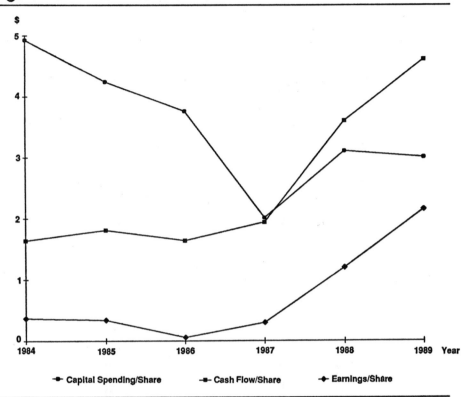

growth and increasing profitability throughout the forecast period, these results can be seen in Tables 14.7 and 14.8.

The implication of these forecasts are that investors may earn an annual return of 18.4 percent between 1990 and 1994 and 18.7 percent between 1990 and 1999 if they were to purchase MCI stock at the beginning of the respective period and sell at the end of the respective period.

United Telecommunications Forecast (UT)

UT operates the second largest non-Bell regulated telephone system in the U.S. In 1989, UT sold off its cellular phone business to Centel

Table 14.7   Forecast; MCI

Year	DDM Stock Price Estimate	Revenues	Net Profit	EPS	CFS	Dividends
1990	41.55	7,800	780	3.06	6.10	0.00
1991	51.85	9,360	1,030	4.00	7.97	0.00
1992	59.23	11,045	1,215	4.67	9.31	0.00
1993	69.54	12,812	1,409	5.57	11.11	1.67
1994	77.88	14,734	1,621	6.41	12.78	2.56
1995	87.46	16,944	1,864	7.37	14.69	3.68
1996	98.47	19,485	2,143	8.47	16.89	4.66
1997	111.15	22,408	2,465	9.74	19.43	5.36
1998	125.72	25,769	2,835	11.20	22.34	6.16
1999	142.48	29,635	3,260	12.88	25.70	7.09

Table 14.8   Forecast Assumptions; MCI

Year	Shares Outstanding	Profit Margin	Revenue Growth	Payout Ratio	PE Ratio
1990	255.0	0.10	0.25	0.00	15
1991	257.6	0.11	0.20	0.00	14
1992	260.1	0.11	0.18	0.00	15
1993	253.0	0.11	0.16	0.30	13
1994	253.0	0.11	0.15	0.40	12
1995	253.0	0.11	0.15	0.50	12
1996	253.0	0.11	0.15	0.55	12
1997	253.0	0.11	0.15	0.55	12
1998	253.0	0.11	0.15	0.55	11
1999	253.0	0.11	0.15	0.55	11

in order to focus its energies on the development of U.S. Sprint. At that time it raised its stake in Sprint to 80.1 percent (previously being 50/50 partners with GTE in this joint venture). In addition to its local telephone service companies, UT also owns 9 percent of SNET and is involved in directory publication.

US Sprint experienced its first operating profit in the last quarter of 1988. During the 1980s, Sprint spent several billion dollars to develop an all digital fiber optic long-distance transmission system to provide an alternative to AT&T's wire line system.

A digital fiber optics system has clear advantages over wire line, microwave, and satellite transmission systems. Fiber optics provides greater transmission fidelity and quality. The advantage of this for voice transmission may be mostly cosmetic, but it provides a serious competitive edge for the transmission of large volumes of data. The transmission of large volumes of data certainly will be one of the fastest growing market segments in telecommunications. In addition, clear superiority in this telecommunications area will provide Sprint with an entree into important business markets. This advantage will be enhanced by Sprint's planned completion of a world-wide fiber optics network.

Fiber optics linkages also have tremendous capacity. Fiber optics capacity is a function of the instruments that produce light signals that travel through the fiber. The expected advances in light source technology are expected to push capacity to new and unknown limits.

Once in place, the maintenance costs of fiber optic lines are expected to be about one-third of those of wire lines.

The key to reaching fiber optic's commercial potential is obtaining sufficient volume. The market for long-distance communication is expected to grow dramatically during the forecast period and beyond. In the late 1980s, Sprint grew at a rate significantly faster than the market as a whole. If this trend continues throughout the forecast period, Sprint's investors will reap bountiful rewards indeed.

The critical question in this matter is to what extent AT&T has the will and ability to protect its market share. AT&T is unlikely to be willing to cede market share to Sprint and MCI indefinitely. In the mind of the telecommunications consumer, AT&T's image of quality is a powerful asset. AT&T certainly has the marketing muscle to differentiate the long distance service "commodity" (if it is such) favorably in the mind of the consumer. It is possible that as a result of economies of scale, AT&T retains a cost advantage over Sprint in providing long-distance service (which is possible, but not necessarily so, because of the difficulties in allocating fixed costs among the various activities of these multifaceted firms).

It is likely to be another seven to ten years before the FCC and Judge Greene would allow AT&T to make unfettered pricing decisions with respect to its long-distance services. The current form of structured regulation sets minimum prices for AT&T long-distance services, which provides an umbrella under which MCI and Sprint are economically viable. This umbrella will surely be lowered over time. The critical factor for Sprint is the rate at which it is lowered.

Following divestiture in 1984, Sprint and MCI did not have equal access to the BOCs (their customers had to dial up to 20 numbers to make a call—equal access being when one can select any long distance carrier by merely dialing "1" and received a significant discount on access charges relative to AT&T. As the BOCs made the technological changes necessary to provide equal access, this discount was removed. Although volume increased throughout the period, earnings lagged as access charges rose and rate reductions were initiated by AT&T. Sprint was additionally handicapped by the fact that during most of this period its system was not complete and had to rely on leased lines (primarily from AT&T), which was expensive (in 1986 accounting for 26 percent of gross revenues) and vitiated Sprint's all fiber optics advantage.

In addition to absorbing the normal array of start-up costs characterizing the creation of a large system, Sprint experienced a major billing snafu which cost it hundreds of millions of dollars in lost revenues. This managerial glich may well have reflected the difficulties in coordinating decisions between two equal partners. The clear shift of operating responsibilities to UT should provide a focus that prevents the repetition of such an unfortunate event.

UT's decision to develop a strategic focus centered on the development of Sprint's optic fiber network is a strong move that bodes well for its future performance. In the short run, loss of the cellular phone operations eliminates a big cash drain and shores up its balance sheet. More importantly, management can now single-mindedly focus on developing the system's potential.

At the end of the 1980s, Sprint was moving strongly to enhance the inherent advantages of its system with an array of conventional (e.g., full operator services handling station-to-station and person-to-person calls and customer assistance in call completion) and new (e.g., an array of 800 services designed to serve the needs of small and medium sized businesses) telecommunication services. UT had expanded its international telecommunication services to the point where it could directly connect to 90 percent of the world's phones.

It is expected that strong price competition will characterize the market for long-distance services throughout the forecast period. Sprint's unique all fiber optics capability will give it some shelter from this competition, but by the middle of the 1990s AT&T is expected to have a comparable all fiber optics system in place. The general fall in the cost of long-distance services will induce this market to grow dramatically throughout the forecast period. By the end of the 1990s, Sprint's share of this market should top out in the 20–25 percent range.

Despite the downward pressure on prices, Sprint's growth in volume is expected to be highly profitable because its operating leverage is so high. The effects of these assumptions can be seen in Tables 14.9 and 14.10.

With the assumption that Sprint is able to capture 23 percent of the long-distance market for $20 billion in revenues, and increase profit margins in the face of fierce price competition, investors can expect a superior 23.2 percent annual return between 1990 and 1994 and a 23.6 percent annual return through 1999.

Communications Satellite Corporation (COMSAT)

COMSAT is the sole U.S. Carrier authorized to operate international satellite facilities. COMSAT has a 26.5 percent interest in the international consortium INTELSAT. COMSAT leases half circuits to U.S. long distance carriers from its Comstar and Marisat satellites. COMSAT's video subsidiary provides in-room TV services, primarily to Holiday Inns.

For the 25 years prior to the mid-1980s, COMSAT was flush with profits from its monopoly position. It provided a service for which there was no effective substitute and sparked a revolution in

Table 14.9   Forecast Assumptions
United Telecommunications Inc.

Year	Shares Outstanding	Profit Margin	Dividend Payout	Revenue Growth
1990	212	6.6%	37%	12%
1991	216	7.0%	37%	15%
1992	221	7.0%	37%	17%
1993	225	7.3%	40%	20%
1994	229	7.5%	40%	20%
1995	234	7.7%	40%	20%
1996	239	8.0%	40%	20%
1997	244	8.0%	45%	20%
1998	248	8.0%	45%	20%
1999	253	8.0%	45%	20%

Table 14.10 Forecast; United Telecommunications Inc.

Year	DDM Stock Price Estimate	Revenues	Net Profit	CFS	EPS	Dividends
1990	38.13	8,750	578	7.65	2.72	1.01
1991	45.19	10,063	704	9.33	3.26	1.21
1992	51.85	11,773	824	10.92	3.74	1.38
1993	63.38	14,128	1,031	13.66	4.58	1.83
1994	76.74	16,953	1,271	16.84	5.54	2.22
1995	93.15	20,344	1,566	20.75	6.69	2.68
1996	114.66	24,413	1,953	25.87	8.18	3.27
1997	136.39	29,295	2,344	31.05	9.62	4.33
1998	162.47	35,154	2,812	37.25	11.32	5.10
1999	193.76	42,185	3,375	44.71	13.32	5.99

the way business organizations thought about the strategic implications of data transmission. COMSAT's transmission system was highly capital intensive and required heavy capital expenditures to maintain and develop the system. This created a financial structure for a service that had very low marginal costs and very high operating leverage. With demand growing by leaps and bounds and without competition COMSAT performed quite well.

The entry of fiber optics technology into this sector of the market in the early 1980s began to erode profits. In addition, COMSAT was forced to restructure during the mid-1980s to shed unprofitable manufacturing and private phone service businesses. This situation led to a significant decline in revenues and cash flows. In 1986, cash flow fell below capital spending. This deficit in funds was financed

Figure 14.8   COMSAT Financial Ratios 1984–1989

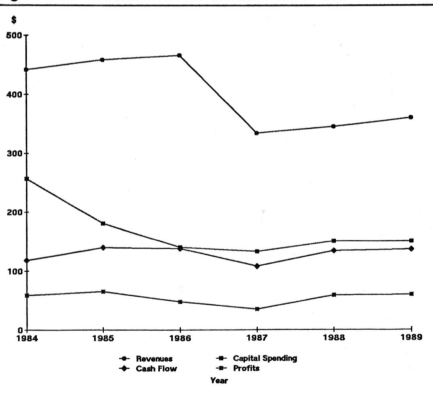

by a jump in the long-term debt ratio from 30.1 percent in 1984 to 39.8 percent in 1985. This decline in sales and profitability began to reverse itself towards 1990. These trends can be seen in Figure 14.8.

The demand for COMSAT's maritime services looks promising and is expected to increase at a 15–20 percent rate throughout the forecast period. In contrast, COMSAT is likely to lose significant market share in its core transmission services to domestic and international fiber optic networks. At the very least, profit margins will be under severe pressure. The company plans to expand its COMSAT Video operations, but these are unlikely to reproduce the old levels of profitability.

The impact of these trends may be seen in Tables 14.11 and 14.12.

As can be seen from these forecasts, COMSAT will grow slowly on the basis of exploiting market niches for which it can provide a unique service. Profit margins will be maintained by FCC-sanctioned price increases in those monopolistic markets.

While COMSAT remains viable in this scenario, the returns to investors will be meager. Annual returns of 5.4 percent are forecast between 1990 and 1994 as well as for the full forecast period.

Table 14.11   Forecast Assumptions; COMSAT

Year	Shares Outstanding	Profit Margin	Revenue Growth	Rayout Ratio	PE Ratio
1990	18.8	0.145	0.040	0.39	10
1991	18.9	0.140	0.040	0.40	10
1992	19.1	0.135	0.030	0.41	10
1993	19.3	0.135	0.030	0.41	10
1994	19.1	0.130	0.030	0.41	10
1995	19.1	0.130	0.030	0.41	10
1996	19.1	0.130	0.030	0.41	9
1997	19.1	0.130	0.030	0.41	9
1998	19.1	0.130	0.030	0.41	9
1999	19.1	0.130	0.030	0.41	9

Table 14.12 Forecast; COMSTAT

Year	DDM Stock Price Estimate	Revenues	Net Profit	EPS	CFS	Dividends
1990	33.50	450	65	3.48	8.40	1.36
1991	33.38	468	66	3.46	8.35	1.38
1992	33.03	482	65	3.40	8.21	1.39
1993	33.44	497	67	3.47	8.38	1.42
1994	33.50	511	66	3.48	8.40	1.43
1995	34.13	527	68	3.59	8.65	1.47
1996	34.78	543	71	3.69	8.91	1.51
1997	35.45	559	73	3.80	9.18	1.56
1998	36.14	576	75	3.92	9.46	1.61
1999	36.85	593	77	4.04	9.74	1.65

Summary

Despite what often appears to be an excess of competitive zeal in their fight for market share, AT&T, MCI, and UT will each experience continuing increases in sales and profits throughout this period.

The increasingly rapid succession of technological advances, and proliferation of new long-distance telecommunications products, will spur a 15 percent annual growth in long-distance service sales (despite a continuing fall in the cost of long-distance services). This strong growth in the size of the market will allow AT&T to gracefully lose its hegemony in the long-distance communications.

Structured competition, accompanied by continued government and judicial review, will ensure the financial success of each of the market participants. Consumers will benefit from the continued introduction of new services, the unbundling of old services, and the tendency for price to be driven to incremental cost of service in most market segments.

Chapter 15

FUTURE RETURNS IN WATER UTILITIES

Performance Overview

At best, investors in water utility stocks may only expect to tread water in the 1990s. In the late 1980s, a deluge of interest flooded this area and water utilities became faddish. This was partially (perhaps primarily) a response to the October 1987 market break. Portfolio managers (having been generally swept over the dam) wished to appear conservative and defensive. The consequent tidal move to water utility stocks innundated these generally thin markets pushing prices up.

If water utility stocks lose their faddish status, investors could take a bath. Current (1989) price levels do not appear adequately supported by dividends or potential increases in earnings. Investors in water utility stocks may be in over their heads at the start of the 1990s.

The returns to investors forecast in Table 15.1 assume smooth sailing in this market. If this sector loses popularity, the storm could be tough to ride out. The only thing certain in this area is that the pool of water utility analysts will continue to make bad puns that leave investors at sea over whether to fish or cut bait.

Table 15.1   Water Utility Forecast TRRs

		TRR	
Rank by TRR 1990-94	Utility	1990-94	1990-99
1	Middlesex Water	17.4%	15.5%
2	SJW Corporation	16.1%	15.1%
3	American Water Works	16.0%	15.3%
4	Consumers Water	15.4%	15.4%
5	E'Town Corporation	14.3%	14.5%
6	United Water Resources	13.8%	13.5%
7	California Water Service	12.5%	12.0%
8	So. California Water	12.1%	12.3%
9	Connecticut Water	10.9%	10.4%
10	Hydraulic Corporation	10.5%	10.6%
11	Philadelphia Suburban	10.4%	8.6%

Market Structure

Water utility stocks are an anomaly. From an investor's standpoint, they do not behave as either equity or debt instruments. Like long-term bonds, water utility stocks do not fluctuate in value as the long-term interest rate changes. Investors are attracted to these stocks by the stability of the dividend and the size of the dividend.

Unlike bonds, water utility stocks do not pay a fixed return. Most firms in the industry have a history of steadily increasing dividends. Relative to industrial and other utility stocks, water utility stocks are little effected by market risk. Water utility stock prices are not a strict function of dividends.

Bonds and water utility stocks appear to be subject to a distinctly different array of market forces. However, water utility stocks constitute an island, standing apart from the mainland of co-variant investment opportunities in other equity instruments.

Water utility stocks in general enjoyed a strong secular upward trend in value during the 1980s. The stock prices of individual water utilities exhibited considerable volatility during this period, reflecting the market's perception of their operating prospects, diversification efforts and the presence of undervalued assets.

Stock price movements among water utility companies appear to be completely independent of broader market forces. Yet their price is not strictly a function of yield either.

The recent upsurge in the popularity of water utility stocks has created a danger for investors. Stock price levels in 1989 among the 11 water utilities analyzed below do not appear to be warranted by current or future earnings or current and future dividend levels.

A mentality has arisen with respect to water utility stocks that they are "defensive." Even though the market had recovered from the October 1987 crash, that experience has left a legacy of anxiety for many investors. The betas (measures of market risk) presented in Table 1 for the water utilities suggest a relative absence of market risk. Many investors apparently feel comforted by their inclusion in a portfolio. Security of yield and low market risk (Table 15.2) have contributed to their popularity among institutions.

The current popularity of water utility stocks as a portfolio component has been reinforced by their strong performance in the 1980s. Table 15.3 indicates that returns ranged from an exceptional 41 percent at United Water Resources to 7 percent at California Water Services. These are certainly great returns from stocks that bear little exposure to market risk.

However, the yield from dividends indicated in Table 15.3 is not suggestive of a desirable selection for one's portfolio when long-term government bonds are yielding 10 percent. The relative attractiveness of water utility stocks during this period rested upon their price appreciation. This effect can be seen more clearly from the annual returns developed in Table 15.4.

The important question for investors then becomes: To what extent will water utility stock prices appreciate in the future? For reasons developed below, only moderate price appreciation may be expected among these stock in the 1990s.

Water Utility Fundamentals

Water utility fortunes in the 1990s will depend on (1) the success of present and future diversification efforts, (2) regulatory responses

Table 15.2   Water Utilities Market Attributes (Spring, 1989)

Utility	Beta	Institutional Ownership	Stock Exchange Listed
American Water Works	0.16	36.2%	NY
California Water Service	0.03	6.1%	OTC
Connecticut Water	0.07	14.9%	OTC
Consumers Water	0.01	10.5%	OTC
E'Town Corporation	−0.03	27.6%	OTC
Hydraulic Corporation	−0.12	27.7%	NY
Middlesex Water	−0.11	12.5%	OTC
Philadelphia Suburban	−0.14	23.7%	NY
SJW Corporation	−0.34	6.4%	A
So. California Water	0.02	21.3%	OTC
United Water Resources	0.24	11.6%	NY

Table 15.3   Water Utilities; Yield, Return and P-E Ratios

Rank by TRR 1989-94	Utility	TRR 1984-88	Yield 1988	P-E 1988
1	United Water Resources	40.6%	4.9%	16
2	American Water Works	32.9%	3.9%	10
3	Middlesex Water	31.9%	6.2%	12
4	Hydraulic Corporation	30.5%	5.3%	14
5	So. California Water	28.7%	7.4%	14
6	SJW Corporation	28.4%	6.0%	12
7	Connecticut Water	25.9%	8.2%	10
8	Consumers Water	25.2%	4.9%	13
9	E'Town Corporation	23.4%	7.0%	11
10	Philadelphia Suburban	14.5%	7.0%	11
11	California Water Service	7.2%	6.3%	10

Table 15.4   Water Utilities TRR 1984–1988

Rank by TRR 1989-94	Utility	TRR (includes dividends) 1984-88	TRR (excludes dividends) 1984-88	Percent of TRR due to Price Change
1	United Water Resources	40.6%	23.0%	56.7%
2	American Water Works	32.9%	24.9%	75.7%
3	Middlesex Water	31.9%	18.8%	58.8%
4	Hydraulic Corporation	30.5%	19.2%	63.0%
5	So. California Water	28.7%	14.7%	51.3%
6	SJW Corporation	28.4%	17.0%	59.7%
7	Connecticut Water	25.9%	10.9%	42.3%
8	Consumers Water	25.2%	16.8%	66.7%
9	E'Town Corporation	23.4%	10.8%	46.3%
10	Philadelphia Suburban	14.5%	4.2%	29.2%
11	California Water Service	7.2%	–0.2%	–3.4%

to the increased costs inherent in the implementation of the Safe Drinking Water Act of 1986, (3) the ability of these firms to realize the value in undervalued assets, and (4) the future pattern of demand for water utility stocks.

Diversification Efforts

While earnings at water utility companies tends to go up over time, considerable year-to-year variance may be encountered. Heavy snows or a wet spring can fill reservoirs. If this is followed by a hot dry summer that necessitates watering the lawn, washing the car, and lots of showers, profits will climb. Dry conditions in the winter and spring bring about water use restrictions during the summer that cause volume and thus profits to fall. The resultant potential for variability in EPS is suggested by the experience of the four firms presented in Figure 15.1. for 1985 through 1989.

To avoid this variability and to avoid the limits placed on earnings by the ROR regulation universal in this industry, most water utilities have experimented with diversification. The majority of the

Figure 15.1   Selected Water Utility Earnings Per Share 1985–1989

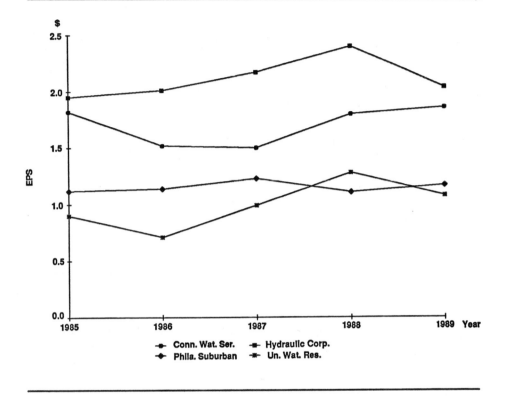

11 firms considered in this Chapter are organized as holding companies for this purpose. Only Consumers Water Company (33 percent), Philadelphia Suburban (30 percent), and the Hydraulic Company (20 percent) currently have revenues from nonregulated activities exceeding 10 percent of total revenues. The thrust of the diversification varies considerably among the firms.

Consumers Water Services has real estate and manufactured housing subsidiaries. Philadelphia Suburban focuses on management information systems and services. The Hydraulic Company is primarily concerned with a forest products enterprise.

The opportunity to diversify is good for stockholders only if those diversification efforts generate a return above that which could be earned by investments of comparable risk. While there is no reason to think that these diversification activities will not meet this test, this is not a strongly held view. If anything, it would be expected that management experience gained in the relatively sheltered existence of a protected monopoly would not be conducive to success in more competitive arenas.

While it appears that, as a group, companies with diversified activities produce better per share earnings than companies without, the correlation is not strong. It may even be that diversification is a consequence, rather than a cause, of higher EPS.

Increasing Costs

Congress amended the Safe Water Drinking Act in 1986 to require the EPA to develop 83 new contamination standards for public drinking water by 1989, with 25 additional standards each year for the following three years. The total impact of these standards on the cost of drinking water is uncertain because the maximum levels of contamination permitted have not yet been set and, in a large number of instances, the appropriate chemical or water treatment procedures to reduce contamination have not been developed.

The potential for increased costs is enormous, but varies significantly from utility to utility depending on the current quality of water provided by that utility. The impact on each water utility will be further affected by the form of the existing rate structure and the amount of embedded capital. The net effect for both companies and consumers alike will be higher costs. The question is whether or not regulatory authorities will permit rates to rise at a sufficient rate to protect or increase earnings.

Regulatory agencies may be forced to allow higher earnings in order to enable firms in the industry to attract the capital necessary to meet the new standards. The industry is sufficiently concerned about financing the necessary capital to bring the quality of water up to these standards that it is questioning the propriety of applying the same formula to its capital expenditure processes that are applied to electric utilities (the same regulatory agency frequently oversees both utilities in a given state). The assumption underlying this concern is that the water utilities do not have the same strong access to capital markets that electric companies enjoy.

The upshot of these concerns is likely to be a squeeze on water company earnings in the intermediate period while regulatory agencies adapt to the new circumstances. This would then be followed by an era of unprecedented (for water utilities) high earnings.

Undervalued Assets

The late 1980s saw a burgeoning of interest in water utilities that owned surplus acreage in areas where the value of the land was considerably higher than was being carried on the books. Realizing such hidden value has proved a difficult task. The regulators must agree that the land is indeed unneeded for future water supply purposes. Even with this approval, the water utility must secure permission to develop the land from appropriate planning and zoning bodies. Where the watershed land represents one of the few expanses of undeveloped woodland in the area, such conversion may be fought by consumerist or environmentalist groups. Even where land may eventually be developed, the gains are likely to be nonrecurring and relatively small compared to operating cash flows.

There is some chance that the higher costs resulting from the Safe Water Drinking Act of 1986 will encourage consolidations and mergers in the industry. The experience of these activities in the 1980s has been that the stockholders of the acquired firms reap significant benefits, i.e., the value of their stock will rise 10 percent to 30 percent. If the infatuation with mergers and acquisitions that characterized Wall Street at the end of the 1980s continues, water utility stockholders could conceivable benefit from this trend.

Future Demand for Water Utility Stocks

Water Utilities came to the attention of the investment community in 1985 and have maintained a comparatively high profile since that time. The gains in trading volume between 1984 and 1985 generally ranged in the 50 percent to 100 percent range. Smaller but still significant increases were recorded in 1986. Trading in water utility shares have remained at about this level since that time.

Historically, dividend yields at water utilities have been on a par with those of telephone utilities and slightly below those of electric and gas utilities. Despite steady increases in the actual level of dividends (Table 15.5) for most firms, dividends yields have been eroded (Table 15.3) by the rise in stock prices.

Note that the dividends from water utility stocks at current price levels alone will not be sufficient to support its price. Indeed, 1990 appeared to see the beginning of a general disenchantment with these stocks. As long as water utility stocks retain their popularity among investors as "defensive" elements in their portfolio, this should not be a problem. However "defensive" water utility stocks might be, the only justification for purchasing them at current price levels is their potential for future price appreciation. If the investment community were to become disenchanted with this sector and their popularity fade, stock prices are likely to fall to levels where their yields are consistent with their historical pattern.

Water Utility Returns

The DDM model applies well to predicting future stock prices in the water utility industry. As suggested in Table 15.4 above, stock price changes have played an important role in determining investor returns. An investor in water utilities certainly does not want to be guided by dividend prospects or yield alone. The relationship between the TRR earned by investors in this industry and the change in stock prices between 1984 and 1988 is depicted in Figure 15.2.

As might be expected from this scatter, the change in stock price is capable of explaining ($R^2 = .86$) most of the variance in the annual return.

Stock prices among water utilities are driven by dividends. The relationship between stock price and dividends among the 11 water utilities considered in this Chapter are illustrated in Figure 15.3.

The level of dividends among these 11 utilities is capable of explaining ($R^2 = .83$) the bulk of the variation in stock prices.

The level of dividends to common shareholders reflects the companies willingness to return a portion of its earnings to its owners. The considerations impacting the selection of a particular payout level depend on cash flows, capital structure, anticipated capital

Table 15.5 Water Utility Dividends

Utility	1984	1985	1986	1987	1988	Percentage Increase 1984-88
American Water Works	$0.40	$0.50	$0.56	$0.64	$0.68	70.00%
California Water Service	$1.50	$1.30	$1.40	$1.50	$1.60	6.67%
Connecticut Water	$1.42	$1.48	$1.49	$1.52	$1.53	7.75%
Consumers Water	$0.64	$0.73	$0.82	$0.90	$0.98	53.12%
E'Town Corporation	$2.60	$2.66	$2.74	$2.82	$2.79	7.31%
Hydraulic Corporation	$1.27	$1.32	$1.37	$1.43	$1.51	18.88%
Middlesex Water	$1.43	$1.52	$1.60	$1.68	$1.74	21.75%
Philadelphia Suburban	$0.88	$0.88	$0.94	$0.94	$0.94	6.82%
SJW Corporation	$1.33	$1.45	$1.57	$1.68	$1.76	32.83%
So. California Water	$1.65	$1.78	$1.88	$1.93	$2.02	22.42%
United Water Resources	$0.67	$0.68	$0.70	$0.77	$0.84	25.37%

**Figure 15.2   Water Utility Total Return–
                 Stock Price Relationship**

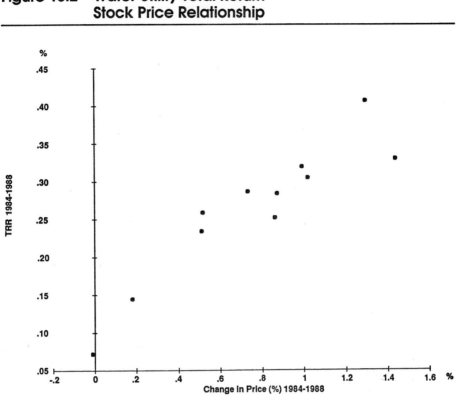

needs, and maintaining a stock price that will attract new capital into the firm.

The potential for dividends over the long-run is a function of earnings. Among these water utilities, dividends are strongly (R^2 = .75) related to EPS. This relationship is depicted in Figure 15.4.

Thus, future returns to investors in the water utility industry are dependent upon increases in earnings that will impact dividend levels, which, in turn, will impact stock prices. Dividends and any change in stock prices will then determine the annual return associated with a particular investment.

Figure 15.3   Water Utility Stock Price–Dividend Relationship

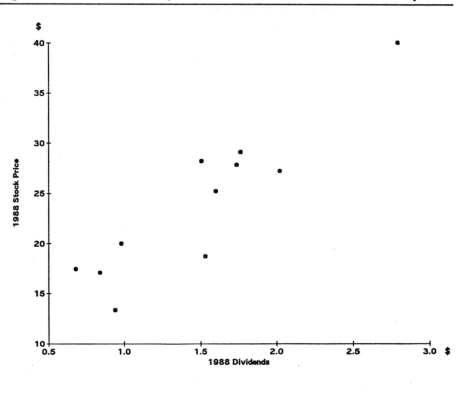

A potential for additional volatility among water utility stocks rises from the fact that the equities for many of these firms are thinly traded. Even where the dividend is secure and the stock price well supported by the dividend, selling pressure could swiftly devalue the stock. The recent popularity of this sector has heightened this danger. To the extent that a ready market exists for these stocks on the basis of their steady flow of dividends, this danger is lessened.

Figure 15.4   Water Utility Earnings Per Share–
**   Dividend Relationship**

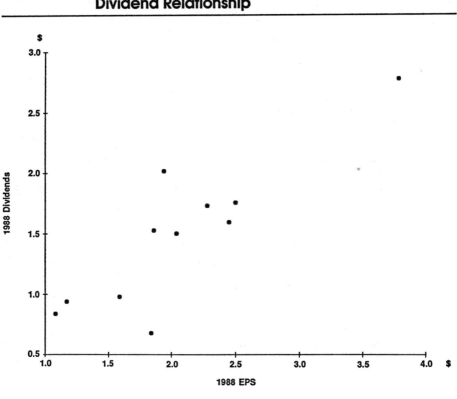

Specific Water Utilities

American Water Works Company, Inc. (AWW)

AWW is a holding company primarily involved in operating its 25 local water service companies. The company has an aggressive strategy of acquiring water systems that are adjacent to its existing systems and will yield economies of scale. AWW also seeks to enter new service areas and provides management services to non-affiliated water service companies.

Existing operations span 500 communities in 20 states serving 1.5 million customers. As the largest water utility, AWW has been able to develop a strong reputation for management and technological expertise. With its exposure to a large number of regulatory bodies, AWW is thus in a strong negotiating position with its regulators. This may prove to be its paramount advantage over time and help it to outperform other water utilities during the 1990s.

Total water capacity at AWW is 1.2 billion gallons per day with 493 gallons of distribution storage. Considerable acreage is owned almost entirely in watersheds. Residential customers consume about 45 percent of its water sales in gallons, but generate 55 percent of its revenues.

The companies operations are geographically diverse. Table 15.6 indicates the diverse nature of AWW's operations.

This diversity will protect AWW from undue fluctuations in its earnings with respect to weather or regulatory problems; the latter aspect may be particularly important as it negotiates with its various regulators over the impact of meeting the Pure Water Drinking Act standards.

These considerations suggest that the coming decade will be a time of continued growth for AWW. The pace of acquisitions should increase somewhat as smaller water companies are hard-pressed to meet the new standards for purity. AWW itself will require significant additions of capital to upgrade its present facilities and to meet these standards. Local regulators will be forced to concede rate increases of sufficient magnitude to cover increased costs and attract necessary capital to the firm. Growth in EPS will be slowed by the need to issue additional stock.

The forecasted returns to investors in AWW are presented in Table 15.7.

These returns yield an investor in AWW a TRR of 16.0 percent between 1990 and 1994. The annual return for the full forecast period is 15.3 percent.

The dividends from AWW are well protected by earnings and a solid balance sheet. Investors in this stock must find that this is sufficient to compensate them for a lack of upside potential, even in the face of significant downside potential in stock price due to the chance of the industry losing its popular aura.

Table 15.6 American Water Works Company Regional Subsidiary Revenues

Region	*Percent of Water Service Revenues*
Eastern Region	24.6%
Mid-America Region	20.1%
Pennsylvania Region	23.6%
Southern Region	20.7%
Western Region	9.5%
New England	1.5%

Table 15.7 American Water Works Company Forecast

Year	EPS	*Payout Ratio*	Dividends	*Stock Price*	Yield
1990	2.03	0.40	0.81	16.18	5.02%
1991	2.17	0.42	0.91	18.00	5.07%
1992	2.32	0.43	1.00	20.00	5.00%
1993	2.56	0.45	1.15	21.00	5.48%
1994	2.81	0.45	1.27	22.50	5.62%
1995	3.09	0.45	1.39	24.00	5.80%
1996	3.34	0.45	1.50	25.00	6.01%
1997	3.61	0.45	1.62	37.00	6.01%
1998	3.90	0.45	1.75	30.00	5.85%
1999	4.21	0.45	1.89	33.62	5.63%

California Water Service Company (CWS)

CWS owns and operates 21 water systems serving a population of approximately 1,350,000 individuals residing in 38 cities and communities in California. Its strategic focus is entirely on providing water service.

The communities served range the length of the state from north of Sacramento to south of Los Angeles. The company maintains over 4,00 miles of mains with an average daily water consumption of over 250 million gallons. In a normal year, approximately 22 percent of the water delivered is purchased. Each of CWS's 21 water systems are regulated as distinct entities by the California Public Utilities Commission.

Figure 15.5   California Water Service Company Income Statement Trends 1980–1989

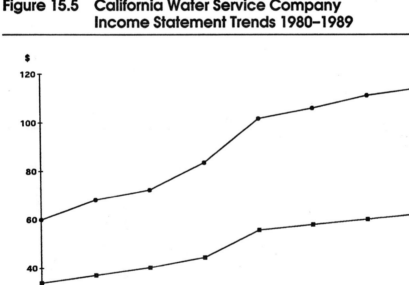

Table 15.8   California Water Service Company Forecast

Year	EPS	Payout Ratio	Dividends	Stock Price	Yield
1990	2.73	0.64	1.75	25.00	7.00%
1991	2.87	0.63	1.81	25.63	7.05%
1992	3.01	0.62	1.87	26.31	7.09%
1993	3.16	0.62	1.96	27.36	7.16%
1994	3.32	0.61	2.02	28.09	7.21%
1995	3.48	0.61	2.13	29.24	7.27%
1996	3.66	0.60	2.20	30.02	7.31%
1997	3.84	0.60	2.30	31.26	7.37%
1998	4.03	0.60	2.42	32.57	7.43%
1999	4.24	0.60	2.54	33.93	7.49%

As a result of population growth, appropriate rate relief, and small acquisitions, a strong growth in revenues has produced steadily increasing net income. These trends may be seen in Figure 15.5.

Continued population growth is likely to spur revenues and earnings throughout the forecast period. Profit margins at CWS were squeezed towards the end of the 1980s by water restrictions necessitated by the drought in the northwestern United States. The impact of the Pure Water Drinking Act is likely to have minimal impact on their operations.

The results of these assumptions are embodied in the forecast presented in Table 15.8.

Steady growth averaging 5 percent in EPS throughout the period earn the investor in CWS an annual return of 12.5 percent between 1990 and 1994 and a comparable return of 12.0 percent between 1990 and 1999.

Connecticut Water Service, Inc.

CONN is a holding Company whose subsidiaries own and operate water companies for 30 towns in Connecticut. The operating companies serve slightly more than 55,000 residential, commercial and

**Figure 15.6   Connecticut Water Service Company
                 Earnings Per Share and Dividend Trends 1984–89**

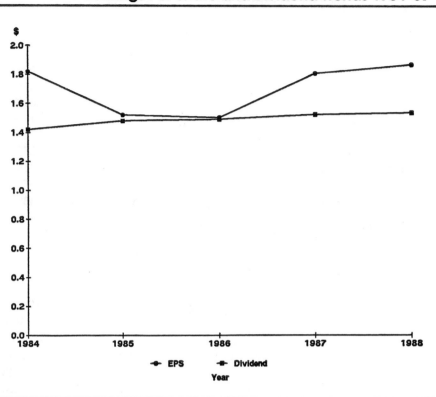

industrial customers. The company has approximately 900 miles of mains and generates operating revenues of less than $30 million.

The stock is thinly traded over-the-counter with 2 million shares outstanding and approximately 5,000 individual stockholders. The company is highly leveraged. CONN borrowed heavily at the end of the 1980s to finance necessary capital expenditures because issuing additional stock would have necessitated a cut in the dividend and disadvantaged existing stockholders.

Net income was only 1.6 times long term interest in 1987. In 1989, CONN had a B+ Standard and Poor's rating. At 8.2 percent, CONN averaged the highest effective yield of all 11 water utilities covered in this Chapter. As can be seen from Figure 15.6, dividends

Table 15.9   Connecticut Water Forecast

Year	EPS	Payout Ratio	Dividends	Stock Price	Yield
1990	1.85	0.80	1.48	17.94	8.25%
1991	1.85	0.80	1.48	17.94	8.25%
1992	1.90	0.78	1.48	17.97	8.25%
1993	1.90	0.78	1.48	17.97	8.25%
1994	1.95	0.76	1.48	17.97	8.25%
1995	1.95	0.76	1.48	17.97	8.25%
1996	1.99	0.76	1.51	18.30	8.26%
1997	2.03	0.76	1.54	18.64	8.27%
1998	2.07	0.76	1.57	18.99	8.28%
1999	2.11	0.76	1.60	19.35	8.29%

almost consume EPS at CONN. While actual cash flow is higher and gives a little more margin than apparent, without significant rate relief CONN is likely to cut the dividend to fund required capital expenditures as it nears the limits of its borrowing capacity.

The difficulties inherent in this situation are compounded by the significant additions to capital spending that will be necessary to comply with the new EPA pure drinking water standards.

The forecast for the financial performance of CONN is presented in Table 15.9.

As indicated in the forecast, little price appreciation can be expected in CONN stock throughout the period. Assuming they are able to keep a moderately large dividend, investors may expect an annual return of 10.9 percent between 1990 and 1994 and 10.4 percent between 1990 and 1999. A high dividend yield is critical to this return.

These results are obtained despite a fall in EPS and a cut in the dividend early in the forecast period. With its current rate structure, expenses are likely to rise more rapidly than revenues. The returns indicated in Table 15.8 assume a moderate amount of rate relief. It remains to be seen whether or not such rate relief is forthcoming.

Consumers Water Company (CONS)

CONS is a holding company whose primary interests are in owning and operating water utilities. Important subsidiaries include a real estate development firm and two companies that manufacture housing. Seventy five percent of total revenue was derived from water utility operations in 1987, compared with 67 percent in 1986.

The company operates 25 separate water systems through 13 companies in seven states (in the Midwest and Northeast areas). In 1987, 198,000 customers were served by its water utilities, generating $60 million in revenue. Operating margins appear high, but the company is highly leveraged. Total interest expense in 1987 was $9,244 million, compared with net income of $8,870 million. Long-term debt was $83 million and short-term debt $21 million in 1987.

Figure 15.7 Consumers Water Company
Earnings Per Share and Dividend Trends 1984–88

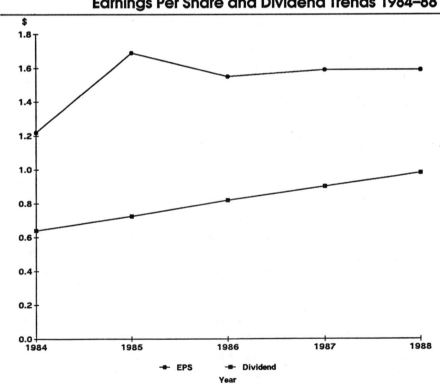

Despite this capital structure, CONS's dividend is amply protected by earnings. This may be seen in Figure 15.7.

This high degree of financial leverage exposes the firm to some volatility in its earnings. The degree of downside exposure is limited by its dividend coverage, but earnings could soar with a fall in interest rates. The sensitivity of its real estate operations to interest rate swings will amplify this volatility. CONS appears to have some undervalued land that gives the firm additional upside potential. From an investor's standpoint, this stock may be a wolf in sheep's clothing.

The forecast for CONS is presented in Table 15.10.

On the basis of moderating interest trends during the first half of the period, CONS investors may look forward to an annual return of 15.4 percent in both forecast periods.

E'Town Corporation

E'Town is a holding company organized in 1985 with its principle subsidiary being the Elizabethtown Water Company (EWC). The EWC supplies retail water service (82 percent of volume) to its customers in 49 municipalities and wholesale water (18 percent of volume) to eight other municipalities and three privately owned re-

Table 15.10   Consumers Water Company Forecast

Year	EPS	Payout Ratio	Dividends	Stock Price	Yield
1990	1.84	0.64	1.18	14.53	8.11%
1991	1.99	0.63	1.25	15.37	8.15%
1992	2.15	0.62	1.33	16.26	8.19%
1993	2.32	0.61	1.41	17.20	8.22%
1994	2.50	0.60	1.50	18.19	8.26%
1995	2.63	0.59	1.55	18.74	8.27%
1996	2.76	0.59	1.63	19.62	8.30%
1997	2.90	0.59	1.71	20.54	8.32%
1998	3.04	0.59	1.80	21.51	8.35%
1999	3.19	0.59	1.88	22.52	8.37%

tail water companies. Under agreement with the State of New Jersey, the EWC is fortunate to have access to ample supplies of water from the Raritan Basin to meet present and future needs. This access removes fluctuations in earnings which would occur with differing weather patterns.

Operating revenues have grown strongly as a result of continuing population and industrial growth in central New Jersey. Costs of expansion combined with the regulation of rates by the Public Utility Commissioners of the State of New Jersey has kept profits flat. These trends may be seen in Figure 15.8.

As is characteristic of this capital intensive industry, return on assets is low. However, E'Town is well leveraged and has experi-

Figure 15.8   E'Town Corporation Income Statement Trends 1981–1987

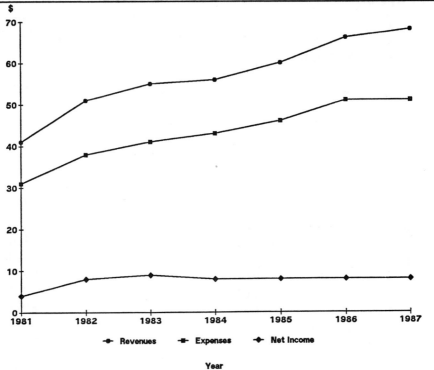

Figure 15.9   Performance Trends 1981-1987

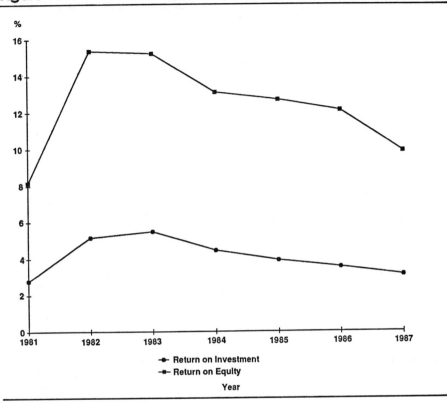

enced returns on equity that compare with those of other water utilities.

A disturbing trend suggested in Figure 15.9 is the tendency for both the ROI and ROE to fall toward the end of the decade. The fall in ROE is especially significant as the reorganization of the company in 1985 permitted a significant increase in financial leverage.

E'Town's management is restless. The returns indicated in Table 15.11 are seen as greatly inferior to those which could be earned by capital employed in the nonregulated areas of central New Jersey's booming economy. E'Town Properties has been created as a real estate subsidiary to enable the firm to increase its returns to share-

Table 15.11   E'Town Corporation Forecast

Year	EPS	Payout Ratio	Dividends	Stock Price	Yield
1990	4.15	0.70	2.91	35.05	8.29%
1991	4.36	0.68	2.96	35.70	8.30%
1992	4.58	0.67	3.07	36.86	8.32%
1993	4.80	0.65	3.12	37.51	8.33%
1994	5.09	0.65	3.31	39.62	8.35%
1995	5.40	0.65	3.51	41.87	8.38%
1996	5.72	0.65	3.72	44.25	8.41%
1997	6.07	0.65	3.94	46.77	8.43%
1998	6.43	0.65	4.18	49.44	8.45%
1999	6.81	0.65	4.43	52.27	8.47%

holders; certain watershed properties have been transferred to E'Town Properties to this end. It remains to be seen if E'Town will be successful in this highly competitive and potentially profitable market.

The forecast developed below expect the contributions of E'Town Properties to be minimal early in the forecast period and to only have a moderate impact on earnings thereafter. It is felt that, despite the ownership of valuable land, E'Town Properties will find the development of this land full of hazards and pitfalls. To the extent that this development effort increases the debt burden at E'Town, the ability of the firm to maintain a constantly increasing dividend may be imperiled.

The resultant forecast is presented in Table 15.11.

The expected pattern of dividends and stock prices will yield investors in E'Town Corporation annual returns of 14.3 percent between 1990 and 1994 and 14.5 percent for the full forecast period.

Hydraulic Company (HC)

HC is a holding company whose primary (80 percent of its revenue) activities are owning and operating water utilities around Bridgeport and Stamford Connecticut, serving 12 separate commu-

Table 15.12 Hydraulic Company Forecast

Year	EPS	Payout Ratio	Dividends	Stock Price	Yield
1990	2.44	0.66	1.61	23.38	6.89%
1991	2.51	0.66	1.66	23.75	6.98%
1992	2.59	0.65	1.68	23.75	7.08%
1993	2.67	0.65	1.73	24.00	7.22%
1994	2.75	0.65	1.79	24.50	7.29%
1995	2.83	0.65	1.84	25.25	7.28%
1996	2.91	0.65	1.89	26.00	7.28%
1997	3.00	0.65	1.95	27.00	7.22%
1998	3.09	0.65	2.01	28.00	7.18%
1999	3.18	0.65	2.07	28.75	7.20%

nities with a combined population of 374,000. HC owns 29 well fields with a combined daily capacity of 76 million gallons which is supplemented by 17 reservoirs with a storage capacity of 25 million gallons.

HC's ability to pump from its wells is sensitive to yearly fluctuations in rainfall. This situation could limit profits in the event of a drought.

HC has diversified into real estate (primarily downtown Bridgeport), timber production (HC owns 20,000 acres of woodland), electricity cogeneration, and management consulting in the area of the privatization of public utility operations.

HC's balance sheet is solid, and its dividend well supported by earnings. While the dividend may be expected to increase steadily throughout the forecast period, the growth in earnings will be sufficiently weak to limit the size of this increase. Thus the price of HC stock may be expected to weaken from current levels in order to generate a yield comparable to that of alternative investments. These trends may be seen in Table 15.12.

As a result of this forecast, investors in HC may anticipate only 10.5 percent TRR between 1990 and 1994 and 10.6 percent between 1990 and 1999.

Middlesex Water Company (MWC)

MWC is a small water utility serving 51,000 customers in North Central New Jersey. The company maintains 634 miles of mains. MWC utilizes five sources of water with a combined daily capacity of 50 million gallons and has a storage capacity of 251 million gallons.

Total revenues are somewhat over $22 million. Returns on investment run around 4 percent and returns on equity hover around 8 percent. Earnings are sensitive to variations in the amount of rainfall and regulatory policies. The company appears committed to a steady increase in the dividend in order to maintain stock values at levels which will permit it to attract new capital to facilitate expan-

Figure 15.10 Middlesex Water Company
Earnings Per Share and Dividends Trends 1984–88

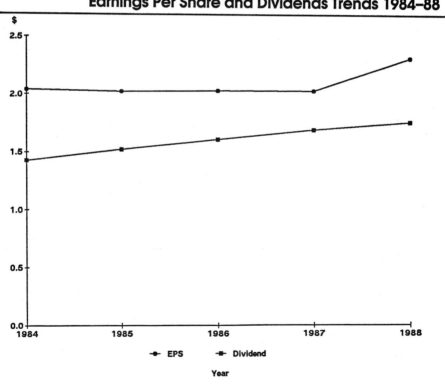

Table 15.13 Middlesex Water Company Forecast

Year	EPS	Payout Ratio	Dividends	Stock Price	Yield
1990	1.22	0.76	0.93	10.00	9.27%
1991	1.27	0.76	0.96	10.50	9.18%
1992	1.32	0.76	1.00	11.00	9.12%
1993	1.37	0.76	1.04	11.25	9.27%
1994	1.43	0.76	1.08	12.00	9.04%
1995	1.48	0.76	1.13	12.50	9.02%
1996	1.54	0.76	1.17	13.00	9.02%
1997	1.61	0.76	1.22	13.50	9.04%
1998	1.67	0.76	1.27	14.00	9.06%
1999	1.74	0.76	1.32	14.50	9.10%

sion. This commitment can be seen in the recent trends in EPS and Dividends in Figure 15.10.

The forecast for MWC is presented in Table 15.13.

As a result of the anticipated trends in stock prices and dividends, MWC will offer one of the higher yields in the industry. This has partially resulted from investor disenchantment that manifested itself in a price decline in early 1990. At current price levels, this solid stock offers investors a good risk-return combination. Investors may anticipate 17.4 percent annual return between 1990 and 1994 and 15.5 percent for the full forecast period.

Philadelphia Suburban Water Company (PSWC)

PSWC has been a holding company since 1969. Nonregulated operating revenues now constitute 30 percent of its total revenues. PSWC's diversification program centers on providing an array of data processing, engineering, and management services to other water companies.

PSWC's water utility subsidiary supplies water service to 59 boroughs in Delaware, Montgomery, and Chester counties in Pennsylvania. The company maintains 2,700 miles of mains and draws its water principally from five rural streams that are tributaries to

Figure 15.11 Philadelphia Suburban Water Company
Earnings Per Share and Dividend Trends 1984–88

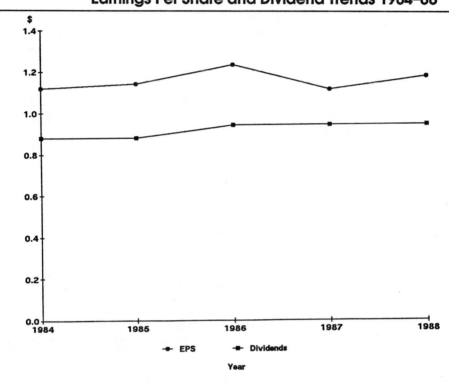

the Schuylkill and Delaware rivers. The company's four major filtration and purification plants have a pumping capacity of 180 million gallons per day.

PSWC's return on assets is 4 percent and its return on equity is 7.6 percent. Despite good growth in its service area, PSWC has not been able to translate this increase to its EPS. Variations in EPS reflect both rate adjustments and variations in earnings due to the weather. This trend can be seen in Figure 15.11.

The key word describing PSWC is stability. Unfortunately, this concept suggests that growth in the future in earnings, dividends, and share price will be slow. This is reflected in the forecast presented in Table 15.14.

Table 15.14   Philadelphia Suburban Water Co. Forecast

Year	EPS	Payout Ratio	Dividends	Stock Price	Yield
1990	1.22	0.76	0.93	13.70	6.77%
1991	1.24	0.78	0.97	14.19	6.84%
1992	1.27	0.76	0.96	14.12	6.83%
1993	1.32	0.75	0.99	14.41	6.87%
1994	1.37	0.72	0.99	14.39	6.87%
1995	1.43	0.69	0.98	14.27	6.85%
1996	1.48	0.66	0.97	14.21	6.84%
1997	1.51	0.68	1.03	14.86	6.93%
1998	1.54	0.65	1.00	14.57	6.89%
1999	1.58	0.62	0.98	14.26	6.85%

The average rate of growth in earnings is expected to advance from 2 percent to 4 percent in 1993 as the implementation of the Pure Water Drinking Act moves into full swing. The increase in earnings occurs when PSWC responds to the resultant increased demands for its management service. EPS is expected to resume its slow growth by 1997.

These trends result in an TRR to investors of 10.4 percent between 1990 and 1994 and 8.6 percent between 1990 and 1999.

SJW Corporation

SJW is a holding company whose principle subsidiary (the SJW Water Co.) provides water service to 200,000 customers in rapidly growing Santa Clara, California. Its other subsidiary (the SJW Land Co.) develops property around company headquarters.

The company currently maintains 2,300 miles of mains. Purchased water ranges between 15 percent and 20 percent of total revenues. Future expansion to accommodate population growth may necessitate additional issues of stock to raise capital. The drought in the Northwest at the end of the 1980s adversely impacted earnings by restricting water consumption. The company remained commit-

Figure 15.12 SJW Corporation
Earnings Per Share and Dividend Trends 1984–88

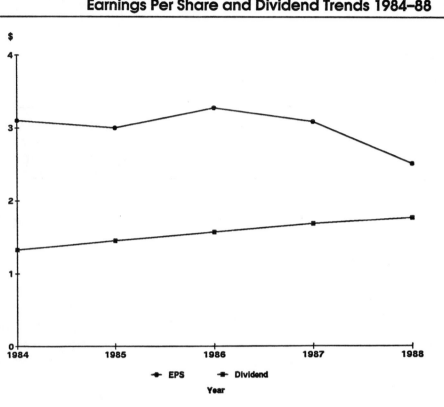

ted to strong increase in dividends during this period. These trends can be seen in Figure 15.12

SJW has strong upside potential (for a water utility). The company has good potential because it services such an affluent and rapidly growing area. The breaking of the drought sooner or later will result in dramatic increases in earnings. These increases in earnings may be somewhat diluted by the need to issue new stock. Throughout this period the company will be aggressively supporting stock price with dividend increases in order to benefit existing stockholders. The result of these trends are embedded in the forecast presented in Table 15.15.

Table 15.15 SJW Corporation Forecast

Year	EPS	Payout Ratio	Dividends	Stock Price	Yield
1990	3.20	0.62	1.98	25.42	7.81%
1991	3.42	0.61	2.09	26.60	7.85%
1992	3.66	0.60	2.20	27.84	7.90%
1993	3.92	0.60	2.35	29.58	7.95%
1994	4.16	0.60	2.49	31.17	8.00%
1995	4.40	0.60	2.64	32.86	8.04%
1996	4.67	0.60	2.80	34.66	8.08%
1997	4.95	0.60	2.97	36.55	8.12%
1998	5.25	0.60	3.15	38.57	8.16%
1999	5.56	0.60	3.34	40.70	8.20%

These results translate into an above average annual return to investors of 16.1 percent in the 1990–94 period and 15.1 percent between 1990 and 1999.

Southern California Water Company (SCWC)

SCWC gathers, purifies and distributes water in ten California counties, three of which are adjacent to Los Angeles. The Company also distributes electricity (11 percent of revenues) in San Bernardino County.

The water distribution system contains 2,600 miles of pipeline and derives water from its own wells as well as purchasing water from the (L.A.) Metropolitan Water District. Rapid population growth in its service area places a constant strain on its ability to provide adequate supplies of water. The hot dry climate in this region produces a high per capita demand for water and periodic water shortages.

ROI tends to be high for the industry (4.5 percent in 1987), although variable. ROE tend to be low (6.9 percent in 1987). The low ROE reflects the relatively low degree of operating leverage in this firm. Increasing the operating leverage would have a significant impact on the profitability of the firm.

**Figure 15.13 Southern California Water Company
Earnings Per Share and Dividend Trends 1984–88**

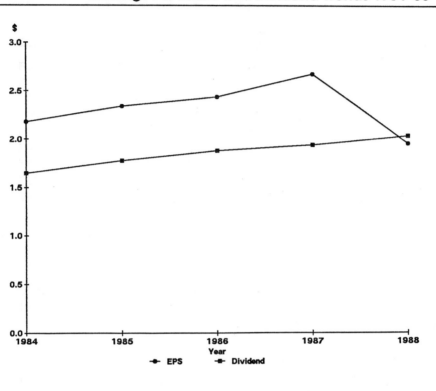

The company has a strong history of increasing EPS and dividends. The dip in EPS in 1988 was the result of accounting adjustments and unfavorable weather conditions. These trends may be seen in Figure 15.13.

The forecast for SCWC is presented in Table 15.16.

As a result of the dip in earnings in 1988 and a high payout ratio, SCWC stock had the highest yield in the industry at the end of the 1980s. As the market regains confidence in SCWC's earnings ability, stock prices are expected to rise sufficiently to lower yields to industry norms. These factors will combine to yields investors a substantial 12.1 percent annual return in the 1990–94 period and 12.3 percent in the 1990–99 period.

Table 15.16   Southern California Water Co. Forecast

Year	EPS	Payout Ratio	Dividends	Stock Price	Yield
1990	2.60	0.78	2.02	31.00	6.50%
1991	2.76	0.76	2.09	32.00	6.55%
1992	2.92	0.75	2.19	33.25	6.59%
1993	3.10	0.75	2.32	34.00	6.83%
1994	3.28	0.75	2.46	35.04	7.03%
1995	3.48	0.75	2.61	35.71	7.11%
1996	3.69	0.75	2.77	38.48	7.19%
1997	3.91	0.75	2.93	40.35	7.27%
1998	4.14	0.75	3.11	42.34	7.34%
1999	4.39	0.75	3.29	44.45	7.41%

United Water Resources (UWR)

In 1983, UWR was organized as a holding company. Its principle subsidiaries (Hackensack Water Company, Spring Valley Water Co., and the Dundee Water Power and Land Co.) are regulated water utilities. Hackensack supplies water to 170,000 customers in 60 New Jersey municipalities located in Hudson and Bergen counties. Spring Valley supplies water to 60,9000 customers in Rockland County, New York. The company's water supplies have historically been subject to periodic shortages, which has given some unevenness to its earnings. The completion of the Wanaque South Project (providing access to the Monksville Reservoir) will effectively droughtproof Hackensack Water and provide greater stability to future earnings.

UWR has moved aggressively to diversify. Its Rivervale real estate subsidiary is growing rapidly and is an important contributor to company profits. The importance of this subsidiary to the operation can be seen from Figure 15.14.

In addition to its real estate activities, UWR is active in environmental testing through its Laboratory Resources subsidiary. UWR also has nonregulated consulting subsidiaries that work with developers in installing water and sewer systems.

**Figure 15.14 United Water Resources Income Statement
                 Trends 1981–1987**

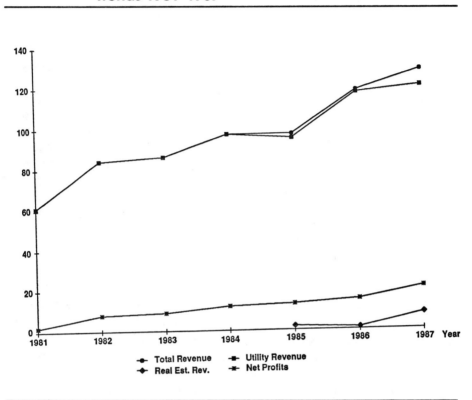

Continued population growth in its service areas will provide steadily increasing income and earnings from its utility operations. While its real estate development activities offer the promise of much higher returns than possible from its regulated activities, real estate development activities are notoriously volatile. The softening of the northern New Jersey real estate market in 1989 and its consequent adverse impact on UWR stock gives investors a foretaste of what is to come. While UWR will remain primarily a water utility, its stock may well manifest some nonutility-like behavior.

The strength of the basic economy in northern New Jersey and Rockland County will probably bring UWR ultimate success in its

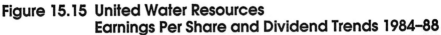

Figure 15.15   United Water Resources
Earnings Per Share and Dividend Trends 1984–88

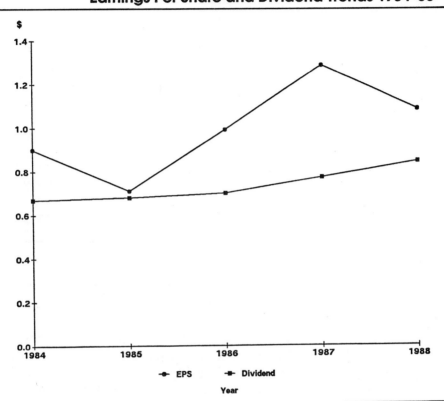

real estate development activities—although much depends on the quality of management. Along the way, investors in UWR should be prepared for a roller coaster ride.

The impact of these trends can be seen in Figure 15.15.

The dip in EPS in 1985 reflected a water shortage at Hackensack Water that is unlikely to reoccur. The dip in EPS in 1988 reflects a softening in the New Jersey real estate market; this will happen again.

The net effect of this exposure is presented in the forecast in Table 15.17.

Table 15.17 United Water Resources Forecast

Year	EPS	Payout Ratio	Dividends	Stock Price	Yield
1990	1.60	0.58	0.93	13.49	6.88%
1991	1.90	0.55	1.05	14.81	7.06%
1992	1.70	0.62	1.05	14.91	7.07%
1993	1.50	0.70	1.05	14.87	7.06%
1994	1.60	0.71	1.14	15.84	7.17%
1995	1.80	0.71	1.28	17.44	7.33%
1996	2.10	0.65	1.37	18.42	7.41%
1997	2.40	0.60	1.44	19.27	7.47%
1998	2.80	0.54	1.51	20.09	7.53%
1999	2.30	0.66	1.52	20.15	7.53%

The results of this forecast yield investors an annual return of 13.8 percent in the 1990–94 period and 13.5 percent in the 1990–99 period.

A critical assumption in this forecast is that stock price remains a function of dividends (as would be expected for a water utility) rather than earnings (which would be expected for a real estate development company). An additional assumption is that any adverse fluctuations in earnings will not be of sufficient magnitude to cause a reduction in dividends. In this context, a conservative approach to paying out dividends at UWR is in the best interests of its stockholders.

Summary

At current and forecasted price levels, water utility stocks do not generally appear to be promising investments. The earnings potential and realizable portion of undervalued assets are more than fully reflected in current price levels. Moreover, these stocks suffer from the legacy of being a "fad" at current price levels and therefore are exposed to considerable downside risk should water utilities fall from favor.

If the bull market of the 1980s continues throughout the 1990s, it is likely that the popularity of water utilities will fade, causing their PE ratios to fall and bringing their dividend yields into line with historical levels. Since the markets are thin, the fall in price may be excessive, boosting dividend yields to historically high levels. Under these circumstances, an investor may do well to consider entering the industry.

Index

A

Agreement on Natural Gas Prices and Markets, 157
Alabama Gas Company, 225
Allegheny Power, 12, 15, 82, 97, 100, 102-104, 116
  stock price forecast, 104
Allowance for Funds Used During Construction, 43-44
Alltel Corporation, 29, 30, 240, 241, 251, 252, 254, 269-271
  stock forecast, 267, 270
American Electric Power, 21, 81, 124, 131, 134
American Telephone. *See* AT&T
American Water Works, 31, 32, 360, 362
  forecast, 371-373
Ameritech, 29, 30, 241, 292, 296
  forecast, 301-304, 305, 306

Anadarko Petroleum Corporation, 200
Arkla, Inc., 24, 26, 167, 215, 221
  stock forecasts, 220, 222
Artificial price structures, 39
Atlanta Gas Light Company, 24, 26, 167, 215, 221
  stock forecast, 222
Atlantic Energy Inc., 12, 15, 82, 123, 134, 136
  stock forecast, 137-138
AT&T, 28, 29, 30, 239, 241, 247-248
  business, data, and consumer products, 341-342
  divestiture of operating companies, 237, 247, 257
  forecast, 329, 334-346
  regulation of, 242, 245
Avoided cost, 89

B

Bad Creek nuclear plant, 139
Baltimore Gas & Electric, 12,
        15, 78, 123, 131, 134, 136
    stock forecast, 138
Bay State Gas Company, 24,
        26, 167, 215, 221
    stock forecast, 222
Bell Atlantic, 29, 30, 241, 255
    forecast, 304, 306-307
Bell Labs, 257
Bellsouth Corporation, 29, 30,
        241, 250, 255
    forecast, 308, 310-313
Bluefield Waterworks, 35-36
Boston Edison, 21, 84, 124, 132,
        134
Boston Gas Company, 224
Brooklyn Union Gas
        Company, 24, 26, 167,
        215, 221
    stock prices, 222-223
Burlington Resources, 24, 26,
        161, 162, 166, 172, 185
    stock forecast, 183-184
Bush, President George, 10, 40
    and deregulation, 10, 88
    proposed acid rain legisla-
        tion, 107

C

Cal Gas, 233
California Water Service
        Company, 31, 32, 360,
        362
    forecast, 374-375
Calvert Cliff, 138

Carolina Power, 12, 15, 81, 123,
        131, 134, 136
    stock forecast, 138-139
Cascade Natural Gas
        Company, 24, 26, 167,
        215
    stock pricing, 223
Cellular mobile telephones,
        249-251
Centel Corporation, 29, 30,
        240, 251, 252, 254,
        281-283
    stock forecast, 279, 281, 282
Centerior Energy, 21, 84, 85,
        124, 132, 134
Central Hudson, 21, 84, 124,
        132, 134
Central Illinois Public Service
        Company, 12, 15, 82, 97,
        100, 103, 116
    stock forecast, 104-105
Central Louisiana Electric
        Company, 12, 15, 81, 95,
        97, 100, 103, 116, 119
    stock forecast, 105
Central Maine, 21, 84, 124, 132,
        134
Central & South West's
        Corporation, 21, 81, 124,
        131, 134
Central Vermont Public
        Service, 12, 15, 81, 123,
        131, 134, 136
    stock forecast, 139
Century Telephone Enter-
        prises, 29, 30, 240, 251,
        252, 254, 285
    stock forecast, 283-284

CILCORP, 12, 15, 82, 97, 100, 103, 116
  stock forecast, 105
Cincinnati Bell Inc., 29, 30, 240, 247, 251, 252-254, 284, 286, 287
Cincinnati Gas & Electric Company, 12, 15, 78, 97, 100, 103, 116
  stock forecast, 105-106
Citizens Utilities Company, 29, 30, 241, 251, 252
  stock forecast, 286-287, 288
City Gas Company, 228
CMS Energy Corporation, 21, 84, 124, 132, 134
Coastal Corporation, 24, 26, 161, 162, 166, 172
  stock forecast, 184-187
Cogeneration subsidiaries, 18
Colonial Penn, 140
Columbia Gas System, 24, 26, 162, 163, 166, 172
  stock forecast, 187-188
Common carriers, 28, 240-241, 257-259
  investment future, 329-357
Commonwealth Edison, 21, 82, 124, 131, 134
Commonwealth Energy System, 21, 84, 124, 132, 134
Communications Act of 1934, 242
Communications Industries, 250
Communications Satellite Corp. *See* COMSAT

COMSAT, 29, 30, 239-240, 241, 257, 258, 259, 329
  forecast, 352, 354-356
Connecticut Natural Gas Corp., 24, 26, 167, 215, 221
  stock forecast, 223-224
Connecticut Water Service, 31, 32, 360, 362
  forecast, 375-377
Consolidated Edison, 12, 15, 81, 123, 131, 134, 136
  stock forecast, 139
Consolidated Natural Gas System, 24, 26, 161, 162, 163, 166, 172
  stock forecast, 190
Consumer prices, increase in, 65
Consumers Water, 360, 362, 364
  forecast, 378-379
Contel Corporation, 240, 241, 251, 252, 254
  stock forecast, 271-272, 273
Contruction work in progress, 44
Consumer activist movement, 5, 9
Consumers Water Company, 31, 32
Contel Corporation, 29, 30
Cost of capital, calculating, 37-38
Cost of service, 36
C-Tec Corporation, 29, 30, 240, 241, 251, 252, 254, 280, 281, 283

stock forecast, 278-279

D

De facto deregulation, 40
Delmarva Power, 12, 15, 82,
        123, 131, 134, 136
    stock forecast, 139
Deregulation, 5, 10
    and breakdown of
        monopoly markets,
        39-41
    and diversified gas
        companies, 171
    and electric utilities, 6, 10
    and Federal Communica-
        tions Commission, 10
    and Federal Energy Regula-
        tory Commission, 10
    and gas utilities, 7, 10, 22
    government philosophy
        toward, 10
    and increased power at
        federal level, 40
    of interstate transmission,
        149
    and natural gas industry,
        168
    and telecommunications, 8,
        10, 245-248
Detroit Edison Company, 21,
        82, 124, 131, 134
Diablo Canyon nuclear plant,
        141
Diamond State Telephone
        Company, 304
Diversification
    of electric utilities, 91-92

of telecommunications, 248
of water utilities, 363-365
Diversified Energies, Inc., 24,
        26, 167, 215, 221
    stock forecast, 224
Diversified gas companies, 7,
        22
    impact of electric industry,
        174, 175
    future energy prices,
        173-176
    investment future, 171-211
    performance, 161-166
    specific forecasts, 183-210
    stock prices, 177-183
Dividend Discount Model
        (DDM), 48-51
    in diversified gas companies,
        176-183
    in nonnuclear electric
        industry, 96, 99-102,
        104
    in nuclear electric industry,
        133, 135, 137
    in water utility industry,
        367-370
Dodd, David, 48
Dominion Resources, 21, 84,
        124, 132, 134
Dow Jones Industrial and
        Dow Jones Utility
        compared, 56-60
DPL Inc., 12, 15, 78, 97, 100,
        103, 116
    stock forecast, 106
Duke Power Company, 12, 15,
        81, 123, 131, 134, 136
    stock forecast, 139-140

Dundee Water Power and
    Land Company, 391
Duquesne Light Company, 21,
    82, 124, 131, 134

E

Eastern Gas & Fuel Associates,
    24, 26, 167, 215, 221
    stock forecast, 224
Eastern Utility Associates, 21,
    78, 79, 124, 130, 131, 134
Electric utilities, 6-7
    average performing, 80, 82,
        83, 84, 85
    capacity, 90-91
    cogeneration subsidiaries,
        18
    and deregulation, 6, 10
    diversification of, 91-92
    dividends forecast, 15-18
    and environmental legisla-
        tion, 92-93
    financial performance,
        1984-1988, 70-72
    fundamentals, 67-91
    future trends, 87
    independent power
        producers, 18
    investor returns, analysis of,
        72-75
    low performing, 83, 84,
        85-87
    mergers, 70
    nonnuclear, 95-119
    nuclear exposure, 5, 18-22,
        121-144

outlook for specific seg-
    ments, 77-87
regulatory environment,
    87-90
speculative, with nuclear
    exposure, 124
stock prices
    forecast, 11-14, 18
    rising, 75-77
strong performing, 80, 81-82,
    83
Elizabethtown Gas Company,
    228
Elizabethtown Water
    Company, 379
El Paso Natural Gas Company,
    183
Empire District Electric, 12, 15,
    81, 97, 100, 103, 116
    stock forecast, 106
Energen Corporation, 24, 26,
    167, 215, 221
    stock forecast, 225
Energy crisis, and impact on
    earnings, 5
Energy sources, 153
Enron Corporation, 24, 26, 162,
    166, 172, 190-192
Enserch Corporation, 24, 26,
    162, 166, 172
    stock forecast, 192-193
Environmental impact of utili-
    ties, 5, 10, 69-70
Equitable Resources, 24, 26,
    162, 166, 172
    stock forecast, 194-195
E'Town Corporation, 31, 32,
    360, 362

forecast, 379-382

F

Fair rate of return, 36
FASB 95, 46
Federal Communications
    Commission (FCC), 10,
    23, 40, 242, 245
Federal Energy Regulatory
    Commission (FERC), 10,
    40, 69
Federal Express, 49
FERC Order 436, 164
Ferris, Charles, 246
Florida Gas, 190
Florida Progress Corporation,
    12, 15, 81, 91, 123, 131,
    134, 136
    stock forecast, 140
Foreign trade, and invest-
    ments, 2
FPL Group Inc., 12, 15, 82, 123,
    131, 134, 136
    stock forecast, 140
Free cash flow, 46
Free Trade Act, 157
Fuel prices, 154

G

Gas and oil exploration, 175,
    180
Gas utilities, 7, 22-23, 24-27
    and deregulation, 7, 10, 22
    diversified gas companies, 7
    dividends forecast, 26-27

local distribution companies,
    7, 213-234
    stock prices forecast, 24-25
General Public Utilities, 12, 15,
    70, 78, 86, 123, 131, 134,
    136, 145
    stock forecast, 140
Graham, Benjamin, 48
Green, Judge, 247, 248, 257, 350
Green Mountain Power, 12, 15,
    81, 123, 131, 134, 136
    stock forecast, 140-141
GTE Corporation, 29, 30, 240,
    251, 252, 254
    sale of Sprint fibre optics
        network, 272
    stock price forecast, 272, 274,
        275
Gulf States Utilities, 21, 83, 85,
    124, 130, 132, 134

H

Hackensack Water Company,
    391
Hadson Corporation, 161, 162,
    195-196
Harris 1 Nuclear plant, 138
Hawaiian Electric Industries,
    12, 15, 77, 96, 97, 100,
    103, 116-118
    stock forecast, 106-107
Houston Industries, Inc., 21,
    81, 124, 131, 134
Houston Pipeline, 190
HRB Singer, 195
Hydraulic Corporation, 31, 32,
    360, 362, 364

forecast, 382-383
Hyperinflation, 9

I

Idaho Power Company, 12, 15,
    82, 97, 100, 103, 116
  stock forecast, 107
IE Industries, 21, 81, 91, 124,
    131, 134
Illinois Bell, 301
Illinois Power Company, 21,
    84, 124, 132, 134
Income, 43-44
Income statement, example, 37
Independent power producers,
    18
Independent telephone compa-
    nies, 23, 240, 261-290
  financial performance,
    251-254
  potential growth companies,
    267, 269-276
  proven growth companies,
    268, 276, 278-289
  range of returns, 263-264
  stock prices, 264-266
  uncertain growth compa-
    nies, 266-267
Indiana Bell, 301
Indiana Energy, Inc., 24, 26,
    167, 215, 221
  stock forecast, 225
Indiana Gas Company, 225
Industrial and public utility
    stocks compared, 6,
    47-48, 55-56

Inflation, and investments, 2,
    5, 9
Interest rates, and investments,
    2
Interstate Power Company, 12,
    15, 80, 82, 97, 100, 103,
    116
  stock forecast, 107
Investment advisory services,
    41
Investment rules, 33-34
Iowa-Illinois Gas & Electric
    Company, 12, 15, 81, 123,
    131, 134, 136
  stock forecast, 141
Iowa Resources Inc., 21, 84,
    124, 132, 134
IPALCO Enterprises Inc., 12,
    15, 81, 97, 100, 103, 116
  stock forecast, 107-108

K

Kansas City Power & Light
    Company, 21, 124, 131,
    134
Kansas Gas & Electric Com-
    pany, 21, 84, 124, 132,
    134
Kansas Power & Light Com-
    pany, 12, 15, 81, 97, 100,
    103, 116
  stock forecast, 108
Kentucky Utilities Company,
    12, 15, 81, 97, 100, 103,
    116
  stock forecast, 108

Kewaunee nuclear plant, 143
KN Energy, 24, 26, 162, 163, 172
    stock forecasts, 196

L

Laboratory Resources, 391
Laclede Gas Company, 24, 26, 167, 215, 221
    stock forecast, 225-226
Local gas distribution companies, 7, 213-234
    specific company forecasts, 220-234
    stock prices and returns, forecasting, 216-220
Long Island Lighting Company, 21, 83-84, 85, 124, 132, 134, 146
Louisiana General Services Inc., 24, 26, 167, 213, 215
    stock forecast, 226
Louisville Gas & Electric Company, 13, 16, 82, 97, 100, 103, 116
    stock forecast, 108

M

Marble Hill nuclear plant, 141
Market ideology, 40
MCI Communications Corp., 28, 29, 30, 241, 242, 257, 258
    forecast, 346-347, 348-349
    investment future, 329, 330

    and regulation 242
MCN Corporation, 215
    stock forecast, 226-227
MDU Resources Group, 13, 16, 84, 97, 100, 103, 116
    stock forecast, 108-109
Mergers, electric utilities, 70, 93-94
Metromedia, 250
Michigan Bell, 301
Michigan Energy Resources Company, 24, 26, 167, 221
Michigan Gas Utilities, 226
Middlesex Water Company, 31, 32, 360, 362
    forecast, 384-385
Middle South Utilities Inc., 21, 84, 124, 132, 134
Midwest Energy Company, 13. 16, 21, 84, 97, 100, 103, 116, 124, 132, 134
    stock forecast, 109
Minnegasco, 224
Minnesota Power & Light Company, 13, 16, 81, 91, 97, 100, 103, 116
    stock forecast, 109
Mitchell Energy and Development, 24, 26, 162, 166, 172
    stock forecast, 197-199
Mitchell, George P., 197, 199
Mobile Communication, 250
Monopoly markets, breakdown of, 39-41
Monopoly pricing, 245

Montana Power Company, 13, 16, 84, 91, 97, 100, 103, 116
  stock forecast, 109-110
Mountain Fuel Supply Company, 231
Mountain States Telephone Company, 322
Munn vs. *Illinois*, 35

N

National Fuel Gas Company, 24, 26, 167, 215. 221
  stock forecast, 227
National Gas Policy Act, 148-149
Natural gas industry, 147-170
  characteristics of, 150
  distribution company performance, 166-170
  diversified gas companies, 161-166, 171-211
  financial performance, 150-151
  fuel prices, 154, 159
  future returns, 151-152
  household consumption, 155
  imports, 157
  local distribution companies, 167, 169
  1990-1999, 158-160
  proven reserves, 158
  structure of, 148-149
  supply-demand fundamentals, 152-158
Natural monopolies, 4

N.E. Utilities, 21, 81, 124, 131, 134
Nevada Power, 13, 16, 82, 97, 100, 103, 116
  stock forecast, 110
New England Electric System, 21, 84, 124, 132, 134
New England Telephone and Telegraph Company, 313
New Jersey Bell, 304
New Jersey Natural Gas, 227
New Jersey Resources Corp., 24, 26, 167, 215, 221
  stock forecast, 227-228
New York Telephone Company, 313
Niagra Mohawk Power Corp., 21, 84, 124, 132, 134
Nicor Incorporated, 25, 27, 167, 215, 221
  stock forecast, 228
NIPSCO Industries Inc., 21, 83, 85, 124, 132, 134
Nonnuclear electric utilities
  DDM estimate, 99, 102
  deregulation of, 96
  dividend forecasts, 116-117
  investment future, 95-119
  stock prices, forecasting, 96, 98-99, 103, 115
  specific forecasts, 104-115
Nonrecurring income, 43
Northern Border, 190
Northern Illinois Gas Company, 228
Northern Natural Gas, 190

Northern States Power
    Company, 13, 16, 81, 123,
    131, 134, 136
  stock forecast, 141
North Shore Gas, 230
Northwestern Bell, 322
Northwest Natural Gas
    Company, 24, 27, 267,
    215
  stock forecast, 229
Nuclear exposure, electric utili-
    ties with, 121-146
  evaluating investment re-
    turn, 144
  forecasting dividends,
    133-137
  forecasting returns, 130-132
  forecasting share prices,
    125-126
  projected total rate of return,
    123
  reliably performing, 133
  and risk, 128-129, 145-146
  speculative, 124
Nuclear power, 5, 18-22, 126-
    129
  cleanup costs, 42
NUI Corporation, 25, 27, 167,
    215, 221
  stock forecast, 228-229
NYNEX Corporation, 29, 30,
    240, 241, 255
  forecast, 313-316, 317-318
  potential acquisition of
    SNET, 274-275
N.Y. State Electric & Gas
    Corp., 21, 84, 124, 132,
    134

O

Ohio Edison Company, 21, 78,
    124, 131, 134
Oil prices, effect on electric
    utilities, 92
Oklahoma Gas & Electric
    Company, 13, 16, 82, 97,
    101, 103, 116, 119
  stock forecast, 110
Oneok Inc., 25, 27, 162, 172,
    199-200
OPEC, 92, 160
Orange & Rockland Utilities,
    Inc., 13, 16, 82, 97, 101,
    103, 116
  stock forecast, 110-111

P

Pacific Bell, 316
Pacific Corporation, 91
Pacific Enterprises Corp., 25,
    27, 167, 215, 221
  stock forecast, 229-230
Pacific Gas & Electric Com-
    pany, 13, 16, 82, 95, 123,
    131, 134, 136
  stock forecast, 141
Pacific Northwest Bell, 322
Pacificorp, 13, 16, 81, 91, 95,
    97, 101, 103, 116
  stock forecast, 111
  merger with Utah Power &
    Light, 93, 111
Pacific Telesis, 29, 30, 241, 250,
    255
  forecast, 316, 318-319,
    320-321

Panhandle Eastern Corp., 25, 27, 162, 165, 172
stock forecast, 200-202
Peach Bottom nuclear plants, 137, 142
Pennsylvania Bell, 304
Pennsylvania Power & Light Company, 13, 16, 78, 123, 131, 134, 136
stock forecast, 141-142
Peoples Energy Corporation, 25, 27, 167, 215, 221
stock forecast 230
Peoples Gas Light & Coke, 230
Phantom income, 43-44
Philadelphia Electric Company, 21, 81, 124, 129, 131, 134, 138
Philadelphia Suburban Water Company, 31, 32, 360, 362, 364
forecast, 385-387
Phillips Petroleum vs. Wisconsin, 148
Piedmont Natural Gas Company, 25, 27, 167, 215, 221
stock forecast, 230-231
Pinnacle West Capital Corporation, 21, 84, 91, 124, 132, 134
Pipelines, 175, 180
Portland General, 21, 80, 81, 124, 131, 134
Potomac Electric Power Company, 13, 16, 95, 96, 97, 101, 103, 116, 118
stock forecast, 111

Power Plant and Industrial Fuel Use Act, 155
Primerit, 232
Providence Energy Corporation, 25, 27, 167, 215, 221
stock forecast, 231
PSI Holdings Inc., 11, 13, 16, 81, 84, 85, 123, 132, 134, 136
stock forecast, 142
Public Service Company of New Hampshire, 34, 70, 83, 85, 124, 130, 132, 134, ·146
Public Service Company of New Mexico, 21, 83, 85, 91, 124, 132, 134
Public Service Enterprise Group, 13, 16, 81, 123, 131, 134, 136
stock forecast, 142
Public Service of Colorado, 13, 16, 84, 123, 132, 134, 136
stock forecast, 142
Public utilities
dividends, future
electric utilities, 15-18
gas utilities, 26-27
telecommunications, 30
water utilities, 32
electric, 67-91, 95-119, 121-146
financial performance, evaluating, 41-47
cash flows, 46-47
expenses, 45
income, 43
interpreting data, 41-42

quality of earnings,
    42-43
investing in, 2-3
investor-owned, 35
natural gas, 147-170
natural monopolies, 4, 34-36,
    47
privately owned, 35
rate making process, 36-39
regulation of, 4, 5
returns 1984-1989, 4
stock prices, determination
    of, 33-35
stock prices, forecasting,
    47-53
stock prices, future
    electric utilities, 11-14,
        18, 52
    gas utilities, 24-25, 52
    telecommunications, 28,
        52
    water utilties, 28, 31-32,
        52
technology impact on, 4
telecommunications,
    235-259
understanding, 4-5
water, 359-395
Public Utilities Regulation Act
    of 1978, 88, 91
Public utility stocks
    and industrial stocks
        compared, 6, 55-56
Puget Sound P & L Company,
    13, 16, 82, 97, 101, 103,
    116
    stock forecast, 111-112

Q-R

Questar Corporation, 25, 27,
    167, 215, 221
    stock forecast, 231-232
Questar Pipeline Company, 231
Railway Express, 49
Rate increases, 37
Rate of return, 35, 36
    real and after-tax, 64-65
    regulation of, 245-247
Reagan, Ronald, 5, 40, 88
Regional holding companies,
    23, 28, 29-30, 240, 247,
    254-257
    capital spending, 296-298
    forecasts, 298-301
        specific, 301-327
    growth and development,
        295-296
    investment future, 291-328
    regulatory reform, 294-295
Regulation of public utilities,
    4, 5
    and artifical price structures,
        39
    changes in 1990s, 69
    electric utilities, 87-90
    historical justification for, 34,
        35
    in natural gas sectors, 22
    and rate making process,
        36-39
    in telecommunications,
        241-248
Revised tariffs, 38
Rochester Gas & Electric
        Corp., 22, 84, 124, 132,
        134

Rochester Telephone Corporation, 29, 30, 241, 251, 252
stock forecast, 275

S

Sabine Corporation, 230
Safe Drinking Water Act of 1986, 363, 365
St. Joe Light and Power Company, 11, 13, 16, 78, 95, 96, 97, 101, 103, 117, 118
stock forecast, 112-113
San Diego Gas & Electric Company, 22, 78, 79, 124, 131, 134, 143
SCANA Corporation, 13, 16, 81, 123, 131, 134, 136
stock forecast, 142-143
SCE Corporation, 13, 16, 81, 123, 131, 134, 136
stock forecast, 143
takeover attempt by, 94
Seagull Energy Corp., 25, 27, 162, 166, 172, 203
stock forecast, 202
Security Analysis: Principles and Techniques, 48
Sierra Pacific Resources, 13, 16, 81, 97, 101, 103, 117
stock forecast, 112
SJW Corporation, 31, 32, 360, 362
forecast, 387-389
SNET. See Southern New England Telephone
Sonat Inc., 25, 27, 162, 172, 204, 205

stock forecasts, 202, 203
South Central Bell Telephone, 308
Southern Bell Telephone, 308
Southern California Gas Company, 229
Southern California Water Company, 31, 32, 360, 362
forecast, 389-391
Southern Company, 22, 82, 124, 131, 134
Southern Indiana Gas & Electric Company, 13, 16, 78, 97, 101, 103, 117
stock forecast, 112
Southern New England Telecommunications, 29, 30
Southern New England Telephone, 240, 241, 247, 251, 252, 254, 276
stock forecast, 274-275
Southern Union Company, 25, 27, 167, 221
South Jersey Gas Company, 232
South Jersey Industries, Inc., 25, 27, 167, 215, 221
stock forecast, 232
Southwestern Bell, 29, 30, 240, 250, 255
forecast, 319, 321-322, 323-324
Southwest Gas Corporation, 25, 27, 167, 215, 221
stock forecast, 232
Speculative electric utilities with nuclear exposure, 124

Spring Valley Water
    Company, 391
Sprint (United Telecommunica-
    tions), 28, 29, 30, 251
Statement of Cash Flows, 46
Stock price determination, 33-
    53
St. Vrain nuclear plant, 142
Susquehanna nuclear units, 141
S. W. Public Service Company,
    13, 16, 97, 101, 103, 116
    stock forecast, 112

T

Tax Reform Act of 1986, 65
Technical factors, and impact
    on stock prices, 3
Technology, and breakdown of
    monopolies, 39
TECO Energy Corporation, 13,
    16, 81, 97, 101, 103, 117
    stock forecast, 113
Telecommunications industry,
    7-8
    bypass, 248-249
    cellular telephone market,
        45, 249-251
    common carriers, 28, 240-
        241, 257-259, 329-357
    competition in, 23
    deregulation, 8, 10, 245-248
    diversification, 248
    environment, 237-238
    financial performance, 238-
        240, 251-259
    forecast, 23, 28
    fundamentals, 235-259

future returns, 240-241
independent operating
    companies, 240,
    251-254
independent telephone
    companies, 261-290
regional holding companies,
    23, 28, 29-30, 240,
    254-257
    investment future, 291-
        328
regulation, 241-248, 294-295
structure, 236-237, 241-251
Tenneco Inc., 25, 27, 161, 162,
    172, 206
    stock forecast, 204-205
Texas Eastern Corporation, 25,
    27, 162, 166
Texas Utilities Company, 22,
    84, 124, 132, 134
Theory of Investment Value, 48
Three Mile Island, 78, 130, 140,
    145
TNP Enterprises, 13, 16, 81, 97,
    101, 103, 117
    stock forecast, 113
Total rate of return, calculat-
    ing, 60-64
Transco Energy Company, 25,
    27, 162, 166, 172, 208
    stock forecast, 205
Transwestern, 190
Trimble 1, 108
Tucson Electric Power Com-
    pany, 14, 17, 84, 97, 101,
    103, 117
    stock forecast, 114

U

UGI Corporation, 25, 27, 167, 215, 221
  stock forecast, 233
Ultrasystems, 195
Unemployment, and investments, 2
Uniform Systems of Accounts Rewrite, 333
Union Electric Company, 22, 78, 124, 131, 134
United Illuminating Company, 22, 84, 124, 132, 134
United Telecommunications (Sprint), 28, 29, 30, 251
  acquisition of fibre optics network, 272
  forecast, 347, 349-352, 353
United Water Resources, 31, 32, 360, 362
  forecast, 391-394
Universal Telephone Service, 244
U.S. West, 29, 30, 241, 255
  forecast, 322, 324-327
Utilicorp United Inc., 11, 14, 17, 82, 95, 96, 97, 101, 103, 117, 118, 145
  proposed merger with MCN, 226
  stock forecast, 114

V-Z

Valero Energy Corporation, 25, 27, 162, 172, 207, 208-209
Vermont Yankee Nuclear Power Corporation, 140

Washington Energy Company, 25, 27, 167, 213, 214, 215, 221
  stock forecast, 233
Washington Gas Light Company, 25, 27, 167, 215, 221
  stock forecast, 234
Washington Natural Gas Company, 233
Washington Water Power Company, 14, 17, 81, 97, 101, 103, 117
  stock forecast, 115
Water utilities, 8
  cost increases, 365-366
  demand for, future, 366-367
  diversification efforts, 363-365
  forecast, 28, 31-32
  fundamentals, 361, 363
  future returns in, 359-395
  market structure, 360-361
  returns, 367-370
  specific utilities, 371-394
  undervalued assets, 366
Western Electric, 247
Wicor Inc., 25, 27, 167, 215, 221
  stock forecast, 234
Williams Companies, 25, 27, 161, 162, 172, 211
  stock price forecast, 209-210
Williams, J., 48
Wisconsin Bell, 301
Wisconsin Energy Corporation, 14, 17, 81, 123, 131, 134, 136, 146
  stock forecast, 143

Wisconsin Gas Company, 234
Wisconsin Public Service Cor-
        poration, 14, 17, 81, 123,
        131, 134, 136, 146
    stock forecast, 143
WPL Holdings Inc., 14, 17, 84,
        123, 132, 134, 136
    stock forecast, 143
Zimmer Nuclear Power Plant,
        105, 106